Questions & Answers

Human Rights
and Civil Liberties

THIRD EDITION

Steve Foster

Principal Lecturer in Law, Coventry University

2010 and 2011

OXFORD
UNIVERSITY PRESS

OXFORD
UNIVERSITY PRESS

Great Clarendon Street, Oxford ox2 6DP

Oxford University Press is a department of the University of Oxford.
It furthers the University's objective of excellence in research, scholarship, and education
by publishing worldwide in

Oxford New York

Auckland Cape Town Dar es Salaam Hong Kong Karachi
Kuala Lumpur Madrid Melbourne Mexico City Nairobi
New Delhi Shanghai Taipei Toronto

With offices in

Argentina Austria Brazil Chile Czech Republic France Greece
Guatemala Hungary Italy Japan Poland Portugal Singapore
South Korea Switzerland Thailand Turkey Ukraine Vietnam

Oxford is a registered trade mark of Oxford University Press
in the UK and in certain other countries

Published in the United States
by Oxford University Press Inc., New York

British Library Cataloguing in Publication Data

Data available

Library of Congress Cataloging-in-Publication Data

Foster, Steve, 1955-

Questions & answers, human rights and civil liberties / Steve Foster. — 3rd ed.
p. cm. —
(Q&A series) "2010 and 2011." Rev. ed. of: Human rights and civil liberties. 2nd ed. 2008.
Includes index.
ISBN 978–0–19–957914–3
1. Civil rights — Great Britain. 2. Human rights. I. Foster, Steve, 1955- Human rights and civil liberties.
II. Title. III. Title: Questions and answers human rights and civil liberties. IV. Title: Human rights
and civil liberties.
KD4080.F67 2009
342.4108'5076 — dc22

2009039591

Typeset by MPS Limited, A Macmillan Company
Printed in Great Britain
on acid-free paper by
Clays Ltd, St Ives plc

ISBN 978–0–19–957914–3

1 3 5 7 9 10 8 6 4 2

Questions & Answers

Human Rights and Civil Liberties

Questions & Answers Series

Series Editors: Rosalind Malcolm and Margaret Wilkie

The ideal revision aid to keep you afloat through your exams

Q&A Company Law
Stephen Judge

Q&A Criminal Law
Mike Molan

Q&A Employment Law
Richard Benny, Malcolm Sargeant,
and Michael Jefferson

Q&A Equity and Trusts
Margaret Wilkie, Rosalind Malcolm,
and Peter Luxton

Q&A EU Law
Nigel Foster

Q&A Evidence
Maureen Spencer and John Spencer

Q&A Family Law
Penny Booth with Chris Barton
and Mary Hibbs

Q&A Human Rights and Civil Liberties
Steve Foster

Q&A International Law
Susan Breau

Q&A Land Law
Margaret Wilkie, Peter Luxton,
and Rosalind Malcolm

Q&A Law of Contract
Adrian Chandler with Ian Brown

Q&A Law of Torts
David Oughton, Barbara Harvey,
and John Marston

Q&A Public Law
Richard Clements and Philip Jones

- **advice on exam technique**
- **summary of each topic**
- **bullet-pointed answer plans**
- **model answers**
- **diagrams and flowcharts**
- **further reading**

Contents

Preface   vii

Table of Cases   ix

Table of Statutes   xix

Table of International and European law   xxi

Table of Secondary Legislation   xxiii

1 Introduction   1

2 Nature and enforcement of human rights and civil liberties   5

3 The European Convention on Human Rights   21

4 The Human Rights Act 1998   45

5 The right to life   63

6 Freedom from torture and inhuman and degrading treatment   81

7 Due process, liberty and security of the person, and the right to a fair trial   95

8 Prisoners' rights   119

9 The right to private life   135

10 Freedom of expression   159

11 Freedom of religion, association, and peaceful assembly   193

Index   217

The Q&A series

Key features

The Q&A series provides full coverage of key subjects in a clear and logical way.

This book contains the following features:

* Questions
* Commentary
* Diagrams
* Bullet point answer plans
* Suggested answers
* Further reading

online resource centre
www.oxfordtextbooks.co.uk/orc/qanda/

Every book in the Q&A series is accompanied by an Online Resource Centre, hosted at the URL above, which is open-access and free to use.

The online resources for this title include revision and exam advice, additional questions and answers, a subject-specific glossary, updates in the law, further reading guidance, and links to websites useful for the study of human rights and civil liberties.

Preface

The study of and interest in human rights and civil liberties has grown tremendously over the past two decades, particularly since the implementation of the Human Rights Act 1998. As a result, a great number of specific human rights courses are taught on undergraduate programmes and most constitutional law courses are dedicating more time and space to human rights issues. In addition, human rights have become central to the law student's study and pervade much of their law studies, not only in constitutional law, but also in areas such as tort, criminal law, and even business law and property subjects, where the student needs to be aware of the impact of the 1998 Act.

The central aim of this book is to provide clear guidance on how to tackle questions, both in essay and problem question form, on human rights and civil liberties. The author has attempted to cover as many aspects of human rights and civil liberties as possible, ranging through the theory of human rights, their protection in domestic and international law, and the protection of specific human rights such as the right to life, freedom from torture, freedom of expression, the right to association and peaceful assembly, the right to privacy, the right to a fair trial, liberty and security of the person and prisoners' rights. Issues relating to freedom from discrimination are covered in chapters on the European Convention on Human Rights, Private Life and Freedom of Association, Assembly and Religion. Chapters on the Human Rights Act, the European Convention, and Freedom of Association also contain questions on the very topical area of terrorism and human rights. Consequently, the book concentrates on civil and political rights as opposed to social and economic rights, mainly because these are the rights protected under the European Convention on Human Rights and the Human Rights Act 1998, which so dominate discussions on human rights and the coverage of human rights issues on most, though not all, human rights courses in undergraduate programmes.

Essentially the book provides the student with guidance on how to prepare, plan, and answer essay- and problem-type questions in the area of human rights and civil liberties, primarily at second or third year undergraduate level—although the text might be useful for those studying on CPE and ILEX courses and those studying human rights as part of another course. To a limited degree it may also provide basic guidance to those studying human rights at postgraduate level, particularly if they have not studied the subject before and are not aware of the British system of protecting rights. In particular it gives guidance on what the module leader is looking for in an answer in this area and how to distinguish between a fair, good, very good, and excellent answer.

For the third edition of the text we have decided to cut down on the length and detail of the answers so as to reflect the fact that they are to be written under examination conditions. We have also decided to omit a number of questions which appeared in the first two editions; although those questions and their answers will appear on the book's website at www.oxfordtextbooks.co.uk/orc/qanda/. We trust that these changes will be welcomed by the reader.

Since the publication of the first and second editions of this text, there have been a great number of new cases and legislative changes affecting the law of human rights, many of which have been incorporated in the answers. Specifically, there has continued to be a good deal of development in areas such as terrorism and the law, privacy and free speech and liberty of the person, and these have been incorporated, along with various other new cases and statutory changes. The text is supported by an accompanying website, which includes regular updates on the law as well as a supplementary reading list. Students are advised to use this site to keep abreast of new developments.

My thanks go to everyone at Oxford University Press who helped in the preparation and publication of this text. The book is dedicated to our children Tom, Ben, and Ella.

Steve Foster
August 2009

Table of Cases

A v B, [2009] 3 All ER 416 ... 175

A v B plc and another [2002] 3 WLR 542, CA (Civ Div); [2001] 1 WLR 2341, QBD ... 143, 151, 152, 153

A v Secretary of State for the Home Department [2005] 2 AC 68, HL; [2002] EWCA Civ 1502; [2003] 2 WLR 564, CA (Civ 564 ... 9, 19, 27, 38, 39, 53, 55, 56, 99, 103

A v Secretary of State for the Home Department (No 2) [2006] 2 AC 221; HL [2004] EWCA Civ 1123; [2005] 1 WLR 414, CA (Civ Div) ... 133

A v United Kingdom (1999) 27 EHRR 611 ... 25, 85, 89

A v United Kingdom (2003) 36 EHRR 51 ... 170

A v United Kingdom (2009) 49 EHRR 29 ... 23, 28, 39, 54, 55, 99, 100, 103, 104

Abdulaziz, Cabales and Balkandali v United Kingdom (1985) 7 EHRR 471 ... 42

ADT v United Kingdom (2001) 31 EHRR 33 ... 29, 41, 137, 156

AF v Secretary of State for the Home Department [2009] 3 WLR 74 ... 104

Ahmed v United Kingdom (1981) 4 EHRR 126 ... 197

Ahmed v United Kingdom [1999] IRLR 188 ... 204

Al-Fayed v United Kingdom (1994) 18 EHRR 393 ... 108

Amann v Switzerland (2000) 30 EHRR 843 ... 138, 146

Amekrane v United Kingdom (1974) 44 CD 101 ... 24

American Cyanamid v Ethicon Ltd [1975] AC 396 ... 166

Amin v Secretary of State for the Home Department [2004] 1 AC 653 ... 75

Anderson v United Kingdom (1998) 25 EHRR CD 172 ... 203

Andronicou v Cyprus (1998) 25 EHRR 491 ... 73, 74

An Application by D [2009] NICty 4 ... 187

Arrowsmith v Jenkins [1963] 2 QB 561 ... 208, 212

Arrowsmith v United Kingdom (1978) 3 EHRR 218 ... 195

Ashindane v United Kingdom (1985) 7 EHRR 528 ... 97

Ashworth Security Hospital v MGN Ltd [2002] 1 WLR 2033 ... 186

Askoy v Turkey (1996) 23 EHRR 553 ... 82, 83

Assenov v Bulgaria (1999) 28 EHRR 652 ... 99

Associated Provincial Picture Houses Ltd v Wednesbury Corp [1948] 1 KB 223 ... 53

Atkas and others v France, Application No 43563/08 ... 196

Attorney-General v Blake [2001] 1 AC 268 ... 176

Attorney-General v English [1983] 1 AC 116 ... 181, 183

Attorney-General v Guardian Newspapers (No 2) [1990] 1 AC 109 ... 49, 165, 175, 176

Attorney-General v Hislop and Pressdram [1991] 1 QB 514 ... 180, 182, 183

Attorney-General v ITN and others [1995] 2 All ER 370 ... 180, 182

Attorney-General v MGN [1997] 1 All ER 456 ... 182

Attorney-General v News Group Newspapers [1987] 1 QB 1 ... 180

Attorney-General v News Group Newspapers [1989] 2 All ER 906 ... 181, 182, 183

Attorney-General v Newspaper Publishing Ltd [1997] 3 All ER 159 ... 177

Attorney-General v Punch and Steed [2003] 1 All ER 289, HL ... 177

Attorney-General v Sport Newspapers [1991] 1 WLR 1194 ... 183

Attorney-General v Times Newspapers [1974] AC 273 ... 179

Attorney-General v Times Newspapers (1983), The Times, 12 February ... 180, 181

Attorney-General v Times Newspapers [1992] 1 AC 191 ... 176

Attorney-General v TVS Television Ltd and Southey and Sons (1989), The Times, 7 July ... 181, 183

Attorney-General's Reference (No 3 of 1973) [1978] 3 All ER 1166 ... 190

Attorney-General's Reference (No 4 of 2002) [2005] 1 AC 264 ... 55

Austin v Commissioner of Police of the Metropolis [2006] 2 WLR 372 ... 210

Autronic AG v Switzerland (1990) 12 EHRR 485 ... 161

B v France (1992) 16 EHRR 1 ... 157

B v United Kingdom (1987) 10 DR 87 ... 128

Bamber v United Kingdom, Application No 33742/96 ... 126, 128

Barthold v Germany (1985) 7 EHRR 383 ... 162

BBC v United Kingdom (1996) 84-A DR 129 ... 184

Beatty v Gillbanks (1882) 15 Cox CC 138 ... 208

Becker v Home Office [1972] 2 QB 407 ... 122

Beech v Freeson [1972] 1 QB 14 ... 170, 172

Beet and others v United Kingdom (2005) 41 EHRR 23 ... 98

'Belgian Linguistics' Case (1968) 1 EHRR 252 ... 42, 43

Bellinger v Bellinger [2003] 2 AC 467 ... 54, 55, 56, 144, 158

Benham v United Kingdom (1996) 22 EHRR 293 ... 98, 107, 113

Blackshaw v Lord [1984] QB 1 ... 170

Blake v United Kingdom (2007) 44 EHRR 29 ... 176

Bonnard v Perryman [1891] 2 Ch 269 ... 170, 172

Boyle and Rice v United Kingdom (1988) 10 EHRR 425 ... 126, 128

Boznao v Italy (1986) 9 EHRR 297 ... 98

Brannigan and McBride v United Kingdom (1993) 17 EHRR 539 ... 28, 37, 38, 99, 103

Brennan v United Kingdom (2002) 34 EHRR 18 ... 107, 113

Broadwith v DPP [2000] Crim LR 924 ... 215

Brogan v United Kingdom (1989) 11 EHRR 117 ... 27, 38, 99, 102, 103

Brooks v Metropolitan Police Commissioner [2005] 1 WLR 1495 ... 111

Browne v Associated Newspapers [2007] 3 WLR 289 ... 152

Broziek v Italy (1989) 12 EHRR 371 ... 107

Brutus v Cozens [1972] 2 All ER 1297 ... 60

Bryan v United Kingdom (1996) 21 EHRR 342 ... 109, 111

Bubbins v United Kingdom (2005) 41 EHRR 24 ... 66, 67

Caballero v United Kingdom (2000) 30 EHRR 643 ... 99

Campbell and Cosans v United Kingdom (1982) 4 EHRR 243 ... 196

Campbell and Fell v United Kingdom (1984) 7 EHRR 165 ... 107, 108, 113, 127

Campbell v MGN [2004] 2 AC 457 ... 143, 151, 152, 153, 154, 2153

Campbell v United Kingdom (1992) 15 EHRR 137 ... 127, 133

Carr v News Group Newspapers Ltd [2005] EWHC 971 ... 151

Castells v Spain (1992) 14 EHRR 445 ... 163

CC v AB [2007] EMLR 11 ... 152, 2153

Centaur Communications v Camelot [1998] 2 WLR 379 ... 185, 186

Chahal v United Kingdom (1997) 23 EHRR 413 ... 50, 78, 80, 82, 85, 86, 91, 92, 93, 94, 98, 99

Chandler v DPP [1964] AC 763 ... 175

Chester v Bateson [1920] KB 829 ... 48, 106

Chief Constable of Greater Manchester Police v Channel 5 Broadcast Ltd [2005] EWCA Civ 739 ... 180

Chorherr v Austria (1993) 17 EHRR 358 ... 58, 210

Choudhury v United Kingdom (1991) 12 HRLJ 172 ... 42, 197, 200

Ciulla v Italy (1991) 13 EHRR 346 ... 98, 101

Condron v United Kingdom (2001) 31 EHRR 1 ... 106, 112

Copland v United Kingdom (2007) 45 EHRR 37 ... 139, 146

Corbett v Corbett [1970] 2 All ER 33 ... 157

Corporate Officer of the House of Commons v Information Commissioner [2009] 3 All ER 403 ... 177

Cossey v United Kingdom (1990) 13 EHRR 622 ... 44, 138, 157

Costello-Roberts v United Kingdom (1993) 19 EHRR 112 ... 84, 137

Cream Holdings v Banerjee and Another [2005] 1 AC 253 ... 166, 167

Cuscani v United Kingdom (2003) 36 EHRR 1 ... 107

D v United Kingdom (1997) 24 EHRR 423 ... 85, 93, 94

De Becker v Belgium (1979–80) 1 EHRR 43 ... 24

Demir v Turkey (2001) 33 EHRR 43 ... 67

Derbyshire County Council v Times Newspapers [1993] AC 534; [1993] 1 All ER 1011 ... 49, 170, 171

Dickson v United Kingdom (2007) 41 EHRR 21 ... 124, 126

Dickson v United Kingdom (2008) 46 EHRR 41 Grand Chamber ... 124

Domenichini v Italy (2001) 32 EHRR 4 ... 127

Doody v Secretary of State for the Home Department [1994] 1 AC 531 ... 123

Douglas and others v Hello! and others [2001] 2

WLR 992 ... 142, 143, 151, 166–7, 2153

Dougoz v Greece (2002) 34 EHRR 61 ... 128

Dowsett v United Kingdom (2004) 38 EHRR 41 ... 112

DP and JC v United Kingdom (2003) 36 EHRR 14 ... 85

DPP v Channel Four Television Company Ltd [1993] 2 All ER 517 ... 185

DPP v Haw (2007), *The Times*, 11 September ... 209

DPP v Jones and Lloyd [1999] 2 All ER 257 ... 209, 213, 214

DPP v Jordan [1977] AC 699 ... 190

Dubowska and Skup v Poland (1997) 24 EHRR CD 75 ... 197

Dudgeon v United Kingdom (1982) 4 EHRR 149 ... 25, 29, 33, 137, 141, 155

Duncan v Jones [1936] 1 KB 218 ... 208, 209, 213

East African Asians Case (1973) 3 EHRR 76 ... 42

EB v France (2008) 47 EHRR 1 ... 157

Edore v Secretary of State for the Home Department [2003] NLJ 998 ... 53

Edwards and Lewis v United Kingdom (2005) 40 EHRR 24 ... 112

Edwards v United Kingdom (2002) 35 EHRR 19 ... 65, 66, 73, 75, 128

ELH and PBH v United Kingdom [1998] EHRLR 231 ... 128

Ellis v Home Office [1953] 2 QB 135 ... 89, 122

Engel v Netherlands (1976) 1 EHRR 647 ... 108, 115

Entick v Carrington (1765) 19 St Tr 1029 ... 48

Evans v United Kingdom (2007) , *The Times*, 2 May ... 65

Ezeh and Connors v United Kingdom (2004) 39 EHRR 1 ... 108, 111, 127

Findlay v United Kingdom (1997) 24 EHRR 221 ... 108, 109, 111

Finucane v United Kingdom (2003) 37 EHRR 29 ... 66

Fox, Campbell and Hartley v United Kingdom (1991) 13 EHRR 157 ... 36, 98, 99, 102

Foxley v United Kingdom (2001) 31 EHRR 25 ... 111

Frette v France (2004) 38 EHRR 1 ... 157

Funke v France (1993) 16 EHRR 297 ... 106

Galloway v Telegraph Group Ltd [2005] EMLR 7 ... 168, 171

Gaskin v United Kingdom (1990) 12 EHRR 36 ... 137, 139, 141

Gay News v United Kingdom (1983) 5 EHRR 123 ... 117, 161, 162, 197, 199

Ghai v Newcastle City Council (2009), *The Times*, 18 May ... 196

Gleaner Company and another v Abrahams [2004] 1 AC 628 ... 172

Glimerveen and Hagenbeek v Netherlands (1980) 18 DR 187 ... 161, 201

Golder v United Kingdom (1975) 1 EHRR 524 ... 25, 50, 107, 110, 122, 123, 124, 126, 133, 138

Goodwin v United Kingdom (1996) 22 EHRR 123 ... 166, 184, 185, 186

Goodwin v United Kingdom (2002) 35 EHRR 18 ... 25, 29, 34, 44, 54, 55, 138, 144, 158

Govell v United Kingdom (1997) EHRLR 438 ... 146

Granger v United Kingdom (1990) 12 EHRR 496 ... 107, 113

Grant v South West Trains [1998] IRLR 508 ... 156

Grant v United Kingdom (2007) 44 EHRR 1 ... 158

Greek Case (1969) 12 YB 170 ... 83

Green v Associated Newspapers [2005] 3 WLR 281 ... 166, 170, 172

Grieves v United Kingdom (2004) 39 EHRR 2 ... 109

Grobelaar v News Group Newspapers [2002] 1 WLR 3024; [2001] 2 All ER 437 ... 170

Guzzardi v Italy (1981) 3 EHRR 373 ... 97

Hachette Filipacchi Associes v France, (2009) 49 EHRR 23 ... 139

Halford v United Kingdom (1997) 24 EHRR 523 ... 138, 146

Hamer v United Kingdom (1982) 4 EHRR 139 ... 34, 126, 128

Handyside v United Kingdom (1976) 1 EHRR 737 ... 9, 15, 19, 28, 29, 33, 34, 58, 60, 159, 160, 161, 162, 188, 189, 190, 198

Harman and Hewitt v United Kingdom (1992) 14 EHRR 657 ... 146

Hashman and Harrap v United Kingdom (1999) 30 EHRR 241 ... 33, 59, 161, 210, 215

Hatton v United Kingdom (2003) 37 EHRR 28 ... 23

Hilal v United Kingdom (2001) 33 EHRR 2 ... 93

Hill v Chief Constable of West Yorkshire [1990] 1 WLR 946 ... 111

Hilton v United Kingdom (1981) 3 EHRR 104 ... 128

Hirst and Agu v Chief Constable of Yorkshire (1987) 85 Cr App R 143 ... 208, 212

Hirst v Attorney-General (2001), *The Times*, 17 April ... 124

Hirst v United Kingdom (No 2) (2004) 38 EHRR 40 ... 124, 126, 128, 129

HLR v France (1998) 26 EHRR 29 ... 92

Hoare v United Kingdom [1997] EHRLR 678 ... 190

HRH Prince of Wales v MGN Ltd [2007] 3 WLR 222 ... 143, 152, 167

HRH Princess of Wales v MGN (unreported) 8 November 1993 ... 142, 154

Hubbard v Pitt [1976] QB 142 ... 207

Hussain and Singh v United Kingdom (1996) 21 EHRR1 ... 127

IA v Turkey (2007) 45 EHRR 30 ... 199

Independent News and Media plc and another v Ireland (2006) 42 EHRR 46 ... 170

Inquiry under the Company Securities (Insider Dealing) Act 1985, Re [1988] 1 All ER 203 ... 185

Interbrew SA v Financial Times [2002] EMLR 24 ... 187

IRC v Rossminster [1980] 2 AC 852 ... 48

Ireland v United Kingdom (1978) 2 EHRR 25 ... 24, 25, 83, 87, 131

Jagger v Darling [2005] EWHC 683 ... 152

Jameel v Wall Street Journal [2005] 2 WLR 1577 CA ... 171

Jameel v Wall Street Journal Europe [2007] 1 AC 359 HL ... 168, 173

Jamil v France (1996) 21 EHRR 65 ... 115

Jasper and Fitt v United Kingdom (2000) 30 EHRR 411 ... 112

Jersild v Denmark (1994) 19 EHRR 1 ... 163, 184, 191

JJ v Secretary of State for the Home Department [2006] 3 WLR 866 ... 97, 104

John v Express Newspapers [2000] 3 All ER 257 ... 186

Jordan v United Kingdom (2003) 37 EHRR 2 ... 65, 66, 75

Kalac v Turkey (1997) 27 EHRR 552 ... 195

Kalashnikov v Russia (2003) 36 EHRR 34 ... 69, 79, 84, 128

Kansal v United Kingdom (2004) 39 EHRR 31 ... 112

Karner v Austria (2004) 38 EHRR 24 ... 156

Kaye v Robertson [1991] FSR 62 ... 141, 142, 143

Keenan v United Kingdom (2001) 33 EHRR 38 ... 24, 66, 89, 90, 128, 129

Kent v Metropolitan Police Commissioner (1981), *The Times*, 15 May ... 208

Khan v United Kingdom (2001) 31 EHRR 45 ... 112, 138, 139, 144, 146, 147

Kirkham v Chief Constable of Greater Manchester Police [1990] 2 QB 283 ... 89

Klass v Germany (1978) 2 EHRR 214 ... 24, 137, 145, 147, 148, 175

Knuller v DPP [1973] AC 435 ... 189, 191

Kokkinakis v Greece (1993) 17 EHRR 397 ... 115, 194, 195

Kunstler v Austria (2008) 47 EHRR 5 ... 200

Kurt v Turkey (1999) 27 EHRR 373 ... 97

Laskey, Jaggard and Brown v United Kingdom (1997) 24 EHRR 39 ... 29, 137

Launder v United Kingdom [1998] EHRLR 337 ... 80, 93

Lawless v Ireland (No 3) (1961) 1 EHRR 15 ... 27, 37, 103

LCB v United Kingdom (1999) 27 EHRR 212 ... 65

Leander v Sweden (1987) 9 EHRR 433 ... 147, 167, 174, 175, 177

Lehideux and Irsoni v France (2000) 30 EHRR 665 ... 60

Liberty v United Kingdom (2009) 48 EHRR 1 ... 138

Lingens v Austria (1986) 8 EHRR 407 ... 25, 163, 164, 167, 169

Lord Advocate v Scotsman Publications Ltd [1990] 1 AC 812 ... 176

Loutchansky v Times Newspapers Ltd and others (No 2) [2002] 1 All ER 652 ... 171, 173

Luedicke, Belkacem and Koc v Germany (1978) 2 EHRR 149 ... 107

Lustig-Prean and Beckett v United Kingdom (2000) 29 EHRR 548 ... 156

McCann v United Kingdom (1995) 21 EHRR 97 ... 24, 64, 66, 68, 69, 72, 74

Macdonald v Ministry of Defence [2004] 1 All ER 339 ... 156

McGlinchey v United Kingdom (2003) 37 EHRR 41 ... 88, 89, 129

McGonnell v United Kingdom (2000) 30 EHRR 289 ... 109, 111

McKennitt v Ash [2007] 3 WLR 194 ... 143, 152, 167

McShane v United Kingdom (2002) 35 EHRR 23 ... 66

McVicar v United Kingdom (2000) 35 EHRR 22 … 171

Madison v Malsbury 1 Cranch 137 (1803) … 17

Malone v Metropolitan Police Commissioner (No 2) [1979] Ch 344 … 48, 50, 141, 142, 146, 148

Malone v United Kingdom (1984) 7 EHRR 14 … 13, 32, 50, 137, 138, 141, 142, 143, 144, 146, 148

Mandla v Dowell Lee [1983] 2 AC 548 … 200

Manossakis v Greece (1996) 23 EHRR 387 … 195

Marckx v Belgium (1979) 2 EHRR 330 … 137

Martin v McGuiness (2003), *The Times*, 23 April … 147

MB v Secretary of State for the Home Department [2006] 3 WLR 839… 109, 111

Mellors v United Kingdom (2004) 38 EHRR 11 … 113

Members of the Gldani Congregation of Jehovah's Witnesses v Georgia, European Court of Human Rights, 3 May 2007 … 197, 199

Mendoza v Ghaidan [2004] 2 AC 557 … 54, 144, 156

Mersey Care NHS Trust v Ackroyd (2007), *The Times*, 26 February … 186

Minelli v Switzerland (1983) 5 EHRR 554 … 106, 112

Modinos v Cyprus (1993) 16 EHRR 485 … 156

Morris v United Kingdom (2002) 34 EHRR 52 … 109

Moss v McLachlan [1985] IRLR 76 … 208, 214

Müller v Switzerland (1991) 13 EHRR 212 … 59, 161, 162, 189, 191

Munjaz v Mersey Care NHS Trust; S v Airedale NHS Trust [2006] 2 AC 148 … 144

Murray v Express Newspapers (2007), *The Times*, 4 October … 154

Murray v United Kingdom (1994) 19 EHRR 193 … 102

Murray v United Kingdom (1996) 22 EHRR 29 … 106, 113

N v Secretary of State for the Home Department [2005] 2 AC 296 … 94

N v United Kingdom (2008) 47 EHRR 39 … 85, 94

Nagy v Weston [1965] 1 WLR 280 … 212

Napier v Scottish Ministers (2004), *The Times*, 13 May … 89, 124–5, 131

New York Times v Sullivan (1964) 376 US 254 … 163

New York v Furber (1982) 485 US 747 … 19

News Verlags v Austria (2001) 31 EHRR 8 … 181

Nicol and Selvanayagam v DPP [1996] Crim LR 318 … 208, 213

Niemietz v Germany (1992) 16 EHRR 97 … 136

Norwood v DPP [2003] EWHC 1564 (Admin); [2003] Crim LR 888; (2003), *The Times*, 30 July … 204

Norwood v United Kingdom (2005) 40 EHRR 11 … 201, 205

Observer and Guardian v United Kingdom (1991) 14 EHRR 153 … 163, 166, 176

Ocalan v Turkey (2003) 37 EHRR 10 … 25

Ocalan v Turkey (2005) 41 EHRR 45 Grand Chamber … 67, 70, 79, 98, 101, 108

O'Hara v Chief Constable of the RUC [1997] 1 All ER 129 … 102

O'Hara v United Kingdom (2002) 34 EHRR 32 … 36, 98, 102, 103

O'Moran v DPP [1975] QB 864 … 205

Orange v Chief Constable of West Yorkshire Police [2001] 3 WLR 736 … 90, 123

Osman v United Kingdom (2000) 29 EHRR 245 … 65, 66, 72, 73, 111

Otto-Preminger Institut v Austria (1994) 19 EHRR 34 … 29, 161, 162, 197, 199

P, C and S v United Kingdom (2002) 25 EHRR 31 … 112

Pabla Ky v Finland (2006) 42 EHRR 34 … 109

Papon v France (2004) 39 EHRR 10 … 89, 131

Peck v United Kingdom (2003) 36 EHRR 41 … 139, 143, 148

Peers v Greece (2001) 33 EHRR 51 … 88, 89, 124, 128, 131

Percy v DPP (2002), *The Times*, 21 January … 209, 213

Perry v United Kingdom (2004) 39 EHRR 3 … 146, 147

PG and JH v United Kingdom (2001), *The Times*, 19 October … 138–9, 146, 147

Piddington v Bates [1961] 1 WLR 162 … 208

PM v United Kingdom (2006) 42 EHRR 45 … 43

Poplar Housing and Regeneration Community Association Ltd v Donoghue [2001] 2 WLR 1546 … 54

Pretty v United Kingdom (2002) 35 EHRR 1 … 30, 44, 56, 65, 136, 141, 195

Price v United Kingdom (2002) 34 EHRR 53 … 89, 129

Quinn v France (1996) 21 EHRR 529 … 98

R (Al-Saadoon and Mufhdi) v Secretary of State for Defence [2008] EWHC 3098 ... 70

R (Al-Saadoon and Mufhdi) v Secretary of State for Defence (2009), *The Times*, 3 February, CA ... 70, 78

R (Amin) v Secretary of State for the Home Department [2004] 1 AC 653 ... 75

R (Animal Defenders International) v Minister of Culture, Media and Sport [2007] EMLR 6 ... 167

R (applicant) v Home Secretary *see* R (applicant) v Secretary of State for the Home Department

R (Baiai) v Secretary of State for the Home Department [2007] 4 All ER 199 ... 42

R (Begum) v Denbigh High School [2006] 1 WLR 3372, CA ; [2007] 1 AC 100 ... 196, 197

R (Brehony) v Chief Constable of Greater Manchester Police [2005] EWHC 640; (2005), *The Times*, 15 April ... 210, 215

R (British American Tobacco) v Secretary of State for Health (2004), *The Times*, 11 November ... 53

R (Carroll and Al-Hasan) v Secretary of State for the Home Department [2002] 1 WLR 545 ... 125

R (Daly) v Secretary of State for the Home Department [2001] 2 AC 532 ... 34, 53, 59, 124, 133

R (Ellis) v Chief Constable of Essex Police (2003), *The Times*, 17 June ... 148

R (Faizovas) v Secretary of State for Justice (2009), *The Times*, 25 May ... 132

R (Farrakhan) v Secretary of State for the Home Department [2002] 3 WLR 481 ... 60

R (Gillan) v Commissioner of Police of the Metropolis [2006] 2 AC 307 ... 104, 210

R (Green) v Westminster Magistrates' Court [2008] HRLR 12 ... 201

R (Hirst) v Secretary of State for the Home Department [2002] 1 WLR 2929 ... 124

R (Laporte) v Chief Constable of Gloucestershire and others [2007] 2 WLR 46 ... 210, 214

R (Launder) v Secretary of State for the Home Department [1997] 1 WLR 839 ... 93

R (Limbuela) v Secretary of State for the Home Department [2004] 3 WLR 561 ... 10

R (Nilsen) v Secretary of State for Home Affairs [2005] 1 WLR 1028 ... 124, 125

R (Persey) and others v Secretary of State for Environment, Food and Rural Affairs [2003] QB 794 ... 177

R (Playfoot) v Millais School Governing Body (2007), *The Times*, 23 July ... 196

R (Prolife Alliance) v BBC [2003] UKHL 23; [2004] 1 AC 185, HL; [2002] 2 All ER 756, CA (Civ Div) ... 167, 191, 200

R (Stanley) v Metropolitan Police Commissioner (2004), *The Times*, 22 October ... 148

R (Swami Suryanada) v Welsh Ministers (2007) CA; [2007] EWCA Civ 893 ... 196

R (Uttley) v Secretary of State for the Home Department [2004] 1 WLR 2278 ... 116

R (Watkins Singh) v Aberdare Girls' High School Governors [2008] EWHC 1865 ... 196

R (Williamson) v Secretary of State for Employment [2005] 2 AC 246 ... 196

R v A (Complainant's Sexual History) [2002] 1 AC 45 ... 51, 54, 59

R v Anderson [1972] QB 304 ... 190

R v Board of Visitors of Hull Prison, *ex parte* St Germain [1979] QB 425 ... 122

R v Bow Street Stipendiary Magistrate, *ex parte* Pinochet Ugarte (No 2) [2000] 1 AC 119 ... 106, 110, 111

R v Bowker [2007] EWCA Crim 1608 ... 116

R v Brentwood Council, *ex parte* Peck [1998] CMLR 697 ... 144

R v Calder and Boyars [1969] 1 QB 151 ... 190

R v Chief Constable of South Yorkshire, *ex parte* LS and Marper [2004] 1 WLR 2196 ... 144

R v Chief Metropolitan Stipendiary Magistrate, *ex parte* Choudhury [1991] 1 QB 1006 ... 42, 200

R v Deputy Governor of Parkhurst Prison, *ex parte* Hague [1992] AC 58 ... 122

R v DPP, *ex parte* Pretty [2002] 1 AC 800 ... 55

R v Home Secretary *see* R v Secretary of State for the Home Department

R v Howell [1982] QB 416 ... 213

R v Jordan and Tyndall [1963] Crim LR 124 ... 205

R v Keogh [2007] 1 WLR 1500 ... 176

R v Lemon [1979] AC 617 ... 199

R v Mental Health Tribunal, *ex parte* H [2001] 3 WLR 512 ... 55

R v Ministry of Defence, *ex parte* Smith [1996] 1 All ER 257 ... 49, 50, 141, 142

R v Morpeth Ward Justices, *ex parte* Ward (1992) 95 Cr App R 215 ... 208

R v Penguin Books [1961] Crim LR 176 ... 189

R v Perrin [2002] EWCA 747 ... 190

R v Ponting [1985] Crim LR 318 ... 175

R v Press Complaints Commission, *ex parte* Ford [2002] EMLR 5 ... 154

R v R [1991] 4 All ER 481 ... 117, 118

R v Secretary of State for the Home Department, *ex parte* Anderson [1984] QB 788 ... 123

R v Secretary of State for the Home Department, *ex parte* Brind [1991] 1 AC 696 ... 49, 50, 53, 165

R v Secretary of State for the Home Department, *ex parte* Greenfield [2002] 1 WLR 545 ... 111

R v Secretary of State for the Home Department, *ex parte* Kurdistan Workers Party [2002] EWHC 644 (Admin) ... 206

R v Secretary of State for the Home Department, *ex parte* Leech [1994] QB 198 ... 123

R v Secretary of State for the Home Department, *ex parte* Mellor [2002] QB 13 ... 123, 124

R v Secretary of State for the Home Department, *ex parte* O'Brien and Simms [2000] 2 AC 115 ... 49, 123, 124, 165

R v Secretary of State for the Home Department, *ex parte* P and Q [2001] 1 WLR 2002 ... 124

R v Secretary of State for the Home Department, *ex parte* Pierson [1998] AC 539 ... 123

R v Secretary of State for the Home Department, *ex parte* Venables and Thompson [1997] 3 All ER 97 ... 123

R v Shayler [2002] 2 WLR 754 ... 55, 59, 167, 175

R v Smethurst (2001), *The Times*, 13 April ... 191

R v Taylor (1998) 93 Cr App Rep 361 ... 179

R v United Kingdom, Application No. 35748/05 ... 158

R v Wakefield LBC, *ex parte* Robertson [2002] 2 WLR 889 ... 143

Racz v Home Office [1984] 2 AC 45 ... 122

Ramzy v The Netherlands, Application No 25424/05 ... 94

Raninen v Finland (1998) 26 EHRR 563 ... 84, 132

Raymond v Honey [1983] AC 1 ... 48, 56, 59, 122, 124, 133

Redmond-Bate v DPP (1999), *The Times*, 23 July ... 209, 212, 213

Rees v United Kingdom (1986) 9 EHRR 56 ... 44, 138, 157

Reeves v Commissioner for the Police of the Metropolis [2000] AC 283 ... 90

Refah Partisi Erbakan Kazan and Tekdal v Turkey (2002) 35 EHRR 3 ... 60, 204

Refah Partisi Erbakan Kazan and Tekdal v Turkey (2003) 37 EHRR 1 ... 196

Reynolds v Times Newspapers [1999] 4 All ER 609 ... 170, 172, 173

Ridge v Baldwin [1964] AC 40 ... 106, 110

Ringeisen v Austria (1991) 1 EHRR 445 ... 108

Robertson v Kaye [1991] FLR 62 ... 151

Robins v United Kingdom (1997) 26 EHRR 527 ... 106, 113

Rodrigues v Home Office [1989] Legal Action 14 ... 88, 122

Rowe and Davis v United Kingdom (2000) 30 EHRR 1 ... 107, 112

Russell, McNamee and McCotter v Home Office (2001), *Daily Telegraph*, 13 March ... 88, 123

S (Publicity), Re [2005] 1 AC 593 ... 151, 167, 2153

S and G v United Kingdom, Application No 17634 ... 191

S and Marper v United Kingdom (2009) 48 EHRR 50 ... 144

S and W, Re [2002] 2 AC 291 ... 54, 59

Saadi v Italy (2009) 49 EHRR 30 ... 94

Sahin v Turkey (2005) 41 EHRR 8 ... 195, 197

Saidi v United Kingdom (1993) 17 EHRR 251 ... 113

Salaman v Turkey (2002) 34 EHRR 17 ... 65

Sander v United Kingdom (2001) 31 EHRR 44 ... 113

Saunders v Punch [1998] 1 WLR 986 ... 186

Saunders v United Kingdom (1996) 23 EHRR 313 ... 106, 112

SC v United Kingdom (2005) 40 EHRR 10 ... 112

Schenk v Switzerland (1988) 13 EHRR 242 ... 113, 147

Secretary of State for Defence v Guardian Newspapers [1985] AC 339 ... 185, 186, 187

Secretary of State for the Home Department v Wainwright [2004] 2 AC 406 ... 142

Selmouni v France (2000) 29 EHRR 403 ... 83

Shaw v DPP [1964] AC 220 ... 189, 191

Sheffield and Horsham v United Kingdom (1999) 27 EHRR 163 ... 157

Silkin v Beaverbrook Newspapers Ltd [1958] 1 WLR 743 ... 172

Silver v United Kingdom (1983) 5 EHRR 347 ... 25, 32, 79, 111, 126, 127, 133, 137, 138

Sim v Stretch (1936) 52 TLR 669 ... 169, 171

SL v Austria (2003) 37 EHRR 39 ... 156

Smith and Grady v United Kingdom (2000) 29 EHRR 493 ... 24, 29, 33, 41, 49–50, 80, 137, 141, 156

Socialist Party v Turkey (1998) 27 EHRR 51 ... 203

Soering v United Kingdom (1989) 11 EHRR 439 ... 25, 50, 67, 69, 76, 77, 78, 84, 85, 86, 91, 92, 93, 94

Stafford v United Kingdom (2002) 35 EHRR 32 ... 97, 100, 127

Stedman v United Kingdom (1997) 23 EHRR CD 168 ... 197

Steel and Morris v United Kingdom (2005) 41 EHRR 22 ... 107, 113, 163, 169, 171

Steel v United Kingdom (1999) 28 EHRR 603 ... 32, 98, 161, 210, 215

Stephens v Avery [1988] 2 WLR 1280 ... 151, 2153

Sunday Times v United Kingdom (1979) 2 EHRR 245 ... 25, 29, 32, 33, 34, 50, 161, 162, 166, 167, 179, 184, 185

Sutherland v United Kingdom (2001), *The Times*, 13 April ... 24, 44, 137, 156

SW and CR v United Kingdom (1995) 21 EHRR 404 ... 115, 116–17

Szuluk v United Kingdom, (2009) *The Times*, 17 June ... 127

T v United Kingdom (1986) 49 DR 5 ... 128

Tammer v Estonia (2003) 37 EHRR 43 ... 169

Tatlav v Turkey, Application No. 50692/99, European Court, 2 May 2006 ... 200

Taylor v United Kingdom [1998] EHRLR 90 ... 116

Theakston v MGN Ltd [2002] EMLR 22 ... 143, 151, 153, 154

Thlimmenos v Greece (2001) 31 EHRR 15 ... 41

Thomas v News Group Newspapers [2002] EMLR 4 ... 150

Thorgeirson v Iceland (1992) 14 EHRR 843 ... 163

Thynne, Wilson and Gunnell v United Kingdom (1990) 13 EHRR 666 ... 50, 80, 99, 127

Times Newspapers v United Kingdom, [2009] EMLR 14 ... 171

Tinnelly v United Kingdom (1998) 27 EHRR 249 ... 108

Tolstoy Miloslavsky v United Kingdom (1995) 20 EHRR 442 ... 34, 163, 169, 170, 172

Tomasi v France (1993) 15 EHRR 1 ... 84, 88, 89

Tsirlis and Koulompas v Greece (1998) 25 EHRR 198 ... 97

Turkington v Times Newspapers Ltd [2001] 2 AC 277 ... 170

Tyrer v United Kingdom (1978) 2 EHRR 1 ... 25, 83, 84, 131

United Communist Party v Turkey (1998) 26 EHRR 121 ... 58, 203

V and T v United Kingdom (2000) 30 EHRR 121 ... 30, 84, 106, 107, 111, 113, 127

Valasinas v Lithuania 12 BHRC 266 ... 84, 88

Van Colle v Chief Constable of Hertfordshire [2008] 3 WLR 593 ... 73

Van Droogenbroek v Belgium (1982) 4 EHRR 443 ... 97

Venables and Thompson v MGN [2001] 2 WLR 1038 ... 142, 151, 167

VgT Verein gegen Tierfabriken v Switzerland (2002) 34 EHRR 4 ... 167

Vilvarajah v United Kingdom (1992) 14 EHRR 248 ... 78, 85, 93

Vo v France (2005) 40 EHRR 12 ... 24, 30, 65

Vogt v Germany (1995) 21 EHRR 205 ... 203

Von Hannover v Germany (2005) 40 EHRR 1 ... 137, 139, 141, 143, 148, 152, 154, 161, 164

Waddington v Miah [1974] 1 WLR 683 ... 48, 56

Wainwright v United Kingdom (2007) 44 EHRR 40 ... 50, 142, 144

Weeks v United Kingdom (1998) 10 EHRR 293 ... 97

Welch v United Kingdom (1995) 20 EHRR 247 ... 115, 116

Westminster CC v Haw [2002] EWHC 2073 ... 209, 212

Wheeler v Leicester County Council [1985] AC 1054 ... 165

Whitfield v United Kingdom (2005) 41 EHRR 44 ... 109, 127

Whyte v DPP [1972] AC 849 ... 188, 190

Willis v United Kingdom (2002) 35 EHRR 21 ... 43

Wingrove v United Kingdom (1996) 24 EHRR 1 ... 29, 162, 197, 199

Winterwerp v Netherlands (1979) 2 EHRR 387 ... 98, 99

Wood v Commissioner of the Police of the Metropolis (2009) *The Times*, 1 June ... 144

Woodward v Hutchins [1977] 1 WLR 760 ... 151

Worm v Austria (1998) 25 EHRR 454 ... 181

X (Mary Bell) and another v News Group
Newspapers and another [2003] EMLR
37 ... 143, 151
X v Morgan Grampian (Publishers) Ltd [1991]
AC 1 ... 185

X v Netherlands (1985) 8 EHRR 235 ... 137
X v United Kingdom (1979) 2 DR 105 ... 128
X v United Kingdom (1982) 4 EHRR 188 ... 99
X, Y and Z v United Kingdom (1997) 24 EHRR
143 ... 157

Z v United Kingdom (2002) 34 EHRR 3 ... 85, 111

Table of Statutes

Anti-Terrorism, Crime and Security Act
   2001 ... 38, 53, 55, 103, 204
   s.28 ... 201
   s.28(4) ... 201

Bill of Rights 1689
   art.9 ... 170

Civil Partnership Act 2004 ... 144, 156
Communications Act 2003 ... 167, 189
Contempt of Court Act 1981 ... 180, 181, 182, 183
   s.2 ... 180, 182
   s.5 ... 176–7, 181, 182
   s.10 ... 184
Crime and Disorder Act 1998 ... 201
Criminal Justice Act 1991 ... 116
Criminal Justice and Immigration Act 2008
   s79 ... 198, 200
Criminal Justice and Public Order Act 1994
   ss.34–38 ... 111
   s.163 ... 148

Data Protection Act 1988 ... 142
Data Protection Act 1998 ... 142, 143
   s.12(4) ... 142
Defamation Act 1952
   s.5 ... 172
Drug Trafficking Act 1986 ... 115, 116

Education Act 1996 ... 196

Freedom of Information Act 2000 ... 173, 174, 175, 177
   s.1 ... 177
   s.23 ... 177
   ss.35–36 ... 177
   s.50 ... 177

Gender Recognition Act 2004 ... 144, 158

Highways Act 1980
   s.137 ... 212
Human Rights Act 1998 ... vii, 1, 21, 25, 45, 46, 47, 50, 51, 52, 53, 56, 57, 58, 59, 72, 76, 77, 80, 81, 86, 87, 95, 119, 120, 121, 123, 125,
130, 131, 133, 135, 140, 141, 142, 143, 144, 150, 164, 165, 166, 169, 194, 203, 207, 209, 211, 215
   s.2 ... 50, 53, 87, 131, 209
   s.3 ... 51, 54, 55, 56, 59
   s.4 ... 51, 55, 58, 61, 209
   s.6 ... 46, 51, 87, 131
   s.7 ... 51, 123
   s.7(1) ... 58
   s.7(3) ... 58
   s.8 ... 51, 88, 90, 123, 124
   s.10 ... 51, 55
   s.12 ... 151, 153, 164, 165, 166, 186, 212
   s.12(2) ... 166
   s.12(3) ... 153, 166, 167
   s.12(4) ... 151, 153, 167, 186

Immigration Act 1971
   s.34 ... 48
Indecent Displays (Control) Act 1981 ... 188, 189
Insolvency Act 1986 ... 112
Interception of Communications Act
   1985 ... 13, 146
   s3(2) ... 138

Magna Carta 1215 ... 48, 110
Mental Health Act 1983
   s.72 ... 55
   s.73 ... 55

Obscene Publications Act 1959 ... 188, 189, 191
   s.4 ... 49, 190
   s.4(2) ... 189
Obscene Publications Act 1964 ... 188, 189
Official Secrets Act 1911 ... 173, 174, 175
Official Secrets Act 1989 ... 55, 167, 173, 174, 175
   s.1 ... 175
   s.4 ... 175
   s.7(3)(a)–(b) ... 175

Police Act 1997 ... 146
   s.89 ... 208, 212
Police and Criminal Evidence Act 1984 ... 49

Prevention of Terrorism Act 1978 ... 27, 38
Prison Act 1952 ... 123, 132, 133, 134, 165
Protection of Children Act 1978 ... 190
Protection from Harassment Act 1997 ... 154
   s.2 ... 154
   s.3 ... 154
Public Order Act 1936
   s.1 ... 205
   s.2 ... 205
Public Order Act 1986 ... 204, 210, 211
   s.5 ... 60, 201
   s.7 ... 201
   s.11 ... 49, 208, 212, 215
   s.12 ... 49, 208, 212, 215
   s.12(1) ... 215
   s.13 ... 49, 208
   s.14 ... 49, 208, 210
   s.14A ... 208, 212
   s.14A(1) ... 213
   s.14A(2) ... 214
   s.14A(9) ... 213
   s.14B ... 208, 212
   s.14B(1) ... 214
   s.14B(4) ... 214
   s.14C ... 208, 212, 214
   s.14C(4) ... 214
   s.17 ... 200
   s.18 ... 200, 201, 204
   s.18(5) ... 201
   ss.19–23 ... 200
Public Order Act 2007 ... 57

Race Relations Act 1976 ... 196
Racial and Religious Hatred Act 2006
   s.1 ... 200, 204
Regulation of Investigatory Powers Act
   2000 ... 144, 146

Security Services Act 1989 ... 146
Serious Organized Crime and Police Act 2005
   s.132 ... 209

Sex Discrimination Act 1975 ... 43
Sexual Offences Act 2003 ... 156
Sexual Offences (Amendment) Act 2000 ... 156
Suicide Act 1961
   s.2(1) ... 55

Terrorism Act 2000 ... 205
   s.1 ... 205
   s.3 ... 205
   s.5 ... 205
   s.11 ... 206
   s.12 ... 206
   s.13 ... 205, 206
   s.44(4)(b) ... 210
   s.123 ... 205
   Sch.2 ... 205
Terrorism Act 2005 ... 104
   s.1 ... 206
   s.44 ... 104

War Crimes Act 1991 ... 117

Bill before Parliament
Constitutional Reform and Government Bill
   2009
   clause 32 ... 210

French legislation
French Declaration of Human Rights ... 16

Hong Kong legislation
Basic Law ... 93

United States legislation
Bill of Rights ... 17, 45
Constitution ... 17
   First Amendment ... 19

Table of International and European law

African Charter on Human and Peoples' Rights (1981) ... 13

American Convention on Human Rights (1969) ... 13, 16

Canadian Charter of Fundamental Rights ... 18

European Convention on the Prevention of Torture (1987) ... 14, 119

European Convention for the Protection of Human Rights and Fundamental Freedoms (1950) ... vii, 1, 2, 6, 7, 9, 12, 13, 14, 19, 21, 22, 26, 28, 31, 39, 45, 46, 47, 50, 51, 53, 55, 56, 57, 58, 59, 67, 68, 69, 71, 77, 78, 80, 81, 91, 92, 95, 109, 119, 120, 121, 122, 123, 125, 126, 130, 131, 135, 136, 140, 141, 142, 143, 144, 145, 148, 154, 155, 158, 160, 164, 169, 197, 198, 202, 206, 207, 211

preamble ... 22

Pt One ... 22, 91

art.1 ... 13, 23, 25, 26, 28, 91

art.2 ... 22, 37, 63, 64, 65, 66, 67, 68, 69, 70, 71, 72, 73, 74, 75, 76, 77, 78, 79, 80, 86, 87, 89, 90, 123, 128

art.2(1) ... 67, 68, 69, 70, 79

art.2(2) ... 63, 64, 66, 68, 71, 74

art.3 ... 22, 24, 30, 37, 38, 42, 63, 67, 69, 70, 76, 77, 79, 80, 81, 82, 83, 84, 85, 86, 87, 88, 89, 90, 92, 93, 94, 123, 124, 125, 128, 129, 130, 131, 132, 133, 134, 196

art.4 ... 23, 129, 130, 132, 134

art.4(1) ... 37

art.4(2) ... 132

art.5 ... 23, 24, 27, 32, 36, 37, 54, 55, 95, 96, 97, 98, 99, 100, 101, 102, 103, 104, 105, 114, 127

art.5(1) ... 38, 98

art.5(1)(a) ... 97

art.5(1)(b) ... 98

art.5(1)(c) ... 98, 101

art.5(1)(f) ... 98

art.5(2) ... 99, 102

art.5(3) ... 38, 97, 99, 102, 103

art.5(4) ... 97, 99, 127

art.5(5) ... 97, 100, 103

art.6 ... 23, 95, 105, 106, 107, 108, 109, 110, 111, 112, 113, 127, 133, 147

art.6(1) ... 107, 110, 112

art.6(2) ... 106, 112

art.6(3) ... 107, 113

art.6(3)(a)–(e) ... 107

art.7 ... 37, 48, 95, 114, 115, 116, 117

art.8 ... 26, 28, 31, 32, 33, 41, 42, 43, 44, 50, 55, 91, 113, 126, 129, 132, 134, 136, 137, 138, 139, 140, 141, 142, 143, 144, 145, 146, 147, 150, 152, 154, 155, 156, 157, 158, 169, 170, 172, 195

art.8(2) ... 29, 133, 137, 138, 146, 147, 156

art.9 ... 23, 26, 28, 31, 33, 42, 43, 193, 194, 195, 196, 197, 198, 199, 200, 201

art.9(2) ... 194, 195

art.10 ... 9, 23, 26, 28, 31, 33, 41, 43, 53, 55, 58, 59, 60, 61, 128, 151, 160, 161, 162, 163, 164, 165, 166, 167, 168, 169, 170, 171, 174, 175, 177, 178, 179, 183, 184, 187, 188, 189, 190, 191, 198, 203, 204, 205, 210

art.10(2) ... 28, 160, 161, 169, 174, 179, 188, 189, 190, 197, 198

art.11 ... 23, 26, 28, 31, 33, 43, 58, 59, 60, 61, 193, 202, 203, 204, 205, 206, 210

art.12 ... 26, 44, 128, 138, 154, 155, 158

art.13 ... 25, 66, 71, 72, 76, 77, 79, 80, 90, 143, 144, 147

art.14 ... 39, 40, 41, 42, 43, 44, 144, 154, 155, 156, 157, 158, 200

art.15 ... 26, 27, 35, 36, 37, 38, 39, 55, 68, 70, 96, 99, 101, 103, 105, 115

art.15(2) ... 68

art.15(3) ... 36, 64

art.17 ... 60, 61, 161, 194, 204, 205

art.19 ... 23

art.28 ... 23

art.31 ... 23

art.33 ... 24

arts.34–35 ... 13, 24

art.38 ... 24

art.41 ... 13, 24

art.43 ... 23

art.47 ... 23

Protocol 1
art.1 ... 43
art.2 ... 43, 196
art.3 ... 124, 128

Protocol 4
  art.2 ... 97
Protocol 6 ... 67, 70, 76, 79
Protocol 11 ... 25
Protocol 12 ... 40, 43, 44, 200
  preamble ... 39
  art.1 ... 43
Protocol 13 ... 67, 70, 76, 79
Protocol 14 ... 23, 25
European Prison Rules (1987) ... 119
European Social Charter (1961) ... 10

Geneva Convention ... 37

International Covenant on Civil and Political
  Rights (1966) ... 9, 12, 119, 120, 131, 133
  art.4 ... 15
  art.6 ... 12, 69
  art.6(2) ... 69
  art.6(5) ... 69
  art.7 ... 12
  art.9 ... 12

art.10 ... 130, 133, 134
art.14 ... 70
art.26 ... 40
art.28 ... 12
art.40 ... 12
art.41 ... 12
Optional Protocol
  art.1 ... 12
International Covenant on Economic, Social and
  Cultural Rights (1966) ... 10, 12, 14
  art.1 ... 12
  art.3 ... 12
  arts.11–13 ... 13
  art.16 ... 13

United Nations Charter (1945) ... 11, 13, 40
  art.68 ... 11
United Nations Minimum Standards on the
  Treatment of Prisoners (1987) ... 14
Universal Declaration of Human Rights
  (1948) ... 11, 12, 22

Table of Secondary Legislation

Employment Equality (Sexual Orientation) Regulations 2003 (SI 2003/1661) ... 156

Prison Rules 1999 (SI 1999/728) ... 74, 129, 133
rr.34–35 ... 133

Introduction

The author has taught human rights and civil liberties, and public law, for over twenty-five years and thus has considerable experience in setting questions, and marking answers, in this area. Answers in this field require the display of a combination of skills from the student and this text hopes to illustrate how the student can best tackle assessment questions which require a sound legal knowledge with an appreciation of the dynamic and sometimes uncertain state of the law.

Answering questions on human rights and civil liberties presents students with two central and related problems. Both relate to the nature of the subject, but the *first* one raises the question of whether they should treat human rights and civil liberties as a traditional legal subject, and when presenting their work whether they need to display the research, writing, and referencing skills needed in other legal subjects such as contract, tort, or criminal law. Many students enrol on human rights courses because they believe it will not involve the study of law and legal materials as such, but rather will simply require them to be interested in topical affairs and then willing to give their own views on matters such as the rights of terrorist suspects and press freedom and the privacy of celebrities. In this respect it should be remembered that the study of human rights and civil liberties *does* involve the study of law and does require the student to become familiar with the relevant legal rules and hard case law. The student cannot, therefore, answer a question on press freedom and privacy without knowing the relevant domestic law on confidentiality and privacy, and the application of the Human Rights Act 1998 and the European Convention on Human Rights. He or she cannot *simply* argue for the public right to know, or the privacy rights of the celebrity, however articulate those arguments are. As we shall see, those social and philosophical arguments, although relevant, can only be presented once the law has been understood and explained appropriately.

The *second* problem relates to how their study and written work in this subject can reflect the political, philosophical, and constitutional characteristics of the subject. Answers to questions in this area not only call for a sound knowledge of the substantive legal issues, above, but also require the student to comprehend and contribute to the arguments surrounding the protection and restriction of human rights and civil liberties. Thus, answers should combine knowledge of the relevant substantive law with a critical appreciation of the arguments for and against the protection of human rights and civil liberties and an awareness of the effect on the subject of constitutional principles such as the rule of law, the separation of powers, the independence of the judiciary, democracy, and government accountability. In addition, when studying international human rights, students must appreciate doctrines such as cultural relativism, state sovereignty, and the margin of appreciation.

Consequently, it is important that the student knows how to incorporate case and statutory and treaty provisions into answers in this area, and how to use such sources to enhance their answers. Equally, the student needs to avoid simply giving a bare account of the law; he or she must be able to articulate arguments about whether those legal rules are compatible with human rights norms, and that will require an appreciation of *established and objective* principles of fairness, such as legality, necessity, proportionality, and concepts such as the rule of law and democracy. Take, for example, the following question:

> 'To what extent does the domestic law of defamation strike a correct balance between freedom of speech and the protection of reputation?'

That question cannot be answered by simply relating the general rules on the law of defamation—the definition of a defamatory statement, the intention required to establish liability, the defences available, the various remedies, etc. First, the student needs to establish what specific aspects of defamation law have human rights implications; reliance on a textbook in tort in this respect may provide the reader with an overall account of the legal principles, but will not allow the student to identify which aspects have a bearing on free speech, individual privacy, press freedom, and the public right to know. It is only if you appreciate the potential effect of defamation law on principles of free speech and privacy that you will be able to pinpoint the actual dilemmas—that large damages awards might curtail free speech, or that the availability of a defence of qualified privilege might encourage press freedom and the public right to know. Secondly, the student will need to combine knowledge of those (relevant) legal rules with an ability to articulate an argument and a conclusion as to whether the law is achieving a correct balance; that will require knowledge of the principles and case law of the European Convention on Human Rights, and will also test the student's ability to articulate the moral arguments (whether public figures should have the right to reputation or whether the press should have immunity in this area) logically and clearly.

The answers provided in this text thus hopefully combine a reasonably thorough account of the relevant law and a sufficiently critical analysis of legal rules and cases within the established and developing arguments for and against the protection of human rights and civil liberties in any given situation. They should also provide the student with a good idea of how answers (both essays and problems) should be structured and presented. Good, clear writing skills are essential in every area of the law, but are especially important when writing essays in this area, where the marker will want a structured and coherent account of the law in addition to well-articulated views on the (often open-ended) political, moral, and constitutional considerations.

Students should also be aware of the factors which distinguish between poor, satisfactory, good, and excellent answers. A *poor* answer will either fail to answer the question (fully) or display confusion with respect to the legal principles, cases, and application of the law to the question. In particular, answers to problem questions which fail to identify the factual and legal problems and/or fail to apply the law to the factual scenario will attract low marks despite the student's knowledge of the general law. It is essential, therefore, that the student reads the question carefully and has acquired a very solid knowledge of the legal areas and cases before attempting the questions. The answer plans and commentaries provided for each question in this text should help you focus in this respect; although obviously you will have to tackle different questions in your actual exam. A *satisfactory* answer will identify the central issues raised in the question and display a reasonably sound knowledge of the law as well as an ability to apply the law to the question; whereas a *good* answer will display a broader and deeper knowledge of the law and greater competence in applying that knowledge to the question. We should also stress at this stage the importance of a clear and appropriate writing style when answering the question. A good, clear style can impress markers, while poor writing skills detract from the quality of the answer and often lead to marks being reduced. Finally, the *excellent* answer will have a variety of qualities: enhanced writing skills; in-depth knowledge of the law and cases; very strong ability to use legal materials to illustrate the answer; and an ability to spot and discuss controversial or complex issues (including spotting all issues raised by the essay question or problem scenario).

A guide as to what would be a satisfactory, good, and then excellent answer to a question is provided below with respect to an answer expected to Question 1 in Chapter 2. Thereafter, the student should apply those basic criteria for each of the essay questions. A similar guide to answering problem questions is provided below with respect to the answer expected of Question 3 in Chapter 4, which again can be used for subsequent problem questions.

Essay Questions (Refer to Question 1 in Chapter 2)

- A satisfactory answer will provide a basic definition of the relevant terms and an outline of the various theories, with some mention of the importance of protection.

- A good answer will draw on a variety of definitions of the terms, comparing and contrasting the terms, and providing various examples under each category. The student will provide a reasonably detailed and clear explanation of rights theory and will appreciate the importance of rights protection as well as the means employed by domestic and international documents to achieve effective protection.

- An excellent answer will explore the terms in detail and provide a number of means by which the distinction can be made between the terms. The student will offer a very clear and critical account of various rights theories, including alternative views, and will provide a number of examples of both domestic and international mechanisms of recognition, tying those in to the earlier part of the essay. The student will also provide case or other examples of how human rights violations are dealt with by adjudication. The answer will be clearly and professionally written and display confidence in the theory of rights protection, as well as the relevant terminology and academic language.

Problem Questions (Refer to Question 3 in Chapter 4)

- A satisfactory answer will identify the Convention rights at issue and give some general advice on the compatibility of the proscription and the prosecution with those rights. The student should show a sufficient awareness of the mechanics of the Human Rights Act 1998 and be able to offer some conclusions on the likely success of the claims.

- A good answer will identify the relevant Convention rights and analyse the importance of those rights and the seriousness of the breach in this scenario, as well as stressing the conditional status of such rights. The answer should offer a clear and thorough explanation of the mechanism by which the proscription, the prosecution, and the Act itself can be challenged by the use of the Human Rights Act and should provide clear and coherent advice as to the likely success of each claim, including any remedy the applicant may have should they fail in their claims.

- An excellent answer will display all the qualities of the good answer, above, but in addition will display an enhanced knowledge of the nature and scope of the relevant Convention rights and of the jurisprudence of both the European and domestic courts in this area. Some knowledge of existing public order laws will assist the student in assessing the legality and necessity of the powers contained in the imaginary Act.

Finally, let us provide a few words of warning. First, this book should not be used as a *substitute* for a textbook on the subject of human rights and civil liberties. There are a number of good texts in this area and students should purchase one and use it throughout their study of the subject, turning to this text to give them guidance on how to put their knowledge of the subject into the context of assessment. The author has included some further reading at the end of each chapter, and whilst this is not by any means definitive, it should give the student a reasonable indication of the type of texts and articles that they should be reading during their study of the subject. Secondly, do not expect the questions in this text to be exactly the same as, or indeed very similar to, the ones that you might face in an examination. Whilst the text offers sample questions of the type you should expect in the exam, you should not rehearse the answers in the expectation that you can present them in the exam. The text is intended to help you acquire general skills in this specific area and to assist you in facing the assessment with more confidence, not to prepare you for your specific examination or to rehearse the answers. Thirdly, the law of human rights and civil liberties changes at a frightening pace; hardly a week will go by without some important case being decided or some statutory change being made or proposed. Students in this area are expected to keep up to date with these developments and to incorporate them into their assessments. In this respect you are advised to consult the newspapers, journals, and legal websites on a regular basis, and to utilize the accompanying website for this text, which will provide regular updates on changes to the law that will affect the questions in this text.

Good luck!

2

Nature and enforcement of human rights and civil liberties

Introduction

Most human rights and civil liberties courses begin with an explanation of the nature and theory of human rights and civil liberties, including their development in both domestic and international law. This aspect of the subject covers the definition of the terms 'human rights', 'civil liberties', and 'fundamental freedoms', the distinction between civil and political and social, economic, and cultural rights, the theoretical and historical development of individual rights, and the various mechanisms by which such rights and liberties can be protected at both national and international level.

A sound knowledge of the theoretical basis of individual human rights is fundamental to the understanding of the substantive law and the student will be expected to appreciate, and provide an answer to, such questions as where such rights come from, what values they promote, whether such rights are democratically justifiable, and how such rights should be balanced with other rights and collective interests. In addition, many courses will dedicate a good deal of time to the manner in which such rights are enforced, both domestically and internationally. Consequently, students need to have a sound knowledge of the various mechanisms for recognizing human rights, the efficacy of those methods, and the variety of constitutional, legal, and moral dilemmas that arise from those methods.

Questions on these theoretical and institutional areas will often appear in coursework and examination questions, and usually appear in essay form. The knowledge needed to answer them can also be usefully employed in other substantive areas of human rights, because it is rarely possible to answer a question on a substantive area of human rights such as freedom of expression or freedom from torture without appreciating the theoretical justification for that freedom, the reasons why the freedom might have to be curtailed, and the mechanisms for enforcement (including the benefits, limitations, and constitutional and legal problems of enforcement).

Those who prefer theory and institutions to black letter law usually favour theory questions, but even those who prefer the latter approach are advised to get to grips with basic theory, for the reason outlined above and the fact that some papers will force the student to attempt at least one question in this area.

Question 1

What do we mean by the terms 'human rights' and 'civil liberties'? Explain and analyse the leading theories on human rights protection and describe how those theories are implemented in national and international human rights documents.

 Commentary

This question is a fairly broad one, requiring the student to appreciate the meaning of human rights and civil liberties, to display a sound knowledge of the variety of theories justifying such rights and liberties, and to explain how those theories are incorporated into both domestic bills of rights and international treaties. Because it has several components it does not require a *detailed* knowledge of the meaning and theory of human rights or of the variety of national and international instruments responsible for protecting such rights. However, the question does require a sound working knowledge of human rights theory and should not be tackled unless the student is confident with these principles and theories and in answering questions that do not invite a substantive, black letter law approach, or, of course, if the question is compulsory!

The question requires the student first to make a distinction between human rights and civil liberties and explain where the terms overlap; and secondly to explain how human rights theory is reflected in the actual machinery for their enforcement. To complete the second task the student needs to appreciate the importance of the constitutional methods of rights protection and the reason why such domestic and international documents put rights first and attempt to give them an enhanced status over other rights or social interests.

The student should have an appreciation of a variety of domestic and international mechanisms, although in most cases students will employ as examples the mechanisms best known to them, such as the International Covenants, the European Convention and, on the domestic front, the English and United States' methods. Finally, although the question is theory-based and does not require an exposition of the substantive law, it is acceptable to work in examples of substantive rights to explain what human rights and civil liberties are and to illustrate their importance and the theory behind them.

Answer plan

- Definition of the terms 'human rights' and 'civil liberties'
- Distinction (and similarities) between human rights and civil liberties
- An explanation of the main rights theories—Locke, Rawls, Dworkin, Bentham
- An explanation of how those theories are incorporated into both domestic and international mechanisms

Suggested answer

The terms 'human rights' and 'civil liberties' refer principally to those rights or moral claims that are regarded as fundamental to the individual's liberty—such as freedom of movement, freedom from torture, and freedom of expression—or basic needs, such as shelter, food, and clothing. Although there is an argument that individuals should respect each other's rights and liberties, human rights and civil liberties refer to those basic rights that are owed by the state to its own, or other states', citizens. There is, accordingly, a belief that each state should respect these individual liberties and needs and that its legal and constitutional system should identify and protect these rights from encroachment and ensure that the individual is provided with such rights. Human rights and civil liberties thus represent the way in which states should treat individuals with respect to their basic liberty, humanity, and worth.

The term 'civil liberties' often refers to those lists of civil and political rights which are contained in documents such as the **European Convention on Human Rights**. These liberties consist of an obligation on the part of the state not to interfere with the individual's basic rights to life, liberty, and property, and include the right to privacy, free speech, freedom from slavery and torture, the right to due process and freedom from arbitrary arrest and, of course, the right to life. The term 'human rights', on the other hand, often refers to the state's obligation to provide the individual with the basic needs of human life—often referred to as social and economic rights and including rights such as food, shelter, clothing, and employment.

The above distinctions are not, however, comprehensive, and sometimes the term 'human rights' can be used in an umbrella sense to refer to both types of right or claim. Equally, documents such as the European Convention refer to 'Human Rights and Fundamental Freedoms', and also makes some mention of social and economic rights, such as the right to education. Further, although civil liberties consist principally of negative rights to be left alone by the state, they often include the state's obligation to provide the physical resources to enable the individual to enjoy that liberty; for example, by providing a court structure and officers to enable an individual to enjoy liberty and a fair trial. Despite this overlap, the terms 'human rights' and 'civil liberties' are often used by scholars to distinguish between positive and negative rights.

The basis of civil liberties is entrenched in the idea of the liberty of the individual and protection from the acts of arbitrary government. Each state should recognize and protect the individual citizen's right to life, liberty, and property, as contained in a variety of domestic bills of rights throughout the world as well as in international treaties.

Although such notions were articulated by philosophers such as Plato and Aristotle, the idea of specific protection of liberty from state interference came to prominence in the so-called 'Age of Enlightenment', in order to control the acts of arbitrary and oppressive governments. During this time, philosophers such as John Locke devised the 'social contract', which has since formed the basic justification for the protection of civil rights. This involves the state agreeing to respect the individual's choice on matters such as religion, private life, and speech, and is based on the inalienable and fundamental character of such liberty. These liberties or rights are bolstered by international treaties and thus are regarded globally as fundamental, and superior to other rights or interests. Thus, for example, the right to free speech and freedom of assembly will be regarded as more important than the right to shop in an area free from the inconvenience of demonstrations. Although the latter interest might, in some circumstances, override our fundamental right, there is no argument that the right to shop has a fundamental status and is, therefore, worthy of inclusion in any domestic or international bill of rights.

The protection of such rights can be justified on a number of grounds. First, under the 'social contract', expounded by such writers as Locke and Rawls, every individual is said to enter into a contract with the state under which the latter agrees to protect the fundamental rights of each citizen. Here the citizen's promise of allegiance to the state is conditional on the retention of fundamental claims, which include the right to life, liberty, and property. Rawls imagines a hypothetical social contract, whereby each individual, not yet knowing his or her ultimate destination or choices, seeks to achieve a society that will best allow him or her to achieve those individual goals. This position may not find favour with the utilitarian view expounded by those such as Jeremy Bentham, which does not see individual liberty as a good in itself, and which condones individual liberty being sacrificed for the greater public good if necessary.

Secondly, human rights can be said to uphold the basic dignity of the individual as a human being; that every human being is deserving of humane treatment, and should not, for example, be subject to torture or other ill-treatment, or to slavery and servitude. Consequently, states violate human dignity when committing any of the above violations, and the restriction of an individual's right of choice, such as freedom of religion, association, and expression, will be regarded as an attack on human worth and dignity, particularly if done on grounds of sex, race, or religion, etc. This justification also ensures that states do not violate the standards of civilized society.

Thirdly, much human rights law is based on the idea of equality and freedom from discrimination. International treaties and domestic bills of rights insist that rights are enjoyed free from discrimination on grounds, such as sex, race, national origin, and religion and domestically specific laws will be passed to ensure that individuals and groups are not subject to unlawful discrimination. For example, Ronald Dworkin believes that every state has a duty to treat all of its citizens with equal concern and respect, ensuring that every person, particularly those, for example, who espouse unpopular views, enjoy these fundamental rights.

Fourthly, the protection of individual liberty and rights can be supported with reference to the rule of law. Under this doctrine, law should be open, clear, and prospective, and government should not interfere with people's rights in an arbitrary fashion. The rule of law also insists on equality, in the equal application of the law to all classes, including government officials, and on due process, including the principles of a fair trial, the presumption of innocence, the prohibition of retrospective penalties, and the guarantee of judicial impartiality and independence. The rule of law not only protects the individual from arbitrary, irrational, and unreasonable interference, but also provides a public good, and society benefits from the application of 'due process' rights such as the right to liberty and security of the person and the right to a fair trial, both of which uphold the principles of legality, the rules of natural justice, and the independence and impartiality of the judiciary. Consequently, anti-terrorism provisions have been subject to both political and legal challenge on the basis that they departed from fundamental principles of liberty and justice (*A v Secretary of State for the Home Department* [2005] 2 AC 68).

Fundamental rights and liberties are contained in both domestic and international instruments and display a reasonably common content. For example, both bills of rights and international treaties will attempt to protect rights such as the right to life, the right to property, the right to a fair trial, and freedom of expression and peaceful assembly. Equally, basic needs such as food, shelter, clothing, and the right to education will be regarded as fundamental, will be accommodated in both the state's legal and constitutional framework, and will be recognized and protected by a variety of international treaties and measures.

With respect to civil and political rights, treaties such as the **European Convention on Human Rights 1950** and the **International Covenant on Civil and Political Rights 1966** adopt the rights theories described above and give a special status to individual freedom and rights. Such rights are given the status of 'fundamental' rights, assuming that they are *normally* more important than the enjoyment of other rights or interests and can only be overridden in exceptional circumstances and under certain prescribed conditions. Thus, these international treaties impose on the state a burden to prove that any interference is legal, necessary, and proportionate. For example, under **article 10** of the European Convention, any interference with freedom of expression has to be prescribed by law and be necessary in a democratic society for the protection of a legitimate aim and the European Court has made it clear that in such cases it is a question of protecting freedom of expression subject to narrowly applied exceptions (*Handyside v United Kingdom* (1976) 1 EHRR 737).

Equally, a domestic bill of rights will give a special legal status to these rights, providing special constitutional recognition and protection, elevating them above regular rights, and protecting them from arbitrary interference. This gives the right the characteristic of an immunity, which should then ensure that the individual's right will start from the strongest position possible, thus normally trumping other rights and interests.

With respect to the protection of social and economic human rights, domestic and international treaties tend not to offer the same degree of legal protection that is available with respect to civil and political rights. Consequently, these treaties are not generally policed by a judicial body capable of making legally binding decisions on alleged violations of such rights. Nevertheless, treaties, such as the **International Covenant on Economic, Social and Cultural Rights 1966** and the **European Social Charter 1961** represent global and regional concern for such rights and the need to ensure their provision in each state. Similarly, the domestic law of the state will often provide enhanced protection, either by passing specific protective law in the fields of social welfare and employment protection, or by linking the violation of such rights with legally enforceable civil and political rights, such as the right to enjoyment of private life or freedom from inhuman and degrading treatment (*R (Limbuela) v Secretary of State for the Home Department* [2004] 3 WLR 561).

Thus, although social and economic rights may be enforced differently and perhaps less effectively, than civil and political rights, both sets of rights share the quality of being fundamental. Consequently, both domestic and international law will recognize their fundamental status and will attempt to ensure their observance in all but the most exceptional circumstances. This stance will reflect the above theories of rights protection and give such claims the status of 'trump' rights.

Question 2

What remedies are available in international law to those whose human rights have been violated? How effective are those remedies and to what extent is it realistic to expect human rights to be protected at a universal level?

 Commentary

This question not only requires an overall knowledge of various international mechanisms for the protection of human rights, but also asks the student to critically appraise the effectiveness of those systems. The student will need to be aware of the various UN treaties and other instruments, as well as the variety of regional treaties for the protection of human rights. In particular, the student needs to explain that certain treaties are enforced via judicial means, that others rely on mechanisms such as state reporting and visits, and that some are purely aspirational, commenting on the effectiveness and limits of each method. In the final part of the question the student needs to be aware of the doctrines of state sovereignty and cultural relativism and their impact on the enforcement of human rights in the international arena and, accordingly, what can reasonably be expected of international human rights protection.

Although the question appears to come in two parts, it might be better for the student to take a critical approach throughout when considering the various mechanisms and then make conclusions as to overall effectiveness at the end.

 ## Answer plan

- Explanation of the international human rights movement, including the various international treaties and other measures offering protection against and redress for human rights violations

- Explanation of the various techniques employed in international law for such protection and redress

- Critical analysis of the efficacy of such treaties and measures

- Consideration of the difficulties facing international law and its machinery in providing such universal protection and the expectations of international law in this area

Suggested answer

Since the end of the Second World War there has been a movement to provide international recognition of human rights and effective protection against human rights violations. Such a movement gives human rights a global significance and provides a mechanism by which all states can agree universal standards on human rights so as to judge the legitimacy of each state's record in protecting such rights. This movement proceeds on the basis that domestic law cannot adequately safeguard an individual's basic rights, and that a general standard of rights needs to be agreed internationally and to be subject to some form of international policing.

The first formal recognition of human rights in the international order was evident in the **United Nations Charter 1945**. Although the Charter was not an international treaty for the protection of human rights, the preamble to the Charter states that the peoples of the United Nations reaffirm faith in fundamental human rights, in the dignity and worth of the human person, and in the equal rights of men and women. Further, **article 1** states that one of the purposes of the United Nations is to promote and encourage respect for human rights and for fundamental freedoms for all without distinction as to race, sex, language, or religion. These declarations are no more than aspirational, yet they support principles of liberty and individual freedom that subsequently formed the content of specific rights treaties. More specifically, **article 68** provides that the Economic and Social Council of the United Nations shall set up commissions for, *inter alia*, the promotion of human rights, and the Council established the Commission on Human Rights (replaced by the Human Rights Council in 2006), who in turn drafted the **Universal Declaration of Human Rights 1948**.

The 1948 Declaration lists a full range of both civil and political and economic and social rights and establishes the UN Commission on Human Rights, who could consider communications revealing a consistent pattern of gross violations of human rights. In addition, the Commission was concerned with the promotion and encouragement of human rights, including undertaking investigations into the position of human rights in particular countries. This enforcement procedure represented a radical departure from the traditions of international law, which stated that such law should not interfere in the domestic affairs of each state, and led to two separate covenants on human rights—the **International Covenant on Civil and Political Rights**, and the **International Covenant on Economic, Social and Cultural Rights**—with their own mechanisms for enforcement.

The **International Covenant on Civil and Political Rights 1966** contains a list of civil and political rights—similar to that found in the more familiar **European Convention on Human Rights**—and is monitored by the Human Rights Committee. This Committee, established under **article 28**, can receive and study reports submitted by the state parties on how they have given effect to the rights recognized in the Covenant (**article 40**). It may also receive communications from other state parties alleging that a state party is not fulfilling its obligations under the Covenant (**article 41**). This latter process requires a declaration from the relevant state recognizing the competence of the Committee to receive and consider such complaints. Further, the Committee has no power to make a binding judgment, although it may use its powers to achieve a friendly settlement between the parties.

More controversially, the Committee may receive communications from individuals claiming to be a victim of a violation of his or her Covenant rights by a state party (**Optional Protocol to the Covenant, article 1**). This is similar to the enforcement mechanism employed under the **European Convention on Human Rights** and communications can be received by an individual, either personally or through another individual, where the victim is prevented from communicating directly, claiming to be a victim. The Committee has the power to declare communications inadmissible, and must be satisfied that the complainant has exhausted all available domestic remedies and that the complaint is not being considered by any other international procedure. The defendant state party has the opportunity to forward its views on the allegations, and if it finds against the state, the Committee has no power to enforce the finding and must leave it to the state to take any remedial action.

With respect to economic and social rights, the UN is also responsible for the **International Covenant on Economic, Social and Cultural Rights 1966**. **Article 1** seeks to recognize these rights by stating that all peoples have the right of self-determination and the right to pursue their economic, social, and cultural development. **Article 3** then states that the state parties undertake to ensure the equal right of men and women to enjoy the rights laid down in the Covenant, which include such rights as the right to work, including the right to just and favourable conditions of work (**articles 6 and 7**); the right to form trade unions (**article 8**); the right to social security (**article 9**); the right to an adequate standard of living, including adequate food, clothing, and housing (**article 11**); the right to enjoy physical and mental health (**article 12**); the right to education (**article 13**); and the right to take part in cultural life (**article 14**). These rights impose a general duty to attempt to ensure the conditions whereby such rights might be realized, reflecting the nature of economic and social rights, which impose a positive obligation on the state to provide resources and which are, therefore, dependant on the economic resources of each individual state. This is duly reflected in the enforcement mechanism in the Covenant, which is based on the principle of self-monitoring and regulation. Under **article 16** of the Covenant the state parties agree to submit (to the UN Committee on Economic, Social and Cultural Rights) reports on the measures that they have adopted and the progress made in achieving the observance of such rights.

In addition to the UN-inspired treaties above, there exist a number of regional human rights documents, which attempt to regulate the recognition and enforcement of human rights in a particular region, such as the **European Convention on Human Rights 1950**, the **African Charter on Human and People's Rights 1981**, and the **American Convention on Human Rights 1969**. These member states share a reasonably common set of values, particularly with respect to the identification and protection of human rights and fundamental freedoms. The most famous of these treaties is the **European Convention on Human Rights and Fundamental Freedoms 1950**, which applies to members of the Council of Europe (and not just to members of the European Union). One of the central aims of the European Convention is to effect incorporation of the Convention and its principles into the domestic law of member states. For example, **article 1** of the Convention provides that the High Contracting Parties undertake to secure to everyone within their jurisdiction the rights and freedoms set out in **Section One** of the Convention.

The most striking feature of the European Convention relates to the machinery for the enforcement of Convention rights and freedoms. Thus, the European Court of Human Rights not only has the power to receive applications from individuals claiming to be a victim of a violation at the hands of a member state (**articles 34 and 35** of the Convention), but may also make judicial declarations on the Convention, which are then binding in international law on any relevant state party who has accepted the compulsory jurisdiction of the Court. This includes the power to award remedies, including compensation, in the form of 'just satisfaction' under **article 41** of the Convention, and several judgments have resulted in a state changing its law and practice so as to comply with the Court's judgment. For example, the United Kingdom Parliament passed the **Interception of Communications Act 1985** following the Court's decision in *Malone v United Kingdom* (1984) 7 EHRR 14, which held that unregulated telephone-tapping was in violation of **article 8** of the Convention.

This judicial method is the exception rather than the norm with respect to international enforcement of human rights, and a more cautious and less confrontational procedure is usually available. For example, as we have seen, the **United Nations Charter** lacks any machinery for the enforcement of the rights it espouses and relies purely on declaring the importance of such rights and their protection by each and every member state. This method can also be bolstered by a body that is responsible for the promotion of particular fundamental rights and in this way human rights might be enhanced by greater awareness and by international support. Thus in 2006 the UN created the Human Rights Council, which supersedes the Commission on Human Rights and which has new powers, including the undertaking of periodic reviews of the state's human rights obligations. Further, under such treaties as the **International Covenants on Civil and Political and Economic, Social and Cultural Rights**, a system of state reporting is adopted, placing the duty on each member state to make periodic reports of the measures adopted within their jurisdiction. This will give the international body the opportunity of reviewing those measures and, in certain cases, of commenting critically. A more proactive method of international enforcement is the one adopted under the **European Convention on the Prevention of Torture 1987**, whereby the European Committee for the Prevention of Torture is charged, *inter alia*, with the duty to make visits to various places where individuals are detained, for the purpose of assessing whether the conditions of such detention constitute torture or inhuman or degrading treatment or punishment.

Although these methods are, arguably, less effective than the method employed under the **European Convention on Human Rights**, they do at least promote international recognition and respect for fundamental rights, often informing domestic law and practice in this area. Further, the European Convention model is essentially only effective when a victim does, and can, bring a violation before the European Court. In other words, the judicial method does not concentrate on addressing or avoiding human rights violations, although it might be said that a finding by the European Court will often change the law and practice of a particular state and force it to improve its standards. Also, some treaties and instruments were never intended to be subject to adjudication, but instead aim to raise awareness of particular rights or specific groups such as women, refugees, prisoners, and children. Thus treaties such as **UN Minimum Standards on the Treatment of Prisoners 1987** are primarily intended to offer guidance to states and state actors on the standard treatment of prisoners. Judicial enforcement in such cases might not be appropriate, although the standards of such measures might have persuasive force in other formal judicial proceedings.

The 'non-judicial' methods also highlight caution in expecting international law to provide full and effective protection against human rights violations. The protection of human rights at international level gives rise to the question of the proper role of international law *vis-à-vis* a state's right to self-determination, and consequently a balance must be maintained between the right of each state to its individual autonomy and the protection of individual fundamental human rights. Even if a state recognizes the legitimacy of international intervention and of fundamental rights, there may be difficulty in achieving a consensus among member states on what rights should be included in such treaties and to what extent they should be protected, particularly with respect to economic and social rights where the state may not have the financial and other resources to comply with its obligations. Consequently, states may be reluctant to commit themselves to judicially enforceable international treaties and will be more comfortable with measures such as state reporting, which do not impose a judicial sanction on the state's breach.

Further, even in the context of judicially enforceable international treaties, there will need to be some accommodation for the state's autonomy and cultural and social differences. Thus, the treaty might allow states to make reservations when ratifying a treaty, or allow it to derogate from its obligations in time of war or other emergency (**article 4 of the International Covenant on Civil and Political Rights**). This will be attractive to states that do not enjoy the political, social, and constitutional stability needed to provide stable fundamental rights and will thus act as an incentive for such states to subscribe to international standards. Equally, the international machinery for enforcing these fundamental rights must allow each member state a certain margin of appreciation or margin of error in how they achieve a proper balance between the protection of human rights and the achievement of other social or individual interests (*Handyside v United Kingdom* (1976) 1 EHRR 737).

In conclusion, international and regional human rights measures aimed at the recognition and protection of fundamental rights, exist for the purpose of globalizing human rights and offering effective protection against their abuse by individual states. However, social, economic, and constitutional differences often militate against the setting of appropriate standards and this is often reflected in the machinery for the enforcement of such international standards. Ultimately, international law can only hope to set globally agreed minimum standards and it would be unrealistic to expect those standards to be rigid, or for international law to offer protection solely consistent with our idea of legal enforcement.

Question 3

What purpose do national bills of rights serve in the protection of human rights and civil liberties? In your opinion, are such documents damaging to the public interest and anti-democratic?

 Commentary

Although the question appears to require simply an explanation of the purposes of domestic bills of rights, it also requires a sound appreciation of the theory and justification of human rights protection, including the history behind the introduction of such theories and mechanisms. The student needs to appreciate the fact that one vital purpose of bills of rights is to enhance the status of individual rights, by putting rights first and preventing them from being violated for the general good. The answer should also explain that these instruments are often supplemented by judicial enforcement, allowing judges to rule on the compatibility of legislative and executive acts which encroach on basic rights and to provide a remedy in the case of violation.

The question then requires the student to explore the argument that such instruments provide too much protection to the individual and too much power to the courts to overrule the wishes of government and the democratically elected parliament. At this stage examples, hypothetical and real, may be provided of instances where the protection of individual liberties and rights may be damaging to the public interest or anti-democratic. The student may then balance the arguments for and against bills of rights and judicial power and come to their own conclusions whether the protection of fundamental human rights is inconsistent with democracy and the general public interest.

 ## Answer plan

- Explanation of the rationale and aims and objectives of domestic bills of rights
- Consideration of the constitutional problems associated with the protection of such rights and liberties
- Consideration of the notion that the protection of human rights is damaging to the greater social interest and/or anti-democratic
- Conclusions on the above arguments, using pro- and anti-human rights arguments and illustrations

Suggested answer

In most cases a state's written constitution will make express provision for the enjoyment of human rights within what is commonly referred to as a bill of rights. This document will contain a number of rights and liberties that are regarded as common to the notion of individual liberty and human worth, and whose enjoyment are central to the control of arbitrary government. Although the content of a bill of rights may vary from state to state, such documents usually cover basic civil and political rights such as the right to life, liberty, and property (**American and French Declarations**). Thus, it is common for a bill of rights to recognize, and then seek to protect, rights such as the right to life, freedom from torture and slavery, liberty of the person, the right to a fair trial, the right to privacy, freedom of expression and the right to peaceful enjoyment of property.

Having identified these rights as constitutionally fundamental, the legal system will then need to decide how and to what extent such rights are to be protected, and in particular what status is to be afforded to them *vis-à-vis* their relationship with other rights and interests. Central to the question of their legal protection will be the extent to which the courts possess power to question or set aside administrative or legislative acts or decisions which are incompatible with their enjoyment. One method for protecting such rights might be to identify the rights and liberties as central to the constitution of the state, thereby giving them some special constitutional standing.

This declaration may be merely aspirational in that the constitution does not provide any mechanism for the *legal* enforcement of these rights or liberties. As this method of recognition does not impose any legal restraint, the state is then left to decide how those rights should be protected within the law.

However, many bills of rights are given legal support by bestowing the ultimate power of interpretation and enforcement to the courts, thereby restricting the power of lawmakers and executive government to interfere with these rights. This 'constitutional' method of protection is evident in the **United States Constitution**, under which the courts have the ultimate power to interpret both the Constitution and the **Bill of Rights** and are allowed to declare legislative acts unconstitutional. For example, in *Madison v Malsbury* 1 **Cranch** 137 (1803), the Supreme Court declared state law that criminalized abortion in violation of the right to private life and thus unconstitutional.

Such bills of rights achieve a number of aims. First, although they are principally aimed at the protection of individual liberty, such documents reflect common interests in, for example, democracy, and the rule of law, and the control of excessive and arbitrary government. Their protection, therefore, is seen as an essential element of the state's constitutional make-up, reflecting fundamental characteristics of that society. Thus, freedom of expression not only recognizes the public's belief in individual self-autonomy, but also promotes the common good in press freedom, democracy, and the public right to know. Secondly, bills of rights can reflect notions of individual liberty as expressed in theories such as the social contract and the right to equality. A bill of rights will ensure that each individual, irrespective of their standing or the choices they make, will enjoy basic rights of liberty, and this will reflect a common belief in individual freedom and equality. Thirdly, bills of rights are capable of protecting minorities, who might otherwise have their fundamental rights abused by government, often with the approval of the majority. Consequently, bills of rights are often relied on by 'vulnerable' groups, such as prisoners, children, women, and immigrants, who might otherwise be left unprotected by the regular law. Fourthly, they allow domestic law to reflect the international obligations of that state and thus to incorporate those treaties into its domestic law. Thus, a bill of rights can often exist side by side with such international treaties, allowing the courts to employ international human rights norms in the adjudication of domestic disputes.

However, bills of rights are seen by some as damaging to society and, specifically, anti-democratic. First, such documents may be seen by some as inconsistent with the main aims of a state's constitution and government: to secure the greatest happiness for the greatest number of people in that state. Under the utilitarian approach no one person's liberty should be allowed to frustrate the pursuit of the common good, and individual rights, therefore, should be enjoyed within the context of attaining the greatest benefit of the majority. Thus, to allow the enjoyment of the right to free expression over the protection of national security or public morals could be viewed as damaging to the principal interests of society, and the prohibition of ill-treatment of an individual might be seen as protecting human dignity at the expense of achieving a greater good, such as obtaining intelligence information from terrorist suspects.

More specifically, some view the giving of power to the courts to become the final arbiters of the law and its compatibility with fundamental human rights as damaging to democratic values. Under legally entrenched bills of rights the legislative and the executive are disentitled from passing or executing provisions that are inconsistent with such rights. Accordingly, the courts are left with the final say as to the interpretation and application of the bill of rights and what weight should be attached to such rights. This may be regarded as in breach of the separation of powers, as the courts can rule on the compatibility of the law or administrative practice with the enjoyment of fundamental rights. More significantly, where the court decision is in conflict with the express wishes of a democratically elected legislature there may be allegations of anti-democratic practice.

Another concern is that bills of rights are used in practice by unpopular and divisive groups. Accordingly, such documents can be seen by some as a 'rogues' charter', there to protect those who have transgressed, or, more commonly, are *suspected* of transgressing society's laws or morals, or who otherwise pose a threat to its security and well-being. Equally, and in relation to the democratic point, above, many people are unwilling to relinquish the power of the authorities to punish and deal with such individuals as they wish and thus disagree that a bill of rights, policed by a court of law, should set the limits of those measures by declaring them excessive or otherwise unlawful.

Are the above concerns justified? First, it needs to be pointed out that many bills of rights do not relinquish ultimate legal power to the courts, and, some bills allow the government the ultimate power to interfere with fundamental rights. For example, under the **Canadian Charter of Fundamental Rights**, the legislature is allowed to pass legislation with a 'notwithstanding' clause, so that legislation is regarded as legitimate notwithstanding the fact that it is inconsistent with the fundamental rights in the Charter. Indeed, under some systems, such as the ones adopted by New Zealand and the UK, the judiciary is merely given the power to interpret legislation, wherever possible, in conformity with fundamental rights, and the legislature retains the power to pass legislation that is clearly inconsistent with such rights. In this way, parliamentary sovereignty is retained and the democratically elected government remains the ultimate arbiter on questions relating to the protection of human rights and civil liberties. There is, therefore, adequate opportunity for the state to 'claw back' its power from the courts, although many would see this tactic as divisive of the very nature of a bill of rights.

Secondly, whatever system is adopted, all legal systems will need to provide for circumstances where it is permissible to violate, or compromise, fundamental rights. This can be done by either placing express exceptions to the scope of a particular right, for example, that the right to life is to be subject to the lawful implementation of the death penalty, or by allowing interferences, provided they possess the characteristics of legitimacy and reasonableness. For example, in the **European Convention on Human Rights**, restrictions on, for example, freedom of speech, are permissible provided they are prescribed by law and necessary in a democratic society for the protection of a legitimate aim, such as national security or public morals (*Handyside v United Kingdom* (1976) 1 EHRR 737). In addition, fundamental rights can be limited by judicial interpretation. For example, although the first amendment to the American Constitution provides that no law shall be passed which abridges freedom of speech, the American courts have limited the enjoyment of freedom of expression by deciding either that certain speech is not within the ambit of the article (*New York v Ferber* 485 US 747 (1982)) or that it can be compromised for certain legitimate reasons.

Thirdly, bills of rights can indeed be defended against allegations that they are anti-democratic. As we have seen, the rights recognized by such documents are central to the tenets of democracy and individual freedom, based on beliefs shared by all citizens. Indeed, in some cases it can be argued that rights such as free speech and peaceful assembly actively promote democracy in that they inform the public and offer a means to challenge government. Further, the bill will provide for occasions when rights conflict with other legitimate aims of the state and consequently a bill of rights might allow individual interests to be compromised on grounds such as national security and public morality provided there is a pressing need to restrict individual freedom. This is particularly so where there exists an emergency such as war or terrorism, when it is legitimate to further restrict such rights in the name of safety and security. Finally, although bills of rights might allow the courts the final say, there will generally exist an understanding between the courts and government with respect to the amount of deference that should be shown by judges when challenging the political judgement of government officials, particularly when such acts have been given direct authority from the democratically elected legislative. There will exist, therefore, a system of 'democratic dialogue', which recognizes that in some cases the courts are not the most appropriate body to rule on the legitimacy or reasonableness of certain acts.

In conclusion, one might use the opinions of Lord Bingham in the case of *A v Secretary of State for the Home Department* [2005] 2 AC 68 to support the proposition that judicial enforcement of human rights is neither socially divisive nor anti-democratic. In that case, his Lordship stressed that, although judges were not elected, the function of independent judges charged to interpret and apply the law was universally recognized as a cardinal feature of the modern democratic state. Thus, constitutional bills of rights bestow on the courts a specific constitutional role: to uphold the rule of law and to safeguard the fundamental and democratic rights of its citizens. Provided that is done in good faith, and due weight is attached to competing social interests when they are threatened by the enjoyment of human rights, then the protection of such rights by a bill of rights should not be regarded as harmful or anti-democratic.

Further reading

Feldman, D, *Civil Liberties and Human Rights in England and Wales*, 2nd edn (OUP 2002), chs 1 and 2.

Harvey, C, 'Talking about Human Rights' [2004] EHRLR 500.

Ministry of Justice, *Green Paper: Rights and Responsibilities: Developing our Constitutional Framework*, CM 7577 (2009).

Smith, R, *Textbook on International Human Rights*, 3rd edn (OUP 2007).

Waldron, J, *The Law* (Routledge 1990), ch 5.

3

The European Convention on Human Rights

Introduction

The **European Convention on the Protection of Human Rights and Fundamental Freedoms 1950** is at the centre of most modern human rights courses for two principal reasons. First, the European Court (and the now defunct Commission) of Human Rights has generated an enormous amount of case law that has informed international human rights law and has resulted in numerous legal and other changes in the United Kingdom as a result of actions brought against the government by aggrieved individuals. Secondly, the European Convention has now been 'incorporated' into (more properly, given effect to) domestic law by the **Human Rights Act 1998** and as a consequence the Convention rights are the central bases of human rights protection in domestic law.

As a consequence most exam papers will contain questions on the European Convention, including its substantive rights and the machinery for enforcement, and all students will be expected to have a sound knowledge of the Convention's content and its influence on human rights protection. In particular, students need to be conversant with the background to the Convention, its machinery for enforcement, the substantive rights contained in the Convention and their different status, and the various principles underpinning those Convention rights, such as legality, necessity, and proportionality. This chapter contains questions on the machinery for enforcement and the principles of human rights adjudication emanating from that machinery. The substantive rights under the Convention will be dealt with in subsequent chapters on the right to life, freedom from torture, due process, the right to private life, freedom of expression, and freedom of religion, association, and assembly.

Question 1

Why was the **European Convention on Human Rights** drafted and ratified? What machinery did the Convention establish for the enforcement of human rights and how effective has the Convention and that machinery been in protecting human rights?

Commentary

The first part of this question asks for a reasonably descriptive account of the history of the Convention and its ratification, requiring an historical appreciation of the Council of Europe and the drafting of the Convention. The student should also appreciate the dual role of the Convention: to establish machinery for the enforcement of human rights and the resolution of human rights disputes, and to ensure that the standards laid down in the Convention were applied in the domestic law of each state.

The real crux of the question lies in the second part and the student should not only be able to fully explain the relevant procedures and mechanisms provided for under the Convention, but also show an appreciation of the system's novelty in allowing individual petition and accepting the compulsory jurisdiction of the European Court of Human Rights. This obviously requires the student to be aware of the more traditional and limited mechanisms of international human rights enforcement.

Answer plan

- Explanation of the history of the setting up of the Council of Europe and the drafting of the European Convention
- Analysis of the aims and objectives of the European Convention
- Explanation of the machinery established under the Convention for protecting human rights, notably the role of the European Court of Human Rights
- Examination of the effectiveness of that machinery, and especially the decisions of the European Court, in protecting human rights within the Council of Europe

Suggested answer

The **European Convention on Human Rights and Fundamental Freedoms 1950** was drafted by the Council of Europe, a body set up after the Second World War to achieve unity among its members in matters such as the protection of fundamental human rights. It was drafted in the light of the atrocities that took place before and during the Second World War and in its preamble the Convention reminds the 'High Contracting Parties' of the common heritage of political traditions, ideals, freedom, and the rule of law shared by their governments. Further, the preamble states that the Contracting Parties should resolve to take steps for the collective enforcement of certain of the rights contained in the **Universal Declaration of Human Rights 1948**, this being one effective way of ensuring future peace and stability.

The aims of the Convention were, therefore, threefold. First, Part One of the Convention identified a number of (mainly) civil and political rights that were felt central to any democratic and civilized society. Thus, Part One refers to rights such as the right to life (**article 2**), freedom from torture and inhuman and degrading treatment (**article 3**), freedom from slavery (**article 4**), and liberty and security of the person (**article 5**). Further, the Convention refers to a number of due process rights, such as the right to a fair trial (**article 6**) and democratic rights such as the right to religion (**article 9**), free speech (**article 10**), and the right to peaceful assembly (**article 11**), such rights being central to a democratic society.

Secondly, the Convention imposed an obligation on each Contracting Party to secure those rights within their own jurisdiction (**article 1**). In this sense, therefore, the Convention attempted to create within each state a culture of human rights protection that is consistent with both the ideals contained in the preamble and the specific rights laid out in the Convention. Thirdly, and most controversially, the Convention established its own machinery for the enforcement of these rights, including the power to receive individual and state applications and the establishment of a Court of Human Rights, empowered to make judicial decisions that would be enforceable on the offending member state. This process reflects the intention of the Convention that states would not be left entirely to their own devices in securing these basic rights and freedoms, but would rather be subject to a degree of international judicial control.

The Convention established three enforcement bodies. First, the European Commission of Human Rights would consider the admissibility and merits of any application made to it, a task now carried out by the European Court, below. Secondly, the Committee of Ministers, consisting of politicians of each state, is charged under **article 46** with supervising the execution of the European Court's judgments. Most recently, the proposed **Protocol 14** will enable the Committee to bring proceedings before the Court where a state refuses to comply with the judgment. Thirdly, **article 19** of the European Convention gives the European Court a judicial role to 'ensure observance of the engagements undertaken by the High Contracting Parties in the Convention and the Protocols'. Thus the European Court decides whether there has been a violation of one of its substantive rights and whether any and sufficient justification existed for any violation. The Court now functions on a permanent basis and is the sole body responsible for deciding the admissibility and merits of application made under the Convention.

The Court consists of Committees, who consider the initial admissibility of applications and have the power (under **article 28**) to strike out cases from its list, and Chambers of the Court, who decide on the admissibility and merits of the application. In addition, the Convention has now established the Grand Chamber of the Court, which has the power to determine applications relinquished to it by a Chamber of the Court (**article 31**). This will occur where the case raises a serious question affecting the interpretation or application of the Convention or a serious issue of general importance. Thus in *A v United Kingdom,* (2009) 49 EHRR 29, the European Court referred the issue of the detention of terrorist suspects to the Grand Chamber. Further, under **article 43** the Grand Chamber acts as an appeal court by considering requests by the parties to a case for referral within three months of the decision, as in *Hatton v United Kingdom* (2003) 37 EHRR 28 on the issue of airport noise and home life. It may also consider requests for advisory opinions under **article 47**.

Applications can either be brought by member states on behalf of individual victims of breaches by another High Contracting Party (**article 33**), or from individual applicants claiming to be victims of a violation of the Convention (**article 34**). With respect to state applications, a member state may bring an application against another state in relation to either its own citizens or those of another state. For example, in *Ireland v United Kingdom* (1978) 2 EHRR 25 an application was brought by the Irish government in relation to the treatment of suspected terrorists by British authorities in army barracks in Northern Ireland, claiming that such treatment constituted a violation of **articles 3 and 5** of the European Convention. State applications must comply with some of the admissibility criteria in **article 35** in that states must exhaust all domestic remedies and applications must be made within six months of the last decision, unless there is a continuing breach (*De Becker v Belgium* (1979–80) 1 EHRR 43).

Article 34 of the Convention provides that the Court may receive applications from any person, non-governmental organization, or group of individuals claiming to be a victim of a violation by one of the High Contracting Parties. A person includes both natural and legal persons, such as companies, but does not include an unborn child (*Vo v France* (2005) 40 EHRR 12). The applicant must be a 'victim' of a breach, meaning normally that he or she must be affected by the alleged violation (*Klass v Germany* (1978) 2 EHRR 214), although it is possible for family and other representatives of the victim to bring proceedings (*Keenan v United Kingdom* (2001) 33 EHRR 38). In addition to the requirement to exhaust all effective remedies and to bring the case within six months, **article 34** allows the Court to declare an application inadmissible if it is anonymous, an abuse of the right of petition, substantially the same as one already investigated under the Convention or other international machinery or 'manifestly ill founded', in other words where the alleged violation is clearly lawful under the Convention. Further, **article 38** allows the European Court of Human Rights to effect a friendly settlement between the applicant and the defendant state and to strike the case out; either on the basis that the state agrees to amend the relevant law or practice (*Sutherland v United Kingdom, The Times*, 13 April 2001), or without any admission of liability (*Amekrane v United Kingdom* (1974) 44 CD 101).

The decisions of the European Court of Human Rights are binding in international law on those states that have accepted the compulsory jurisdiction of the Court and place a duty on the state to comply with the judgment. Under **article 41** the European Court is empowered to award just satisfaction, to place the victim into the position had the violation not occurred in the first place. Any such award can include pecuniary damages to compensate for any direct financial loss such as loss of property, and non-pecuniary loss, where the applicant has suffered because of the nature of the violation, for example, for physical or mental distress (*Smith and Grady v United Kingdom* (2000) 29 EHRR 493). In some cases the Court will regard the judgment itself as just satisfaction and offer no damages award (*McCann v United Kingdom* (1995) 21 EHRR 97). The Court can also compensate for legal costs and expenses 'actually, necessarily and reasonably incurred by the applicant'.

With respect to the effectiveness of the Convention and its machinery, it could first be argued that the creation of a full-time Court via **Protocol 11**, is testimony to the success of that machinery. Indeed, the Convention may have become a victim of its own success. **Protocol 14,** yet to be ratified, attempts to deal with the increasing caseload by allowing in certain cases a single judge to decide on admissibility and three-men committees to decide on admissibility in the case of repeated violations. Further, cases can be declared inadmissible where the applicant has not suffered a serious disadvantage and where respect for human rights does not require the court to examine the merits of the case. Indeed, if the Court is now acting as an international court of appeal, this conflicts with the original intent of the Convention, which was that the Convention would enforce duties on the state itself and that the Court would only be used as a last resort.

Secondly, it cannot be denied that the decisions of the European Court have had an enormous impact on the protection of the human rights of certain groups such as prisoners (*Golder v United Kingdom* (1975) 1 EHRR 524), those facing expulsion from the state (*Soering v United Kingdom* (1989) 11 EHRR 439), children (*Tyrer v United Kingdom* (1978) 2 EHRR 1 and *A v United Kingdom* (1999) 27 EHRR 611), and sexual minorities (*Dudgeon v United Kingdom* (1982) 4 EHRR 149) and *Goodwin v United Kingdom* (2002) 35 EHRR 18). These cases have highlighted human rights abuses of such groups, and have provided the victim with a remedy that would not have been available in domestic law.

Thirdly, the decisions of the European Court of Human Rights have had a considerable influence on the establishment of international human rights norms. Thus, the Court has established firm principles of legality and proportionality with respect to areas such as the death penalty (*Ocalan v Turkey* (2003) 37 EHRR 10), ill-treatment of detainees (*Ireland v United Kingdom* (above)), the extra-territorial liability of state parties (*Soering v United Kingdom* (above)), and freedom of the press (*Sunday Times v United Kingdom* (1979) 2 EHRR 245 and *Lingens v Austria* (1986) 8 EHRR 407). The principles enunciated in these cases have been accepted by other international agencies, such as the Human Rights Committee, and continue to inform the content and application of domestic human rights law.

Fourthly, the obligation imposed by **article 1** of the Convention on each member state to secure human rights within their own jurisdiction has led to the incorporation of Convention rights and principles into the domestic law of individual states. Although the European Court has not insisted on such in order for the state to offer effective remedies under **article 13** (*Silver v United Kingdom* (1983) 5 EHRR 347), incorporation represents one of the essential aims of the Convention and of the Council of Europe. Consequently, the passing of the **Human Rights Act 1998**, although not representing full incorporation of the Convention, is to be welcomed as providing a more effective and immediate remedy for human rights violations.

However, the number, and success rate, of applications brought before the European Court should not be used as the sole measure of the Convention's success. Such figures illustrate the ability of the Court to hear adjudications and make binding decisions, which should in turn inform and change domestic law. On the other hand, the fact that so many applications continue to be brought, particularly against established member states, might indicate that the central aim of the Convention—of providing effective domestic protection against the violation of human rights—is not being realized. Further, the machinery provided under the Convention might be criticized for concentrating on judicial remedies to deal with established violations to the exclusion of monitoring and investigative procedures that might prevent violations taking place. In conclusion, therefore, although the Convention and its machinery for enforcement may be seen by many as a panacea of international legal protection against human rights abuse, it is clear that it needs to exist alongside wider and different mechanisms of protection, such as education and state reporting, which are intended to address and improve the human rights records of each state.

Question 2

To what extent does the European Court of Human Rights attempt to strike a balance between on the one hand ensuring that member states comply with the standards laid down by the Convention, and on the other respecting the autonomy of each member state and its legal system?

 Commentary

This question tackles the balance between state autonomy—the right of states to control their own affairs and to make their own decisions on human rights issues—and the monitoring of human rights protection via the **European Convention on Human Rights**. The area is quite popular with courses that concentrate on international human rights, but this type of question is increasingly popular on courses studying the European Convention.

The question is principally about the 'margin of appreciation', a doctrine established by the European Court of Human Rights to ensure that each member state is given an element of discretion in how they implement and apply Convention standards in their own domestic law. To answer the question, the student needs to be aware of the relationship between the Convention machinery for enforcement and state autonomy, and in particular of **article 1** of the Convention, which places the primary duty to protect Convention rights on the member states themselves. The student will then need to examine the relevant case law where the margin of appreciation has been applied and modified by the European Court of Human Rights, particularly with respect to the conditional rights contained in **articles 8–12** of the Convention. The question also calls for an examination of the doctrine (the margin of error) with respect to **article 15** of the Convention—which allows states to derogate from their Convention obligations in times of war and other emergencies. There is also room to consider whether the doctrine plays a role in the determination of absolute rights, such as the right to life and freedom from torture.

Answer plan

- Explanation of the general conflict between state sovereignty and the universal protection of human rights

- Examination of the machinery for the enforcement of human rights contained in the Convention with respect to its relationship with the state's domestic law

- Identification of the Convention provisions allowing state derogation and the role of the margin of error

- Critical examination of the doctrine of the margin of appreciation and the setting of common European standards by the European Court of Human Rights

- Conclusions as to the balance between enforcing human rights standards and respecting state autonomy

Suggested answer

Any international or regional human rights treaty requires the acceptance of universal standards and seeks to measure the legality of each state's laws and practices with those standards. This inevitably threatens the state's power to protect the human rights of those within its jurisdiction in a manner that is consistent with the community values of that state. This conflict between international and domestic values is particularly acute in the **European Convention on Human Rights 1950**, where each state's obligations is monitored by a Court of Human Rights that has the power to rule on the compatibility of state law with Convention rights. Assuming the state has agreed to the jurisdiction of the Court, the latter is then faced with the question of whether it is to apply international norms in disregard of the state's various values, or whether it will allow the state a level of discretion as to how it will realize its obligations under the Convention.

The European Court has recognized this friction and has devised mechanisms by which it can show a level of respect to each member state, whilst maintaining its function in ensuring that the values laid down in the Convention are recognized and respected by that state. Although many commentators, in particular Timothy Jones, have criticized this concept as devaluating the rights in the Convention, these mechanisms are now clearly part of the European Court's jurisprudence and are used extensively in assisting the Court in its function of establishing a violation of the Convention.

First, and most specifically, the European Court has shown a good deal of deference when interpreting and applying **article 15** of the Convention, which allows states to derogate from their Convention obligations in times of war or other public emergency threatening the life of the nation. Although the Court has insisted that these measures will need to correspond to a very pressing social need and meet a strict test of proportionality, it has also recognized that the state should have a good deal of discretion in such cases. Thus, in *Lawless v Ireland (No 3)* (1961) 1 EHRR 15, in deciding whether detention without trial for five months was justified within **article 5**, the Court stressed that the respondent government should be afforded a certain 'margin of error' or appreciation in deciding what measures were required by the situation. Accordingly, it was not the Court's function to substitute for the government's assessment any other assessment of what might be the most prudent or most expedient policy to combat terrorism.

This deference was clearly evident in the case of *Brannigan and McBride v United Kingdom* (1993) 17 EHRR 539, which involved a challenge to the United Kingdom's derogation of **article 5(3)** following the European Court's decision in *Brogan v United Kingdom* (1989) 11 EHRR 117—which held that provisions contained in the **Prevention of Terrorism Act 1978** failed to guarantee the right of detained persons to be brought promptly before a judge or other officer. The Court held that the derogation was justified, even though it had not been lodged before the Court's decision in *Brogan*, and that the government were entitled to keep open the possibility of finding a means of ensuring greater conformity with the Convention. Thus, provided the Court is satisfied that the Convention rights are safeguarded against arbitrary interference—in *Brannigan* the Court noted the availability of the remedy of the *habeas corpus*—it will respect the state's assessment of the situation as well as the proportionality of the specific measures. However, the recent decision of the House of Lords in *A v Secretary of State for the Home Department* [2005] 2 AC 68 shows that there is a limit to judicial deference even in this sensitive area; the decision of the domestic courts being confirmed by the Grand Chamber of the European Court (*A v United Kingdom*, (2009) 49 EHRR 29).

More generally the European Court might want to offer some discretion to a member state when deciding whether a potential violation is justified for reasons of other individual or state interests. In particular, the conditional rights contained in **articles 8–11** of the Convention require the Court to decide whether an interference with a right is 'necessary in a democratic society' for the purpose of achieving a legitimate aim. In *Handyside v United Kingdom* (1976) 1 EHRR 737 the European Court stressed that the machinery of the Convention is subsidiary to the national systems safeguarding human rights, leaving to each state, in the first place at least, the task of securing the rights and liberties in the Convention. Thus, provisions such as **article 10(2)** leave to each state a 'margin of appreciation', given both to the domestic legislature and to the bodies called upon to interpret and apply the laws. This margin of appreciation goes hand in hand with its powers to give the final determination on whether a restriction is compatible with the Convention right.

This margin of appreciation will allow the member state to defend its laws and practices against alleged violations even though such laws are not enforced with the same rigour in other states. Although the doctrine may militate against the establishment of a common standard of protection in Europe, it exists for a number of reasons. First, the doctrine recognizes that the Court's role under the Convention is subsidiary to the system adopted and carried out by each member state. This is born out by **article 1** of the Convention, which provides that the principal obligation to secure Convention rights is placed on the High Contracting Parties. Secondly, the doctrine allows the Court to apply an element of judicial reticence and to respect the law and decision-making of a particular state when determining whether something is necessary and proportionate.

Thirdly, in certain cases it is difficult to decide whether a particular law and its application is 'necessary in a democratic society' because of the problem in establishing a common European standard by which the necessity of a particular law or practice can be measured. For example, one would not expect domestic laws on obscenity to display a common standard among member states, and thus the Court should respect the different cultural and social conditions prevailing in each state.

Nevertheless, the doctrine is a potential threat to the universal enforcement of human rights and has been applied with caution. Further, it does not apply equally in all contexts. The Court has afforded a wide margin of appreciation in cases where matters of public morality are at issue, and in *Handyside* (above) the Court held that the states, by reason of their direct and continuous contact with the vital forces of their countries, were in a better position than the international judge to give an opinion on the exact content of the requirements of morals, as well as to the necessity of any restriction or penalty intended to meet those requirements. This reluctance to interfere on moral issues is also evident in cases involving blasphemous speech (*Wingrove v United Kingdom* (1996) 24 EHRR 1 and *Otto-Preminger Institut v Austria* (1994) 19 EHRR 34).

On the other hand, the Court has applied a narrower margin of appreciation where the restriction in question impinges on the enjoyment of the individual's right to private life. Thus, in *Dudgeon v United Kingdom* (1982) 4 EHRR 149 it held that the prohibition on homosexual acts via the criminal law concerned a most intimate aspect of private life, and accordingly there had to exist particularly serious reasons before interference with that right could be justified under **article 8(2)** of the Convention. In such circumstances the Court held that it was not sufficient that the majority of society merely disapproved of such conduct and would object to a change in the law. Similarly, in *Smith and Grady v United Kingdom* (2000) 29 EHRR 493 the Court held that a prohibition on homosexuals from remaining in the armed forces could not be justified solely on the basis of the negative attitudes of heterosexuals towards homosexuals. Although the European Court is prepared to allow some margin to member states in the control of private sexual life (*Laskey, Jaggard and Brown v United Kingdom* (1997) 24 EHRR 39), it has taken an increasingly robust approach in this area (*ADT v United Kingdom* (2001) 31 EHRR 33). This is particularly true with respect to the legal and civil status afforded to transsexuals in domestic law (*Goodwin v United Kingdom* (2002) 35 EHRR 18).

The Court has also given a narrow margin of error in the area of press freedom, recognizing that most laws which impinge on press freedom display a reasonably common European standard, and accepting that press freedom is fundamental to the operation of any democratic state and thus requires the greatest degree of protection. For example, in *Sunday Times v United Kingdom* (1979) 2 EHRR 245 the Court accepted that the laws of contempt of court displayed a relatively common approach, allowing the Court to more easily judge the necessity of any particular interference so that in such a case a more extensive European supervision corresponds to a less discretionary power of appreciation. Equally, because the Court regarded the duty of the press to inform the public on matters of great public interest as essential to democracy, it submitted the law and the measure in question to the utmost scrutiny.

Although the doctrine of the margin of appreciation in its strict sense applies only to the enforcement of conditional rights, there is evidence that the Court will offer some element of discretion in the interpretation and application of more absolute rights, such as the right to life and freedom from inhuman and degrading treatment or punishment. This will offer each state an area of discretion to pass and administer laws that might otherwise infringe Convention rights. For example, in *Pretty v United Kingdom* (2002) 35 EHRR 1 the Court noted that there was no general right to die under **article 2** of the Convention, and that even though some states practised controlled euthanasia there was no obligation on any state to introduce such a right. Further, in *Vo v France* (2005) 40 EHRR 12 the Court confirmed that the right to life did not on its proper interpretation cover the right of the unborn child, noting that there was still a considerable amount of difference of opinion among member states as to when 'life' begins. Equally, in determining applications under article 3, the Court has offered an area of discretion with respect to penal policy. For example, in *V and T v United Kingdom* (2000) 30 EHRR 121, in finding that there had been no violation of **article 3** when two young boys were given life sentences for murder, the Court recognized that there was no fixed or common agreement among European states on the minimum age for incarceration.

In conclusion, despite strong criticisms, the doctrines of the margin of appreciation and the margin of error have become important principles in the Court's jurisprudence and case law. Accordingly, it has been employed by the Court to balance its role in upholding the Convention rights of the individual with the desire to ensure that the appropriate level of autonomy of each member state is respected. Although the doctrine appears to be unwieldy and discretionary, there have emerged some guiding principles determining the extent of the doctrine and its application, and ensuring that each state complies with the essence of the Convention rights whilst being permitted an element of discretion. Although the notion of a flexible enforcement of human rights in each state appears to contradict the universal nature of such rights, such a notion is essential in recognizing the autonomy of each state's legal culture and, provided the margin is not extended unduly, is not inconsistent with the aims of the European Convention.

Question 3

With reference to relevant case law, explain the importance of the following principles and doctrines with respect to the role of the European Court of Human Right's role in protecting human rights:

'Prescribed by or in accordance with law';

'Necessary in a democratic society';

'The doctrine of proportionality'.

Commentary

The question is reasonably straightforward and is also nicely broken down for the student. The introduction to the answer should explain where these principles appear and illustrate the context in which they arise—in the justification of *prima facie* violations of so-called 'conditional rights', contained in **articles 8–11** of the Convention. The question calls for relevant case law, and should not be attempted unless the student has a very sound knowledge of the cases under each principle.

The student should not just deal with each principle in turn, but should attempt to explain how each one assists the European Court of Human Rights in adjudicating on human rights cases by upholding principles of legality, the rule of law, democracy, and reasonableness. The question clearly calls for an analysis of the European Court's jurisprudence, and students should avoid detailed discussions of domestic case law on these principles, although some reference to domestic authorities may be useful to illustrate the scope of the Court's jurisprudence.

Answer plan

- General explanation of the role of the European Court within the Convention machinery
- Explanation of the term 'prescribed by/in accordance with law' and an analysis of relevant case law
- Explanation of the term 'necessary in a democratic society' as interpreted and applied by the European Court of Human Rights
- Explanation of the doctrine of proportionality and its impact on human rights adjudication, as applied by the European Court of Human Rights

Suggested answer

Some rights contained in the European Convention can be interfered with in certain circumstances provided the interference possesses certain characteristics of legality and reasonableness. Thus, once the European Court has established that the applicant's Convention rights are engaged and have been breached, it must then decide whether any restriction on that right is permissible. For example, the rights contained in **articles 8–11** of the Convention, guaranteeing rights such as private life, religion, freedom of expression, and the right to association and peaceful assembly, state that everyone has the right to, say, freedom of expression, but in the next paragraph provide that such rights are subject to such restrictions that are prescribed by law (or in the case of **article 8**—guaranteeing the right to private and family life—'in accordance with law') and necessary in a democratic society for the protection of one of a number of legitimate aims. These qualifying paragraphs recognize that the enjoyment of certain fundamental rights is not absolute. However by insisting that any restriction is 'prescribed by law' and 'necessary in a democratic society' these qualifications are restricted and must meet generally recognized standards of legality and fairness in order to be permissible.

Prescribed by/in accordance with law

With respect to the requirement that a restriction is 'prescribed by law' or 'in accordance with law', any interference with a Convention right must first be justified by reference to some provision of domestic law. For example, **article 5** of the Convention allows interference with a person's liberty and security of the person, but only in accordance 'with a procedure prescribed by law', which means that the law not only has a legitimate source, but that it complies with the fundamental ideals of the rule of law in that it is sufficiently fair, impartial, and clear (*Steel v United Kingdom* (1999) **28 EHRR 603**). Consequently, any restriction on a Convention right that lacks such a legal basis will be automatically unlawful under the Convention, however necessary that provision may be.

The phrase 'in accordance with the law', employed in **article 8**, was considered by the European Court in *Malone v United Kingdom* (1984) **7 EHRR 14**. For a measure to be in accordance with law it had to first have a sufficiently established legal basis, secondly be accessible so that those affected by it can find out what the law says, and thirdly be formulated with sufficient certainty to enable people to understand it and to regulate their conduct by it. Consequently the Court found that the rules relating to telephone tapping, being included in secret administrative guidance, were not in accordance with law.

In *Malone* (above) the European Court held that there must be a measure of legal protection against arbitrary interference by public authorities with the right in question. Consequently, as the process of telephone tapping was controlled by administrative regulation rather than formal law subject to judicial supervision, it found that such measures were unlawful under **article 8**. The Court also stressed that provisions must be sufficiently independent of those who administer them. Further, the requirement that the rule has to be accessible, insists that a person who is likely to be affected by the rule should have access to it. Thus, in *Silver v United Kingdom* (1983) **5 EHRR 347**—a case involving the regulation of prisoners' correspondence via administrative guidance produced by the Secretary of State for the Prison Service—the European Court held that restrictions on prisoners' correspondence authorized by non-legal and non-published Standing Orders were not in accordance with law.

In addition, law should be sufficiently certain and clear and in *Sunday Times v United Kingdom* (1979) **2 EHRR 245** the Court held that a norm cannot be regarded as a law unless it is formulated with sufficient precision to enable the citizen to regulate his conduct. Thus, a person must be able (with appropriate advice if necessary) to foresee, to a degree that is reasonable in the circumstances, the consequences which a given action may entail. The Court stressed that those consequences need not be foreseeable with absolute certainty, accepting that most laws are inevitably couched in terms which, to some extent, are vague, and that the legal provisions do not have to be in statutory form, but could derive from the common law. Thus, in the *Sunday Times* case, although the common law of contempt of court was inevitably uncertain and dependent on interpretation, a person could, by examining its application via the case law, predict with a sufficient degree of certainty whether the publication of an article would be caught by the law. Conversely, if a rule is so vague that its meaning and extent cannot be reasonably predicted, then the rule will not be regarded as law. Thus, in *Hashman and Harrap v United Kingdom* (1999) 30 EHRR 241 the European Court held that the power of the domestic courts to order a person to desist in conduct that was *contra bones mores* (conduct which is seen as wrong in the eyes of the majority of contemporary citizens), failed to give sufficient guidance to the applicants as to what conduct they were not allowed to partake in.

Necessary in a democratic society

All restrictions on the rights contained in **articles 8–11** of the Convention must be 'necessary in a democratic society' for achieving one of the legitimate aims listed in the article. This involves the Court considering the merits of the relevant domestic legal provision and subjecting such laws to a test of necessity and reasonableness to ensure that the interference can be justified for some greater public or individual good. In *Handyside v United Kingdom* (1976) 1 EHRR 737 the Court established that it must first inquire whether there is a 'pressing social need' for the restriction. Secondly, it must ask whether that restriction corresponds to that need, and finally, whether it is a proportionate response to that need and, whether the reasons advanced by the authorities are relevant and sufficient. The Court has also stressed that in deciding whether a restriction is necessary it is not faced with a choice between two conflicting principles, but with a principle of, for example, freedom of expression subject to a number of exceptions, which must be narrowly interpreted (*Sunday Times v United Kingdom* (above)).

In *Handyside v United Kingdom* (above) the European Court held that the word 'necessary' did not mean 'absolutely necessary' or 'indispensable', but neither did it have the flexibility of terms such as 'useful' or 'convenient'. Instead, in the Court's view, there must be a 'pressing social need' for the interference and any interference must be proportionate to the protection of a legitimate aim (see below). Thus, although a member state does not have to show that society could not possibly do without the legal restriction, the Court will not accept a restriction merely because it provides a useful tool in achieving a social good. For example, in *Smith and Grady v United Kingdom* (2000) 29 EHRR 493 the European Court was not satisfied that in practice the ban on homosexuals in the armed forces served any real purpose of maintaining national security via an effective national fighting force.

Thus, the Court insists that there is strong objective justification for the law and its application, that the member state can point to a real social harm and that the employment of that law is necessary to achieve that aim. For example, in *Dudgeon v United Kingdom* (1982) 4 EHRR 149 the European Court noted that, as opposed to the time when legislation prohibiting homosexual conduct was passed in Northern Ireland, there was evidence of a greater understanding and tolerance of such conduct. Accordingly, a blanket prohibition of such conduct, irrespective of the age of the participants, did not correspond to a pressing social need. The European Court's review, however, may be weakened when it recognizes that the state should be provided with a wide margin of appreciation. For example, in *Handyside v United Kingdom* (above) the Court accepted that the prosecution in the English Courts of an obscene publication was justified even though the publication was freely available in most other European states.

Proportionality

In assessing the necessity of any restriction the doctrine of proportionality ensures that a fair balance is achieved between the realization of a social goal, such as the protection of morals, and the protection of the fundamental rights contained in the Convention. In *Handyside* (above) the Court insisted that any restrictions should be strictly proportionate to the legitimate aim being pursued and that the restriction in question does not go beyond what is strictly required to achieve that purpose. The extent to which the Court is prepared to conduct such an inquiry may well depend on the importance of the right that has been interfered with, the extent to which the right was violated, the urgency of the pressing social need, and the sanction imposed on the right user. For example, in *Tolstoy v United Kingdom* (1995) 20 EHRR 442 the European Court held that the award of £1.5m damages in a libel action was a disproportionate interference with freedom of expression, as it would have a chilling effect on freedom of the press.

It is also clear that the doctrine of the margin of appreciation may play a vital role in determining the extent of the Court's interference, and indeed the Court has adopted a number of approaches in determining the necessity and proportionality of restrictions depending on the context of the decision. Thus, where the Court feels that there is little evidence of a common European approach to the matter (such as in cases concerning public morality), and wishes to give the state a wide margin of appreciation, it has simply asked whether the state has advanced relevant and sufficient reasons for the interference (*Handyside v United Kingdom* (above)). Conversely, where the Court is intent on thorough scrutiny, and where there is evidence of a common European standard, it might ask whether the domestic authorities had available to them a less restrictive alternative than the one applied to the applicant. Such an approach is usually taken when the Court is faced with restrictions on press freedom (*Goodwin v United Kingdom* (1996) 22 EHRR 123) or the public right to know (*Sunday Times v United Kingdom* (above)). The Court and Commission have also asked whether the restriction destroys the very essence of the Convention right in question (*Hamer v United Kingdom* (1982) 4 EHRR 139).

The need to establish necessity and proportionality bestows a potentially wide power on the European Court to judge the acceptability of state law and practice, arguably taking the European Court beyond a mere reviewing function, and in *R (Daly) v Secretary of State for the Home Department* [2002] 2 AC 532, Lord Steyn observed that the doctrine of proportionality requires the reviewing court to assess the balance that the decision-maker had struck and requires attention to be directed to the relevant weight accorded to the interests and considerations. Such powers may, of course, be restricted by the domestic principle of judicial deference and, with respect to the European Court's powers it could be argued that similar deference might be shown by the Court employing the doctrine of the margin of appreciation.

Conclusion

The fact that restrictions on Convention rights have to be prescribed by law, and to be necessary and proportionate in their application, is central to the Convention's aim of ensuring that fundamental human rights are not violated unless there are legitimate and pressing reasons for doing so. The requirement that restrictions are prescribed by law insists that even formal law must be prospective, accessible, and clear. Further, the need to show that restrictions are necessary in a democratic society and proportionate, recognizes that rights should not be interfered with unless there is a pressing and urgent need to do so and that such rights should not be compromised on grounds of convenience or simply because their enjoyment is not countenanced by the majority. Although the European Court's application of these principles is tempered somewhat by the application of the doctrine of the margin of appreciation, such principles act as a safeguard against unlawful and unnecessary interference with basic rights.

Question 4

Critically examine the extent to which **article 15** of the European Convention allows member states to derogate from their obligations under the Convention in times of war or other emergency.

 Commentary

This question considers the right of a member state to depart from or reduce its human rights obligations under the Convention in times of war or other public emergency. This type of question has become very popular given the United Kingdom government's efforts to safeguard the state and the public from the threat of terrorism, and references should be made to recent legislation and its review by the domestic courts.

The answer should begin with the general wording of **article 15** and, in particular, its rationale. At this point the student should identify the scope and extent of **article 15**, noting when it can and cannot apply and what Convention articles are not covered by it. Then, via the use of cases, the student can explain what discretion member states are left with in this area and the extent to which the European Court of Human Rights is prepared to regulate its use by states. The case law will primarily be that of the European Court, although a discussion of domestic affairs and recent domestic decisions with respect to detention without trial will be particularly apposite.

Answer plan

- Explanation of the rationale behind **article 15** and how human rights might be compromised in times of war and emergency
- Examination of the wording of **article 15** and its restrictions and limitations
- Critical examination of the monitoring of state derogation under **article 15**, together with relevant case law of the European Court of Human Rights and recent domestic decisions in this area
- Conclusions as to the scope of the power of derogation and its compatibility with the protection of fundamental human rights.

Suggested answer

Article 15 provides that member states can derogate from their obligations under the Convention during times of war or other public emergency threatening the life of the nation. This article reflects the fact that war and other emergencies place extra pressure on states in terms of maintaining social order and that individual liberty might need to be compromised in the light of threats to such order and national integrity. For example, if a state is threatened by war or by internal or external terrorism it may be necessary to provide officials with extra powers with respect to the arrest and questioning and detention of individuals suspected of endangering the order of that society. Similarly, during such times it might be necessary to place restrictions on the right to association, freedom of movement, or freedom of expression. This power of derogation is in addition to the increased area of discretion given by the European Court to states in the control of serious crime, including acts of terrorism (*Fox, Campbell and Hartley v United Kingdom* **(1991) 13 EHRR 157** and *O'Hara v United Kingdom* **(2002) 34 EHRR 32**), although it has stressed that such circumstances should not destroy the very essence of the due process rights contained in **article 5** of the Convention.

As derogation measures will have an increased impact on the enjoyment of individual rights and liberties, it is essential that any measures are subject to limitations and judicial control. As recent events in the United Kingdom and the United States have shown, our fundamental rights and liberties can be under the greatest threat during such times and governments can often overreact and impose unnecessary and draconian measures, which may threaten the very democratic values that such rights purport to uphold, including the need to control arbitrary government. Accordingly, the right of derogation under **article 15** is circumscribed by a number of rules that limit the power of derogation and place it under the control of the Convention's supervisory organs.

First, under **article 15(3)**, the Convention provides that any High Contracting Party using the right of derogation must keep the Secretary-General of the Council of Europe informed of the measures which it has taken, along with the reasons for derogation. In addition, the state must inform the Secretary-General when such measures have ceased to operate and that the provisions of the Convention are being fully executed.

Secondly, if the derogation is challenged before the European Court, it must be satisfied not only that an emergency threatening the life of the nation exists, but that any measures taken are *strictly required* by the exigencies of the situation. Thus, by using the phrase *strictly required*, **article 15** indicates that the measures must correspond to a very pressing social need and meet a strict test of proportionality. Thus, although the member state will be afforded a wide margin of error in such situations, **article 15** gives the Convention organs the right to monitor the emergency situation and to provide some objective review of the emergency and the relevant measures. This will allow the Court to take into account the seriousness of a state departing from fundamental standards of rights protection, whilst offering some margin of discretion to that state.

Thirdly, the measures taken by the member state must not be inconsistent with its other obligations under international law. This provision ensures that any derogation must comply with other internationally accepted standards applying to war or other emergency situations, such as the obligations imposed under the Geneva Convention. Fourthly, no derogation is allowed in respect of certain Convention rights, such as **article 2** (the right to life), although an exception is made in respect to deaths resulting from lawful acts of war, **article 3** (prohibition of torture and inhuman or degrading treatment or punishment), **article 4(1)** (prohibition of slavery or servitude), or **article 7** (prohibition of retrospective criminal law). This reflects the view that there are certain rights which should never be transgressed, even in the defence of the state and of social justice.

The extent to which a proper balance between human rights and social order is maintained during such situations, will depend primarily on how the European Court monitors the use of **article 15**, and the European Court has stated that it will offer states a wide degree of discretion in this area. In *Lawless v Ireland (No 3)* **(1961) 1 EHRR 15**, the applicants claimed that their internment without trial was in breach of their right to liberty of the person, whilst the state argued that such measures were justified because of the emergency situation existing in Ireland. Although the Court found that the detention of the applicant without trial for a period of five months was in violation of the right to be brought promptly before a court for trial or release, it held that the government was entitled to derogate from its obligations by virtue of the existence of a public emergency. Although the Court stressed that the measures governments can take when derogating are strictly limited to what is required by the exigencies of the situation, it held that the respondent government should be afforded a certain margin of error or appreciation in deciding what measures were required by the situation, and that it was not the Court's function to substitute for the government's assessment any other assessment of what might be the most prudent or most expedient policy to combat terrorism.

The decision in *Lawless* suggests that the European Court would be loath to interfere with the judgment of the state or to subject its measures to intense review. Further, in that case the Court stressed that it must arrive at its decision as to the compatibility of the measures in the light of the conditions that existed at the time that the original decision of derogation was taken, rather than reviewing the matter retrospectively. This judicial reticence was evident in the case of *Brannigan and McBride v United Kingdom* **(1993) 17 EHRR 539,** concerning the United Kingdom's derogation in relation to **article 5** following the European Court's decision in *Brogan v United Kingdom* (1989) **11 EHRR 117**, where it had held that detention provisions contained in the **Prevention of Terrorism Act 1978** were in contravention of **article 5(3)** of the Convention. Following that decision, the government lodged a derogation in respect of **article 5(3)** because of the emergency position in Northern Ireland. Those measures and the derogation were challenged in *Brannigan and McBride* (above), but the Court held that they were justified despite the derogation only being lodged after the Court's decision in *Brogan*. Accepting that there was an emergency situation, it held that the derogation was not invalid merely because the government had decided to keep open the possibility of finding a means in the future, other than employing **article 15**, of ensuring greater conformity with its Convention obligations. The Court also found that there were effective safeguards, such as the availability of *habeas corpus*, to safeguard against arbitrary action, and consequently such measures were strictly required by the situation.

It is quite clear from these cases that the doctrine of the margin of error will force the European Court to take a 'hands off' approach and allow the state wide latitude in compromising human rights for the sake of social order. However, the recent domestic events surrounding the challenge of provisions allowing detention without trial have shown that the domestic judiciary will be unwilling to relinquish their role of safeguarding basic rights, even in times of emergency. In *A v Secretary of State for the Home Department* [2005] **2 AC 68** a challenge was made to provisions in the **Anti-terrorism, Crime and Security Act 2001**, which provided for an extended power to arrest and detain foreign nationals suspected of terrorism and whose removal was not possible because they would face ill-treatment in violation of **article 3** of the Convention if returned to that particular country. The government had consequently derogated from **article 5(1)** of the European Convention, but, a majority of the House of Lords held that the measures allowing indefinite detention without trial or charge were incompatible with the United Kingdom's obligations under the Convention and could not be excused within **article 15**. The majority of their Lordships accepted that there existed a 'public emergency threatening the life of the nation' so as to allow derogation, adding that great weight should be given to the judgment of the Home Secretary and Parliament because they had to exercise a pre-eminently political judgement and that as a consequence the court's role in scrutiny would be smaller. Lord Hoffmann, dissenting, believed that the government had equated a situation where there was a threat of serious physical damage and loss of life with one where there was a threat to the life of the nation. In Lord Hoffmann's view the real threat to the life of the nation came not from terrorism but from laws such as those in issue.

However, the majority then held that the measures taken were not strictly required by the exigencies of the situation. Lord Bingham conceded that during terrorism difficult choices had to be made and that the decision of a representative democratic body demanded a degree of respect, but stressed that even in a terrorist situation neither the Convention organs nor the domestic courts were willing to relax their residual supervisory role. The measures were disproportionate because they did not deal with the threat of terrorism from persons other than foreign nationals, in other words United Kingdom nationals, and permitted suspected foreign terrorists to carry on their activities in another country provided there was a safe country for them to go to. Lord Bingham concluded that, if the threat posed by UK nationals could be addressed without infringing the right to personal liberty, it had not been shown why similar measures could not adequately address the threat posed by foreign nationals.

Their Lordships also held that the measures were in violation of **article 14** of the European Convention, which provides that Convention rights should be enjoyed without discrimination, because the provisions allowed foreign nationals to be deprived of their liberty but not UK nationals, and the appellants were thus treated differently because of their nationality or immigration status. Subsequently, the Grand Chamber of the European Court upheld those findings on **article 15**, refusing to interfere with the government's assessment of the emergency or the House of Lords' findings on necessity (*A v United Kingdom*, (2009) 49 EHRR 29).

The decisions of the House of Lords and the Grand Chamber confirm that human rights must be enjoyed despite the existence of an emergency and that the courts' role in safeguarding such rights should not be diminished to the point that a government is allowed to compromise human rights at their discretion and without strong and cogent evidence and justification. Although both courts accept that the question of whether an emergency exists is primarily political, they are adamant that the proportionality of such measures is for the courts to determine. Equally importantly, the decision highlights the fact that the violation of basic rights can be as damaging to democratic principles as the threats to social order themselves.

In conclusion, **article 15** has the potential to endanger the protection of fundamental human rights and to undermine the central aims of the European Convention, particularly if it is not effectively monitored. Although the article's use is limited in its scope and subject to examination by the Council of Europe and the European Court, the case law of the Court thus far suggests that the European Court will offer states a very wide margin of appreciation, leaving each state to decide what measures to take to deal with the emergency situation. However, the decision of the House of Lords in *A v Secretary of State for the Home Department* (above)—and the subsequent decision of the Grand Chamber in that case—clearly indicates that the state will not be left with an unlimited discretion in this area. Those decisions display a robust approach in ensuring that a state of emergency is not used as an excuse for departing from the essential values underlying the Convention and the rights contained in it.

Question 5

'... all persons are equal before the law and are entitled to the equal protection of the law;' (preamble to **Protocol No 12** to the European Convention).

How effective is **article 14** of the **European Convention on Human Rights** as a vehicle for guaranteeing freedom from discrimination?

Commentary

This question is concerned with the effectiveness of **article 14** of the Convention in protecting individuals from discrimination. The student needs to appreciate the limited scope of **article 14** in prohibiting discrimination, and to discuss the gaps in that provision as well as examining its interpretation and application.

The answer should begin by explaining the importance of equality and freedom from discrimination, identifying how that right relates to the enjoyment of other human rights. The student can then examine the wording and scope of **article 14**, along with the relevant case law of the European Court in this area; students can also cite domestic decisions in the post-Human Rights Act era in illustration. The student can examine the possible reforms to **article 14**, comparing it with **article 26** of the **International Covenant on Civil and Political Rights 1966**, before drawing conclusions as to its general effectiveness.

Answer plan

- Brief explanation of the basis of equality and freedom from discrimination and how discrimination impacts on the enjoyment of other human rights

- Examination of **article 14** and **Protocol No 12** of the European Convention and their relationship with other substantive articles

- Examination of relevant case law of the European Court of Human Rights under **article 14**

- Critical analysis of the scope and effectiveness of the Convention provisions and any relevant case law

- Conclusions as to the effectiveness of protection against discrimination under the Convention

Suggested answer

Equality and freedom from discrimination lie at the heart of all domestic and international treaties on human rights. Most constitutions will contain a declaration to the effect that all people are born equal and should receive equal protection under the law and this principle is reflected in the preamble of the **United Nations Charter 1945**, which 'reaffirms faith in the equal rights of men and women . . . ' This reflects the notion of the 'social contract' theory, ensuring that every person is allowed to enjoy their fundamental rights, and Ronald Dworkin's idea that every state has a duty to treat all of its citizens with equal concern and respect. Every person, therefore, has a moral right to be treated equally and in particular to enjoy their human rights free from discrimination on grounds such as race, sex, or social status; consequently, discriminatory treatment is viewed as an affront to human dignity and worth.

Protection from discrimination can be achieved in a number of ways. For example, the law might provide for a general clause, as contained in **article 26 of the International**

Covenant on Civil and Political Rights 1966, which provides that all persons are equal before the law and are entitled without discrimination to the equal protection of the law. This can then be buttressed by domestic laws which ensure that individuals and groups are not subject to unlawful discrimination, and which then provide the individual with a specific remedy on violation of those laws. This method ensures that all laws, including those impacting on fundamental human rights, are interpreted and applied equally and that the individual is given effective protection against discrimination, irrespective of whether the perpetrator is a public or private body. Alternatively, a national constitution or international treaty might contain a clause which ensures the enjoyment of fundamental human rights irrespective of discrimination, leaving domestic law to pass specific legislation protecting identified groups.

This latter approach is adopted by **article 14 of the European Convention on Human Rights,** which provides that the enjoyment of Convention rights and freedoms shall be secured without discrimination on any ground such as sex, race, colour, language, religion, political, or other opinion, national or social origin, association with a national minority, property, birth, or other status. **Article 14** ensures that no one is denied the enjoyment of those rights on any of the above grounds and applies equally to the situation where the equal treatment of individuals has a discriminatory effect (*Thlimmenos v Greece* (2001) 31 EHRR 15). The article can also be used as the guiding principle when the European Court is considering the legality and necessity of any restriction on those rights. Thus, if a person is denied freedom of expression purely because of his political affiliation, there could be a violation of **article 10** of the Convention because of the lack of necessity of that interference, and of **article 14** because of its discriminatory basis. **Article 14** thus complements the other Convention rights, rather than providing a 'freestanding' and separate right not to be discriminated against.

Article 14 can, therefore, be used in addition to (or in conjunction with) claims made under other articles of the Convention, and in certain cases the Court will find it unnecessary to make a separate ruling on **article 14.** For example in *Smith and Grady v United Kingdom* (2000) 29 EHRR 493 the European Court found a violation of the applicants' right to private life when they had been dismissed from the armed forces because of their sexual orientation. Consequently, after finding that their treatment was not justified by the need to maintain the morale of the armed forces, the Court found it unnecessary to consider whether that treatment constituted a violation of **article 14.** In such cases, therefore, the Court has already considered the discriminatory effect of the violation in determining the legality and proportionality of the interference and thus does not need to consider the claim separately under **article 14.** Similarly, in *ADT v United Kingdom* (2001) 31 EHRR 33, having found that the applicants had only been penalized (for committing gross indecency) because they were men, the Court held that such a penalty was an unnecessary and disproportionate interference with private sexual life under **article 8,** making it unnecessary to consider **article 14.**

However, this does not mean that **article 14** has no individual impact on the enjoyment of Convention rights. It is possible that an applicant will succeed under **article 14,** even where the claim on the substantive right alone would have failed because, without the discrimination, the interference would have been lawful and necessary. In such a case article 14 can be used in conjunction with another Convention right to establish a violation (*'Belgian Linguistics' Case* (1968) 1 EHRR 252). This was illustrated in *Abdulaziz, Cabales and Balkandali v United Kingdom* (1985) 7 EHRR 471. In this case the applicants claimed that the government's refusal to give permission to their spouses to enter and remain in the United Kingdom constituted an unlawful interference with the right to private and family life under article 8 of the Convention. The European Court held that because a state had a wide margin of appreciation in refusing to allow non-national spouses to enter the country, any interference with article 8 was necessary in a democratic society. However, as the rules relating to the entry of such persons into the country were applied more harshly to women who wished to bring their husbands into the country, the Court concluded that there had been a violation of article 14. A similar decision was made by the domestic courts in *R (Baiai) v Secretary of State for the Home Department* [2007] 4 All ER 199 with respect to the Home Secretary's efforts to control sham marriages.

That decision shows that the principles underlying article 14 have a pervasive influence on all Convention rights and can thus inform the Convention's general jurisprudence. Thus, in certain cases a discriminatory decision might constitute a violation of another Convention article. For example, in the *East African Asians Case* (1973) 3 EHRR 76 the European Commission held that to publicly single out a group of persons for differential treatment on the basis of race might, in certain circumstances, constitute a special form of affront to human dignity, and thus constitute degrading treatment within article 3 of the Convention. In that case, therefore, it held that the government's refusal to allow the applicants leave to enter the country had been made on grounds of their race and colour and thereby subjected them to inhuman and degrading treatment within article 3.

However, the scope of article 14 is severely curtailed by the requirement that any complaint under article 14 must be related to an alleged violation of another Convention right. In other words the complaint must at least engage another Convention right. This is starkly illustrated in the European Commission's decision in *Choudhury v United Kingdom* (1991) 12 HRLJ 172. The applicants had attempted to bring blasphemy proceedings against a publisher for vilifying the Islamic faith, but the domestic courts held that the law only protected the Anglican faith (*R v Chief Metropolitan Stipendiary Magistrate, ex parte Choudhury* [1991] 1 QB 1006). The applicants' claim under the European Convention was declared inadmissible because the Commission held that article 9 of the Convention (guaranteeing the right to freedom of religion) did not include a positive obligation on behalf of the state to protect religious sensibilities via effective blasphemy laws. Further, with respect to the claim under article 14, it held that because there was no positive obligation of a state to protect the right to be free from offence under article 9, it could not be a breach of article 14 to deny someone that protection even on grounds forbidden under article 14.

That decision is difficult to reconcile with the European Court's decision in the *'Belgian Linguistics' Case* (above), where it was held that although a person had no right to demand that the state create separate educational establishments, once a state had set up such an institution, it could not lay down discriminatory entrance requirements.

In any case, the decision in *Choudhury* illustrates the shortcomings of **article 14**, in comparison with the more general protection provided by **article 26** of the International Covenant, which would have protected the applicants in that case. This gap might be filled by the ratification of **Protocol No 12** of the Convention, concerning the prohibition on discrimination. The protocol was established to facilitate the further promotion of the principle of equality and **article 1 of Protocol 12** provides that the enjoyment of any right set forth *by law* shall be secured without discrimination on any of the grounds identified in **article 14** of the Convention. This extends freedom from discrimination beyond the enjoyment of Convention rights to the enjoyment of any legal right in domestic law, and is complemented by the guarantee that no one shall be discriminated against by a public authority on any such ground. This, combined with the general right under **Protocol 12**, would extend the protection offered by specific UK discrimination law such as the **Sex Discrimination Act 1975** and would thus offer a general, albeit conditional, human right to be free from discrimination.

In addition, although **article 14** does not contain any qualifying provisions, as in **articles 8–11** of the Convention, it is clear that the enjoyment of Convention rights without discrimination is not absolute. Consequently, **article 14** does not secure complete equality of treatment and in the *'Belgian Linguistics' Case* (above) the European Court held that **article 14** is only violated where the difference in treatment has no objective or reasonable justification. Furthermore, although any difference in treatment must pursue a legitimate aim, and must be reasonably proportionate in achieving that aim, the Court is prepared to afford a margin of appreciation to each state to reflect its social and cultural values. Thus, in the *'Belgian Linguistics' Case* (above) it held that there would be no breach of **article 14** (together with **article 8** and **article 2 of the First Protocol**) when domestic law stated that, generally, state-funded schools would only teach in the designated official language of their region.

This qualifies the impact of **article 14**, and in that case the Court stressed that the effect of **article 14** (in conjunction with other articles) was not to *guarantee* the right to enjoy the Convention right, but to ensure that it is secured by each state without discrimination. The enjoyment of Convention rights is, therefore, subject to justified exceptions, which need to be assessed in relation to the aims and effects of the measures under consideration and the principles that normally prevail in a democratic society. Clearly, any distinction needs to be based on legitimate grounds and cannot be justified if the difference in treatment is explainable only on the basis of discrimination. Thus, in *Willis v United Kingdom* (2002) 35 EHRR 21 the Court held that the exclusion of men from entitlement to the Widowed Mother's Allowance constituted a violation of **article 14** and **article 1 of the First Protocol**; the only reason for being refused the benefits was that he was a man and that distinction was not based on any objective and reasonable justification. This illustrates that differential treatment must be based on reasonable and objective factors and that the state must provide substantive justification in this respect. For example, in *PM v United Kingdom* (2006) 42 EHRR 45, Article 14 was violated when tax relief in respect of maintenance payments to a child were denied because the applicant had not been married to the girl's mother. The Court held that although the purpose of the deductions made it easier for married fathers to support a new family, it was difficult to see why unmarried fathers would not have similar difficulties.

On the other hand, in some cases the Court has been reluctant to interfere, preferring to defer to the state's assessment. Thus, in *Pretty v United Kingdom* (2002) **35 EHRR 1** it held that there had been no violation of **article 14** when the applicant had been denied her right to terminate her life. Although the Court accepted that she had been discriminated against, because she was not (due to her physical state) able to personally exercise her self-autonomy, there existed objective and reasonable justification for not distinguishing in law between those who are and those who are not physically capable of committing suicide and thus not allowing her partner to assist her. This approach may be justified because of the sensitive nature of the issue at hand—in the *Pretty* case the right to life and the legal issues surrounding euthanasia. In such a case, therefore, the Court will be reluctant to interfere with the state's discretion where there is room for other, acceptable views.

The case law on **article 14**, therefore, remains fluid, reflecting the Court's willingness to offer a margin of appreciation with respect to other Convention articles. Thus, for some time the Court allowed member states to decide whether they would afford full civil status to transsexuals (*Rees v United Kingdom* (1986) **9 EHRR 56**), or allow such individuals the right to marry (*Cossey v United Kingdom* (1990) **13 EHRR 622**). In those cases the Court used a restrictive approach to **articles 8 and 12** to uphold the legality of any discrimination against such individuals. However, as social conditions changed the Court has changed its stance, holding that such discrimination was unjustifiable (*Goodwin v United Kingdom* (2002) **35 EHRR 18**), and a similar approach has been evident when considering different age limits for heterosexuals and homosexuals (*Sutherland v United Kingdom, The Times*, **13 April 2001**).

In conclusion, **article 14** offers a general protection against unjustified discriminatory interference with the enjoyment of an individual's fundamental human rights. This is not a freestanding right not to be discriminated against, although the ratification of **Protocol No 12** by all member states, including the United Kingdom, would assist in the fuller recognition of equality under the law. Further, the qualification of **article 14** by the recognition of objective and reasonable discrimination dilutes the impact of the article in challenging discriminatory practices. Such qualifications, as of other Convention rights, are inevitable, although the margin of appreciation in this area needs to reflect the Court's desire to provide a more uniform and stricter protection of human rights and human dignity.

Further reading

Harris, DJ, O'Boyle, M, Warbrick, C, and Bates, E, *The Law of the European Convention on Human Rights*, 2nd edn (OUP 2009).

Janis, M, Kay, R, and Bradley, A, *European Human Rights Law: Text and Materials*, 3rd edn (OUP 2008).

Mowbray, A, *Cases and Materials on the European Convention on Human Rights*, 2nd edn (OUP 2007).

4

The Human Rights Act 1998

Introduction

The **Human Rights Act 1998** it at the heart of most domestic civil liberties courses in the United Kingdom and it is not possible to succeed on such courses without a thorough knowledge of the Act and its provisions as well as the reason for the passing of the Act and its case law. The Act came into force in October 2000 and gave further effect (many teachers and authors do not like the use of the word incorporation in this context) to the substantive rights contained in the **European Convention on Human Rights**, allowing domestic courts to employ the principles and case law of the Convention when determining disputes which raise an individual's Convention rights. As a result of the Act the courts can now officially take into account the case law of the European Court and Commission of Human Rights, have further powers of interpretation to ensure that legislation is compatible with the Convention and can, in rare cases, declare legislation incompatible with the Convention. The Act does not, however, rid the **British Constitution** of the doctrine of parliamentary sovereignty and the Act should not be viewed as an overriding bill of rights in the sense that we understand the **USA Bill of Rights**. It is essential that students understand the true nature and scope of the Act and the relationship between the Act and the European Convention—the latter system and machinery continues as before but hopefully there will be less recourse to it because of the more effective system of rights protection introduced by the 1998 Act.

Because the Act builds upon the common law tradition for protecting civil liberties, it is essential that the student has a sound knowledge of the traditional system and its deficiencies and it is quite common for questions to be set comparing and contrasting the traditional system with the post-Act era. Thus, students should be aware of the traditional system and of the cases that have been brought against the UK highlighting the deficiencies of that system. With respect to the Act itself, questions will be asked about the central provisions of the legislation and about the employment of those provisions in case law decided under the Act. The most topical and common areas of examination are those addressing the new powers of the courts under the Act and the constitutional significance of those powers, the possible 'horizontal' effect of the Act and its application to private disputes, the meaning of 'public authorities' within s.6 of the Act, and the various remedies available under the Act to victims of Convention violations. It is unlikely that students will be asked simply to outline the main provisions of the Act and much more likely that they will be asked to consider the legal and constitutional dilemmas posed by the Act; students should thus be fully conversant with those central arguments.

Problem questions on the Act and its application are also common. In these cases the student will not only need to be conversant with the Act's provisions and its case law, but will also have to show the necessary skills in advising the respective parties as to the application of those provisions and the likely success of any action. This will involve the interpretation of hypothetical pieces of legislation and the application of principles such as legality and proportionality to the facts of the case. These are not easy skills, particularly as the answers to those exercises are often open-ended—for example, is it necessary in a democratic society to ban a publication that the authorities claim is depraving and corrupting its readership? In addition, the question may expect you to be conversant with a substantive area of law or Convention article in order to ask the question—for example if the question relates to freedom of expression or peaceful assembly. In that case, the student needs to know the essential case law of the European Convention as well as the procedure and provisions under the Act, although the substantive area will have been covered in the module.

Although the provisions, principles, and case law of the European Convention are central to an understanding of, and application of the Act, it is important that the student identifies which jurisdiction the question is aimed at. Thus, if the question refers to the provisions of the 1998 Act, the student should not spend his or her time talking about the Convention machinery and the cases decided by the European Court and Commission for Human Rights. Rather, the question is asking how the *domestic law* is going to be affected by the provisions of the Act and the giving effect to the Convention by the Act. Thus, if the questions ask for an appraisal of the case law under the Human Rights Act, it is not appropriate to discuss the case law of the European Court, unless that case law has been specifically referred to by the domestic courts in making their decision.

Question 1

To what extent did English law recognize human rights and civil liberties before the passing of the **Human Rights Act 1998**? Why was this 'traditional' method regarded as unsatisfactory and how did the 1998 Act address any deficiencies of the traditional system?

 Commentary

This question asks you to consider the manner in which human rights and civil liberties were recognized and protected before the **Human Rights Act 1998**, and whether this system was satisfactory. It then asks you to consider how the 1998 Act made good any deficiencies of that system. It is a popular myth that there existed no human rights and civil liberties law before the passing of the Human Rights Act and that all violations had to be taken before the European Court and Commission of Human Rights. In fact, before the 1998 Act there existed a relatively sophisticated and effective system of rights protection—through both statute and judicial protection—much of which has survived the Act. This question asks you to consider the various ways in which rights and liberties were upheld in the pre-Act era but, equally importantly, it asks you to identify the shortcomings of a system that had no charter of rights and no special or entrenched human rights law. In order to assess the efficacy of the traditional system you will need to consider the cases brought before the European Convention machinery against the United Kingdom as well as the general calls for reform before the passing of the 1998 Act. This should highlight the deficiencies of the old system, including the gaps filled by the 1998 Act itself.

The diagram below compares the domestic law's protection of human rights in both the pre- and post-Human Rights Act era:

	Pre-Act	Post-Act
Applicability of the ECHR	No direct effect—Convention had persuasive influence	Convention rights given effect by Act—can be raised directly
Case law of the European Court and Commission	Courts reluctant to apply case law of the Convention	Duty under **s.2** to take into account case law of the Court and Commission
Interpretation of statutes	Presumption against interference with fundamental rights	Must interpret legislation in light of Convention rights wherever possible
Validity of primary legislation	No power to question or set aside an Act of Parliament	Power of higher courts to declare Act of Parliament incompatible with ECHR
Validity of secondary legislation	Power to declare secondary legislation *ultra vires* and invalid	As pre-Act and power to declare it incompatible with Convention rights and invalid unless clearly authorized by parent Act
Development of common law	Indirect and persuasive influence	Horizontal effect of convention rights in private law
Review of executive action	Power to strike it down as illegal/irrationality/breach of natural justice	As pre-Act plus proportionality and breach of Convention rights

 Answer plan

- The position of residual civil liberties under the traditional common law method
- The advantage and efficacy of that method
- The drawbacks of that system

- The United Kingdom's record before the European Court of Human Rights *vis-à-vis* such deficiencies
- Proposals for reform and a comparison with the Human Rights Act method

Suggested answer

Despite the lack of a bill of rights and any formal recognition of human rights, the United Kingdom has a long tradition of civil liberties, dating back to the Magna Carta 1215, which recognized the right of access to the courts and the right to a fair trial. This method—under which liberty was protected by the traditional courts and by Parliament and where the individual had the right to do anything provided it was not prohibited by the law—was preferred to the American style bill of rights by writers such as Dicey, who claimed that the formal mechanism could not guarantee a remedy on its breach.

Liberty and fundamental rights (of property and the person) were thus part of the constitutional heritage and would be protected by the courts from arbitrary interference by government. For example, in *Entick v Carrington* (1765) 19 St Tr 1029, the courts insisted that government showed legal authority in the form of statute or case law to justify its actions, so as to safeguard individual rights from unlawful interference. However, the courts could not interfere when Parliament had clearly intended to encroach upon individual rights, and, in *IRC v Rossminster* [1980] 2 AC 852, the House of Lords held that it was not the role of the courts to strike down unpopular legislation that unambiguously violated individual rights—in this case allowing tax authorities arbitrary powers of entry and search. In addition, the courts' powers were restricted to upholding rights that were recognized by the law, and in *Malone v MPC (No 2)* [1979] Ch 344 it was held that police authorities did not have to justify the act of telephone tapping by reference to legal provisions as such an act did not transgress any established legal right.

Despite these limitations, the courts were prepared to safeguard civil liberties by interpreting statutes and developing the common law in the light of fundamental human rights. In respect of statutory interpretation, although the courts were, and still are, powerless to strike down an Act of Parliament, they could assume that Parliament did not intend to interfere with fundamental rights and interpret the statute accordingly. Thus, the courts refused to allow government officials to pass secondary legislation that interfered with access to the courts, refusing to believe that Parliament would have sanctioned such a power. (See, for example, *Chester v Bateson* [1920] KB 829 and *Raymond v Honey* [1983] AC 1.) This included the power to interpret ambiguous legislation in the light of the **European Convention on Human Rights**, and in *Waddington v Miah* [1974] 1 WLR 683 the House of Lords interpreted **s.34 of the Immigration Act 1971** in a manner which avoided the provision having retrospective effect, which would have contravened **article 7** of the Convention.

With respect to the common law, the courts could develop legal rules and defences in the light of fundamental human rights. For example, in *Attorney-General v Guardian Newspapers (No 2)* [1990] 1 AC 109 the House of Lords established that government could not injunct the press unless it was able to show a powerful countervailing interest to override freedom of expression. Similarly, in *Derbyshire County Council v Times Newspapers* [1993] AC 534 the House of Lords decided that democratically elected local authorities could not sue in defamation because such an action would have a chilling effect on freedom of expression.

Judicial protection was particularly evident in the area of judicial review, where courts could assume that certain actions that interfered with human rights were not within the relevant statutory powers, declaring such actions *ultra vires*. For example, in *R v Secretary of State for the Home Department, ex parte O'Brien and Simms* [2000] 2 AC 115, the House of Lords interpreted prison regulations in such a way that prohibited the prison authorities from denying prisoners the right to visits from journalists, such a prohibition denying prisoners their right of access to justice. Similarly, when applying the principle of irrationality the courts would insist that the greater the interference with human rights, the greater the justification that had to be put forward to the courts by the decision-maker (*R v Ministry of Defence, ex parte Smith* [1996] 1All ER 257).

In addition to the courts' role, Parliament itself could and did bestow individual rights by passing legislation with the purpose of granting rights or freedoms, for example the various anti-discrimination laws, and data protection legislation, which were often passed to comply with standards laid down by European or international law. Further, certain legislation provided limits to the power of public officials, for example the **Police and Criminal Evidence Act 1984**, or defences to criminal charges which violated basic human rights—see for example **s.4 of the Obscene Publications Act 1959**, providing for the defence of public good to a charge of obscenity. Of course, Parliament could equally use its powers to pass legislation to interfere with liberty and human rights; see, for example, the restrictions placed on peaceful assembly by **ss.11–14 of the Public Order Act 1986**.

Despite these safeguards, the traditional system suffered from many disadvantages, many of which were exposed by applications brought under the European Convention. In addition to the inherent problem of parliamentary sovereignty, which allowed Parliament the theoretical, and often practical, power to interfere with human rights, the old system had the following drawbacks. First, although the courts had the power to review decisions that violated human rights, and to develop the law in a human rights-friendly manner, they lacked the express power to apply the principles and case law of the European Convention. For example, in *R v Secretary of State for the Home Department, ex parte Brind* [1991] 1 All ER 696, the House of Lords stated that the courts could not apply the Convention unless there was an ambiguity in the Act; equally they could not subject decisions to the doctrine of proportionality, applied by both the European Court of Human Rights and the European Court of Justice. The refusal to employ proportionality was highlighted in the case of *Smith and Grady v United Kingdom* (2000) **29 EHRR** 493, where the European Court held that the inability of the applicants to claim in the domestic courts that interferences with their right to private life were disproportionate (*R v Ministry of Defence, ex parte Smith* (above)) was a violation of their right to an effective remedy for breach of Convention rights. Secondly, some judges applied the law in a way that failed to give adequate weight to that issue. For example, in *Sunday Times v United Kingdom* (1979) 2 EHRR 245 the European Court noted that the domestic courts should not have committed a newspaper for contempt for commenting on ongoing litigation unless it was absolutely certain to interfere with those proceedings, whereas the domestic courts felt that the action could be taken if there was a real risk of such interference.

Thirdly, the traditional system only protected rights that were specifically recognized by statute or the common law. The common law had, and still has, failed to develop a specific law of privacy and in *Malone v United Kingdom* (1984) **7 EHRR 14**, the government was held liable for an act of telephone tapping, which constituted an interference with the applicant's right to private life under **article 8**, but which did not require authorization because the police had not broken any enforceable legal right (*Malone v MPC* (above)). This refusal to develop a common law of privacy was again highlighted in *Wainwright v United Kingdom* (2007) **44 EHRR 40**, where the European Court held that the domestic laws of trespass failed to provide adequate safeguards against arbitrary interferences with the applicants' privacy. Fourthly, the lack of an enforceable bill of rights allowed Parliament and the courts to ignore the rights of certain unpopular and under-represented groups. Thus, in a series of cases the European Court found violations of both the rights of prisoners (*Golder v United Kingdom* (1975) **1 EHRR 524** and *Thynne, Wilson and Gunnell v United Kingdom* (1990) **13 EHRR 666**), and persons subject to deportation or extradition (*Chahal v United Kingdom* (1997) **23 EHRR 413**) and *Soering v United Kingdom* (1989) **11 EHRR 439**).

The **Human Rights Act 1998** was passed in the context of the government's unsatisfactory record under the European Convention, and amid calls for a more robust system of human rights protection that could more effectively challenge both the acts of government and excessive parliamentary legislation. Specifically, the Act was passed to give 'further effect' to the European Convention and its case law, and to make domestic law and practices more Convention-compliant. Thus, although the Act preserves the general notion of parliamentary sovereignty, many of its provisions allow the courts, and Parliament, to implement a system more akin to that of the European Convention and its values.

First, **s.2** allows domestic courts and tribunals to take into account the case law of the European Court and Commission when adjudicating on cases raising Convention rights. In particular, this allows the courts to employ the doctrine of proportionality, rejected as a ground for review before the Act was passed (*Brind* (above)). Although the courts are not bound to *follow* such case law, it is expected that they will do so and thus decide cases in a manner more akin to the European Court, thus avoiding, where possible, subsequent applications to Strasbourg. Secondly (under **s.3**), the courts are given increased powers of statutory interpretation, allowing them to interpret legislation in favour of Convention rights *wherever possible*. This allows them to read a provision as Convention-compliant wherever that is possible, it no longer being necessary to show that the provision was ambiguous (*R v A* [2002] 1 AC 45). Thirdly, although the Act does not allow the courts to strike down incompatible (and clear) primary legislation (or secondary legislation which is clearly permitted by clear primary legislation), higher courts are allowed under **s.4** to issue declarations of incompatibility in respect of such provisions. This can expose legislation that may be inconsistent with the Convention and its case law, and under **s.10** of the Act the relevant Minister can use a power to introduce legislation that rectifies that inconsistency.

Fourthly, the Act has created a rights-based system, which, in contrast to the traditional system, is based on protecting human *rights* as opposed to residual *liberties*. **Section 6** of the Act makes it unlawful for public authorities (including the courts) to violate Convention rights and **ss.7 and 8** of the Act provide a remedy to the victim of such violations. Although these rights are not available where the violation is expressly and clearly authorized by primary legislation, individuals can seek a remedy that is consistent with those available under the Convention. In addition, it is hoped that the Act will persuade government and Parliament (as well as the courts) to adopt a more rights-conscious approach in the carrying out of their respective functions.

In conclusion, although the **Human Rights Act 1998** has not fundamentally altered the United Kingdom's constitutional arrangements, it has put in place a method of human rights protection which is more consistent with the principles and case law of the **European Convention on Human Rights**. Such principles can, of course, be displaced by express and clear legislation, but in the absence of such derogations the courts are entitled to assume that Parliament and the administration intend to comply with the standards laid down in the Convention. The 1998 Act has created a different rights culture and has armed the courts with greater powers to interpret statutes and develop the common law in line with the principles of legitimacy and proportionality. Thus, although some of the traditional principles have remained, the Act has eradicated many of the deficiencies of the traditional system, making it more compatible with human rights norms and international law.

Question 2

With respect to the role of the courts in the protection of human rights, what constitutional difficulties have been highlighted by the passing and implementation of the **Human Rights Act 1998**? In your opinion, are the courts' powers under the Act 'unconstitutional'?

Commentary

This question asks the students to examine the constitutional implications of the courts' powers of human rights enforcement and to consider, subjectively, the 'constitutionality' of those powers. The question is, therefore, not asking for a 'black letter' answer and the student should not simply outline the main provisions of the Act. To answer the question the student needs to appreciate the Act's potential constitutional dilemmas—the difficulty of applying 'European' principles and case law in the resolution of legal disputes; the changing constitutional role of the courts; the loss, if any, of parliamentary sovereignty; and the effect of the Act on the separation of powers and the rule of law. The student will need a good working knowledge of the Act's provisions, but more importantly will need to appreciate its aims and the constitutional arguments surrounding its passing and of its particular provisions. The post-Human Rights Act case law can be considered either to illustrate specific constitutional problems or to further a particular argument relating to the Act's constitutionality.

When offering your opinion on constitutionality, be careful only to consider the constitutional issues raised by the Act itself. You may come to whatever conclusion you wish, provided you show an appreciation of the issues and of both sides of any particular argument. Your conclusions should be supported by clear logic and, where appropriate, by legal authority and examples. In particular, any conclusion should draw on the central arguments raised in the main body of the answer.

Answer plan

- Brief explanation of the traditional method of rights protection before the **Human Rights Act 1998** and the inadequacy of that method
- Examination of the various changes made to the powers of the courts under the Act
- Critical examination of post-Act case law highlighting any constitutional issues arising from such provisions
- Consideration of the constitutionality and democratic legitimacy of the courts' powers under the Act
- Conclusions on whether the Act and its applications is consistent with the Constitution

Suggested answer

As bills of rights attempt to put rights first, many question whether individual rights should have an enhanced status over and above other individual rights and social claims, and whether judges should have the power to strike down parliamentary or executive acts that are alleged to be incompatible with such fundamental rights. These dilemmas are particularly acute in the United Kingdom where the British Constitution and the traditional common law system of rights protection are subject to the doctrine of parliamentary sovereignty, thus limiting the constitutional role of the judges.

The passing of the **Human Rights Act** raised a number of constitutional arguments from those who felt that the traditional system would be replaced by one allowing judges to employ European human rights principles that would undermine national sovereignty and the general public good. Although these fears were largely groundless, principally because of the method of incorporation of the **European Convention on Human Rights** chosen under the 1998 Act, as some of the Act's provisions were intended to shift the balance of power from government and Parliament to the courts, the Act raised genuine constitutional concerns.

The main constitutional arguments revolve around the new powers of the courts to resolve human rights disputes by going beyond its traditional constitutional role of simply applying the law and instead allowing them to judge the merits and reasonableness of particular laws and practices. This includes the courts' power, under **s.2** of the Act, to consider the case law of the European Convention and to apply the doctrines of necessity and proportionality when judging the compatibility of legislative or other acts that infringe the applicant's Convention rights. The Act allows the courts to adopt the principle of proportionality that had been rejected as part of the common law powers of review in *R v Secretary of State for the Home Department, ex parte Brind* [1991] 1 AC 696, and in *R (Daly) v Secretary of State for the Home Department* [2002] 1 AC 532. Lord Steyn held that there was a material difference between *Wednesbury* review and proportionality, the latter requiring the reviewing court to assess the balance that the decision-maker had struck, and requiring attention to be directed to the relevant weight accorded to the various interests. Further, any limitation of the right had to be necessary in a democratic society, in the sense of meeting a pressing social need and being truly proportionate to any legitimate aim being pursued. Despite this, Lord Steyn did not believe that there had been a shift to merits review and in *Edore v Secretary of State for the Home Department* [2003] NLJ 998, it was held that given the margin of discretion available to decision-makers, there was often room for two possible proportionate outcomes in a particular situation.

Accordingly, the courts may still be prepared to offer decision-makers, including Parliament, a great degree of discretion. For example, in *R (British American Tobacco and others) v Secretary of State for Health, The Times,* 11 November 2004, the High Court held that regulations banning the advertising of tobacco products were proportionate and compatible with **article 10** as they were proportionate to promoting health by restricting advertising. Conversely, the House of Lords took a more robust approach in *A and others v Secretary of State for the Home Department* [2005] 2 AC 68 in deciding that the detention of foreign nationals under the **Anti-terrorism, Crime and Security Act 2001** was a disproportionate response to the threat of terrorism and not strictly required by the exigencies of the situation. Lord Bingham held that the traditional *Wednesbury* approach was no longer appropriate and the domestic courts themselves had to form a judgment whether a Convention right was breached. Further, given the importance of **article 5**, judicial control of the executive's interference with individual liberty was essential and the courts were not precluded by any doctrine of deference from scrutinizing such issues. Their Lordships' views appear to be vindicated by the decision of the Grand Chamber of the European Court in *A v United Kingdom*, (2009) 49 EHRR 29.

Similar constitutional concerns have been raised regarding the courts' powers under s.3 of the Act to interpret both primary and secondary legislation 'so far as is possible' in a way that is compatible with Convention rights. Although this provision gives the court a greater power to interpret legislation, it is expressly provided that **s.3** does not affect the validity of any incompatible primary legislation, or the validity, continuing operation, or enforcement of any incompatible subordinate legislation if primary legislation prevents removal of the incompatibility. Consequently, whether parliamentary sovereignty is compromised, and whether the courts extend their powers by legislating, will depend on the extent to which they use their interpretation powers under the Act. A robust approach was taken by the House of Lords in *R v A (Complainant's Sexual History)* [2002] 1 AC 45, where the House of Lords held that although the adoption of traditional principles of statutory interpretation could not solve the problem of the *prima facie* excessive inroad on the right to a fair trial, the interpretative obligation under **s.3** of the **Human Rights Act 1998** applied even where there was no ambiguity and placed a duty on the court to strive to find a possible interpretation compatible with Convention rights. **Section 3** required the courts to proceed on the basis that the legislature would not, if alerted to the problem, have wished to deny the right to an accused to put forward a full and complete defence.

However, in *Poplar Housing and Regeneration Community Association Ltd v Donoghue* [2001] 2 WLR 1546, Lord Woolf CJ warned that **s.3** does not entitle the courts to legislate, and that a court should not radically alter a statute in order to achieve compatibility. Further, in *Re S and W* [2002] 2 AC 291, the House of Lords stressed that the 1998 Act maintained the constitutional boundary between the interpretation of statutes and the passing and repeal of legislation, and that a meaning that departed substantially from a fundamental feature of an Act of Parliament was likely to have crossed the boundary.

Nevertheless, there is still a good deal of judicial argument regarding the scope of s.3 and the extent to which the courts should use their powers to amend incompatible legislation. Thus, in *Bellinger v Bellinger* [2003] 2 AC 467 the House of Lords held that it was not possible to use **s.3** to interpret the words 'man and woman' to include a person who had undergone gender reassignment, so as to comply with the decision of the European Court in *Goodwin v United Kingdom* (2002) 35 EHRR 18. Yet in *Mendoza v Ghaidan* [2004] 2 AC 557 the House of Lords held that the words 'as his wife or husband' could be interpreted to mean 'as if they were his wife or husband' so as to give a homosexual the right to inherit his partner's tenancy. Notably, Lord Millett dissented on the grounds that it was for Parliament to change a law that was quite clearly not intended to cover same-sex relationships. **Section 3** clearly raises questions of the constitutional role of interpretation and in *Attorney-General's Reference (No 4)* [2005] 1 AC 264 the House of Lords held that it was possible to read down a statutory provision so as to avoid incompatibility, even though Parliament had intended a consequence inconsistent with the Convention. Having regard to its intention in passing **s.3** of the **Human Rights Act 1998**, it was permissible to assume that other statutory provisions should not be incompatible with a person's Convention rights.

Similar constitutional issues are raised with respect to the power of the courts, under **s.4** of the Act, to declare primary and secondary legislation incompatible. The Act does not allow the courts to strike down or disallow primary legislation; they simply have the power to make a declaration of incompatibility, leaving Parliament with the choice to amend or repeal the relevant law, under the procedure laid down by **s.10** of the Act. Although **s.4** provides the Court with a seemingly wide power to challenge legislation, this power has, thus far, been used with a good deal of caution and the courts have shown some reluctance to question primary legislation passed by the democratically elected Parliament. For example, in *R v Shayler* [2002] 2 WLR 754 the House of Lords held that the **Official Secrets Act 1989** was compatible with **article 10** of the Convention despite the absence of a public interest defence, and in *R v DPP, ex parte Pretty and another* [2002] 1 AC 800, the House of Lords held that **s.2(1) of the Suicide Act 1961** was not incompatible with the European Convention.

Despite this general reticence, there have been occasions where the courts have been prepared to grant declarations of incompatibility. Thus, in *R v Mental Health Tribunal, ex parte H* [2001] 3 WLR 512 the Court of Appeal found that **ss.72 and 73 of the Mental Health Act 1983** were incompatible with **article 5** of the European Convention, because they placed the burden of proof on a restricted patient to show that he was no longer suffering from a mental disorder warranting detention. In particular, the courts will be prepared to issue such declarations where the law appears to be in conflict with a clear decision of the European Court. Thus in *Bellinger v Bellinger* (above) the House of Lords held that legislation which did not recognize the right of transsexuals to marry was incompatible with **article 8** of the Convention and relevant case law of the European Court (*Goodwin v United Kingdom* (above)). More controversially, in *A and others v Secretary of State for the Home Department* (above) the House of Lords held that detention provisions of the **Anti-terrorism, Crime and Security Act 2001** were incompatible with **article 5** of the European Convention and were not justified under **article 15** of the Convention, which allows derogation in times of war or other emergency threatening the life of the nation. The decision was seen by many as being in breach of the separation of powers by not offering the government and Parliament appropriate deference on matters of national security and public safety, but the decision was confirmed by the European Court in *A v United Kingdom* (above).

The above provisions no doubt increase the courts' powers to provide redress for human rights violations, but are they unconstitutional? First, the courts have always had the constitutional power to safeguard human rights against arbitrary interference, including the power to interpret legislation in line with human rights norms (*Waddington v Miah* [1974] 1 WLR 683), and to assume that Parliament did not intend to interfere with fundamental rights (*Raymond v Honey* [1983] AC 1). Consequently, s.3 of the Act can be seen to be no more than statutory recognition of this power. Secondly, although the courts now have the power to apply Convention law and principles, and to declare legislation incompatible with Convention rights, it should not be forgotten that this power has been bestowed by Parliament itself, who through the Act has expressed an intention that the court's constitutional powers be extended in this area. Thus in *A v Secretary of State for the Home Department* (above) Lord Bingham rejected any assertion that the court's interference would be undemocratic, noting that the courts had been given a wholly democratic mandate by Parliament.

Thirdly, the Act has been carefully constructed so as to avoid any direct conflict with the doctrine of parliamentary sovereignty. Thus, the courts have no power to strike down any incompatible primary le gislation, or secondary legislation clearly authorized by primary legislation. The ultimate legislative power is thus still vested in Parliament and it still has the power to pass new legislation, correcting the court's interpretation. Fourthly, although the doctrines of necessity and proportionality no doubt depart from the more restrictive traditional grounds of review, there is evidence that the courts are willing to display a good deal of judicial deference where they feel that a matter is better resolved by a government official or by Parliament itself (*Bellinger* (above) and *Pretty v United Kingdom* (2002) 35 EHRR 1).

Finally, it could be argued that such powers are constitutional in a more general sense because it is accepted in most jurisdictions that the courts' constitutional role includes the power to strike down legislative and executive acts that conflict with fundamental constitutional rights.

In conclusion, the 1998 Act has extended the power of the courts in the area of human rights protection, and such powers raise constitutional concerns. However, given the scope and content of the Act, in particular its retention of parliamentary sovereignty, it would be wrong to allege that these new powers are unconstitutional. The Act was passed for the specific purpose of giving effect to the rights and principles of the European Convention, and unless the courts deliberately or clearly seek to go beyond that remit, these powers should be viewed as entirely constitutional.

Question 3

In February 2009, in response to the formation and activities of a number of right-wing extremist groups, Parliament passed the (imaginary) Public Order (Proscription of Associations)

Act 2009. The Act made it an offence to belong to, to assist in the recruitment and organization of, or to take part in the activities of any group that has been proscribed by the Secretary of State under the Act. Under s.2 of the Act, the Secretary of State may proscribe any group if he has reasonable grounds for believing that such a group advocates the use of violence for the purpose of expressing the views or agenda of such a group, or where the agenda or activities of such a group are such that they would cause gross offence to any racial or religious group, or to any members of such group. Acting under s.2 of the Act, the Secretary of State proscribed a group known as Freedom Against Religious Terror, which suggested banning all 'extremist' religious groups that advocated religious following above the enjoyment of individual liberty. The head of the group had recently been found guilty of arson after burning down an Islamic Centre, and several members of the group had been found guilty of assaults on a number of Muslims. In July 2009, Boris and Billy, both members of the group, were arrested for distributing leaflets produced by the group outside the local town hall. The leaflets attempted to recruit new members and invited people to a proposed rally to promote 'religious tolerance and the freedom of the individual'. They were both subsequently charged under the Act, for recruiting and taking part in the activities of a proscribed group, and at their trial they claimed that the Act, the group's proscription and the proceeding were contrary to their Convention rights.

Advise Boris and Billy as to what Convention rights might be at issue and how those rights might be raised in the domestic courts by employing the relevant provisions of the **Human Rights Act 1998**. In particular, how might the **Public Order Act 2009**, the Secretary's proscription, and the prosecution be challenged under the **Human Rights Act 1998**, and what are their chances of success?

 ## Commentary

This question tests the student's ability to apply their knowledge of the **Human Rights Act 1998** and a number of the principles of the **European Convention on Human Rights** in a hypothetical problem scenario. Although the scenario raises possible violations of the rights of association and assembly and freedom of expression, the student does not need an in-depth knowledge of those rights or the relevant case law of the European and domestic courts. Thus, although the student should be aware of the basic principles surrounding those rights and of some principal case law in the area, the question is principally testing the student's knowledge of the machinery for the enforcement of human rights under the 1998 Act, the principles of legality and reasonableness that the courts will use in resolving the case, and of any remedies available to the victims of any violation.

The student should first identify which Convention rights are engaged in the claim, explaining the importance of that right and its status; in particular, whether it is an absolute or conditional right and whether there may be any justification for its violation. The student should then explain to Boris and Billy what procedure they would use in challenging the Act and any decision made under the Act, and what role the 1998 Act and the relevant Convention rights would have in making and resolving any claim. The answer should then deal in turn with the legality and compatibility of the Secretary of State's proscription, the prosecution and the parent Act itself, explaining how the **Human Rights Act** and the courts' powers under that Act could be used to assist Boris and Billy's claim.

Answer plan

- Identification of any Convention rights that may have been breached in the scenario
- Explanation of the process by which Boris and Billy can raise those rights under the **Human Rights Act**, together with the various powers of the courts to adjudicate and rule on those issues
- Identification and consideration of the possible challenges to the Act, the Secretary's proscription and the prosecution
- Consideration of the likely chances of success with reference to relevant case law under the European Convention and the 1998 Act

Suggested answer

The Convention rights at issue

The proscription of a particular group under the 2007 Act engages the right to freedom of association under **article 11**, a right regarded as a fundamental aspect of any democratic society (*United Communist Party v Turkey* (1998) 26 EHRR 121). Further, as the Act makes it an offence to take part in the activities of a proscribed group, and in particular Boris and Billy were charged under the Act for distributing leaflets publicizing the agenda and forthcoming rally of the group, the right to peaceful assembly under **article 11** of the Convention and the right to freedom of expression under **article 10** are also engaged. Again, both those rights are regarded as essential to democracy (*Handyside v United Kingdom* (1976) 1 EHRR 737 and *Chorherr v Austria* (1993) 17 EHRR 358). These rights are conditional and can be violated provided the interference is prescribed by law, pursues a legitimate aim, and is necessary in a democratic society for the purpose of achieving that aim.

The mechanism for challenge

With respect to the Secretary of State's proscription, under the 1998 Act, Boris and Billy are able to challenge the decision via judicial review, and under **s.7(3)** of the **Human Rights Act** can rely on the provisions of the 1998 Act in such proceedings provided they are 'victims' of any potential violation of their Convention rights, which they clearly are. With respect to the prosecution, **s.7(1)** of the Act provides that a person can rely on their Convention rights 'in any legal proceedings'. Thus, Boris and Billy's prosecution could be challenged on that basis in the trial itself, by arguing that the conditions of liability under the Act have not been met in this case. Further, Boris and Billy could argue that the 2009 Act itself is incompatible with their Convention rights—although the Crown Court cannot issue a declaration of incompatibility under **s.4** of the 1998 Act (under **s.4** such a right only applies to the High Court and above), Boris and Billy may ask the High Court to decide the compatibility of the prosecution as a preliminary issue (*R v Shayler* [2002] 2 WLR 754).

The Home Secretary's proscription

The Home Secretary's act of proscription can be challenged via judicial review, or collaterally during the trial. As the Secretary's power is derived from the 2009 Act, Boris and Billy would argue that the proscription was *ultra vires*, using the **Human Rights Act** and the relevant Convention rights to argue that the Secretary has acted unlawfully. Thus it could be argued initially that Parliament did not intend to interfere with the rights of political groups, or groups with a genuine political agenda, and that **s.2** of the 2009 Act should be construed so as to exclude such groups. However, although a court can assume that Parliament did not intend to violate fundamental human rights (*Raymond v Honey* [1983] AC 1), it would appear impossible to construe **s.2** of the 2009 Act in that way. Although **s.3** of the **Human Rights Act** allows the courts to adopt a strained interpretation to ensure compatibility (*R v A* [2002] 1 AC 45), to interpret **s.2** of the 2009 Act so as to exclude political groups would be in conflict with the clear intention of the Act, which was to proscribe any group, political or otherwise, who used violence or whose agenda or activities caused gross offence. Such interpretation, therefore, would amount to judicial legislation (*Re S and W* [2002] 2 AC 291).

The Secretary of State does not appear to have identified which of the two grounds under **s.2** he has relied on in proscribing the group. Although the Secretary may have evidence of violence on behalf of the group, (see below), the group would not appear to fall into the second category because the group's existence would not be likely to cause gross offence, as opposed to mere annoyance and affront, to any religious group. If the Secretary's duty to identify the grounds of proscription was mandatory, then the proscription would be unlawful. Further, Boris and Billy could also argue that the Secretary's act of proscription in this particular case was unlawful and disproportionate since he did not have grounds for believing that the group met either of the relevant criteria. Since the 1998 Act came into force a claimant can now rely on the doctrine of proportionality, employed by the European Court of Human Rights when assessing the necessity of any interference with Convention rights (*R (Daly) v Secretary of State for the Home Department* [2002] 1 AC 532). However, there would appear to be ample grounds for believing that the group did advocate the use of violence for the purpose of expressing its views and its agenda, and given the power vested in the Home Secretary, his decision would appear to be both rational in the traditional sense, and a proportionate use of such powers.

If those grounds of challenge failed, Boris and Billy could then seek to challenge the 2009 Act itself, seeking a declaration from the court under **s.4** that its provisions are incompatible with Convention rights. The court would, having established that there had been a *prima facie* breach of their Convention rights, consider first whether the relevant provisions of the 2009 Act are sufficiently clear to be 'prescribed by law' under **articles 10 and 11** of the Convention. In this respect it may be argued that the wording of **s.2** of the Act, particularly the words 'cause gross offence to any racial or religious group, or to any member of such group' is vague and subjective, and provides an individual with insufficient guidance as to what sort of group would come within the terms of the section (see, for example, *Hashman and Harrap v United Kingdom* (1999) 30 EHRR 241). Although such phrases as 'gross offence' can be clarified by subsequent case law (*Müller v Switzerland* (1991) 13 EHRR 212), it might be argued that a prosecution under this provision at such an early stage of the Act's life, would result in the conclusion that the provision is too vague to be prescribed by law. On the other hand, it might be found that the phrase 'gross offence' is readily understandable by everyone and that the court would merely apply a common-sense interpretation to such a phrase (as in the word 'insulting' used in what is now **s.5 of the Public Order Act 1986**, see *Brutus v Cozens* [1972] 2 All ER 1297). Further, although the Secretary is given a good deal of discretion in deciding to proscribe, that discretion is phrased objectively ('reasonable grounds for believing') and would be subject to intense judicial review.

Assuming the Act passes the above test, the Court would then ask whether the Act and its provisions pursued any of the legitimate aims recognized in **paragraph 2 of articles 10 and 11** of the Convention. In this respect it would be argued that **ss.1 and 2** of the Act pursued a variety of legitimate aims such as the protection of the rights of others, public safety, the prevention of crime and disorder and, to a limited extent, the protection of morals. Finally, it would need to be decided whether the Act and its application in this particular case was necessary in a democratic society, in other words whether there was a pressing social need to pass and apply the Act and whether its application to Boris and Billy was truly proportionate to achieving any of the above legitimate aims (*Handyside v United Kingdom* (above)). The court would consider a number of matters, such as the level of judicial deference it should offer to the Secretary (*R (Farrakhan) v Secretary of State for the Home Department* [2002] 3 WLR 481), the importance and extent of the violation, the importance of the legitimate aim, and whether any other, less intrusive measures were available to the government and the police to deal with the activities of such groups.

The court would need to be shown convincing evidence that the draconian step of proscription was really necessary, and that the normal criminal law, which would punish individuals for committing specific illegal acts other than mere association with a particular group, would be totally inadequate to deal with the threats posed by such groups. Although the European Court has accepted that a state may proscribe an organization, such measures would be regarded as exceptional, applicable only when the groups pose a real threat to the security of the state or its citizens (*Refah Partisi Erbakan Kazan* and *Tekdal v Turkey* (2002) 35 EHRR 3). In addition, the Home Secretary could rely on **article 17** of the European Convention, which states that the enjoyment of Convention rights does not extend to activities aimed at the destruction of the rights of others. Although the views of such groups are unlikely to be regarded as an activity for this purpose (*Lehideux and Irsoni v France* (2000) 30

EHRR 665), the violent activities of the group in our scenario might be sufficient to engage **article 17**.

It is likely that the court would regard the power of proscription under the 2009 Act, and its application in this case as disproportionate. First, although there was some evidence of violence on behalf of a number of such groups, including the one in this scenario, there does not appear to be sufficient evidence to suggest that the normal criminal law and police powers are inadequate to deal with the dangers posed by such groups. In particular, it is not clear why offences such as incitement to racial or religious hatred, and the variety of racially or religiously aggravated offences under public order legislation, cannot be used effectively against such groups without having recourse to the drastic step of proscription. Secondly, although there is evidence that several of its members have been acting violently and unlawfully, otherwise the group's mandate appears to be entirely peaceful and advocates a reasonable, although controversial, agenda. Finally, following the act of proscription the Act has the ability to interfere with entirely peaceful and non-provocative behaviour such as distributing leaflets. Although such effects might be the natural product of proscribing dangerous groups, such effects should only ensue in the most exceptional circumstances, which it could be argued do not exist in our scenario.

The prosecution under the Act

As the success of the prosecution is dependent on the legality of the Secretary's proscription, Boris and Billy could raise the same arguments of interpretation and compatibility of that power, as outlined above. Further, it could be argued that **s.2** of the 2009 Act should be interpreted so that the word 'activities' meant unlawful and violent activities, so as to exclude entirely peaceful activities such as distributing leaflets. However, as Boris and Billy were clearly 'assisting in the recruitment' of the organization, the argument appears redundant, unless the charge is solely for taking part in the activities of the group. Given the clarity of the provisions of the 2009 Act, the court would have no option but to find that Boris and Billy have clearly committed an offence under the Act. Accordingly, Boris and Billy's remedy would be to seek a declaration of incompatibility under **s.4** of the 1998 Act.

Conclusions

Despite the courts' powers to interpret and apply the Act in a Convention-friendly manner, it appears that both the proscription and the prosecution were within the scope of the 2009 Act and, considering the scope of the Act and the Secretary's powers, appear to have been exercised proportionally. The most likely successful challenge would be to the 2009 Act itself on the grounds that the power of proscription was incompatible with **articles 10 and 11** of the Convention. It is suggested that the power of proscription is incompatible with **article 10**, and that the provisions be declared incompatible with the Convention as far as their application to this case is concerned. This would not affect the validity of the proscription, or of the legality of Boris and Bill's prosecution or subsequent conviction.

Further reading

Amos, M, *Human Rights Law* (Hart 2006), Part 1.

Clayton, R and Tomlinson, H, *The Law of Human Rights*, 2nd edn (OUP 2009), chs 3, 4, and 5.

Wadham, J and Mountfield, H, *Blackstone's Guide to the Human Rights Act 1998*, 5th edn (OUP 2009).

5

The right to life

Introduction

The right to life is regarded as the most fundamental of all human rights and is recognized and protected in all international and regional human rights treaties concerned with the protection of civil and political rights. Students are likely to receive questions on a number of areas relating to the right to life, ranging from the importance of the right itself, the content and scope of **article 2 of the European Convention on Human Rights**, the exceptions under **article 2(2)** of the Convention, the procedural aspects of the right, and a number of specific areas such as the death penalty, the rights of the unborn child, and the right to die.

Students should have a thorough knowledge of the case law of the European Court of Human Rights in this area and must also be conversant with the developing case law in domestic law in areas such as inquiries into death and the political and legal discussions on the right to die and euthanasia. Some knowledge of other international treaty provisions, and some case law, may also be useful. Questions may come in the form of essays or hypothetical problems and it is becoming common for questions to concentrate on specific and topical areas, such as abortion and the right to life, euthanasia, and the death penalty. It is also not uncommon for a question to combine issues under both the right to life and freedom from torture guaranteed under **article 3** of the Convention.

Question 1

By the use of the case law of the European Court of Human Rights, critically examine how **article 2** of the **European Convention on Human Rights** has protected the individual's right to life.

 ## Commentary

This question is quite broad and reasonably straightforward, although it does require the student to identify the essential issues relating to the scope of **article 2** and to answer the question in a critical and analytical manner. The student will be expected to have a very sound overall knowledge of the different aspects of **article 2** and, in particular, of the relevant case law of the European Court of Human Rights, and the answer should cover as many facets of the article as possible.

The student should begin by identifying the fundamental character of the right to life and why its protection is so important. The answer should then examine the wording of **article 2**, identifying the duties that it imposes on member states, as well as the specific exceptions to the general right. The student can then examine the case law of the European Court with a view to explaining how the right and its exceptions have been interpreted and applied by the Court. The student should take a critical and analytical approach, discussing controversial topics such as the right to die, the rights of the unborn child, the procedural protection offered by the article, and the death penalty. In particular, the question should critically examine the relevant case law of the Court under **article 2(2)**, where the Convention permits life to be taken away intentionally in exceptional circumstances.

Finally, the student should reach some critical conclusions with respect to the success of the European Court in protecting the right to life, drawing on the examples referred to in the main body of the essay.

 Answer plan

- General explanation of the importance of the right to life
- Examination of the wording and scope of **article 2**
- Critical examination of the case law of the European Court of Human Rights with respect to the interpretation and application of **article 2**
- Conclusions with respect to the extent of protection of the right to life under **article 2** by the European Court

Suggested answer

Article 2 of the European Convention on Human Rights provides that 'everyone's right to life shall be protected by law and that no one shall be deprived of his life intentionally (save in the execution of a sentence of a court following his conviction of a crime for which the penalty is provided by law)'. **Article 2** protects the most fundamental of all human rights, as the enjoyment of all other rights depends on the preservation of the individual's life. Thus the European Court of Human Rights, in *McCann v United Kingdom* (1995) 21 EHRR 97, noted that together with **article 3** (the prohibition of torture) it enshrines one of the basic values of all democratic societies in the Council of Europe. The right is regarded as absolute in the sense that under **article 15(3)** it cannot be derogated from even in times of war and other public emergency (except in respect of deaths resulting from lawful acts of war).

Despite this, the Convention provides for a number of exceptions justifying the taking of an individual's life (see below), and, the scope of the article is subject to judicial interpretation and application. As a consequence the level of protection afforded to this fundamental right is dependent on the European Court, who will need to decide whether particular claims fall within the ambit of the article's protection. For example, in *Vo v France* (2005) 40 EHRR 12 the Grand Chamber of the European Court decided that on the proper interpretation of **article 2** an unborn child was not 'a person', there being no European consensus on the nature and status of the embryo/foetus (confirmed in *Evans v United Kingdom* (2008) 46 EHRR 34). Similarly, in *Pretty v United Kingdom* (2002) 35 EHRR 1 the Court held that the right to life did not include the right to die, the principal thrust of **article 2** being the state's obligation to preserve life. The Court thus refused to treat the right to life as part of a more general human right of self-determination.

On the other hand, the Court has adopted a positive approach with respect to the state's obligation under **article 2** and the circumstances in which the article is engaged. It is clear that **article 2** covers deaths caused by the deliberate, or negligent acts, or omissions, of the state (*McCann v United Kingdom* (above)), and that in cases where the state or state actors have allegedly been involved in the victim's death, the Court will place a burden of proof on it to explain the circumstances of the death (*Jordan v United Kingdom* (2003) 37 EHRR 2). A positive duty to protect individuals from unreasonable environmental hazards was also accepted in *LCB v United Kingdom* (1999) 27 EHRR 212. Specifically, in cases where it has been shown that the individual entered state custody in good health, the Court has stressed that the state has a strong duty to provide a satisfactory account of the events (*Salaman v Turkey* (2002) 34 EHRR 17). This obligation is supported by the state's procedural obligations, examined below, and reflects the values and importance of **article 2** and the necessity of imposing strict duties on the state to protect the lives of those within its jurisdiction.

Article 2 not only imposes a negative duty on the state not to interfere with a person's right to life, but also places a positive duty on the state to ensure that an individual's life is not taken unnecessarily, including having in place appropriate criminal laws and proper procedures to ensure that persons are deterred from committing such acts and are appropriately sanctioned. This duty is not absolute and an applicant would need to show that there was a real risk of a violation of **article 2**, and in *Osman v United Kingdom* (2000) 29 EHRR 245, the European Court held that although the state had a positive obligation to take preventive operational measures to protect an individual whose life is at risk from the criminal acts of another, that obligation should not impose an impossible and disproportionate burden on the state.

However, although *Osman* represents the Court's caution in this area, it will be prepared to find liability in clearer cases. Thus, in *Edwards v United Kingdom* (2002) 35 EHRR 19, the Court found a violation of **article 2** when the applicant's son had been stamped and kicked to death by his violent cell mate, the Court finding that the cell mate posed a real and serious risk to the applicant's son and that the prison authorities had not been properly informed of the cell mate's medical history and perceived dangerousness. In addition, **article 2** can be engaged where the individual has taken his or her own life, although the Court requires a specific and real risk of self-harm. Thus, in *Keenan v United Kingdom* (2001) **33 EHRR 38**, in finding that there had been no violation of **article 2** when the applicants' son committed suicide in prison, the Court noted that he had not been formally diagnosed as schizophrenic and was, therefore, not considered an immediate risk while in detention.

The Court has also developed extensive case law with respect to the state's duty to carry out a proper investigation into any deaths that have occurred within their jurisdiction. In *Jordan and others v United Kingdom* (above), the Court held that **article 2** required there to be some form of effective official investigation when individuals had been killed as a result of the use of force, thus ensuring the state's accountability for deaths in their jurisdiction. Further, any investigation had to be capable of leading to a determination of whether the force used in such circumstances was justified, and to the identification and punishment of those responsible. In addition, the investigation would need to be undertaken with reasonable expedition. The Court has also stressed the importance of the independence of any investigation, and in *McShane v United Kingdom* (2002) **35 EHRR 23** held that an inquiry into the lawfulness of a civilian's death during a disturbance in Londonderry was in violation of **article 2** because the police officers investigating the incident were not independent of the officers implicated in the incident. The Court has also stressed the need for the availability of civil remedies in the case of established liability (*Edwards v United Kingdom* (above)), and in *Finucane v United Kingdom* (2003) **37 EHRR 29** the Court noted the need for publicity of the proceedings and the need for the DPP to give reasons for his decision not to prosecute those suspected. This procedural aspect of **article 2** is supported by **article 13**—guaranteeing an effective remedy—*Bubbins v United Kingdom* (2005) **41 EHRR 24**.

However, the Court has been prepared to offer member states a much wider area of discretion in deciding whether the state has violated the substantive duty to protect life. This has been noted in cases such as *Osman* (above) and is also apparent when the Court is judging the legitimacy of state action under the exceptions permitted under **article 2(2)**. This provides that the deprivation of life will not be in contravention of **article 2** when it results from the use of force which is no more than absolutely necessary in cases such as the defence of any person from unlawful violence, or in order to effect a lawful arrest or to prevent the escape of a person from lawful detention. In *McCann v United Kingdom* (above), the European Court noted that **article 2** included a stricter and more compelling test of necessity than, for example, when deciding whether an interference with freedom of speech is necessary in a democratic society, so that the Court must subject deprivations of life to the most careful scrutiny. Nevertheless, it drew a distinction between the actual shooting of the terrorist suspects and the planning of the operation leading to the shootings, finding that although the SAS members had used no more force than was necessary in the circumstances, there had been a violation of the right to life through the careless planning of the operation by the administrative authorities. This suggests that the Court is more likely to find a breach of **article 2** when there has been a breach of procedure, or an error in the overall decision-making process, rather than where there is an alleged error of judgement on behalf of an individual state official, although in the recent case of *Bubbins v United Kingdom* (above), where the police had shot dead the applicant's brother mistakenly believing that he was a burglar, the Court granted the authorities a margin of discretion and found that it had not been established that there had been a failure to plan and organize the operation in such a way as to minimize to the greatest extent possible any risk to the right of life. Despite this general reluctance to gainsay the judgement of state actors who have used fatal force for the protection of the safety of others, the Court has insisted that life is not taken away arbitrarily (*Demir and others v Turkey* (2001) 33 EHRR 43).

The Court has also played a role in assessing the legality of the death penalty under the Convention. Although **article 2** expressly provides for the existence of the death penalty, unless the member state has ratified **Protocols 6 or 13** prohibiting such, the Court has nevertheless accepted that the death penalty may violate other provisions of the Convention. In particular, in *Soering v United Kingdom* (1989) **11 EHRR 439** the Court held that the death penalty might, in appropriate circumstances, give rise to liability under **article 3** of the Convention, which prohibits inhuman and degrading punishment. More controversially, in *Ocalan v Turkey* (2005) **41 EHRR 45**, the Grand Chamber of the Court noted that it could be argued that the member states had agreed through their practice to modify the second sentence of **article 2(1)** in so far as it permitted capital punishment in peacetime and that the death penalty could be regarded generally as inhuman and degrading and thus contrary to **article 3**.

In conclusion, it is clear that the European Court regards the right to life as the most fundamental of all Convention rights. As a consequence it has interpreted **article 2** liberally so as to impose the most stringent duties on the state to preserve life and to protect it from dangers posed by state actors, other private individuals and, in certain cases, by the victim himself. In addition, the Court has developed the procedural aspect of **article 2**, imposing on the state strict duties to investigate deaths in their jurisdiction. In contrast the Court has shown a greater reluctance to interfere with the decisions of state actors when life has been taken for the purpose of achieving public security or of effecting lawful arrest. The scope of the state's obligations, and the extent of its liability remain controversial, and it appears that even in the most fundamental of human rights the Court is prepared to allow it to be compromised and to offer a good deal of discretion to member states on how they fulfil their duties under **article 2**.

Question 2

Is the death penalty consistent with both the principles of the absolute character of the right to life under **article 2** and of the Convention generally?

Commentary

This question requires the student to address the absolute character of **article 2**; and more specifically, whether the death penalty is consistent with the wording and spirit of **article 2** and of the Convention as a whole.

The student needs to appreciate the fundamental character of the right to life and the extent to which it can, if at all, be violated. Students need to appreciate the fact that **article 2** is a non-derogable right under **article 15**, and must also consider the exceptions to the rights, permitted both expressly under the article and impliedly by the process of interpretation by the European Court. The main part requires an examination of the wording of **article 2**, the various optional protocols prohibiting the death penalty, as well as any case law of the European Court suggesting that the death penalty may be in breach of the Convention. The student should concentrate on the European Convention and its case law, but may refer to more universal arguments for and against the death penalty.

Answer plan

- Explanation of the wording and scope of **article 2** of the European Convention
- Consideration of the absoluteness of the general right to life
- Examination of the legality of the death penalty within **article 2** and relevant protocols
- Consideration of the case law of the European Convention with respect to the compatibility of the death penalty with various articles of the Convention

Suggested answer

Although it has been accepted by the European Court that **article 2** of the Convention, which provides that everyone's right to life shall be protected by law, protects the most fundamental of human rights (*McCann v United Kingdom* **(1995) 21 EHRR 97**), the right to life is not absolute in every sense. First, the right is absolute in the sense that it cannot be derogated from even in times of war or other public emergency, as **article 15(2)** exempts the right to life from the general derogation provisions. However, even in this sense **article 15(2)** excludes deaths arising from lawful acts of war, thus making it clear that there may be circumstances where it is permissible to take life and thus interfere with this most fundamental of all human rights.

Further, the Convention recognizes that the right to life may be compromised in peacetime, providing in **article 2(2)** a number of circumstances that provide justification for the taking of a person's life. Thus, in addition to the exception provided for by the death penalty in **article 2(1)** (see below), **article 2(2)** provides that the deprivation of life shall not be regarded as inflicted in contravention of **article 2** when it results from the use of force which is no more than absolutely necessary in the following circumstances: in defence of any person from unlawful violence; in order to effect a lawful arrest or to prevent the escape of a person lawfully detained; or in action lawfully taken for the purpose of quelling a riot or insurrection.

However, the European Court has made it clear that the exceptions must be strictly and narrowly construed so that the use of fatal force should be regarded as absolutely necessary for the purpose of achieving any of the aims listed in the second paragraph of the article (*McCann v United Kingdom* (above)).

The right to life is, of course, compromised by the existence of the death penalty in domestic law. However, although such a sentence clearly falls within the scope of the right to life, **article 2** appears to legitimize it. Thus the second sentence of **article 2(1)** provides that no one shall be deprived of his life intentionally *save in the execution of a sentence of a court* following his conviction of a crime for which this penalty is prescribed by law. This would appear to reflect the position of the death penalty in international law, in that, although there may exist a universal movement for its abolition, it is not automatically in violation of international human rights law. Thus, **article 6 of the International Covenant on Civil and Political Rights 1966** appears to accommodate the death penalty by providing that in countries where the death penalty has not been abolished, a sentence of death can only be imposed for the most serious crimes and pursuant to a final judgment by a competent court. **Article 6** also presses for its abolition by providing (in **article 6(6)**) that nothing shall delay or prevent the abolition of the death penalty.

However, despite **article 2** appearing to accept the legitimacy of the death penalty, such a sentence may still be in violation of the European Convention or other international human rights treaties. First, the death penalty may constitute a violation of an individual's Convention rights other than the right to life. In *Soering v United Kingdom* (1989) 11 **EHRR 439**, the European Court held that although the death penalty itself was not in violation of the Convention, the manner of its execution and the circumstances surrounding the death penalty may be inconsistent with **article 3**, which prohibits torture and inhuman and degrading punishment. Thus, in that case it held that the subjection of a young man of limited mental ability to the death row phenomenon constituted inhuman and degrading treatment within **article 3**. Similarly, there would be a violation of **article 3** if the death sentence prisoner had been or was to be kept in intolerable prison conditions awaiting his death sentence (*Kalashnikov v Russia* (2003) 36 EHRR 34). This possibility is highlighted in **article 6(2)** of the International Covenant, which provides that the sentence should not be inconsistent with other provisions of the Covenant. Further, **article 6(5)** of the Covenant provides that pregnant women and persons under 18 shall not be sentenced to death, and it is probable that the European Court would regard such sentences as in violation of **article 3** of the European Convention.

Secondly, the exception to the right to life provided in **article 2** only applies where a death sentence has been passed by a court of law, and after the individual has been convicted of a prescribed criminal offence. Accordingly, if the death penalty occurred without due process then not only will there be a potential violation of **article 6** of the Convention, guaranteeing the right to a fair trial, but also a violation of **article 2**, which guarantees protection against the arbitrary taking of life by insisting that the law and the criminal process comply with principles of legitimacy and natural justice. Again, this is stressed in **article 6** of the International Covenant so that a death sentence in violation of a right to a fair trial under **article 14** of the Covenant would breach the right to life.

Thirdly, optional **Protocol No 6 of the European Convention** provides for member states to abolish the death penalty so that no one shall be condemned to such penalty or be executed. Once a member state signs this Protocol then the exemption contained in **article 2** ceases to operate and the death penalty would be contrary to the member state's Convention obligations. In addition, the deportation or extradition of a person to face the death penalty in another country would appear to be in violation of their Convention responsibilities, assuming that on the facts there is a real risk that the applicant would be executed. Such is the desire in the Council of Europe to eliminate the death penalty in domestic law that all states have now ratified **Protocol No 6**, and many have ratified **Protocol No 13**, which extends the abolition of the death penalty in wartime.

Despite the above, on the face of it the death penalty would not automatically or *per se* be in violation of either the Convention or more general international human rights norms. However, the decision of the European Court in *Ocalan v Turkey* (2005) 41 **EHRR 45**, provides some grounds for arguing that the death penalty is inevitably in violation of **article 3** and thus would always be incompatible with the Convention, whether the state has signed **Protocol No 6 (and 13)** or not. In that case the Grand Chamber of the European Court observed that in the light of recent developments in this area it could be argued that the member states had agreed through their practice to modify the second sentence of **article 2(1)** in so far as it permitted capital punishment in peacetime. Accordingly, the Court felt that it could be argued that the death penalty would be regarded as inhuman and degrading punishment within **article 3** whatever the circumstances and that the express words of **article 2** should be read against the total prohibition of torture and other ill-treatment by **article 3**. This observation was not central to that case as the applicant had not been executed and subsequently Turkey had abolished the death penalty; although the Grand Chamber held that **article 2** should now be read to prohibit the death penalty during peacetime, it also held that, until **Protocol No 13** is ratified by all states, **article 3** did not prohibit the death penalty *per se*.

The traditional stance—that the death penalty is not *per se* in violation of international law—was reaffirmed in a domestic law decision. In *R (Al-Saadoon and Mufhdi) v Secretary of State for Defence* [2008] EWHC 3098 the High Court held that it was not unlawful for British troops to hand over two Iraqis to the Iraqi authorities to face the death penalty. Although the court noted that the death penalty was outlawed in the UK it stated that it was not in breach of the European Convention or international law and thus the UK authorities were obliged to hand over the individuals. The decision was upheld on appeal to the Court of Appeal: *The Times*, 3 February 2009, where the court stated that there was insufficient evidence that international law prohibited executions by hanging because it was in violation of the prohibition of inhuman treatment.

In conclusion, although the right to life under **article 2** is clearly fundamental, and is absolute in the sense of not allowing derogation under **article 15**, there are circumstances where it is acceptable to intentionally take life and the express exceptions contained in the article clearly provide for this. More specifically, although the death penalty is not in violation of the Convention or international law *per se*, the accommodation of the death penalty in **article 2** of the Convention has been compromised by so many exceptions and by state practice that in reality a Council of Europe state allowing it would find itself in violation of its obligations under the Convention. Theoretically, however, it is not inconsistent with the principles of the Convention and of general international human rights norms.

Question 3

Fred was a serving prisoner at Greentree Prison. In January 2005 Fred came into possession of a handgun and took three fellow prisoners and a prison officer hostage in the prison kitchen. Fred remained in the kitchen for three days and when his demands for release were refused, he shot and killed Peter, one of the prisoners. On hearing the gunshot, prison officers and police moved into the kitchen and found Peter dead on the floor, with Fred hovering over him with the gun in his hand. Two policemen immediately fired shots and killed Fred. It subsequently transpired that several prison officers suspected that Fred had a gun in his possession, but felt that there was insufficient evidence to search his cell. The Prison Service held an internal inquiry into the incident but attached no blame to the Prison Service for either death. A request for a public legal inquiry was made by both Fred's and Peter's families, but was refused by the Secretary of State.

Advise both families of any claim they may have with respect to **article 2 of the European Convention on Human Rights.**

 Commentary

This question covers three specific aspects of the right to life as guaranteed under **article 2** of the European Convention: first, the extent of the state's obligation to protect a person's life from a threat posed by another private individual; secondly, the circumstances in which it is permissible to take life intentionally under the exceptions provided under **paragraph 2 of article 2**; and thirdly, the state's procedural obligations under **article 2**, as well as its obligation under **article 13** to provide an effective remedy for breach of an individual's Convention rights. Students need a sound knowledge of the case law of both the European Court and the domestic courts in these areas, and need to be able to apply any principles arising from such cases to the particular facts.

The answer should begin by explaining the broad scope of **article 2**, the obligations it imposes on member states, and how those obligations may be relevant to the families' claims. The student can then deal with each family's claim in turn, beginning with Peter's death and the potential liability of the state for that death under **article 2** of the Convention, using any relevant case law of the European Court. The answer should then consider the possible claims of Fred's family under both the procedural and substantive aspects of **article 2**. Again, students should refer to the growing amount of case law of the European Court in this area. The answer should conclude by giving both families clear and accurate advice with respect to the likely success of those claims.

Answer plan

- General explanation of the substantive and procedural rights contained in **article 2** of the European Convention and the potential legal actions available to the families
- Examination of the possible liability of the state under **article 2** for the death of Peter, using relevant case law
- Examination of the possible liability of the state under **article 2** for the shooting of Fred, using relevant case law
- Examination of the possible breach of the state's procedural obligations under **article 2**, with respect to the failure to prosecute and the legality of the inquiry
- Conclusions as to the likely success of all claims

Suggested answer

Introduction

The scenario raises the question of the state's liability for the deaths of Peter and Fred under **article 2 of the European Convention on Human Rights**. Because the events took place after the **Human Rights Act 1998,** a claim under **article 2** can be made under the Act in the domestic courts. The proceedings may be brought under the Act by the families of Peter and Fred, because they will be regarded as 'victims' of a violation of the Convention. **Article 2** of the Convention provides that everyone's right to life shall be protected by law, and this imposes an obligation on the state not to take life arbitrarily or unnecessarily (*McCann v United Kingdom* (1995) 21 EHRR 97), as well as to secure a person's life from acts and threats of other individuals (*Osman v United Kingdom* (2000) 29 EHRR 245). In addition, **article 2** places a procedural obligation on the state to carry out an effective investigation into any death that may engage the state's obligations under **article 2** and this duty is bolstered by **article 13** of the Convention, which guarantees the right to an effective remedy before a national authority for those whose Convention rights have been violated.

Peter's death

Peter's family representatives will argue that his death engages the state's liability and that the state has taken insufficient care for the protection of Peter's life. **Article 2** places a positive duty on the state to ensure that an individual's life is not taken unnecessarily, whether the act in question is one of a state actor or a private citizen (*Osman v United Kingdom* (above)). This also involves the duty to take measures to ensure that foreseeable and real risks to the life of an individual do not materialize, and in this case it would have to be established that the authorities had failed to take the appropriate standard of care ensuring that Peter's right to life was adequately protected against the unlawful actions of Fred.

In *Osman* (above) the European Court held that **article 2** imposed on the state a positive obligation to take preventative operational measures to protect an individual whose life is at risk from the criminal acts of another, but noted that that obligation should not impose an impossible and disproportionate burden on the authorities. In such cases it is necessary that an applicant can show that the authorities did not do all that was reasonably expected of them to avoid a real and immediate risk to life. On the facts, although the applicants could point to a series of missed opportunities to neutralize the threat of attack by an individual, the police could not be criticized for attaching greater weight to the presumption of innocence or failing to use their powers because they felt that they lacked the appropriate standard of suspicion. Similarly, in *Van Colle v Chief Constable of Hertfordshire* [2008] 3 WLR 593, the House of Lords held that there was no violation of **article 2** when the police authorities had failed to protect the life of a vulnerable witness who should have been on a secure witness protection scheme. In their Lordships' view the murder had been the action of a disturbed and unpredictable individual and it could not be reasonably said that the police should from the information available to them at the time, have anticipated that the assailant constituted a risk to the claimants' life that was both real and imminent.

The government would argue that although prisons by their nature impose a serious risk of harm, even fatal harm, to their inmates, the prison authorities should not be held responsible for the unlawful and unforeseeable act of an inmate. In addition, the Court usually gives some discretion to the authorities with respect to the manner in which they carry out their operations (*Andronicou v Greece* (1998) 25 EHRR 491), and this might defeat the claim that the police and the prison authorities acted negligently in not securing Peter's release within the three days of his incarceration at the hands of Fred. However, *Osman* and *Andronicou* might be distinguished because the incident took place in prison, a state-controlled institution, and because prison officers suspected that Fred was armed and thus a specific danger to other inmates. In *Edwards v United Kingdom* (2002) 25 EHRR 19, the Court accepted that the state owes a specific duty under **article 2** to safeguard the lives of those in detention from the actions of fellow inmates. In that case the applicant's son had been killed by his cell mate, who had a history of violent outbursts and assaults and who had been diagnosed as schizophrenic. The European Court found that the cell mate posed a real and serious risk to the applicant's son and that the prison authorities had not been properly informed of the cell mate's medical history and perceived dangerousness.

On that basis it could be strongly argued that Peter's death could reasonably have been avoided and that he was killed in circumstances disclosing a violation of **article 2**. In particular, the prison authorities had failed to take action when they suspected Fred of being in possession of a gun and as a result Fred was a known danger to others, including his fellow prisoners. The question then would be whether the prison authorities acted reasonably in not searching Fred's cell and giving precedence to his presumption of innocence and his residual privacy as a prisoner. In the present case the possession of a gun by a prisoner in a prison would pose a specific and direct threat, and the authorities have wide powers to search cells under the Prison Rules. It is likely therefore that the European Court would find that the authorities had failed in their duty under **article 2** and thus should be liable for Peter's death.

Fred's death

Article 2(2) of the Convention provides that the deprivation of life shall not be regarded as inflicted in contravention of **article 2** when it results from the use of force that is no more than *absolutely necessary* in the defence of any person from unlawful violence or in order to effect a lawful arrest. The government will argue that shooting Fred in these circumstances was absolutely necessary to arrest Fred and to prevent him from causing further fatal harm, whilst the families will argue that more careful planning of the operation, and a less hasty reaction by the two police officers, would have avoided Fred's death.

The issue of whether absolutely necessary force has been used was considered in *McCann v United Kingdom* (above), where three IRA terrorists were shot dead by SAS officers when it was suspected that they were to detonate a bomb in Gibraltar. In that case the Court held that it must subject deprivations of life to the most careful scrutiny and that the term 'absolutely necessary' meant that a strict and compelling test of necessity should be used. On the facts the Court held that although the soldiers could not be faulted for using fatal force, nevertheless the intelligence authorities had been negligent in the planning of the operation and had fed misinformation to the soldiers. Consequently, the Court held that, given the negligence of the overall operations, the deaths were not unavoidable. The decision in *McCann* suggests that the Court is more likely to find a breach of **article 2** when it has found a breach of procedure or an error in the overall decision-making process, rather than where there is an alleged error of judgement on behalf of an individual state official. Thus, in the present case, if it was alleged that Fred's death was caused by the, perhaps, over-zealous acts of the police officers, rather than incompetence of the overall planning of the operation, the European Court may be reluctant to find the state liable under **article 2**.

On the other hand, if the Court was satisfied that the whole operation had been handled without proper care then it may be more willing to find the government in violation of its substantive obligations under **article 2**. However, the decision of the European Court in *Andronicou v Greece* (above) suggests that the Court may be prepared to afford a reasonable amount of discretion to the authorities. Here the police forcibly entered premises and shot dead an armed man and his fiancée, who he had been keeping hostage. The Court found that there had been a number of areas of concern with respect to the rescue operation, but nevertheless concluded that there had been no violation of **article 2** because it had not been shown that the operation had not been planned in a way that minimized to the greatest extent possible any risk to the victims' lives. It could be argued that despite the margin of discretion given to the police and other authorities when carrying out an operation to defend the lives of others, the killing of Fred by the police officers when Fred did not appear to be a danger to the officers or anyone else could be described as reckless, perhaps suggesting inexperience or a lack of care on behalf of those officers. In that case the Court might conclude that the use of fatal force was not absolutely necessary.

The investigation into the deaths

Article 2 imposes a duty on every member state to carry out a proper investigation into any deaths that have occurred within their jurisdiction and which may be in violation of its general duty under that article. In *Jordan v United Kingdom* (2003) 37 EHRR 2, the Court held that where the events in issue lay within the knowledge of the authorities, strong presumptions of fact would arise in respect of injuries and deaths and that the burden of proof would be on the state to provide a satisfactory and convincing explanation. The obligation under **article 2** required some form of effective official investigation when individuals had been killed as a result of the use of force.

Although the Court did not specify the exact form of any inquiry, it did lay down some essential requirements of effectiveness: it should be carried out by persons independent of those implicated in the events; it should be capable of leading to a determination of whether the force used in such circumstances was justified, and to the identification and punishment of those responsible; the authorities must take reasonable steps to secure the evidence concerning the incident, including eyewitness testimony; and it should be carried out with sufficient promptness and reasonable expedition. Further, in *Edwards v United Kingdom* (above), the Court stressed the need for openness and for relatives to be allowed to participate in any inquiry, including the ability to attend and to be represented at it. These principles have been upheld in domestic law and in *Amin v Secretary of State for the Home Department* [2004] 1 AC 653 the House of Lords quashed the decision of the Home Secretary not to order a public inquiry into the death of a prisoner at the hands of a racist and violent cell mate, the court noting that the Prison Service's investigation did not enjoy independence, had been conducted in private, and had not been published.

Conclusions

Although it is difficult to predict the outcome of cases that turn on their particular facts, it is suggested that following the decision in *Edwards* the domestic court would find a violation of **article 2** in respect of Peter's death and that despite the area of discretion given to the authorities with respect to lethal shootings, that there had been a similar violation with regards to Fred's death. In addition, applying the principles from cases such as *Jordan*, there would appear to be a clear violation of the procedural duties under **article 2** in respect of both deaths, coupled with the lack of an effective remedy for the relatives, leading to a violation of **article 13** of the Convention.

Question 4

In May 2005 John, a 20-year-old citizen of the United Islands of Montrovia (a small group of islands in the South Pacific), landed illegally in the United Kingdom, having escaped from a remand prison in his home country whilst awaiting trial for murder. The United Kingdom has an extradition agreement with the United Islands and has agreed to extradite any person, provided that person would not be subjected to the death penalty upon extradition. John claimed that he would be subject to the death penalty if convicted, although the authorities in the United Islands assured the British authorities that no person under the age of 21 had ever been sentenced to death (even though the death sentence was, theoretically, applicable to anyone over the age of 18 where the circumstances of the murder were sufficiently serious to warrant the death penalty). The Home Secretary decided to extradite John and his application for judicial review of that decision, and his claim under the **Human Rights Act 1998** was refused on the basis that the Home Secretary was entitled to believe that the death penalty would not be imposed. He now makes a claim under the European Convention, claiming that his extradition would constitute a violation of **articles 2, 3, and 13** of the Convention. Advise John as to the process involved in that application and as to the likely success of his claim.

 Commentary

This question is principally concerned with the liability of a state under **articles 2 and 3** of the European Convention for threats to an individual's right to life and subjection to ill-treatment in another state. The student needs to be aware of the so-called '*Soering*' principle, whereby a member state can be held responsible for a violation of an individual's human rights outside that state's territory. The student must also appreciate the arguments surrounding the legality of the death penalty under the European Convention, in particular whether the death penalty is contrary to **articles 2 and 3** of the Convention, and the position where the expelling state has ratified **Protocols Nos 6 and 13** of the European Convention.

Specific to the facts of the case the student needs to address the questions of whether there is a real risk of John being subjected to the death penalty, and if so whether such would contravene **articles 2 and 3** of the Convention. In particular, the student needs to examine whether the United Kingdom is a party to **Protocols 6 and 13** of the Convention, and whether that would forbid his extradition in this case. Finally, the student needs to appreciate the scope of **article 13,** guaranteeing an effective remedy in domestic law for the violation of Convention rights, and whether the domestic judicial review proceedings fell short of the protection of that article. All arguments and conclusions should be supported by relevant case law under both **articles 2 and 3**, and **article 13** of the Convention.

The events appear to have taken place after the **Human Rights Act 1998** had come into force and thus the Act has been applied directly to the events. This may be important with respect to the European Court's willingness to interfere with the domestic authorities' decisions and the effectiveness of the review proceedings *vis-à-vis* **article 13** of the Convention.

 Answer plan

- Explanation of the '**Soering**' principle and its possible application in this case *vis-a-vis* the application procedure under the **European Convention on Human Rights**
- Consideration of whether there was a real risk of John being sentenced to death
- Consideration of the possible illegality of the death penalty if it was carried out and the UK's liability for executions outside its territory
- Consideration of a possible breach of **article 13** with respect to the adequacy of the judicial preview proceedings

Suggested answer

Introduction

John's possible extradition to the United Islands of Montrovia by the United Kingdom government raises the question whether such a measure would engage the UK's liability under **article 2** of the Convention, which provides that everyone's right to life shall be protected by law, and **article 3**, which provides that no one shall be subject to torture or inhuman or degrading treatment or punishment. Convention case law (*Soering v United Kingdom* (1989) **11 EHRR 439**) accepts that the expelling state can, in certain circumstances, become responsible for the violations of the receiving state, even where the latter state is not a party to the Convention. In *Soering* the Court established that a member state could be liable for the breach of an individual's Convention rights in another territory where there existed a real risk that if that individual was removed from the member state he or she would face treatment in violation of the Convention. Thus, as John is presently within the United Kingdom's jurisdiction, the government is responsible for securing the enjoyment of his Convention rights and must not expose him to an unnecessary risk of a violation of his rights under **articles 2 and 3**.

In addition, John's failure to succeed in the domestic judicial review proceedings raises the question of whether there has been a violation of **article 13** of the Convention, which guarantees an effective remedy for any violation of a person's Convention rights.

The death penalty

John's claim in respect of the death penalty would succeed provided the European Court was satisfied that there was a real risk that John would lose his life at the hands of the Montrovian authorities, and that his death would be in violation of any of the substantive rights of the Convention. In other words, that there was a real risk of the death penalty being carried out in this case, and that the death penalty or the manner of its execution was incompatible with the Convention.

Dealing with the factual question, it was established in *Soering v United Kingdom* (above) that there had to be a *real risk* that the applicant would face, in that case, ill-treatment in violation of the Convention, as opposed to a mere possibility (*Vilvarajah v United Kingdom* (1992) 14 EHRR 248). In John's case it could be argued by the government (and presumably this was argued in the judicial review proceedings) that John's execution was a mere, or perhaps in the circumstances a remote, possibility. Thus, it would be argued that given the fact that it had been told by the Montrovian authorities of the policy regarding the execution of persons under the age of 21, the government was entitled to conclude that there was no realistic possibility of John facing the death penalty if convicted of murder. Further, it could be argued that there is still uncertainty as to whether John will be convicted of murder, and more importantly, whether the circumstances of this alleged murder were sufficiently serious to warrant the death penalty. On the other hand, John would argue that the fact that the death penalty remains on the domestic statute books, and thus available in theory, amounts to a sufficient risk.

The fact that the death penalty could in theory be granted, would be insufficient for the Court to establish a real risk in this context, although the Court will not take the promises of the government or the Montrovian authorities at face value, and will search for further evidence in order to assess the risk. For example, in *Chahal v United Kingdom* (1997) 23 EHRR 413 the Court found there was a real risk of the applicant being subjected to torture, despite assurances to the contrary from the relevant Indian authorities, the Court taking into account the recent human rights record of that country and the troubles which still existed in a particular region of the country. In this case the Court would investigate the human rights record of Montrovia and the feasibility of relying on the assurance given to the government. Further, the Court would need to clarify this assurance; for example, by asking whether anyone under the age of 21 had ever been convicted of murder, and whether, if they had, there had existed mitigating circumstances that had spared the convicted prisoner the death penalty. On a technical point, the Court would also want to be satisfied that the age exemption applies to not only those who were under 21 at the time of the offence, but also to those who were under that age after being found guilty and at the time of any execution.

If the Court was satisfied that there existed a real risk of John being executed, the Court would then have to examine whether such an execution would be in violation of the Convention. **Article 2** appears to accept the legitimacy of the death penalty because it provides that no one shall be deprived of his life intentionally save in the execution of a sentence of a court following his conviction of a crime for which the penalty is provided by law. Despite this, John might still claim that his execution would be in breach of his Convention rights so as to engage the liability of the United Kingdom government.

First, although the death penalty itself may not be in violation of the Convention or international law (*R (Al-Saadoon and Mufhdi) v Secretary of State for Defence, The Times,* 4 February 2009, the manner of its execution and the circumstances surrounding the death penalty may be inconsistent with **article 3**, which prohibits torture and inhuman and degrading punishment. Thus, in *Soering* the Court held that the subjection of a young man of limited mental ability to the death row phenomenon constituted inhuman and degrading treatment within **article 3**. A similar claim could also be made if the prison conditions under which the prisoner is kept are inhuman or degrading (*Kalashnikov v Russia* (2003) **36 EHRR 34**). Secondly, the exception provided in **article 2** only applies where the death sentence has been passed by a court after the individual has been convicted of a criminal offence. Accordingly, if it can be shown that John will receive the death penalty without due process then there will be a violation of **article 2**, guaranteeing protection against the arbitrary taking of life.

Thirdly, **Protocol No 6** of the European Convention provides for member states to abolish the death penalty so that no one shall be *condemned to* such penalty or be executed. Once a member state signs this Protocol then the exemption contained in **article 2** ceases to operate and the death penalty would be contrary to the member states' Convention obligations. As the United Kingdom has signed it, any death penalty carried out in the jurisdiction of the United Kingdom would certainly be contrary to that Protocol, and states who deport or extradite a person to face the death penalty in another country would appear to be in violation of their Convention responsibilities, assuming that on the facts there is a real risk that the applicant would be executed.

Finally, following the decision of the European Court in *Ocalan v Turkey* (2005) **41 EHRR 45**, there may be an argument that the death penalty is in violation of **article 3** and thus incompatible with the Convention, whether the state has signed **Protocol No 6** or not. In that case the Grand Chamber of the European Court held that in the light of recent developments in this area the member states had agreed through their practice to modify the second sentence of **article 2(1)** and thus it could be argued that the death penalty would be regarded as inhuman and degrading. However, it was not willing to regard the practice as being in violation of **article 3** *per se* until all member states had signed **Protocols 6 *and* 13**. As the United Kingdom is a party to both, the extradition would be in breach of its obligations, provided the Court finds that there was a real risk of John facing the death penalty. On the facts, therefore, it appears that John's extradition would be in breach of the UK's obligations under the Convention.

The claim under article 13

Article 13 of the Convention provides that everyone whose Convention rights are violated shall have an effective remedy before a national authority. **Article 13** requires that where an individual has an arguable claim under the Convention, he should have a remedy before a national authority in order both to have his claim decided, and, if appropriate, to obtain redress (*Silver v United Kingdom* (1983) **5 EHRR 347**).

John's main argument, therefore, is that the judicial review proceedings did not allow him to raise his claims under **articles 2 and 3** of the Convention and that the courts gave insufficient weight to those arguments, irrespective of whether those claims would have succeeded. Although the European Court does not insist that a domestic court has the power to substitute its opinion for that of the original decision-maker, the reviewing court should have adequate powers to question the original decision (*Thynne, Wilson and Gunnell v United Kingdom* (1990) 13 EHRR 666). Further, an individual should be able to argue his or her case in accordance with Convention principles, including whether the restriction was unnecessary or disproportionate (*Smith and Grady v United Kingdom* (2000) 29 EHRR 493). With particular relevance to John's case, the domestic court must not be precluded from examining the facts of the case, or of looking behind the reasons given by the decision- maker. Accordingly, in *Chahal v United Kingdom* (above) there was a clear violation of **article 13** when a decision to deport the applicant was not reviewed solely with reference to the question of the risk to the applicant of ill-treatment in breach of **article 3** and the domestic court was limited to asking whether the Home Secretary had balanced the risk with issues of national security. Similarly, in John's case if the domestic courts had not reviewed the evidence of the Home Secretary in assessing the risk of John's Convention rights being violated, and had instead relied on the Home Secretary's assessment of the fact and the risk, then there would be a clear violation of **article 13**.

On the other hand, if the proceedings were full and complied with **article 13** and the decision of the Home Secretary was consistent with the evidence, then the European Court might defer to him and the domestic courts (*Launder v United Kingdom* [1998] **EHRLR 337**). Thus, as the domestic decision was made after the **Human Rights Act 1998** came into force, provided the court subjected the decision to a suitably stringent test, then there would be no violation of **article 13**. Since October 2000 the courts are bound to apply the case law and principles of the Convention and are thus more likely to reach decisions that are compatible with Convention rights. This in turn will comply with **article 13**, despite the Act failing to give direct effect to it under the 1998 Act.

Conclusions

In conclusion, whether there has been a violation of **articles 2 and 3** of the Convention depends principally on whether the European Court is satisfied there was a real risk of John being subjected to the death penalty. If that is the case, the death penalty and its circumstances appear to be clearly in violation of John's Convention rights. The question is whether the judicial review proceedings allowed the domestic courts to assess those risks in line with the principles and case law of the European Convention, and thus whether they were an effective remedy under **article 13** of the Convention.

Further reading

Harris, D, O'Boyle, K, Warbrick, C, and Bates, E, *The Law of the European Convention on Human Rights*, 2nd edn (OUP 2009), ch 2.

Mowbray, A, *Cases and Materials on the European Convention on Human Rights*, 2nd edn (OUP 2007), chs 4 and 5.

Yorke, J, 'The Right to Life and Abolition of the Death Penalty in the Council of Europe' [2009] ELR 205.

6

Freedom from torture and inhuman and degrading treatment

Introduction

The prohibition of torture and other ill-treatment is regarded as a fundamental tenet of human rights law and the topic is covered in many human rights courses, particularly in the post-Human Rights Act era. The prohibition of torture and other ill-treatment is dealt with in a variety of international treaties and other instruments and the student has to be aware of these documents, their different methods of enforcement, and the principles and values underlying their existence. In particular, it is likely that the student is going to be asked questions about the prohibition of torture, etc in the context of the **European Convention on Human Rights** and the recent domestic case law under the **Human Rights Act 1998**. Questions may also relate to the application of this right in particular contexts, such as the rights of prisoners, asylum seekers, those subject to deportation and extradition, and with respect to corporal punishment.

Questions will usually be in essay form, but sometimes the student will be required to apply the substantive law and theoretical principles to hypothetical factual situations. In either case, it is essential that students appreciate both the theoretical basis of the right and the limitations of its scope and application. The subject is an emotive one and the student should not be drawn into making rash and personal statements, unsupported by legal or reliable academic authority. A knowledge and application of relevant case law will assist the student in remaining focused and objective.

Question 1

By the use of case examples, explain how the European Court of Human Rights has interpreted and applied **article 3** of the European Convention. What particular difficulties does the European Court face in interpreting and applying this provision?

Commentary

This question requires the student to be aware of the relevant case law of the European Court and Commission of Human Rights in respect to **article 3** of the Convention. However, the question cannot be answered simply by relating the facts and decisions in the relevant cases, and the student needs to be aware of the main aims of **article 3** and the importance of the article in the context of human rights protection. In particular, the student needs to appreciate the moral, jurisdictional, and legal dilemmas facing a judicial body such as the European Court of Human Rights when deciding whether there has been a violation of the article on the facts of a particular case.

It is necessary to begin the essay by explaining the wording and rationale of **article 3** and referring to its absolute status, although such an introduction should be as brief as possible to allow sufficient time to be dedicated to the specific question. The cases should be chosen carefully so that the essential issues and dilemmas referred to in the question are addressed. The student can choose particular areas, such as deportation, corporal punishment, conditions of detention, mistreatment in detention, etc, but must ensure that those cases illustrate the difficulties facing the European Court in interpreting and applying this provision. The essay should conclude with some observations as to how successfully the European Court has tackled these problems and some views as to whether the case law is sufficiently coherent.

Answer plan

- Explanation of the wording, scope, and rationale of **article 3**
- Explanation, via relevant case law, of the process by which the European Court decides cases under this provision and an overview of the problems it faces
- Consideration of the various specific legal, jurisdictional, and moral difficulties facing the Court in resolving claims, using various cases and examples in illustration
- Conclusion as to the success of the European Court's efforts to solve the above dilemmas

Suggested answer

Article 3 of the European Convention on Human Rights provides that no one shall be subject to torture or inhuman or degrading treatment or punishment. The prohibition of such treatment appears absolute, supported by the fact that the state's obligations under **article 3** cannot be derogated from in times of war or other emergencies threatening the life of the nation. The Court has also strengthened the status of **article 3** by implying a procedural obligation to investigate suspected acts of ill-treatment taking place in its jurisdiction (*Askoy v Turkey* (1996) 23 EHRR 553).

In *Chahal v United Kingdom* (1997) 23 EHRR 413, the Court stated that the article enshrined one of the most fundamental values of a democratic society, and that although it recognized the immense difficulties faced by states in protecting their territory from acts of terrorism, it prohibited torture and other ill-treatment irrespective of the applicant's conduct. Consequently, there can be no justification for any violation, whatever the benefits arising from the relevant act or practice. For example, in *Tyrer v United Kingdom* (1978) 2 EHRR 1 it was held that judicial corporal punishment was contrary to **article 3**, despite claims that birching had a deterrent effect on juvenile crime.

The absolute nature of this article thus gives rise to a number of dilemmas. Most significantly, the European Court of Human Rights must define the terms 'torture' and 'inhuman or degrading treatment or punishment', and then determine whether the act or practice in question meets the necessary threshold. In the *Greek Case* (1969) 12 YB 170, torture was defined as an aggravated and deliberate form of inhuman treatment causing very serious and cruel suffering, whereas inhuman treatment covered treatment that deliberately caused severe mental or physical suffering. The Commission then defined degrading treatment or punishment as that which grossly humiliates a person before others, or drives him to act against his will or conscience. This was applied in *Ireland v United Kingdom* (1978) 2 EHRR 25 with respect to the so-called 'Five Techniques', which involved *inter alia*, intense noise, wall-standing, and deprivation of food and sleep. The Court found that the application of the techniques constituted both inhuman and degrading treatment within **article 3** because they caused if not bodily injury, at least intense physical and mental suffering and acute psychiatric disturbances and were such as to arouse in their victims feelings of fear, anguish, and inferiority capable of humiliating them and possibly taking away their physical or moral resistance. On the other hand the Court held that the techniques did not constitute torture because they did not amount to deliberate treatment causing very serious and cruel suffering.

A finding of torture is reserved for the most aggravated and deliberate forms of inhuman treatment or punishment, the distinction lying in the intensity of the acts and, possibly, the intention of the perpetrators. Having defined the terms, the Court must then determine whether the facts reveal a violation by considering both the level of harm suffered by the victim and the acceptability of such treatment. For example, in *Askoy v Turkey* (above) the Court held that there had been torture when the applicant had been strung up in a cell, blindfolded, and had electrodes attached to his genitals, and in *Selmouni v France* (2000) 29 EHRR 403 the Court made a finding of torture when the applicant had been subjected to repeated physical and verbal assaults, had been urinated on by an officer, and had been threatened with a blow lamp.

In *Selmouni* (above) the Court held that the Convention is a living instrument that must be interpreted in the light of present-day conditions. Accordingly, the Court held that the increasingly high standard being required in the area of human rights required a greater firmness in assessing breaches of the fundamental values of democratic societies, and that certain acts which in the past were classified as inhuman and degrading treatment as opposed to torture could now be classified differently in the future. It is arguable, therefore, that the treatment in *Ireland* (above) might now be regarded as torture, although the lack of physical violence used against the suspects in that case might militate against such a finding. The Court has also held that for an act to be 'inhuman' there must have been a sufficiently serious attack on the victim's physical, mental, or psychological well-being. Thus, in *Tomasi v France* (1993) 15 EHRR 1, where the applicant had been hit in the stomach, slapped, and kicked, had his head knocked against the wall, and been left naked in front of a window for several hours, the Court found that having regard to the number of blows and their intensity, such treatment was both inhuman and degrading.

In deciding whether treatment or punishment is 'degrading' within **article 3**, the Court has held that the humiliation or debasement involved must reach a particular level, such an assessment being relative and dependent on all the circumstances of the case, including the age of the victim (*Tyrer v United Kingdom* (above)). It is clear, therefore, that not all forms of ill-treatment that have a humiliating effect on the applicant will be in violation of **article 3**, and that the Court can take into account whether the treatment complained of is part and parcel of a necessary and civilized social order. For example, although arrest, detention, and imprisonment may degrade a person, they are regarded as perfectly acceptable under the Convention provided there are no aggravating circumstances. Accordingly, the Court has held that a life sentence of imprisonment imposed on a young person did not constitute inhuman or degrading treatment under **article 3** (*V and T v United Kingdom* (2000) 30 EHRR 121), and in *Raninen v Finland* (1998) 26 EHRR 563 it held that the handcuffing of prisoners is not automatically in violation of the Convention. On the other hand, in *Tyrer* (above) the Court labelled judicial corporal punishment as institutionalized violence, involving an unjustifiable assault on a person's dignity.

Other than those cases (as in *Tyrer*) where the treatment is unlawful *per se*, the Court will inquire into the extent of the ill-treatment, its duration, and the suffering of the individual applicant. Thus, in *Costello-Roberts v United Kingdom* (1993) 19 EHRR 112 the beating of a young boy on the posterior with a slipper by a teacher, causing minor bruising, did not constitute a violation of **article 3** as the physical and psychological effects of the punishment were not long-lasting. Again, in the context of prison conditions, the Court must be satisfied that the treatment of the prisoner goes beyond the normal harsh conditions associated with incarceration (*Valasinas v Lithuania* (2001) 12 BHRC 266). The Court must look at all the circumstances, adopting common standards of acceptability and the effect that the conditions are having on the individual prisoner (*Kalashnikov v Russia* (2003) 36 EHRR 34).

The Court may face particular problems in identifying the scope and application of the article; for example, whether a member state can be held responsible for an act of ill-treatment committed outside its jurisdiction and at the hands of another state. In *Soering v United Kingdom* (1989) 11 EHRR 439, the European Court held that a decision of a member state to extradite a person might engage the responsibility of that state where there were substantial grounds for believing that if extradited such a person would be faced with a real risk of being subjected to breaches of **article 3**. Thus, in that case the Court held that there was a real risk that the applicant, a young

German national, could be subjected to the death row phenomenon if extradited to the United States, and accordingly found the United Kingdom government in violation of **article 3**.

Such cases involve the Court determining the factual question of whether the risk is real, and it has to make a distinction between a real risk and a mere possibility. For example, in *Chahal v United Kingdom* (above) the European Court held that there was a real risk that the applicant would face torture at the hands of Indian authorities, despite assurances made by the Indian government to the contrary. In the Court's view the evidence was sufficient to lead to the conclusion that his deportation, if allowed, would lead to a violation of **article 3**. In contrast, in *Vilvarajah v United Kingdom* (1992) **14 EHRR 248** the European Court found that at the time of the government's deportation of the applicants back to Sri Lanka during the civil war, there did not exist a real risk of their ill-treatment. Although the Court held that it had a duty to rigorously examine the existence of the risk in view of the absolute character of **article 3**, in its opinion there were no distinguishing factors in the case of the applicants so as to enable the Secretary of State for the Home Department to foresee that they would be ill-treated on their return.

Despite the caution shown in cases like *Vilvarajah*, the Court has extended the *Soering* principle to cases where the receiving state's actions would not necessarily constitute a violation of the Convention itself, but where, nevertheless the applicant would suffer inhuman or degrading treatment. In *D v United Kingdom* (1997) **24 EHRR 423** a citizen of St Kitts in the West Indies, who had entered the United Kingdom illegally and had been sentenced to six years' imprisonment for importing drugs, contracted AIDS whilst in prison. On his release he claimed that his deportation would constitute a violation of **article 3** because his home country lacked the facilities to provide him with adequate medical care. It was held that given the applicant's current condition and the inadequate medical facilities in that country, his removal by the United Kingdom to a country where he would face the risk of dying in the most distressing circumstances amounted to a violation of **article 3**. This controversial decision has been qualified in subsequent cases and in *N v United Kingdom* (2008) **47 EHRR 39**, it was held that **article 3** does not require member states to afford medical treatment to all suffering from life-threatening diseases and that the decision in *D* was exceptional.

The Court has also imposed a positive obligation on the state to ensure that a person does not suffer ill-treatment at the hands of others, including private individuals. For example, in *A v United Kingdom* (1999) **27 EHRR 611**, the United Kingdom was held liable for the ill-treatment of the applicant at the hands of his stepfather because the domestic law allowed the stepfather to rely on a defence of reasonable chastisement, thereby providing the applicant with inadequate protection against subjection to inhuman or degrading punishment. Similarly, in *Z v United Kingdom* (2002) **34 EHRR 3** the failure of social services to provide adequate protection against physical and other abuse at the hands of the applicants' family was held to constitute a violation of **article 3**. However, the Court will only engage the state's liability when there is clear evidence that the authorities should have been aware of the abuse (*DP and JC v United Kingdom* (2003) 36 EHRR 14).

In conclusion, the Court has adopted a flexible approach in the interpretation and application of **article 3**. Whilst recognizing that **article 3** is fundamental and absolute (*Chahal* (above)), and that its meaning and application can adapt to new and enhanced ideals of human rights protection, it has insisted that the suffering of the applicant must reach a particular level, and that any suffering must exceed that which normally ensues from acceptable punishments and practices such as arrest and incarceration. The Court has also shown some ingenuity by the adoption of the *Soering* principle and the application of **article 3** to cases where private individuals perpetrate the ill-treatment. The article's interpretation and application have thus given rise to a number of legal, jurisdictional, and moral dilemmas and at times the Court has had to compromise human rights for the sake of pragmatism.

Question 2

In February 2009, Harry and Barry were taken into police custody following their arrest for theft and assault involving three old-age pensioners. Both were clearly under the influence of drugs at the time of their arrests and both were placed in police cells. After three hours, a police officer entered the cell and was attacked by Barry. Four officers then entered the cell and administered severe beatings to both Barry and Harry. Both were then taken to another cell, which was full of vomit and excrement and told that they could stay there for the night. They were refused permission to go to the toilet and were forced to urinate in the cell on three occasions before they were released. They were both subsequently charged with assault and Harry received a prison sentence of six months. Whilst in prison, the prison warders told Harry's cell mate that he had beaten up three old ladies and the same evening Harry was stripped and beaten up by three inmates at the prison. He also complained that when he had asked for medication to help him deal with his drug addiction he had been refused on the grounds that 'you can just bloody well suffer'. The following day, Harry told the prison doctor that he could stand no more of this place and that he felt suicidal. The prison decided not to put him in the medical centre, but placed him in a single cell and that night he committed suicide. Advise Barry, and Harry's family as to any action they might have under the **Human Rights Act 1998** and what would be the likely success of any claim.

 Commentary

Although the scenario takes place in a prison context, the question tests the student's knowledge of **articles 2 and 3** of the European Convention, rather than their expertise on prisoners' rights. Consequently, although a student with a sound knowledge in that area might be more conversant with the specific and relevant case law, such study is not essential in order to tackle this question. Students would be advised to deal with each issue as it occurs in the scenario, perhaps under separate sub-headings.

In order to answer the question the student needs a sound knowledge of **articles 2 and 3**, the relevant principles underlying those rights, and the relevant decisions of both the European Court and Commission of Human Rights and any domestic cases in areas such as ill-treatment of detainees and the duty of care owed towards detainees by state and prison authorities. The student will also need to explain how the case may be brought under the 1998 Act. Specifically, the student needs to know whether the state can be liable for human rights violations committed by individual citizens (in this case fellow prisoners).

 ## Answer plan

- Explanation of the scope and extent of **articles 2 and 3** of the European Convention and identification of their possible application in this scenario
- Consideration of the treatment of both prisoners in police custody and any likely violation of **article 3**
- Consideration of Harry's treatment in prison and any likely violation of **article 3** of the Convention
- Consideration of Harry's suicide and any likely violation of **articles 2 and 3** of the Convention
- Concluding advice on all the incidents, including the likelihood of success of the family's action under the European Convention

Suggested answer

Introduction

The scenario raise issues under **articles 2 and 3 of the European Convention on Human Rights**. After the passing of the **Human Rights Act 1998**, both prisoners may bring proceedings claiming a breach of their Convention rights either directly, as victims, under **s.6** of the Act, or indirectly by bringing a private action and using any relevant Convention rights in claiming that the prison authorities had broken common law duties. In either case the domestic courts must, under **s.2** of the 1998 Act, consider the case law of the European Court and Commission of Human Rights in determining that claim.

Harry and Barry's treatment in police custody

Harry and Barry's arrest and detention raise issues under **article 3**, which prohibits inhuman and degrading treatment and punishment. For treatment to be inhuman there has to be a sufficiently serious attack on the victim's physical, mental, or psychological well-being, and in *Ireland v United Kingdom* (1978) 2 EHRR 25 the Court held that such treatment had to cause, if not bodily injury, at least intense physical and mental suffering and acute psychiatric disturbances. In that case, the Court recognized that degrading treatment was that which aroused in their victims feelings of fear, anguish, and inferiority capable of humiliating and possibly taking away physical or moral resistance. Despite the Court's more robust approach in this area, we will not consider whether any of the treatment amounted to torture, which the European Court has defined as deliberate inhuman treatment causing very serious and cruel suffering.

The fact that the arrests were made when they were under the influence of drugs imposes a specific duty on the police authorities. In *McGlinchey v United Kingdom* (2003) 37 EHRR 41 the European Court held that the prison authorities had violated **article 3** when they had provided inadequate medical care to deal with a prisoner's withdrawal symptoms; the authorities had a duty to make proper provision for the prisoner's health and well-being in the form of requisite medical assistance. This matter will be dealt with directly with respect to Harry's treatment in prison, but Harry and Barry's subsequent treatment in the prison cell may well be exacerbated by the fact that both have drug problems and are under the influence of drugs at the relevant time. Further, both prisoners appear to have been left in the cell for three hours, without enquiry into their mental and physical health. However, in the absence of evidence that the influence of drugs had a substantial impact on their mental or physical health, it would be difficult to find a violation of **article 3** solely on this ground.

The attacks on Harry and Barry by the police officers after Barry had attacked an officer raises issues under the domestic law of assault and **article 3**. At common law an officer will commit an assault if he uses force on a prisoner without authority, or where he has authority but uses excessive force (*Rodrigues v Home Office* [1989] **Legal Action 14**). Although Barry had used force on an officer, the beatings appear to be a punishment and not related to self-defence, and are too excessive to be related to the maintenance of order. The scenario is similar to the domestic case of *Russell, McNamee and McCotter v Home Office, Daily Telegraph,* **13 March 2001**, where it was held that prisoners had been unlawfully assaulted by prison authorities after they had been captured after escape. This represents the case law of the European Court of Human Rights and in *Tomasi v France* (1993) **15 EHRR 1** it was held that any wrongful and unnecessary use of force by state authorities on those in detention would constitute at least degrading treatment. Further, depending on the extent of the injuries, the court in our case might find that Harry and Barry were subjected to inhuman treatment. In *Tomasi* the detainee had been hit in the stomach, slapped and kicked, had his head knocked against the wall, and been left naked in front of a window for several hours, and in those circumstances the Court found such treatment was both inhuman and degrading. Because the prisoners in our case are under the influence of drugs, such beating might amount to inhuman treatment; thus affecting the measure of damages, and any just satisfaction under s.8 of the 1998 Act.

With respect to the condition of the cell, although for a claim to succeed under **article 3** the conditions of detention must go beyond the level that is inevitable from the fact of incarceration (*Valasinas v Lithuania* (2001) **12 BHRC 266**), unacceptable conditions of detention can amount to a breach of **article 3**. For example, in *Peers v Greece* (2001) **33 EHRR 51**, where the applicant complained that he had been detained in a cramped cell which had little natural light and no ventilation and which had an open toilet, the Court found that these conditions denoted a lack of respect for the applicant, capable of humiliating and debasing him.

Although Harry and Barry were only required to occupy the cell overnight, the fact that human beings were placed in a cell that was full of vomit and excrement, particularly as it appears to have been done as some form of punishment or on the basis of administrative convenience, suggests that the threshold of article 3 has been met. The situation was exacerbated by the fact that the authorities refused to allow them to go to the toilet, which meant that they had to urinate in front of each other on three occasions. In *Peers* (above), the Court found that it was unacceptable that each cell mate had to relieve themselves in an open toilet in front of each other, and in *Napier v Scottish Ministers, The Times,* 13 May 2004, the Scottish courts held that conditions in Barlinnie Prison, including the lack of adequate sanitary conditions involving 'slopping out', amounted to violation of article 3.

Harry's treatment in prison

Whilst in prison the prison authorities owe Harry a duty of care under the law of negligence to take care for his safety, and this includes a duty to protect him from foreseeable harm caused by fellow inmates (*Ellis v Home Office* [1953] 2 QB 135). By informing other prisoners of the nature of Harry's offence, it was reasonably foreseeable that he might be attacked and the authorities appear to have failed in their duty towards Harry in this respect. Also under article 3 member states owe a positive obligation to protect individuals from an unacceptable risk of ill-treatment at the hands of others (*A v United Kingdom* (1999) 27 EHRR 611), and although this duty should not place an unreasonable burden on the state, the prison officers appear to have subjected Harry to an unacceptable and avoidable risk of ill-treatment. Further, the attack by the prisoners appears to clearly cross the threshold under article 3, and given the fact that he was stripped, it could be argued that the treatment amounted to inhuman treatment (*Tomasi v France* (above)).

The failure to provide Harry with medication to deal with his drug addiction raises issues under article 3. Although there is no right under the Convention to be released from prison simply because one is ill (*Papon v France* (2004) 39 EHRR 10), prison and police authorities owe a duty under the Convention to provide adequate medical and other assistance to those in detention and who have special needs (*Keenan v United Kingdom* (2001) 33 EHRR 38 and *Price v United Kingdom* (2002) 34 EHRR 53). More specifically, in *McGlinchey v United Kingdom* (above), the European Court held that there had been a violation of article 3 when the inmate had died in prison after receiving inadequate medical care to deal with her withdrawal symptoms. In our case, the authorities have deliberately refused to offer assistance, and the remarks of the officer suggest that there may have been a definite intention to humiliate Harry. Accordingly, there appears to be a clear violation of article 3 in this respect.

Harry's suicide

Harry's suicide raises issues under articles 2 and 3 of the European Convention. The common law has imposed a duty on prison and police authorities to safeguard a prisoner's life from acts of self-harm (*Kirkham v Chief Constable of Greater Manchester Police* [1990]

2 QB 283) and this extends to prisoners who are not suffering from mental illness at the time of the suicide (*Reeves v Commissioner for the Police of the Metropolis* [2000] AC 283). This duty is also relevant to the state's obligation to protect the right to life under **article 2** of the Convention, although in *Orange v Chief Constable of West Yorkshire Police* [2001] 3 WLR 736 the Court of Appeal held that such a duty only applied where the prisoner was a clear suicide risk and the authorities have failed to take all reasonable steps to avoid the act of self-harm. This caution is shown in the European Court's decision in *Keenan v United Kingdom* (above). Here a prisoner with mental problems had committed suicide in prison after being placed in a segregation block for breach of the prison rules. Noting that the prisoner was not considered an immediate risk while in detention, the Court held that the state authorities had made a reasonable response to his conduct, placing him in hospital care and under watch when he showed suicidal tendencies.

In our case, as opposed to *Keenan*, the authorities do not appear to have conducted any professional inquiry into the risk of suicide, and thus the state's liability under **article 2** might be satisfied in the circumstances. In any case, the authorities appear to have violated **article 3** by refusing to refer him to the medical centre and by placing him in a single cell. Thus, in *Keenan*, although the Court did not find a violation of **article 2**, it nevertheless found a violation of **article 3** with respect to the prisoner's treatment and lack of proper medical and psychiatric care.

Conclusion

Harry and Barry's treatment appears to amount to a number of violations of both domestic law and of **article 3** of the European Convention. Specifically, the police assaults amount to degrading and, possibly, inhuman treatment, and by being placed in a cell full of vomit and excrement they appear to have been subjected to degrading treatment and punishment. Given the attacks on their dignity and the threats to their health, they would expect to get substantial compensation for non-pecuniary loss under the principles of just satisfaction now contained in **s.8** of the Human Rights Act 1998. Further, the prison authorities appear to have clearly breached their duty of care with respect to Harry by disclosing information that led to his assault and by failing to provide him with adequate medical care. Finally, his suicide would appear to engage the liability of the authorities under both **articles 2 and 3**. Again, Harry's family would expect to receive substantial just satisfaction, and in *Keenan* the Court stressed that family representatives should be able to claim such loss if the state was to fulfil its duty under **article 13** of the Convention to provide an effective remedy for breach of the victim's Convention rights.

Question 3

Critically examine the case law of the European Court of Human Rights with respect to claims made by those facing deportation or extradition to countries where they face the risk of ill-treatment.

Commentary

There is a wealth of case law from the European Court of Human Rights dealing with allegations made by those subject to deportation or extradition that they will face the risk of human rights violations at the hands of the receiving country. This question not only asks the student to detail that case law, but also to analyse it critically with a view to assessing whether such case law offers adequate protection against such violations.

To answer the question the student needs to appreciate the so-called *Soering* principle, whereby a member state of the Council of Europe can attract liability for actual or potential violations of Convention rights by another state, whether a party to the Convention or not. The student also needs to appreciate the limitations of that principle and how the European Court has attempted to balance the human rights of the individuals concerned with state interests in immigration and crime detection and prosecution. The student can then judge whether the European Court has achieved an appropriate balance in that respect.

 Answer plan

- Introduction to the possible human rights violations in cases of deportation and extradition
- Consideration of the jurisdictional and legal difficulties raised in such cases
- Critical examination of the relevant case law of the European Court and Commission in this area
- Conclusions with respect to the level of protection afforded under the European Convention to such victims

Suggested answer

The removal of individuals from a state might result in the person being parted from his family, thus engaging the right to private and family life under **article 8** of the European Convention. Equally, removal will impact on the person's liberty and security of the person because some form of detention will have taken place pending removal (*Chahal v United Kingdom* (1997) **23 EHRR 413**). In addition, deportation or extradition can often subject individuals to a real risk of their fundamental rights being infringed by the receiving state, raising the question whether the removing state can be held responsible for such violations.

Article 1 of the European Convention provides that every member state shall secure the rights and freedoms defined in **Part One** of the Convention to everyone within their jurisdiction. This raises the jurisdictional question of whether a member state can be responsible for actual or anticipated violations of human rights committed by other countries, and in particular whether an individual who is facing expulsion can bring proceedings against the expelling state in respect of violations which are to take place at the hands of the receiving state. In *Soering v United Kingdom* (1989) **11 EHRR 439**, the European Court held that a decision of a member state to extradite a person might engage the responsibility of that state under the Convention where there were substantial grounds for believing that if extradited such a person would be faced with a real risk of being subjected to breaches of **article 3**. In *Soering*, the United States had sought the extradition of a young German national, who was wanted to stand trial for the murder of his girlfriend's parents. The government was given an assurance that the prosecutors would forward the views of the British government that he should not face the death penalty and the government agreed to his extradition. The Court held that exposure of the applicant to the Death Row phenomenon constituted a violation of **article 3** so that extradition in this case would constitute a violation of **article 3**.

In *Soering* the European Court accepted that the Convention did not govern, or impose its standards on, states that were not a party to it. Nevertheless, it accepted that there were good grounds for engaging the responsibility of a member state where it has expelled a person from its jurisdiction and where there are substantial grounds for believing that that person faces a real risk of being subjected to a violation of **article 3**. Further, although the Court accepted that it was not normal to pronounce on potential future violations of the Convention, it was necessary to depart from that rule in order to ensure the effectiveness of the safeguard provided by **article 3**. The *Soering* principle was affirmed in the later case of **HLR v France (1998) 26 EHRR 29**, where the Court held that given the absolute character of **article 3** it could not rule out the possibility that a state may be responsible for the acts of private individuals.

The European Court must address two fundamental and related questions: whether there is a real risk that the applicant will in fact be subjected to the alleged treatment; and whether such treatment is in violation of **article 3**. In these cases the Court must decide whether the applicant faced a *real risk* that he would be subject to conditions or treatment in violation of his Convention rights. However, the prohibition under **article 3** is absolute, and once substantial grounds have been shown for believing that an individual would face such a risk, the activities of the person, however undesirable, cannot be a material consideration. In *Chahal v United Kingdom* (above) the applicant, who had indefinite leave to stay in the United Kingdom, had previously visited the Punjab and had been subjected to torture by the Punjab police. On his return to the United Kingdom the applicant became a prominent member of the British Sikh community and the Secretary of State for the Home Department believed that he was involved in a number of acts of intimidation and terrorism and deported him on the grounds that his presence was not conducive to the public good. The European Court held that, despite assurances given by the Indian government to the British government that the applicant would have no reason to expect to suffer mistreatment at the hands of the Indian authorities, the evidence, including continued international allegations of continued abuse and the fact that the applicant's high profile would make him a target for such mistreatment, meant that his deportation would lead to a violation of **article 3**.

Although the Court has stressed that the obligations under **article 3** cannot be qualified by the behaviour of the applicant, or the pressing need to enforce relevant immigration and deportation policies, it has insisted that there is evidence of a real risk of ill-treatment. Thus, in *HLR* (above), the European Court held that there was no such risk despite the general situation of violence pertaining in Colombia at that time. The applicant must be subjected to both a direct and specific risk, and this allows the Court to display deference to the domestic authorities in balancing the Convention rights of such applicants with the general interests of the community and in accepting diplomatic assurances with respect to such risks.

This was illustrated in *Vilvarajah v United Kingdom* (1991) 14 EHRR 248, where the applicants, Sri Lankan Tamils, had entered the United Kingdom and unsuccessfully claimed political asylum because of the civil war in that country. The applicants alleged that they were subjected to ill-treatment on their return and claimed that their return to Sri Lanka exposed them to a real risk of ill-treatment in violation of **article 3**. The European Court held that the general unsettled situation in Sri Lanka at the time of the applicants' deportation did not establish that they were at greater risk than any other young Tamils who were returning there; the applicants had established only a possibility rather than a clear risk of ill-treatment. Although the Court held that it had a duty to rigorously examine the existence of the risk in view of the absolute character of **article 3**, there were no distinguishing factors in the case of the applicants so as to enable the Secretary of State for the Home Department to foresee that they would be ill-treated on their return.

Similarly, the Court offers states some discretion in deciding whether it is able to rely on diplomatic assurances made by the receiving state. Thus, in *Launder v United Kingdom* [1998] EHRLR 337 the European Commission for Human Rights upheld the extradition of an individual from the United Kingdom to Hong Kong despite his claims that he would be subjected to an unfair trial and the death penalty by the Chinese government, who had recently taken over the territory. This upheld the decision of the House of Lords in *R (Launder) v Secretary of State for the Home Department* [1997] 1 WLR 839, who had held that the Home Secretary was entitled to accept assurances from the authorities that the **Basic Law of Hong Kong** would be adhered to on the transfer of power. However, the Court has been prepared to make a thorough investigation into the potential risk and to rule on the acceptability of that risk. Thus, in *Chahal* (above) the Court rejected the government's pleas, accepted by the domestic courts, that it was not unreasonable for the Home Secretary to rely on the assurances given by the Indian authorities with respect to the risk of Chahal facing further torture.

The Court has extended the *Soering* principle to the subjection of individuals to intolerable and unlawful prison conditions (*Hilal v United Kingdom* (2001) 33 EHRR 2). More controversially, in *D v United Kingdom* (1997) 24 EHRR 423 the Court applied the principle to cases where the receiving state would not necessarily be in violation of the Convention. In this case the applicant, a citizen of St Kitts in the West Indies, had entered the United Kingdom illegally and had been charged with the importation of drugs. He was sentenced to six years' imprisonment and during his sentence he contracted AIDS. On his release he was ordered by the Home Secretary to be returned to his home country. The applicant claimed that because of the lack of medical and other care facilities in that country he would face intolerable conditions in violation of **article 3**. The Court held that on the facts his removal to a country where he would face the risk of dying in the most distressing circumstances amounted to the subjection of the applicant to inhuman treatment.

The decision in *D v United Kingdom* (above) has been limited by subsequent decisions, and the Court has attempted to place the enjoyment of the individual's rights under article 3 alongside the member state's right to execute its lawful and necessary immigration policies. Thus, in *N v United Kingdom* (2008) 47 EHRR 39, the European Court agreed with the House of Lords (*N v Secretary of State for the Home Department* [2005] 2 AC 296) when it held that the deportation of an asylum-seeking Ugandan citizen suffering from AIDS/HIV to Uganda was not in breach of article 3, even though access to medical treatment and facilities was problematic. The House of Lords had held that exceptional circumstances were required to apply the decision in *D*—the test being whether the applicant's medical condition had reached such a critical state that there were compelling humanitarian grounds for not removing him to a place which lacked the medical and social services which he would need to prevent acute suffering. Further, article 3 could not be interpreted so as to require contracting states to admit and treat AIDS sufferers from all over the world for the rest of their lives.

The *Soering* principle has had its critics and in particular it is argued it should be relaxed in the context of terrorism and that states should be able to deport or extradite suspected terrorists to another country despite the risk of ill-treatment. Thus, in *Ramzy v The Netherlands* (Application No 25424/05), the Court is being asked to reconsider its inflexible approach in *Chahal* in this context. In the meantime in *Saadi v Italy* (2009) 49 EHRR 30, it was held that the considerable difficulties facing states with respect to terrorist violence did not call into question the absolute nature of article 3, and that the argument that the risk had to be established by solid evidence where the individual was a threat to national security was not consistent with article 3 and its absolute nature. The test was whether there were substantial grounds for believing that there was a real risk that those found guilty of terrorist offences had been subjected to torture and here the authorities had failed to investigate relevant allegations of such.

In conclusion, the *Soering* principle has provided the European Court with an opportunity to extend and enhance its supervisory role with respect to article 3. The principle has also informed domestic law and practice and has expanded the state's duty to uphold the fundamental human rights of those within its jurisdiction, even where the threat emanates from another state or its citizens. However, the Court has adopted a cautious approach, insisting that the risk of ill-treatment is real and specific, as opposed to fanciful or general. This caution has resulted in the Court compromising the full impact of the principle, whilst allowing it to interfere in cases where there is a real risk of the applicant being subjected to a violation of what the Court regards as a most fundamental and absolute human right. The outcome of the proceedings in *Ramzy* (above) will, therefore, prove particularly significant.

Further reading

Clayton, G, *Textbook on Immigration and Asylum Law*, 3rd edn (OUP 2008).

Clayton, R and Tomlinson, H, *Law of Human Rights*, 2nd edn (OUP 2009), ch 8.

Cooper, J, *Cruelty: An Analysis of Article 3* (Sweet and Maxwell 2002).

Due process, liberty and security of the person, and the right to a fair trial

Introduction

This chapter contains questions on **articles 5–7 of the European Convention on Human Rights,** commonly known as the 'due process' rights. These articles—which safeguard the rights of individual liberty, the right to a fair trial, and freedom from retrospective criminal law—impact heavily on matters such as police powers and the criminal and civil process, and students can be tested on these areas as part of the European Convention or its case law, or within the study of the domestic law on matters such as individual liberty and the right to a fair trial. The questions below concentrate on the principles and the case law of the European Convention, although they require a knowledge and appreciation of post-Human Rights Act domestic case law. In addition, students may be expected to display some knowledge of English law principles such as the rules of natural justice, studied earlier in their course.

These articles, particularly **articles 5 and 6,** are very wide-ranging and cover a number of aspects of each respective right. Consequently they have engendered a tremendous amount of case law—in addition, **article 6** is easily the most contested article. Students need to have a sound knowledge of this case law and to keep up to date in this respect. However, they should also avoid simply learning the cases without reference to the principles and concepts underlying each article. Most essay questions in this area will, therefore, require both an appreciation of the importance of these rights and an ability to analyse the jurisprudence of the domestic and European Courts. Thus, students should be careful to take an analytical approach and attempt to extract certain themes from the ever-growing case law, not losing sight of the fundamental principles of justice and liberty when answering such questions.

It is relatively common to include problem-type questions in this area, usually when the articles are being studied as part of the domestic law on matters such as police powers or a fair trial. As this text concentrates more on Convention rights, the questions below are all essay type.

Question 1

What rights does **article 5** of the European Convention grant to the individual and what limitations does that article place on the infringement of such rights? What values and human rights principles does **article 5** uphold?

 ## Commentary

The first part of the question is relatively descriptive and requires the student to be aware of the wording of the article, its component parts, and its general scope and purpose. The student should, therefore, begin by exploring the meaning of liberty and security of the person, distinguishing it from other rights, such as freedom of movement. The student can then explain the component parts of **article 5** and the range of rights it offers, giving relevant legal authority throughout. The answer can then move on to explaining what controls are placed on the state by this article in restricting its power to interfere with basic liberty.

The second part of the question is more difficult and analytical, requiring the student to discuss the principles and values underlying the article and its wording. The student will be expected to identify themes such as the control of arbitrary power, upholding the rule of law and legal certainty and the separation of powers, which run through the article and its wording and which can be illustrated by reference to the case law of the European Court and, where appropriate, of the domestic courts. The student can draw on a variety of examples for this purpose, but will be expected to cover areas such as powers of arrest, questioning and detention, the release of prisoners, and the use and control of powers of arrest and detention in times of emergency (including the possible use of derogation powers under **article 15** of the Convention). The student need not wait until the end of the essay before addressing these issues, but can identify them throughout the answer, and then summarize them in a neat conclusion.

 ## Answer plan

- Examination and explanation of the wording of **article 5**, its scope and application
- Examination of the rights bestowed by **article 5**, together with relevant case law
- Examination of the restrictions imposed on liberty of the individual, together with the limitations placed on such restrictions
- Analysis of the aim of **article 5** and any human rights values and principles evident from the wording of the article, using relevant case law

Suggested answer

Article 5 of the European Convention provides that everyone has the right to liberty and security of the person. The right under **article 5** must be distinguished from the general right of freedom of movement, guaranteed by **article 2 of the Fourth Protocol** (*Guzzardi v Italy* **(1981) 3 EHRR 333**), although certain restrictions placed on an individual's freedom of movement can constitute a deprivation of liberty if they hamper the enjoyment of a normal life (*JJ v Secretary of State for the Home Department* **[2006] 3 WLR 866**). Further, **article 5** is not engaged by a claim of the *conditions* under which a person is detained (*Ashindane v United Kingdom* **(1985) 7 EHRR 528**).

Article 5 is concerned with protecting individuals from arbitrary arrest and detention by the state and gives precedence to liberty; placing the burden of proof on the state to justify any deprivation. Thus, in *Kurt v Turkey* **(1999) 27 EHRR 373** the European Court held that a state, having assumed control over an individual by taking him into detention, must account for the whereabouts of that person, adopting effective measures to safeguard against the risk of disappearance and conducting a prompt and effective investigation into any claim of illegality.

Article 5 envisages that an individual may lawfully be deprived of their liberty in given situations, provided it is done in accordance with a procedure prescribed by law. Thus, all deprivations of liberty must comply with the essential characteristics of the rule of law and with the procedural and substantive principles of fairness and justice. Further, the article provides specific protection when people are deprived of their liberty, including the right to be brought before a judicial authority (**article 5(3)**), to question the continued lawfulness of that detention (**article 5(4)**), and to receive compensation for unlawful detention (**article 5(5)**).

For example, **article 5(1)(a)** provides for the lawful detention of a person after conviction by a competent court. By insisting that any detention is 'lawful', and that any detention be approved by a 'competent' court, the article ensures that the individual is protected by the general principles of due process. Any conviction must have a sufficient basis in domestic law, the relevant court must not interpret and apply the law in an arbitrary fashion (*Tsirlis and Koulompas v Greece* **(1998) 25 EHRR 198**), and there must be a sufficient connection between the court's finding of guilt and the subsequent detention. This ensures that an individual is only in detention as a result of a judicial ruling, rather than at the discretion of the executive, although the executive may have a supervised role in detaining individuals (*Van Droogenbroek v Belgium* **(1982) 4 EHRR 443**). **Article 5** also allows detention after the expiry of a fixed period of imprisonment within an indeterminate term, provided any further detention or recall is sufficiently connected to the original sentence and its objectives (*Weeks v United Kingdom* **(1998) 10 EHRR 293**). However, there must be a causal connection between the sentence and the subsequent detention, and in *Stafford v United Kingdom* **(2002) 35 EHRR 32** the Court held that there had been a violation of **article**

5(1) when a prisoner sentenced to imprisonment for murder was being detained on the order of the Home Secretary because he posed the risk of committing non-violent crimes on his release.

Article 5(1)(b) permits the arrest or detention of a person who has not complied with a court order when such arrest or detention is required for the fulfilment of an obligation that is prescribed by law. The European Court has insisted that a specific legal obligation has been breached, although in *Steel v United Kingdom* (1999) 28 EHRR 603 it held that the general powers to bind over an individual in order to keep the peace were compatible with **article 5**. The Court will also ensure that the domestic court's decision to detain is not taken in arbitrary fashion, and although a detention would not be unlawful simply because the tribunal had made an error of law (*Benham v United Kingdom* (1996) 22 EHRR 293), in *Beet and others v United Kingdom* (2005) **41 EHRR 23**, it was held that there had been a violation of **article 5** when poll tax defaulters were imprisoned after the magistrates had not properly considered whether the applicants were wilful defaulters.

Article 5(1)(c) allows for lawful arrest or detention for the purpose of bringing a person before a competent legal authority, either on reasonable suspicion of them having committed an offence or when it is necessary to prevent them committing an offence. The arrest must be for the purpose of enforcing the criminal law against that individual (*Ciulla v Italy* (1991) 13 EHRR 346), and the suspicion for any arrest must be based on legitimate and objective grounds. Thus, in *Fox, Campbell and Hartley v United Kingdom* (1991) 13 EHRR 157, the European Court held that a reasonable suspicion presupposes the existence of facts that would satisfy an objective observer that the person might have committed the offence. Although it will offer a margin of discretion to the authorities, particularly in cases of suspected terrorism (*Ocalan v Turkey* (2005) 41 EHRR 45), this should not undermine the essential safeguards provided by **article 5** and must not stretch the notion of reasonableness so as to impair those safeguards (*O'Hara v United Kingdom* (2002) 34 EHRR 32).

Article 5 allows the detention of persons such as minors, those of unsound mind, vagrants, and those seeking to enter the country unlawfully. With respect to the detention of those of unsound mind, the Court has stated that such a person must not only be reliably shown to be of unsound mind, but that the mental disorder must warrant compulsory confinement and that such disorder must persist if the detention is to continue (*Winterwerp v Netherlands* (1979) 2 EHRR 387). Similarly, with respect to the detention of unlawful entrants, or those who are to be deported (article 5(1)(f)), the Court has stated that an arrest or detention will be unlawful if the state authorities have acted in bad faith or have employed illegal means (*Boznao v Italy* (1986) 9 EHRR 297). Further, domestic law must ensure that the detention has not been ordered for arbitrary reasons, and that it is not excessive in length (*Quinn v France* (1996) 21 EHRR 529). However, the Court is prepared to take a flexible approach provided it is satisfied that a lengthy detention was necessary in the circumstances (*Chahal v United Kingdom* (1997) 23 EHRR 413).

Article 5 also provides specific rights to those who have been arrested or detained. For example, under **article 5(2)** everyone shall be informed properly of the reasons for an arrest and of any charge against him. Again, the Court has provided some area of discretion, and in *Fox, Campbell and Hartley v United Kingdom* (above), it was held that the full reasons for arrest need not be given immediately on or after arrest and that in the present case it was sufficient that they were arrested 'on suspicion of being terrorists' and then questioned about specific acts and allegations. Thus, the European Court is prepared to adopt a flexible approach, particularly in the context of terrorist offences, provided the essential values of **article 5** are adhered to and no serious injustice is evident.

Article 5(3) provides that everyone arrested or detained shall be brought *promptly* before a judge or other officer authorized by law to exercise judicial power, that individual then being entitled either to a trial within a reasonable time, or to release pending trial. This does not prohibit pre-trial detention, provided there are sufficient safeguards against arbitrary or unnecessary loss of liberty, but in **Caballero v United Kingdom (2000) 30 EHRR 643** it was held that automatic denial of bail pending trial was in violation of this right. **Article 5(3)** was at the centre of the House of Lords' decision in *A v Secretary of State for the Home Department* **[2005] 2 AC 68** with respect to the detention of foreign suspects at Belmarsh prison, and the European Court defended this right in a similarly robust fashion (***A v United Kingdom*, (2009) 49 EHRR 29**). Thus, in **Assenov v Bulgaria (1999) 28 EHRR 652** the European Court held that the 'other officer' employed in **article 5(3)** must be independent of the executive and the parties to any act, and in **Brogan v United Kingdom (1989) 11 EHRR 117** the Court held that the detention of suspected terrorists for periods between four-and-a-half and six days violated the notion of promptness laid down in **article 5(3)**. Such a ruling, however, is subject to a government's right of derogation under **article 15** (***Brannigan and McBride v United Kingdom* (1993) 17 EHRR 539**).

Article 5(4) of the Convention provides further protection to the individual by stating that everyone deprived of their liberty by arrest or detention shall be entitled to take proceedings to test the lawfulness of that detention. This should be done speedily and a court should be able to order that person's release if it is found to be unlawful. This allows an individual to challenge any detention before a court of law to ensure that the detention is consistent with principles of due process. Although **article 5(4)** does not confer a right of appeal where the original detention is imposed by the court, it allows the individual to question the evidence upon which that individual has lost his liberty (*Chahal v United Kingdom* (above) and *A v United Kingdom* (above)).

In *Winterwerp v Netherlands* (above), the Court stressed that a review must not be limited to the bare legality of the detention, and must be available at reasonable intervals. In **X v United Kingdom (1982) 4 EHRR 188**, the European Court held that a review should be wide enough to bear on those conditions that are essential for the lawful detention of the individual; for example, whether the detention of a patient was still necessary in the interest of public safety. This provision was used in ***Thynne, Wilson and Gunnell v United Kingdom* (1990) 13 EHRR 666**, where the Court held that the decision to release discretionary life-sentence prisoners once their tariff had expired should be subject to judicial supervision and should not be subject to executive discretion, albeit one which was subject to (limited) judicial review. That principle was applied more recently with respect to mandatory life-sentence prisoners (*Stafford v United Kingdom* (2002) 35 EHRR 32); the Court noting that the Home Secretary's role was inconsistent with notions of the rule of law and the separation of powers.

Finally, **article 5(5)** provides that everyone who has been arrested or detained in breach of **article 5** shall have an enforceable right to compensation. This provision encapsulates the principle that where there is a right there should be a remedy, and is of particular importance where the arrest or detention is lawful in domestic law, precluding the domestic courts from granting a remedy (*A v United Kingdom* (above)).

Article 5 thus enshrines many of the fundamental values that underpin the European Convention. The requirement that any arrest or detention has to be prescribed by law ensures that a person only loses his liberty within strict rules of domestic law, and that those laws possess the essential qualities of law and of the rule of law. In particular, the article protects individuals from arbitrary executive discretion and ensures that loss of liberty is regulated and supervised by an independent and impartial body. These principles have been robustly applied by the European Court, although it has been prepared to offer some flexibility in sensitive cases, such as the prevention of terrorism.

Question 2

To what extent should freedom from arbitrary arrest and detention be lawfully compromised in the context of the fight against terrorism?

 ## Commentary

This type of question has become increasingly popular in recent times, particularly since the passing of new anti-terrorism provisions in domestic law and the legal challenge to such in the House of Lords. The question concerns the interplay between the protection of individual liberty and the control of terrorism and is asking the student to explore relevant human rights principles and case law to examine the extent to which the terrorist context can and should deprive the individual of protection against arbitrary arrest and detention.

The student should begin by briefly explaining the notion of liberty of the person and the dangers of arbitrary and unlawful interferences with that right, along with the normal safeguards contained in **article 5** of the European Convention together with relevant case law. The student can then move on to examine the extent to which those principles are compromised in the context of terrorism. This will involve an examination of the relevant case law under **article 5**, as well as the specific provision under **article 15** for states to derogate from their normal obligations under **article 5** of the Convention in times of war and other national emergencies. The relevant case law of the European Court can then be examined, along with relevant domestic cases, most notably recent decisions of the House of Lords with respect to executive detention and stop and search.

Answer plan

- Definition of arbitrary arrest and detention and explanation of how **article 5** of the European Convention guarantees against them
- Examination of relevant case law where **article 5** rights can be compromised in cases of terrorism
- Specific examination of **article 15** of the Convention allowing derogation in times of national emergency
- Explanation and critical examination of domestic anti-terrorism provisions and case law
- Analysis of the above principles and any case law so as to examine the extent to which terrorist threats can compromise such rights

Suggested answer

The right to be free from arbitrary arrest and detention is at the heart of notions of liberty and the control of excessive government. **Article 5** of the European Convention provides that everyone has the right to liberty and security of the person, and although this right can be compromised in a number of situations, that article ensures that any *prima facie* violation conforms to standards of procedural justice. The question arises, however, whether such a right and the restrictions on its interference apply (less stringently) in the context of the fight against terrorism, and whether individual liberty should take second place to national security and safety.

With respect to **article 5**, a number of European Court decisions suggest that the state might be provided with a greater area of discretion when using its arrest and detention laws in the context of terrorism. **Article 5(1)(c)** allows for lawful arrest or detention of a person effected for the purpose of bringing a person before a competent legal authority on reasonable suspicion of having committed an offence or when it is reasonably considered necessary to prevent the commission of such. The article insists that this power is exercised in good faith and for the purpose of bringing a person before the courts (*Ciulla v Italy* **(1991) 13 EHRR 346**). This safeguard is particularly important in times of emergency, where the state may be tempted to abuse the power of arrest and detention for strategic purposes (*Ocalan v Turkey* **(2005) 41 EHRR 45**). Similarly, the Court insists that suspicion for arrest is capable of being justified on legitimate and objective grounds.

These requirements were examined in the context of terrorist offences in *Fox, Campbell and Hartley v United Kingdom* (1990) 13 EHRR 157. The applicants had been arrested and detained for periods between 30 and 44 hours under provisions which allowed a person to be arrested on suspicion of being a terrorist and to be detained for up to 72 hours. They were then released without charge. The European Court held that in general the phrase 'reasonable suspicion' presupposes the existence of facts that would satisfy an objective observer that the person might have committed the offence. What might be regarded as reasonable would depend on all the circumstances of the case, and in respect of terrorist offences the test would differ from conventional crime. However, it stressed that the context of terrorism could not impair the essence of reasonableness and the state would need to furnish at least some information which could satisfy the Court that the arrested person was reasonably suspected of having committed the offence.

Those principles were applied in *Murray v United Kingdom* (1994) 19 EHRR 193, where the Court accepted that due to the difficulties inherent in the investigation of terrorism the reasonableness of the suspicion could not always be judged according to the same standards that were applied in cases of conventional crime. However, it has subsequently noted that such a context gives the authorities a wide, but not unlimited, discretion and that the investigation of terrorist crime could not stretch the notion of reasonableness (*O'Hara v United Kingdom* (2002) 34 EHRR 32). In that case the European Court approved of the decision of the House of Lords in *O'Hara v Chief Constable of the RUC* [1997] 1 All ER 129, where it was accepted that a police constable could have a reasonable suspicion for arrest despite not being aware of all possible information. This stance has been applied to the definition of 'offence' within article 5(1). Thus, in *Brogan v United Kingdom* (1989) 11 EHRR 117, it held that it was sufficient to arrest a person on suspicion of being 'involved in terrorism', as that phrase was defined in the relevant legislation and the applicants had been questioned about specific acts and allegations.

Article 5(2) provides that everyone arrested shall be informed properly of the reasons for his arrest, and of any charge against him, but an individual need not be supplied with full information of the reasons for arrest at the actual time of that arrest, particularly in the terrorist context. Thus, in *Fox, Campbell and Hartley v United Kingdom* (above), it was held that an interval of a few hours between the arrest and the provision of reasons did not necessarily violate article 5(2). Further, although the Court accepted that merely telling the applicants that they were being arrested on suspicion of being terrorists was not sufficient to comply with article 5, the fact that they were questioned in relation to specific acts and allegations complied with the requirement that people should be informed promptly.

The Court has, however, shown less deference with respect to the requirement under article 5(3) that everyone arrested or detained be brought promptly before a judge to exercise judicial power and to be entitled to trial within a reasonable time or to release. In *Brogan v United Kingdom* (above), the applicants had been arrested on suspicion of involvement in acts of terrorism and had been detained for periods between four-and-a-half and six days, eventually being released without charge. The Court concluded that even the shortest of the periods involved in this case was inconsistent with the notion of promptness laid down in **article 5(3)**, and involved a serious weakening of the procedural guarantee and very essence of the right. A similar breach was found in *O'Hara* (above), where the applicant had been held for six days and 13 hours before his eventual release. The right under **article 5(3)** has also been buttressed by the separate right under **article 5(5)** to be compensated for unlawful deprivation of liberty, a right that is inevitably denied to the individual who has been subject to lawful, but excessive detention under domestic terrorism laws (*A v United Kingdom*, (2009) 49 EHRR 29).

A state may also rely on **article 15** of the Convention, which allows it to derogate from its Convention obligations during times of war or other public emergency threatening the life of the nation. Although **article 15** only allows derogation measures that are strictly required by the exigencies of the situation, the European Court has been prepared to offer the state a certain margin of error or discretion in this area. Thus, in *Lawless v Ireland* **(1961) 1 EHRR 15**, it held that a respondent government should be afforded a certain margin of error or appreciation in deciding what measures were required. Importantly, it was not the Court's function to substitute for the government's assessment any other assessment of what might be the most prudent or most expedient policy to combat terrorism. Accordingly, in this case, although the Court found that detention without trial for a period of five months was in violation of **article 5(3)**, it held that the Irish government was entitled to derogate because of the existence of a public emergency.

A similar 'hands-off' approach was adopted in *Brannigan and McBride v United Kingdom* **(1993) 17 EHRR 539**, which challenged the United Kingdom's derogation in relation to **article 5(3)** following the European Court's decision in *Brogan v United Kingdom* (above). In *Brannigan and McBride* the European Court held that the derogation was justified, even though it had not been lodged before the Court's decision in *Brogan*. The Court accepted the government's contention that there was an emergency situation, and that the derogation was not invalid merely because the government had decided to keep open the possibility of finding alternative means of complying with its Convention obligations. The Court was also satisfied that effective safeguards such as the availability of *habeas corpus* were available to the applicants.

However, recently a more positive and dynamic approach has been adopted. In *A v Secretary of State for the Home Department* [2005] 2 AC 68 the House of Lords considered the government's derogation of **article 5** of the Convention with respect to the power under the **Anti-terrorism, Crime and Security Act 2001** to detain foreign terrorist suspects who could not be removed from the country because of the risk of ill-treatment at the receiving country. Overruling the Court of Appeal, their Lordships held that the measures were incompatible with the United Kingdom's obligations under the European Convention.

With respect to whether there existed a public emergency threatening the life of the nation, the majority of their Lordships accepted that there was such a threat, stressing that great weight should be attached to the judgement of the Home Secretary and Parliament because they had to exercise a pre-eminently political judgement (Lord Hoffmann dissented, believing that there was merely a threat of serious physical damage and loss of life and concluding that the real threat to the life of the nation came not from terrorism but from the terrorism laws). However, their Lordships held that the measures taken were not proportionate and strictly required by the exigencies of the situation. Lord Bingham noted that even in a terrorist situation the domestic courts were not precluded from scrutinizing the relevant issues and deciding on the proportionality and necessity of emergency measures. These measures were disproportionate because they did not deal with the threat of terrorism from persons other than foreign nationals and permitted suspected foreign terrorists to carry on their activities in another country provided there was a safe country for them to go. Further, in their Lordships' view, if the threat posed by UK nationals could be addressed without infringing the right to personal liberty, it had not been shown why similar measures could not adequately address the threat posed by foreign nationals. In the subsequent proceedings in Strasbourg (*A v United Kingdom* (above)), the European Court refused to interfere with the House of Lords' assessment and also found that the provisions denied the applicants an effective remedy in challenging their detentions, because of the reliance on 'closed' evidence not made available to the detainees' lawyers. This decision was relied on by the House of Lords in *AF v Secretary of State for the Home Department* [2009] 3 WLR 74, in holding that controlees should be provided with a minimum amount of evidence in such proceedings.

The decisions of the House of Lords and the European Court in *A* suggests that the courts will be reluctant to interfere with political decisions of the government, such as whether to declare an emergency situation and put into place emergency provisions. However, whereas the European Court formerly showed deference in respect to the proportionality and necessity of specific measures, it appears that it will not now be prepared to abandon its review role in this respect and will staunchly defend the fundamental values of individual liberty and the control of arbitrary detention. This approach has been continued by the domestic courts, with some reserve, with respect to the legality of non-derogable control orders, introduced by the **Terrorism Act 2005** after the government's defeat in the House of Lords (*JJ v Secretary of State for the Home Department* [2006] 3 WLR 866). However, an alarming level of discretion was given by their Lordships with respect to stop-and-search powers under **s.44 of the Terrorism Act 2005** (*R (Gillan) v Commissioner of Police of the Metropolis* [2006] 2 AC 307), and that case has been referred to the European Court.

In conclusion, both the European and domestic courts have insisted that the minimum standards laid down in **article 5** of the Convention should not be unduly abandoned in the context of terrorism. However, the European Court has been prepared to compromise those standards in such a context, both in the interpretation of **article 5**, and under **article 15** of the Convention, which allows for derogation in times of public emergency. Nonetheless, the decisions in *A* suggest that the courts will not offer an unlimited margin of error to the government and will stoutly defend liberty against any arbitrary interference.

Question 3

'In the determination of his civil rights and obligations or of any criminal charge against him, everyone is entitled to a fair and public hearing within a reasonable time by an independent and impartial tribunal established by law' (**Article 6** of the European Convention).

What values does that article seek to uphold and in particular how has the European Court and Commission of Human Rights interpreted the following phrases:

'Criminal charge' and 'civil rights and obligations'

'Independent and impartial tribunal'?

 ## Commentary

This question is split into two parts, the second part asking the student to explain and comment on three specific components of **article 6**. The student should begin by outlining the content of **article 6** of the Convention and giving an overall view of the procedural protection it offers to the individual involved in either criminal or civil proceedings. The student should then identify the various constitutional and human rights values that the article seeks to uphold—such as the rule of law, the independence of the judiciary, and the presumption of innocence—and explain the importance of those values within the context of human rights and the European Convention. Relevant case authority should be quoted as and when necessary.

The second part of the question then asks the student to explain how particular phrases contained in **article 6** have been interpreted and applied by the European Court of Human Rights, and how that interpretation has shaped the scope of the article's protection of the individual's right to a fair trial. The student needs to be conversant with the large body of case law in this area and should explain and assess that case law in respect of each phrase in turn. The student should not just list the cases, but should be able to apply that case law in the context of a critical appraisal of the scope of **article 6** and its protection.

 ## Answer plan

- Consideration of the general wording and scope of **article 6**
- Consideration of the values and principles embodied in **article 6**, along with relevant case law

- Analysis of the Court and Commission case law on the respective terms, along with relevant case law

- Conclusion as to the scope of **article 6** and the interpretation of those respective terms

Suggested answer

Introduction

Article 6 of the European Convention guarantees the right to a fair trial, ensuring what is commonly referred to as 'due process'. This article guarantees that legal rights are resolved within the objective law, and is thus regarded as one of the most fundamental human rights within the Convention. **Article 6** mirrors the rules of natural justice, which have been applied in English domestic law (*Ridge v Baldwin* **[1964] AC 40**), and which demand minimum standards of procedural fairness from the law and the legal process. For example, it is fundamental that a person should have a hearing before an impartial and unbiased court or tribunal (*R v Bow Street Stipendary Magistrate, ex parte Pinochet Ugarte (No 2)* **[2000] 1 AC 119**), along with the right of access to the courts (*Chester v Bateson* **[1920] KB 829**). **Article 6** thus provides a general right to a fair trial and more specific due process rights, such as the presumption of innocence and the right to legal representation.

Article 6 guarantees the general right to a fair and public hearing within a reasonable time by an independent and impartial tribunal established by law. This ensures independence and objectivity and guarantees openness and public confidence in the justice system (which can be qualified only in exceptional cases). This right to speedy and effective justice requires the state to take measures to ensure that the courts provide reasonably prompt remedial action (*Robins v United Kingdom* **(1997) 26 EHRR 527**). **Article 6(2)** also upholds the presumption of innocence and liberty by providing that a person charged with a criminal offence shall be presumed innocent until proved guilty according to law. This prevents any finding of guilt based on conjecture or presumption (*Minelli v Switzerland* **(1983) 5 EHRR 554**). The Court has also recognized the right against self-incrimination (*Funke v France* **(1993) 16 EHRR 297**), stating that the right lies at the heart of the notion of a fair trial, having close links with the presumption of innocence contained in **article 6(2)** (*Saunders v United Kingdom* **(1996) 23 EHRR 313**). The Court has also accepted a qualified right of an accused to remain silent (*Condron v United Kingdom* **(2001) 31 EHRR 1**), although such a right is not absolute (*Murray v United Kingdom* **(1996) 22 EHRR 29**).

Article 6 allows the parties to participate effectively in the proceedings, and in *V and T v United Kingdom* **(2000) 30 EHRR 121** the Court held that there had been a violation of **article 6** when two 11-year-old boys charged with murder had been subjected to an adult-like trial that made it almost impossible for them to comprehend the proceedings or to consult effectively with counsel. Equally, both parties have the right to access and to present relevant evidence to the court, enjoying this right equally with the opposing party (*Rowe and Davis v United Kingdom* (2000) 30 EHRR 1). The Court has accepted that equality of arms is a fundamental aspect of the right to a fair trial, and this is supplemented by the right to legal representation, guaranteed by **article 6(3)(c)** (*Steel and Morris v United Kingdom* (2005) 41 EHRR 22), and the right to examine witnesses, conferred under **article 6(3)(d)**.

Article 6(3) provides a number of specific due process rights which complement and strengthen the general right to a fair trial. For example, **article 6(3)(a)** provides that every person has the right to be informed promptly, in detail, and in a language which he understands, of the nature and cause of any accusation made against him (*Broziek v Italy* (1989) 12 EHRR 371). Further, **article 6(3)(b)** provides the right to have adequate time and facilities for the preparation of one's defence, the extent of such a right depending on all the circumstances of the case, including the complexity of the charge (*Luedicke, Belkacem and Koc v Germany* (1978) 2 EHRR 149).

More specifically **article 6(3)(c)** guarantees the right to defend oneself in person or through legal assistance of one's own choosing, and, in appropriate cases, confers the right to free legal assistance for the purpose of presenting legal arguments. This provision upholds access to justice, although the Court has stressed that the right to legal representation is not absolute and depends on factors such as the seriousness of the charge (*Campbell and Fell v United Kingdom* (1984) 7 EHRR 165) and the complexity of the proceedings and legal arguments (*Benham v United Kingdom* (1996) 22 EHRR 293). This provision also guarantees the right to have unimpeded legal assistance during detention and interrogation (*Brennan v United Kingdom* (2002) 34 EHRR 18), and **article 6(3)(c)** provides that if a person has not sufficient means to pay for legal assistance he should be given it free if the interests of justice so require. **Articles 6(1) and 6(3)(c)** should be read together and there will a violation of both provisions if a fair trial could not be conducted without free legal assistance (*Granger v United Kingdom* (1990) 12 EHRR 496). Such rights allow the individual to effectively participate in the proceedings and **article 6(3)(e)** guarantees the right to have the free legal assistance of an interpreter if the individual cannot understand or speak the language used in court (*Cuscani v United Kingdom* (2003) 36 EHRR 1).

Article 6 has been interpreted in a manner consistent with fundamental principles of access to, and the achievement of, justice. For example, the European Court has held that **article 6** contains an implied right of access to the courts and to legal advice (*Golder v United Kingdom* (1975) 1 EHRR 524) and has held that the right to a fair trial includes the right to a fair sentence (*V and T v United Kingdom* (above)). All these cases underlie the values of the rule of law, legal accountability, and due process, which underpin all other Convention rights.

'Criminal charge' and 'civil rights and obligations'

Article 6 applies only to proceedings where the applicant is either facing 'a criminal charge', or where his or her 'civil rights and obligations' are subject to determination. The Court has taken a liberal approach in interpreting 'civil rights and obligations', and in *Ringeisen v Austria* (1991) 1 EHRR 445 it held that for the article to be engaged it was not necessary that both parties to the proceedings were private individuals, provided the proceedings were to determine the private rights and obligations of the parties. Consequently, civil actions brought against public authorities would fall within the scope of **article 6**, and in *Ringeisen*, the fact that the proceedings were classified as 'public', and were dealt with in an administrative tribunal, was not of vital consequence, because the applicant's private (property) rights were being adjudicated upon. Similarly, the fact that what is at issue is the determination of the applicant's statutory rights (to be free from discrimination), will not deny the claim the characteristic of a civil claim (*Tinnelly v United Kingdom* (1998) 27 EHRR 249). Proceedings are only excluded where they fail to impinge on the applicant's civil rights, for example where they are purely administrative (*Al-Fayed v United Kingdom* (1994) 18 EHRR 393).

The Court has adopted a similarly flexible approach in interpreting the phrase 'criminal charge'. In *Engel v Netherlands* (1976) 1 EHRR 647 it held that in determining whether a charge fell within **article 6**, it should address the following questions: first, whether the offence in question had been *classified* as criminal within the domestic legal system; secondly, the *nature* of the offence; and thirdly, the *severity of the punishment*. The classification of the offence was one, but not the decisive, factor in making that distinction. Rather, the Court is more concerned with whether the charge itself, and the accompanying penalty, have the *characteristics* of a criminal offence.

The principles have been applied in the context of prison disciplinary proceedings, which are formally classified as disciplinary proceedings. For example, in *Campbell and Fell v United Kingdom* (above), it held that prison disciplinary proceedings would amount to a criminal charge if the offence and the penalty were consistent with criminal proceedings—the applicants had been charged with very serious offences of mutiny and gross personal violence to a prison officer, and had received over 500 days of loss of remission as a penalty. This protection was extended to less grave offences in *Ezeh and Connors v United Kingdom* (2004) 39 EHRR 1. A similar rationale has been applied with respect to courts martial, discussed below (*Findlay v United Kingdom* (1997) 24 EHRR 221).

'An impartial court or tribunal'

A fundamental aspect of the right to a fair trial is the existence and appearance of an impartial court or tribunal. The Court has insisted that the judge or court is free from bias, or any reasonable appearance or fear of bias, and this principle applies irrespective of considerations of national security or convenience (*Ocalan v Turkey* (2005) 41 EHRR 45). Thus, in *Findlay v United Kingdom* (above) it was held that the body must present an appearance of independence and thus must be subjectively free of personal prejudice or bias and offer sufficient safeguards to exclude any legitimate doubt in this respect.

In *Findlay* the applicant had faced a court martial and, *inter alia*, had been sentenced to two years' imprisonment. The convening officer, who took the decision to charge him, appointed the prosecuting officer and the members of the court martial, all of whom were inferior in rank to him. In addition, the President of the court was on the convening officer's staff and the convening officer acted as confirming officer to whom the applicant unsuccessfully asked for a reduction in sentence. The Court held that the close link between the convening officer and the members of the court and his sentencing powers amounted to a clear violation of **article 6**. Despite a number of legislative changes, the Court has found various violations of **article 6**, highlighting in particular the inadequate training of court officers (*Morris v United Kingdom* (2002) 34 EHRR 52) and the appointment of insufficiently independent personnel (*Grieves v United Kingdom* (2004) 39 EHRR 2). The Court has taken a similarly robust approach with respect to prison disciplinary proceedings that engage **article 6** (*Whitfield and others v United Kingdom* (2005) 41 EHRR 44).

The principles of impartiality and independence have also been applied to judicial decisions taken by officers who have an interest or position in government. For example, in *McGonnell v United Kingdom* (2000) 30 EHRR 289 the Deputy Bailiff of Guernsey (a senior judge in the Royal Court, but also the President of the States of Election, of the States of Deliberation, and of the state legislative committees) had acted as the sole judge in the applicant's planning permission application. The Court held that there had been a clear violation of **article 6**, noting that any direct involvement in the passage of legislation or of executive rules was likely to be sufficient to question the judicial impartiality of someone who subsequently determined a dispute that raised matters of policy. However, the Convention does not prohibit all executive decision-making (*Pabla Ky v Finland* (2006) 42 EHRR 34), and in *Bryan v United Kingdom* (1996) 21 EHRR 342 it was held that, if the decision is sufficiently policy-based and was subject to appropriate judicial review of administrative action, the safeguards of **article 6** would be satisfied. This approach has been adopted by the domestic courts in the post-Human Rights Act era (*MB v Secretary of State for the Home Department* [2006] 3 WLR 839).

Despite the compromise allowed in cases such as *Bryan*, the Court has taken a consistently strict approach with respect to the requirements of impartiality and independence. Such an approach helps to uphold the central feature of the rule of law and general notions of justice.

Question 4

What conclusions can one draw with regard to the compatibility of domestic law with the right to a fair trial with respect to cases brought against the United Kingdom under the **European Convention on Human Rights**?

Commentary

This question calls for a very general overview of cases brought against the United Kingdom under **article 6** of the Convention. There has been a wealth of cases brought under **article 6** on matters such as access to the courts, the presumption of innocence, the impartiality of the court and of judges, availability and access to evidence and witnesses, appeals, legal representation, and remedies and sanctions. The student needs to be aware of a good range of cases brought under this article and should include both successful and unsuccessful applications, although he or she will have to be reasonably selective, presenting the most well-known and influential cases. At this stage of the question the student may wish to present the cases under a variety of headings, as above.

The question also requires a critical assessment of those cases so as to provide an effective analysis of the compatibility of domestic law and procedure in this area with respect to **article 6** and its values. This will require a close examination and analysis of the case law, identifying any common themes of violations and drawing conclusions as to the compatibility of such law and procedure with the general values contained in **article 6**.

 Answer plan

- Brief explanation of the purpose and content of **article 6**
- Examination of the case law of the Convention with respect to alleged violations of **article 6** brought against the United Kingdom
- Identification of central values within **article 6** of the Convention and relevant case law
- Analysis of the above cases to test the general compatibility of domestic law and practice with **article 6**

Suggested answer

Article 6 of the European Convention guarantees the right to a fair and public hearing before an independent and impartial tribunal. This right is fundamental to the notions of justice and equality underpinning both the Convention and domestic law. Such a right has long been accepted in English law (since **Magna Carta 1215**) and is reflected specifically in the rules of natural justice (*Ridge v Baldwin* **[1964] AC 40** and *R v Bow Street Stipendiary Magistrate, ex parte Pinochet Ugarte (No 2)* **[2000] 1 AC 119**).

Despite judicial recognition of this right as a constitutional fundamental, there have been many successful applications brought against the United Kingdom government alleging violations of the right to a fair trial. These cases have concerned a number of specific areas of due process, but have also raised issues with respect to the basic right of access to a judicial remedy. Thus, in *Golder v United Kingdom* (1975) 1 EHRR 524, the Court confirmed that **article 6(1)** contained an implied right of access to the courts and legal advice, and held that there had been a violation of **article 6** when a prisoner had been refused permission to consult a solicitor with a view to bringing civil proceedings. The Court has questioned the domestic law's compromise of this right with respect to groups such as prisoners (*Silver v United Kingdom* (1983) 5 EHRR 347) and bankrupts (*Foxley v United Kingdom* (2001) 31 EHRR 25), and has provided procedural protection to prisoners with respect to fairness at prison disciplinary proceedings (*Ezeh and Connors v United Kingdom* (2004) 39 EHRR 1). In contrast, the domestic courts had classified such proceedings as disciplinary and thus falling outside **article 6** (*R v Secretary of State for the Home Department, ex parte Greenfield* [2002] 1 WLR 545).

The Court has also questioned domestic laws that preclude a party from bringing proceedings against public authorities, and in *Osman v United Kingdom* (2000) 29 EHRR 245 it held that the application of a blanket ban prohibiting civil actions against the police in negligence (*Hill v Chief Constable of West Yorkshire* [1990] 1 WLR 946) constituted a disproportionate restriction on the applicant's right to a fair trial under **article 6**. However, similar immunities have been upheld by the European Court as part of the legitimate substantive law (*Z v United Kingdom* (2002) 34 EHRR 3) and the domestic courts have upheld these in the post-Human Rights Act era with respect to the duty of care owed by the police (*Brooks v Metropolitan Police Commissioner* [2005] 1 WLR 1495). Despite the latitude shown by the European Court in this area, the above cases suggest that domestic law may have been inconsistent in its protection of due process.

Similarly, although the domestic rules of natural justice have protected the right to a fair trial free from bias and the *appearance* of bias (*R v Bow Street Stipendary Magistrate, ex parte Pinochet Ugarte (No 2)* (above)), the government has been found in violation of those principles. For example, in *McGonnell v United Kingdom* (2000) 30 EHRR 289 there had been a violation of **article 6** where the Deputy Bailiff of Guernsey, who carried out roles in all three organs of government, acted as the sole judge in relation to a planning permission application. The Court has taken a similarly robust approach in respect of the impartiality of courts martial, and in *Findlay v United Kingdom* (1997) 24 EHRR 221 it stressed that any such tribunal must be subjectively free of personal prejudice or bias and must offer sufficient safeguards to exclude any legitimate doubt in this respect.

The principles in *McGonnell* and *Findlay* do not, however, preclude an executive officer from making a judicial decision, provided that such a decision is subject to sufficient judicial review (*Bryan v United Kingdom* (1996) 21 EHRR 342). This would appear to legalize many quasi-legal, decision-making processes, and in *MB v Secretary of State for the Home Department* [2006] 2 WLR 839 the Court of Appeal held that control orders effected by the Home Secretary were not in breach of **article 6** provided they were subject to appropriate review by the courts.

Article 6 guarantees the right of effective participation in the proceedings, and in *V and T v United Kingdom* (2000) 30 EHRR 121 it was held that there had been a violation when two 11-year-old boys, charged with murder, had been subjected to an adult-like trial. In the Court's view, the conditions of the trial made it almost impossible for the applicants to understand the proceedings or to effectively consult with their lawyers. Further, in *SC v United Kingdom* (2005) 40 EHRR 10, it held that if a young person faced a criminal trial, it was essential that he should be tried in a specialist tribunal which was able to give full consideration to and make proper allowance for his age and his personal difficulties.

Similarly, the Court has found many violations with respect to the party's inability to present their case effectively during domestic legal proceedings. For example, in *P, C and S v United Kingdom* (2002) 25 EHRR 31 it was held that there had been a violation of **article 6(1)** when the parents of a child felt to be in danger from the mother were not legally represented in either care order or adoption proceedings relating to the child. The Court has been particularly keen in ensuring that the parties to a dispute have the right to present and have access to all relevant evidence before the court. For example, in *Rowe and Davis v United Kingdom* (2000) 30 EHRR 1 it held that **article 6** had been violated when the domestic court had refused, on the grounds of public interest immunity, to order the disclosure of a document at the applicants' trial for murder that referred to evidence given against them by a police informant. Exclusion of evidence on such grounds has been approved of in appropriate cases, provided its application does not interfere with the fundamental right to a fair trial (*Jasper and Fitt v United Kingdom* (2000) 30 EHRR 411), but the decisions in *Dowsett v United Kingdom* (2004) 38 EHRR 41 and *Edwards and Lewis v United Kingdom* (2005) 40 EHRR 24 suggest that the application of public interest immunity in criminal proceedings should be the exception rather than the norm.

Such cases suggest that domestic law often fails to strike an appropriate balance between the individual's right to a fair trial and the successful prosecution of crime. For example, **article 6(2)** states that everyone charged with a criminal offence shall be presumed innocent until proved guilty according to law (*Minelli v Switzerland* (1983) 5 EHRR 554) and that the accused should be protected from self-incrimination. However, in *Saunders v United Kingdom* (1996) 23 EHRR 313 it held that the use by the prosecution at the applicant's trial of statements given under legal compulsion during a statutory investigation violated **article 6**. This decision was followed in *Kansal v United Kingdom* (2004) 39 EHRR 31, where it was held that the use at a subsequent criminal trial of answers given under compulsion under the **Insolvency Act 1986** breached **article 6** of the Convention.

The Court has also examined cases concerning the domestic law's erosion of the 'right to silence'. For example, in *Condron v United Kingdom* (2001) 31 EHRR 1 the European Court affirmed that the right to silence lay at the heart of the notion of a fair procedure and found a violation of **article 6** when the trial judge had given a direction to the jury that might have left them at liberty to draw an adverse inference from the applicant's silence. However, the domestic law in this area (**ss.34–38 of the Criminal Justice and Public Order Act 1994**) appears to be generally in line with the Convention, provided ultimately the applicant receives a fair trial and has received appropriate legal advice. Therefore, in *Murray v United Kingdom* (1996) 22 EHRR 29 the Court held that article 6 did not prevent the applicant's silence from being taken into account in assessing the prosecution's evidence provided there are sufficient safeguards. The Court has also taken a liberal approach to the use of unlawfully obtained evidence (*Schenk v Switzerland* (1988) 13 EHRR 242), and in *Khan v United Kingdom* (2001) 31 EHRR 45 it was held that although evidence used against the applicant in his criminal trial had been obtained in violation of article 8, and the applicant's conviction was based solely on the use of that evidence, the admission of such evidence did not violate article 6, because the trial court had carefully assessed the evidence to see whether its inclusion had caused substantive unfairness.

The Court has been particularly damning where the applicant has been denied legal representation and legal aid. Article 6(3) states that a person has the right to defend himself against any criminal charge and specifically the right to the legal assistance of a person of his own choosing. This right is not absolute, but the Court has found the government in breach on several occasions. For example, in *Benham v United Kingdom* (1996) 29 EHRR 293, article 6 was violated when the applicant had not been provided with legal representation when charged with 'culpable neglect' in failing to pay his community charge, because the charge was not legally straightforward and the applicant's liberty was at stake. Similarly, in *Campbell and Fell v United Kingdom* (1984) 7 EHRR 165, it was held that there had been a violation of this provision when prisoners facing serious disciplinary charges had not been allowed to be legally represented during the hearing. The Court has also found a violation with respect to the denial of pre-trial legal assistance (*Brennan v United Kingdom* (2002) 34 EHRR 18). In addition, article 6(3) specifically provides that if a person has not sufficient means to pay for legal assistance he should be given it free when the interests of justice so require. This provision was violated in *Granger v United Kingdom* (1990) 12 EHRR 496, where a person of limited intelligence had been refused legal aid and the right to be provided with counsel at appeal. Further, in *Steel and Morris v United Kingdom* (2005) 41 EHRR 22 it held that the inability of the applicants to obtain expert legal representation in a long and complicated libel case was in violation of their right to a fair trial.

In addition to the cases above, a number of provisions and practices have been found to be in violation of article 6. These have included convictions based on the findings of a biased juror (*Sander v United Kingdom* (2001) 31 EHRR 44), the delay of legal proceeding, both civil (*Robins v United Kingdom* (1997) 26 EHRR 527) and criminal (*Mellors v United Kingdom* (2004) 38 EHRR 11), the refusal to allow defence witnesses (*Saidi v United Kingdom* (1993) 17 EHRR 251), and the setting of executive sentences (*V and T v United Kingdom* (2000) 30 EHRR 121). Many of these cases might be described as one-offs, where the law or the court has failed to achieve justice in that particular case. However, many other cases, including those concerning the use of public interest immunity and the denial of legal assistance, indicate the domestic law's willingness to compromise due process rights.

Question 5

Why is **article 7** of the European Convention so fundamental to due process? By the use of case law explain how effectively that article has protected individuals from retrospective criminal law and sanctions.

Commentary

This question principally requires a critical examination of **article 7 of the European Convention on Human Rights,** which protects the individual from retrospective criminal charges and penalties. In particular, the student will need to examine the case law of the European Court and Commission of Human Rights in this area to examine the extent of the protection of **article 7,** although students can also use any relevant domestic decisions to the extent that they give guidance on the scope of **article 7.** The student may also highlight other articles under the Convention, such as **article 5** and the variety of conditional rights, which give protection against arbitrary and retrospective interferences with an individual's Convention right via criminal sanctions.

The student should begin by examining the objectives of **article 7** and its importance with respect to the Convention's values, including the rule of law and the regulation of arbitrary criminal law. The answer should then examine the wording of **article 7,** including any restrictions contained in **paragraph 2** of the article, as well as any limitations inherent in **article 7's** interpretation. Extensive use should be made of the leading case law of the European Court and Commission in this area, being careful to explain those decisions in the context of the question and its remit. There has also been some post-Human Rights Act case law that can be analysed in order to explain and critically assess the scope of the protection afforded by **article 7.** The examination of **article 7** can also be supplemented by reference to other Convention articles and relevant case law, protecting an individual from retrospective penalties. The student should end the answer by making some general and specific conclusions regarding the extent of the Convention's protection against retrospective criminal law and sanctions.

Answer plan

- Explanation of the wording and scope of **article 7** of the Convention
- Explanation of the democratic and constitutional values embodied in **article 7** and its relationship with other articles in the Convention
- Detailed consideration of the case law of the European Court and Commission with respect to applications brought under **article 7** and other articles
- Analysis of the effectiveness of **article 7** and the relevant case law in upholding the rule of law and the principles against retrospectivity

Suggested answer

A fundamental aspect of rule of law and the protection of individual liberty is that law should be prospective, as opposed to retrospective. In other words it should regulate the *future* conduct of the individual and should not be applied retrospectively to regulate conduct which at the time of commission was not regulated by clear law. This is particularly fundamental in relation to the criminal law, where an individual's liberty and other rights are subject to sanction by the law. Accordingly, **article 7** of the European Convention upholds the principle that there shall be no punishment without law by stating that no one shall be held guilty of any criminal offence on account of any act or omission which did not constitute a criminal offence under national or international law at the time when it was committed. Further, it guarantees that the law does not impose a heavier penalty than the one that was applicable at the time that the criminal offence was committed.

The European Court has stated that **article 7** occupies a prominent place in the Convention system of rights protection, noting that **article 15** of the Convention, which allows states to derogate from its obligations in times of war or other emergency, does not apply to **article 7**, which must be adhered to in all circumstances (*SW and CR v United Kingdom* (1995) 21 EHRR 404). Further, it has stated that the article not only prohibits retrospective application of criminal law to the accused's disadvantage, including the principle that the law should not be construed by analogy to that person's disadvantage, but also embodies the principle that only the law can define a crime and prescribe a penalty (*Kokkinakis v Greece* (1993) 17 EHRR 397).

Article 7 only applies with respect to 'criminal offences', and in this respect the European Court has applied the same test as it has in relation to **article 6** in determining whether a person is facing a criminal charge (*Engel v Netherlands* (1976) 1 EHRR 647). Consequently, the Court has not restricted the scope of the article to cases which are formally recognized as criminal within domestic law, and has used the same flexible test in interpreting the phrase 'penalty' (*Jamil v France* (1996) 21 EHRR 65). The meaning of the word 'penalty' was considered in detail in the case of *Welch v United Kingdom* (1995) 20 EHRR 247, where the applicant had been convicted of a number of drug offences and where, in addition to imposing a custodial sentence, the trial judge had imposed a confiscation order under the **Drug Trafficking Act 1986**. These measures had come into force after the applicant's arrest but before his conviction and the applicant argued that this violated **article 7**. The Court held that in determining whether there existed such a penalty, it should take into account factors such as whether the measure was imposed following conviction for a criminal offence, the nature and purpose of the measure (including how it is characterized under domestic law), the procedures involved in making and implementing the provision, and its severity. Applying those criteria to the facts of the case, the Court held that there was a strong indication of a regime of punishment and that taking into account a combination of punitive elements involved in the measure, the confiscation order was a penalty within **article 7**.

In *Welch*, the European Court held that the confiscation proceedings were clearly retrospective as they were made in respect of offences committed before the statutory provision came into force. However, this decision was distinguished in the subsequent case of *Taylor v United Kingdom* [1998] EHRLR 90, which again concerned the use of confiscation powers under the 1986 Act, above. The applicant had been found guilty of drug offences with respect to offences committed between 1974 and 1979, and was subsequently convicted of similar offences committed between 1990 and 1993. At his subsequent trial the judge made a confiscation order in respect of all offences and the applicant argued that this contravened **article 7** of the Convention. The European Commission declared his case inadmissible, finding that the penalties imposed on him in the proceedings were essentially for the later offences. Further, the Court noted that the applicant must have been aware that at the time of committing the later offences he was liable to a confiscation order covering the earlier proceeds, as the 1986 Act was then in force.

The decision in *Taylor* illustrates the danger of a restrictive interpretation of **article 7** and this concern is evident in the House of Lords' decision in *R (Uttley) v Secretary of State for the Home Department* [2004] 1 WLR 2278. The case concerned the power of the domestic courts (under the **Criminal Justice Act 1991**) to impose licences on certain prisoners in addition to their fixed sentence, which it was alleged were incompatible with **article 7**. The Court of Appeal held that the imposition of a one-year licence on a prisoner who had served a 12-year sentence for rape and sexual assault was retrospective because the licence applied with respect to acts committed before the Act came into force. He had, therefore, been subjected to a heavier penalty within **article 7**. The Court of Appeal decision was then overturned by the House of Lords, who held that **article 7** referred to the maximum penalty prescribed by law for the offence in question at the time when it was committed, which in the prisoner's case was life imprisonment. In their Lordships' views **article 7** did not refer to the penalty that would *probably* have been imposed on a particular offender at the time. These decisions, it is argued, are based on semantics and ignore the true spirit of **article 7**. Similarly, in *R v Bowker* [2007] EWCA Crim 1608, the Court of Appeal held that it was not in violation of **article 7** to subject a defendant to a harsher penal regime than the one existing at the time of the offence, provided the law itself had not been changed.

A fundamental principle of **article 7** is that a person should foresee the consequences of his action. This principle is threatened when the law is uncertain and thus subject to novel interpretation and application by the courts. This situation would clearly offend against the principle of retrospectivity unless the new interpretation was the result of the natural and foreseeable development of a specific legal rule. The European Court faced this problem in the famous case of *SW and CR v United*

Kingdom (above), concerning the criminalization of marital rape. The applicants had been found guilty of the rape of their wives as a result of a decision of the domestic courts that a husband could no longer rely on the traditional principle of marital immunity (*R v R* [1991] 4 All ER 481). They argued that this decision violated **article 7** as they had in effect been convicted of conduct that at the time of commission did not constitute a criminal offence. The European Court held that **article 7** will not be violated if the constituent elements of an offence are not essentially changed to the detriment of the accused, and where the progressive development of the relevant legal rule is reasonably foreseeable. In the present case the Court found that the traditional immunity granted to husbands had been eroded by a steady number of case authorities, and that the decision of the House of Lords in *R v R* had merely followed that pattern of cases. Consequently, as those cases had been well documented, the Court held that it was inconceivable that either applicant believed that the course of action he embarked upon was lawful.

Further, in that case the European Court held that the abandonment of the unacceptable idea of a husband being immune against prosecution for rape of his wife could not be said to be at variance with **article 7**. In the Court's view, the abandonment of the immunity was in conformity with the fundamental objectives of the Convention, based on the respect for human dignity and human freedom, and of the civilized concept of marriage. Accordingly, the protection afforded by **article 7** does not extend to conduct that violates the fundamental notions underlying the Convention. This is reflected in the second paragraph of the article, which does not provide protection for conduct that is criminal according to the general principles of law recognized by civil nations. This would apply to acts such as torture, and would appear to ensure the compatibility of legislation such as the **War Crimes Act 1991**.

The decision in *SW and CR* accepts that the law will invariably be subject to interpretation and application to new cases, and that although this may act to the detriment of the accused, such an interpretation will not necessarily offend **article 7** and the principles of legal certainty. Thus, in *Gay News v United Kingdom* (1983) 5 EHRR 123 the European Commission held that although the domestic courts must not create new, retroactive criminal offences, or extend existing offences to encompass conduct which was lawful at the time of its commission, it was not in violation of **article 7** for the courts to clarify the requirements of an established offence. In that case the applicant's conviction for blasphemy had been upheld when the House of Lords had confirmed that liability for the offence was strict and did not rely on the intent of the author. In rejecting his application as inadmissible, the Commission held that the decision of the House of Lords did not amount to the creation of new law. Rather, the House of Lords had clarified the law, and the applicants could have foreseen such an interpretation with appropriate legal advice.

In conclusion, **article 7** seeks to protect the most fundamental aspect of criminal justice by prohibiting retrospective law and penalties. This provision is strengthened by other Convention articles, which, along with **article 7**, ensure that any interference with a person's liberty and rights complies with the rule of law. However, the European Court has been prepared on occasions to take a pragmatic approach to the interpretation of these articles, which, it is suggested, has compromised the absolute character of these rights.

Further reading

Amos, M, *Human Rights Law* (OUP 2006), chs 9 and 10.

Clayton, R and Tomlinson, H, *Law of Human Rights*, 2nd edn (OUP 2009), chs 10 and 11.

Emmerson, B and Ashworth, A, *Human Rights and Criminal Justice*, 2nd edn (Sweet and Maxwell 2007), Part 2.

8

Prisoners' rights

Introduction

Prisoners' rights is a growing area and a topic covered on more and more human rights courses. Prisoners' actions have generated a great deal of case law, both under the **European Convention on Human Rights** and in the domestic courts, and a knowledge of this area is essential to understanding many of the human rights principles applied by the courts in the determination of rights disputes. The scope of the topic is determined by the definition of prisoner: some courses will include in that definition anyone in detention and thus include the rights of anyone who is in detention against their will, including detainees at police stations and people under house arrest, while others define prisoners as those who are lawfully detained in prison after a fair trial. These questions concentrate on the rights of those prisoners during incarceration, including such rights as the right to life, freedom from torture and other ill-treatment, the right to private and family life, freedom of speech, and the right to vote, as well as a variety of due process rights such as the right to bring legal proceedings while in prison, the right to be given reasons in respect of decisions which affect them, and the right to a fair trial during disciplinary proceedings.

Students need to be aware of the judicial protection of such rights via public and private law actions, and that with the passing of the **Human Rights Act 1998** prisoners may now use the Act and their Convention rights to challenge various prison practices and decisions, either by bringing a direct action under the 1998 Act or by using the Act, and the case law of the European Convention, to strengthen their public or private law claims.

In particular, students need to be aware of the impact of the **European Convention on Human Rights**, with respect both to the incorporation of the Convention into domestic law via the **Human Rights Act 1998** and the impact of the case law of the European Court and Commission of Human Rights in this area on the vindication of prisoners' rights. More specialist courses may also expect knowledge of other international treaties and documents such as the **International Covenant on Civil and Political Rights, the European Convention on the Prevention of Torture,** and the **European Prison Rules.**

Questions in this area may be aimed at any or all of the above aspects and the student should have an understanding of how each aspect is related to the other. For example, to answer a question on the public law rights of prisoners, one has to be aware not only of the principles and grounds of judicial review and the relevant case law, but also the rules relating to the application of the **Human Rights Act** to such actions, including the extent to which the case law of the European Convention can be used to determine such a dispute. The diagram below should be helpful in this respect. It is also quite common to have questions directed at a specific area of prisoners' rights, such as prison discipline, release and recall, and correspondence. Finally, many questions will ask for a critical analysis of the law and its application, requiring students to appreciate the theory of prisoners' rights and the arguments for and against their protection.

Prisoners' rights — possible legal claims

Domestic law

Civil actions (e.g. negligence and assault)
1. To enforce the prisoner's private law claims
2. Civil action in the County or High Court
3. The European Convention relevant to decide whether the authorities are liable and in considering the level of damages

Public law actions (i.e. judicial review)
1. To enforce the prisoner's public law claims
2. Initiated by an application for judicial review
3. Prisoner must have 'sufficient interest' and the action must be against a public body
4. Provisions of the Human Rights Act 1998 (below) apply to such proceedings if the prisoner is a 'victim'
5. Damages also available if there has been a distinct breach of the prisoner's private law rights

Actions under the Human Rights Act 1998
1. Prisoner must be a 'victim'
2. Action must be brought against a public authority
3. Courts must apply the principles and case law of the Convention
4. Courts must interpret statutory provisions in line with the Convention
5. Higher courts may award a 'declaration of incompatibility'
6. Courts have the power to award just satisfaction for breach of Convention rights

International law

The European Convention on Human Rights
1. Prisoners may bring proceedings before the European Court
2. The UK is bound to comply with the Court's judgments
3. After the 1998 Act, Convention rights can be enforced directly in the domestic courts
4. Prisoner must exhaust all domestic remedies before applying to the Court

The International Covenant on Civil and Political Rights
1. UN Covenant binding in international law and containing a list of civil and political rights
2. UK is not a party to the protocol allowing individual applications to be made to the Human Rights Committee
3. UK's obligations are enforced via a state reporting mechanism
4. Covenant has persuasive authority in the domestic courts

Question 1

Critically examine the extent to which prisoners' rights have been protected in domestic law. By the use of case law explain how their protection has been enhanced in the post-Human Rights Act era.

Commentary

This question is quite broad, requiring an appreciation of prisoners' rights, a knowledge of and critical analysis of how they have been protected in domestic law (as opposed to under the **European Convention on Human Rights**—although a discussion of how the Convention has informed UK law will be required), and an explanation, via relevant case law, of how those rights have been enhanced after the coming into operation of the **Human Rights Act 1998.** The question requires students to briefly identify the nature and characteristics of prisoners' rights, including, briefly, the rationale of protecting such rights. The main part requires the student to critically assess how such claims are accommodated in domestic law by statute and by the judiciary (the student may also consider, briefly, non-judicial means such as the prison complaints system and the Prisons Ombudsman). Finally, the student should explain to what extent the case law in the post-Human Rights Act era has enhanced the protection of those rights. In relation to this part, students are not expected to conclude that the Act has automatically enhanced such rights, but should carefully consider the extent to which the Act has indeed led to greater protection. This will depend on their conclusions to the first part of the question and it may be quite feasible to conclude that the Act has had little effect. The second part can be answered by considering the post-Act case law in general or by looking at specific areas and cases, but in either instance the student should select their cases carefully and not just provide a list of all cases decided in that period. The student may also consider any legislative changes introduced in this era.

Answer plan

- The definition and scope of prisoners' rights
- Justification for the protection of prisoners' rights
- Examples of prisoners' rights, using relevant **European Convention** and **Human Rights Act** provisions
- Critical account of the methods of enforcement in domestic law via statute, actions in public and private law
- Case law under the **Human Rights Act,** and any relevant legislative changes, as evidence of any enhanced protection of such rights

Suggested answer

The question is concerned with the extent to which a lawfully detained prisoner can claim his or her fundamental rights despite (lawful) incarceration.

Prisoners' rights may refer to the prisoners' civil and political rights, the prisoner claiming that he or she retains those basic rights despite incarceration, save the inevitable interference with freedom of movement and personal liberty. This claim is supported by both the European Court (see *Golder v United Kingdom* (1975) 1 EHRR 524), and by the statement of Lord Wilberforce in *Raymond v Honey* [1983] AC 1 that a prisoner retains all basic rights save those which are taken away either expressly or by necessary implication. In addition, prisoners may claim basic human needs, such as the right to decent food, clothing, and accommodation in prison, the state having a duty to protect the prisoners' dignity by providing those resources.

Whatever the nature of prisoners' rights, they can be justified on several bases. First, the inherent dignity of every individual demands that they be treated with dignity and respect irrespective of their predicament or past actions. Secondly, they can be justified with reference to the rule of law, requiring the prison authorities to justify the use of their powers by reference to clear and fair legal regulation and demanding that such officials be legally accountable for misuse of their powers. Thirdly, the protection of prisoners' rights might serve a number of penal purposes, such as the rehabilitation of the prisoner.

Domestically, in the absence of a bill of rights and any clear and comprehensive system of statutory protection, such rights have principally fallen to be protected by the courts, although there do exist several quasi-legal remedies such as recourse to the internal complaints mechanism and the Prisons Ombudsman. First, a number of private law actions are available to prisoners, and, in *Ellis v Home Office* [1953] 2 QB 135 it was accepted that the prison authorities owed the prisoner a duty to take reasonable care for his or her safety, thus enabling the prisoner to sue in the tort of negligence. It is also possible for the prisoner to sue in the tort of assault (*Rodrigues v Home Office* [1989] Legal Action 14) and for misfeasance in a public office (*Racz v Home Office* [1984] 2 AC 45). However, in *R v Deputy Governor of Parkhurst Prison, ex parte Hague* [1992] AC 58 the House of Lords held that the fact of imprisonment precluded the prisoner from suing in the torts of false imprisonment and breach of statutory duty.

The prisoner is allowed to bring proceedings in public law (judicial review) to ensure that the prison authorities act within their legal powers. Although early case law seemed to suggest that the decisions of such bodies were not reviewable (*Becker v Home Office* [1972] 2 QB 407), later decisions accepted that the prison authorities were susceptible to judicial review and the principles of natural justice. Thus, in *R v Board of Visitors of Hull Prison, ex parte St Germaine* [1979] QB 425 the Court of Appeal held that some disciplinary powers were amenable to judicial review, and in *ex parte Hague* (above) it was accepted that, at least in theory, all prison decisions affecting prisoners were reviewable.

Using judicial review the courts have declared a variety of practices and policies *ultra vires*, often on the basis that the rule or decision was contrary to the prisoner's fundamental rights. For example, in *Raymond v Honey* (above) a rule that stopped a prisoner from taking legal action until he or she had exhausted the internal procedures was declared *ultra vires* the **Prison Act 1952** on the grounds that the rule-making powers in the Act did not envisage a policy that interfered with the prisoner's right of access to the courts. This decision was influenced by the case law of the European Court of Human Rights (*Golder v United Kingdom* (above)) and in subsequent cases, rules which interfered with the prisoner's right of access to legal advice and access to the courts were declared void on that basis (see *R v Secretary of State for the Home Department, ex parte Anderson* [1984] QB 788 and *R v Secretary of State for the Home Department, ex parte Leech* [1994] QB 198).

Judicial review has also been employed to protect the rights of prisoners with respect to release and recall and executive sentencing. (See, for example, *R v Secretary of State for the Home Department, ex parte Pierson* [1998] AC 539, where the House of Lords held that the Home Secretary did not have the power to increase an executive sentence, and *R v Secretary of State for the Home Department, ex parte Venables and Thompson* [1997] 3 All ER 97, where the House of Lords held that the Home Secretary could not take into account public opinion in setting the minimum term for two boys found guilty of murder.) In addition, in *Doody v Secretary of State for the Home Department* [1994] 1 AC 531 the House of Lords held that the Home Secretary must give reasons for his decision to set a minimum term.

Using this process the courts have been able to uphold a prisoner's Convention rights. For example, the courts have recognized the prisoner's right of freedom of expression and in *R v Secretary of State for the Home Department, ex parte O'Brien and Simms* [2000] 2 AC 115 the House of Lords struck down a policy which stopped direct contact between journalists and prisoners on the basis that it interfered with the prisoners' right to use journalists to expose a possible miscarriage of justice. However, they were not allowed to use such principles or case law directly. Consequently, the courts often sided with the prison authorities and held that any interference was rational and lawful. (See, for example, *R v Secretary of State for the Home Department, ex parte Mellor* [2002] QB 13, which upheld the decision of the Home Secretary to refuse a prisoner's request to artificially inseminate his wife.)

The passing of the **Human Rights Act 1998** made the Convention directly applicable in domestic courts and a prisoner may (under **s.7**) bring a direct action against the prison authorities (a public authority) claiming that his or her Convention rights have been violated or to continue to bring judicial review proceedings, relying on Convention principles, such as proportionality and legality. The prisoner will also be entitled (under s.8) to 'just satisfaction' if the court decides that his Convention rights have been violated. In addition, the prisoner may use the Convention and its case law to strengthen his claim in private law. For example, in *Russell, McNamee and McCotter v Home Office, The Daily Telegraph*, 13 March 2001 it was held that an assault by prison officers on an escaping prisoner was not only actionable at common law, but also constituted inhuman treatment under **article 3** of the Convention. **Articles 2 and 3** of the Convention will also be relevant in determining negligence claims brought by prisoners (*Orange v Chief Constable of West Yorkshire* [2001] 3 WLR 736).

There is indeed evidence that prisoners' rights will be enhanced by the Act. In *R (Daly) v Secretary of State for the Home Department* [2001] 2 AC 532 Lord Steyn noted that the doctrine of proportionality called for a much more intensive review on behalf of the courts and stressed that any interference with Convention rights had to be necessary in a democratic society and be proportionate to any legitimate aim. The prisoner can thus expect the courts to scrutinize the legality and proportionality of restrictions on their rights to a greater extent. For example, in *R v Secretary of State for the Home Department, ex parte P and Q* [2001] 3 WLR 2002 the Court of Appeal found that a blanket policy which meant that female prisoners were separated from their babies after eighteen months was unlawful as it gave too little weight to the mother's right to private and family life under **article 8** of the Convention. The willingness of the court in this case to ensure that a proper balance is achieved can be contrasted with the decision in *Mellor* (above) and suggests that prisoners' rights will not be so easily compromised on the grounds of prison discipline and public policy.

The Act should also ensure that prisoners' rights are not violated purely on the grounds of incarceration. Certain pre-Act case law suggested that prisoners could forgo certain rights, such as freedom of expression, by implication. Thus, in *O'Brien and Simms* (above) the House of Lords held that prisoners could not expect to enjoy the general right to freedom of expression. Such views appear to be contrary to the jurisprudence of the European Court of Human Rights (*Golder v United Kingdom* (above)) and post-Act case law suggests that any interference with a prisoner's Convention rights needs to be justified solely on the grounds permitted by the Convention itself. This approach is reflected by the decision in *R (Hirst) v Secretary of State for the Home Department* [2002] 1 WLR 2929, where it was held that a blanket policy forbidding prisoners from directly accessing the media was disproportionate to the aim of achieving good order and discipline in prisons.

On the other hand, in *R (Nilsen) v Secretary of State for Home Affairs* [2005] 1 WLR 1028 the Court of Appeal held that the prison authorities could take into account factors beyond prison order and discipline in deciding to restrict the claimant's right to freedom of expression. Equally, in *Hirst v Attorney-General, The Times,* 17 April 2001 the domestic courts referred to public policy arguments in deciding that the disenfranchisement of prisoners was not contrary to **Article 3 of the First Protocol** of the European Convention, a decision overturned by the European Court in subsequent proceedings (*Hirst v United Kingdom (No 2)* (2004) 38 EHRR 40). Such decisions appear to go against the principles laid down in cases such as *Golder* and *Raymond v Honey*, above, and the recent decision of the Grand Chamber of the European Court in *Dickson v United Kingdom* (2008) 46 EHRR 41 reaffirms the principle that restrictions on prisoners' fundamental rights must be proportionate and give proper weight to such rights.

With respect to prison conditions, the lack of any statutory protection in this area made it difficult for prisoners to challenge the legality of the conditions of incarceration. However, prisoners can now rely directly on **article 3** of the Convention, which prohibits inhuman and degrading treatment, and the increasing case law of the European Court in this area. (See, for example, *Peers v Greece* (2001) 33 EHRR 51.) Thus, in *Napier v*

Scottish Ministers, The Times, **13 May 2004** the Scottish Courts awarded damages to a remand prisoner who had been subjected to the harshness of prison conditions, including the regime of 'slopping out'. **Article 3** can also been used to challenge such practices as force feeding and strip searches, although in *R (Carroll and Al-Hasan) v Secretary of State for the Home Department* [2002] 1 WLR 545 the Court of Appeal held that such searches were not contrary to **article 3** provided they were carried out sensitively.

In conclusion, the **Human Rights Act 1998** should provide a more formal mechanism by which prisoners can vindicate their civil and political rights. In addition, prisoners will be able to rely on the principles of administrative justice and their civil law claims, which should also be enhanced by the Convention and its case law. This enhanced judicial enforcement should also raise the public and political profile of such rights, leading to reforms in areas such as prison conditions and discipline and perhaps persuading Parliament to recognize such rights as the right to vote in primary legislation. However, as the case of *Nilsen* (above) suggests, there is still some evidence of judicial reluctance in this area, which has not been affected by the Act's implementation.

Question 2

By the use of case law, critically examine how successfully the European Court and Commission of Human Rights have protected prisoners' rights.

 Commentary

This question requires the student to consider the massive amount of case law of the European Court and Commission of Human Rights in the area of prisoners' rights. Those bodies have dealt with cases on the right to life, freedom from torture and ill-treatment, prison conditions, release of prisoners, prison discipline, correspondence, visits, and other aspects of family and private life. Students should not attempt this question unless they have a fairly comprehensive knowledge of such case law, although they should not just list the cases in an attempt to cover them all. They can, therefore, be selective and cover the most important cases, or make it clear that they are only going to cover a number of areas in any detail. The question asks how successful the Court and Commission have been in protecting such rights and thus the student needs to consider the success rate of prisoners in this area as well as the reforms that have resulted from the judgments. They will also need to identify where the Court and Commission have been most successful—for example, in relation to access to the courts and the release of prisoners—as well as those areas where those bodies have taken a less robust approach—until recently, prison conditions, and certain aspects of the prisoner's right to family life.

Answer plan

- The definition of prisoners' rights and a brief consideration of the Convention rights relevant to prisoners
- Case law demonstrating the areas of prisoners' rights that have been upheld by the European Convention machinery
- The effectiveness of the Court and Commission in upholding those rights
- Changes to domestic law and practice resulting from the Convention case law
- Areas where the Convention machinery has been unsuccessful in protecting prisoners' rights

Suggested answer

Prisoners have used the European Convention to protect a wide range of human rights, including the right to life, freedom from torture and inhuman and degrading treatment and punishment, liberty and security of the person, the right to private and family life, and the right to vote. Many of these cases have been successful and have resulted in changes to domestic law and practice in areas such as prisoners' correspondence (*Silver v United Kingdom* (1983) 5 EHRR 347), the right to marry (*Hamer v United Kingdom* (1982) 4 EHRR 139), and the right of access to lawyers and the courts (*Golder v United Kingdom* (1975) 1 EHRR 524).

The European Court and Commission have stated that prisoners retain their basic rights despite incarceration, and have insisted that any restriction on the prisoner's Convention rights must be justified within the terms of the Convention. For example, in *Golder v United Kingdom* (above) the Court stressed that there were no implied restrictions on the prisoner's right to correspondence under **article** 8 of the Convention and that any interference with the right has to be in accordance with law and necessary in a democratic society. This approach is taken in respect of other rights, such as freedom of expression (*Bamber v United Kingdom*, **Application No** 33742/96), the right to vote (*Hirst v United Kingdom (No 2)* (2004) 38 EHRR 40), and the enjoyment of private life (*Silver v United Kingdom* (above)), although the Court has recognized that the enjoyment of these rights may have to be compromised by reasonable prison regulations (*Boyle and Rice v United Kingdom* (1988) 10 EHRR 425).

This general stance was threatened by the decision of the Court in *Dickson v United Kingdom* (2007) 44 EHRR 21, where it was held that it was permissible for the authorities to take into account public confidence in the penal system in placing restrictions on the prisoner's right to family and private life. However, on appeal to the Grand Chamber ((2008) 46 EHRR 41), it was held that before such rights are interfered with the authorities and the courts must adopt a suitable balance between the prisoner's right and the competing public interests.

With respect to the right of access to the courts and the protection of legal correspondence, in *Golder v United Kingdom* (above) the Court held that preventing a prisoner from writing to a solicitor in order to bring a civil action against a prison officer was a disproportionate interference with the prisoner's right of correspondence and access to the courts. This was followed in *Silver v United Kingdom* (above) and *Campbell v United Kingdom* (1992) 15 EHRR 137, and in the latter case the Court held that any interference with the prisoner's right of correspondence with his lawyer had to be justified by a pressing social need, such as the need to ensure that such correspondence was genuine and not a threat to prison security. The Court has also upheld the prisoner's right of medical correspondence (*Szuluk v United Kingdom, The Times,* 17 June 2009) and of general correspondence (*Silver v United Kingdom* (above)), insisting that any restrictions on prisoner's correspondence should be measured by clear and regular law rather than executive or judicial discretion (*Domenichini v Italy* (2001) 32 EHRR 4).

Prisoners have employed **article 5** of the Convention in challenging a number of rules regarding their release at the discretion of administrative officials. In *Thynne, Wilson and Gunnell v United Kingdom* (1990) 13 EHRR 666 the Court held that there had been a violation of **article 5(4)** of the Convention—which guarantees the right to challenge the lawfulness of one's continued detention—when three discretionary life-sentence prisoners had been denied release by the Home Secretary on the grounds that he still felt them to be a risk to the public. Once the punitive period of the sentence was complete the prisoners had the right for their continued detention to be determined by a court-like body, which should have the power to order, rather than recommend, release. This principle was upheld in the context of young offenders detained at Her Majesty's Pleasure in *Hussain and Singh v United Kingdom* (1996) 21 EHRR 1 and *V and T v United Kingdom* (2000) 30 EHRR 121, and with respect to mandatory sentences for murder in *Stafford v United Kingdom* (2002) 35 EHRR 32 the Court overruled its previous case law and found that the power of the Home Secretary to determine the prisoner's release on grounds of public safety was inconsistent with the notion of the separation of powers and thus in violation of **article 5**. Such prisoners now have the right to have their release determined by a court-like body, such as the Parole Board and the Discretionary Lifer Panel.

With respect to prison discipline, the Court has held that prisoners will be entitled to the protection of **article 6**, guaranteeing the right to a fair trial by an independent tribunal, where the disciplinary charges amount to a 'criminal charge'. In *Campbell and Fell v United Kingdom* (1984) 7 EHRR 165, the Court held that the prisoner had been subjected to a criminal charge when he had been given 570 days loss of remission after having been found guilty. Accordingly, the prisoner was entitled to legal representation under **article 6(3)** of the Convention and there had been a violation when this had been refused. More significantly, in *Ezeh and Connors v United Kingdom* (2004) 39 EHRR 1 the Grand Chamber of the European Court held that there had been a similar violation of **article 6** when additional days (up to 40 days) had been imposed on the prisoners and their request for legal representation had been denied. Further, the decision of the European Court in *Whitfield v United Kingdom* (2005) 41 EHRR 44, held that a governor's disciplinary decision did not satisfy the requirement of impartiality laid down in **article 6**.

The European Court has accepted that the state has a duty to protect the prisoner's life from attack by state officials, and that it must take steps to protect the prisoner from fellow inmates. For example, in *Edwards v United Kingdom* (2002) 35 EHRR 19, the Court found a violation of **article 2** when a violent cell mate who, according to the Court should not have been housed with the victim, had beaten the applicants' son to death in his cell. The Court also found that the state has a duty to conduct a proper investigation into a prison death and in that case there had been no such effective investigation. In addition, the Court has found that liability under **article 2** might be engaged where a prisoner takes his own life due to the negligence of the prison authorities. Thus, in *Keenan v United Kingdom* (2001) 33 EHRR 38 the Court accepted that the prison authorities would have a duty under **article 2** to ensure that prisoners do not take their own lives.

The European Court and Commission have also been successful in recognizing the democratic rights of prisoners. The Commission recognized that the prisoner retains his fundamental right of free speech. For example, in *T v United Kingdom* (1986) 49 DR 5 the Commission held that there had been a violation of **article 10** when the prisoner's freedom of expression was restricted as part of a disciplinary punishment. Further, in *Bamber v United Kingdom* (above), it was accepted that a regulation which stopped a prisoner from contacting the media interfered with the prisoner's **article 10** rights. In addition, the Court recognized that prisoners have the *prima facie* right to vote in the recent case of *Hirst v United Kingdom (No 2)* (above), where it was held that the blanket disenfranchisement of convicted prisoners was an arbitrary and disproportionate violation of **article 3 of the First Protocol** to the Convention.

Despite these successes, the Court and Commission have shown a more hands-off approach in the challenge to prison conditions and various aspects of the prisoner's right to private and family life. Thus in *Boyle and Rice v United Kingdom* (above) it was accepted that the prisoner's visiting rights are necessarily curtailed in regulations which reflect the ordinary and reasonable requirements of imprisonment. Specifically, in *X v United Kingdom* (1979) 2 DR 105 and *ELH and PBH v United Kingdom* [1998] EHRLR 231 it was held that the denial of a prisoner's conjugal rights was not in violation of the prisoner's family and private rights. However, the Court's deference in this area is not absolute and in *Hamer v United Kingdom* (above) the Commission held that the denial of the convicted prisoner's right to marry struck at the very essence of the right to marry as guaranteed under **article 12**.

With respect to prison conditions, the early case law of the European Commission displayed a marked reluctance to apply **article 3**. Thus in cases such as *Hilton v United Kingdom* (1981) 3 EHRR 104 and *B v United Kingdom* (1987) 10 DR 87 it was ruled that although the conditions of imprisonment were unsatisfactory (and had been deemed such by the European Committee on Torture), they did not cross the threshold required for it to find a violation of **article 3**. More recently the European Court has delivered a number of judgments in favour of the prisoner. Thus, in *Peers v Greece* (2001) 33 EHRR 51 it was held that the subjection of the applicant to unsanitary, cramped, and dark conditions amounted to inhuman and degrading treatment, and similar judgments were made in *Dougoz v Greece* (2002) 34 EHRR 61 and *Kalashnikov v Russia* (2003) 36 EHRR 34. The Court has taken a particularly robust approach with respect to mentally and physically disabled prisoners, insisting that such prisoners receive proper treatment and attention (*Keenan v United Kingdom* (above), *McGlinchey v United Kingdom* (2003) 37 EHRR 41, and *Price v United Kingdom* (2002) 34 EHRR 53).

In conclusion, the case law of the European Court and Commission has resulted in a number of high-profile and successful claims being brought by prisoners, which have not only secured changes in the domestic law, but have also led to a marked change in judicial attitudes in the domestic courts. The Court has taken a robust approach in areas of prisoners' correspondence, access to the courts, prison discipline, and the release of life-sentence prisoners and, to a lesser extent, the prisoner's right to life. There is also evidence that the Court is prepared to find certain conditions and practices inconsistent with **article 3**, especially where the prisoner has special physical or mental needs. However, the Court is still prepared to offer prison authorities a wide margin of error in certain areas, such as prison visits (particularly conjugal visits). Notwithstanding this area of discretion, the recent decision in *Hirst v United Kingdom (No 2)* (above) reflects the Court's view that prisoners are entitled to the enjoyment of their Convention rights and that such rights are not lost automatically on incarceration.

Question 3

In January 2010 the Home Secretary introduced some changes to the Prison Rules. Prisoners found guilty of a breach of prison discipline, and who showed via that conduct a complete disregard of prison administration and respect to other prisoners, were subject to new punishments to be introduced by the Rules. This would involve being removed to an annexe of the prison and being forced to endure conditions 'below those expected in normal prison life', including 'slopping out', the prohibition of any association with those other than the prisoners' cell mates and the application of army-type work and exercise schedules. The Rules also allow for all correspondence to be opened and read, and prohibit all visits during the period of the punishment. Stan and Rodney, two category C prisoners, were found guilty of persistently harassing other prisoners and were subjected to the new rules for two weeks, being released under supervision at the weekend to clear the snow off football grounds. Whilst travelling to and from the prison Stan and Rodney were chained to each other.

Stan and Rodney now bring legal proceedings challenging the legality of those Rules and their application. In particular they refer you to the following:

Article 3 of the European Convention on Human Rights—No one shall be subject to torture or to inhuman or degrading treatment or punishment.

Article 4 of the European Convention on Human Rights—No one shall be held in slavery or servitude.

Article 8 of the European Convention on Human Rights—Everyone has the right to respect for his private and family life, his home, and his correspondence.

Article 10 of the International Covenant on Civil and Political Rights—All persons deprived of their liberty shall be treated with humanity and with respect for the inherent dignity of the individual.

Advise the prisoners whether they can make a claim under any of these provisions and the likely success of those claims in domestic law.

 Commentary

This question requires students to appreciate the various international law provisions for protecting prisoners' rights and the possible application of those principles in domestic proceedings. The student will need to be conversant with the provisions of and the case law under the **European Convention on Human Rights**, in particular the standards inherent in **articles 3, 4, and 8** of the Convention and any relevant case law, and of the application and scope of **article 10** of the **International Covenant**. Initially the question asks the student whether those provisions can be used in domestic law proceedings, in other words whether those provisions are directly or indirectly enforceable and the method by which the domestic courts would or could use those principles to resolve the claims brought by the prisoners. The question also requires the student to be conversant with the principles and case law relating to each particular provision, so as to enable the student to provide constructive advice as to the likely success of the prisoners' claims.

It is advisable to answer the question in relation to individual headings so that the prisoners' claims can be dealt with separately under each article. The author can then use these headings to deal with the prisoners' claims in domestic law. This should enable the student to provide a coherent answer, dealing with the relevant points clearly and in order.

 Answer plan

- Consideration of proceedings under the **Human Rights Act 1998** or judicial review
- Consideration of whether various international law provisions are applicable in such proceedings
- Consideration of the principles and scope of those provisions and of any relevant case law
- Application of those principles and case law to the facts of the case
- Conclusion as to the likely success of the various claims

Suggested answer

Introduction

The prisoners' claims are in public law and should be pursued either directly under the **Human Rights Act 1998** or via judicial review. Both procedures will be open to the prisoners because the Home Secretary will be a 'public authority' under **s.6** of the 1998 Act and a 'public body' for the purpose of judicial review, and the prisoners are victims under the 1998 Act, and have sufficient interest to bring a claim in judicial review. Bringing proceedings under judicial review will allow the prisoners to utilize not only their rights under the **European Convention on Human Rights**, but also the general grounds of judicial review such as *ultra vires*, and, possibly any rights they may have under the **International Covenant on Civil and Political Rights 1966**.

Article 3 of the ECHR

Article 3 is a scheduled right under the **Human Rights Act 1998** and thus the prisoners can claim a violation of that article in the domestic proceedings. In such a case under **s.2** of the **Human Rights Act 1998** the court would need to take into account the case law of the European Court and Commission of Human Rights in considering whether there has been a violation on the facts.

The European Court in *Ireland v United Kingdom* (1978) 2 EHRR 25 defined torture as deliberate inhuman treatment causing very serious and cruel suffering; inhuman punishment or treatment such that it causes intense physical or mental suffering or acute psychiatric disturbance; and degrading treatment or punishment such as to arouse feelings of fear, anguish and inferiority capable of humiliating the victim and of taking away his or her physical or moral resistance. Whether there is a violation has to be decided by reference to all the relevant circumstances of the case, including the age and health of the applicant (*Tyrer v United Kingdom* (1978) 2 EHRR 1). Relevant factors in our case might be the reason for the treatment or punishment, the health and age of the prisoners, and the period of the alleged ill-treatment. In particular, to come within **article 3**, the suffering or humiliation endured by the applicant must go beyond that inevitable element of hardship associated with a legitimate form of treatment or punishment, and, in particular, must exceed the harshness normally associated with incarceration (*Papon v France* (2004) 39 EHRR 10).

We shall first consider the general conditions of imprisonment imposed by the new rules and their compatibility with that article. The court can take each claim separately, but is also likely to consider the cumulative effect of each claim in determining whether there was a violation of **article 3**. For example, in *Peers v Greece* (2001) 33 EHRR 51 it held that the applicant had been subjected to inhuman and degrading treatment when he was forced to share a cramped and poorly lit and ventilated cell with another prisoner and was also forced to share toilet facilities with that prisoner. Similarly, in *Napier v Scottish Ministers, The Times*, 13 May 2004 the Scottish courts found a violation of **article 3** when a remand prisoner with a skin complaint had been subjected to conditions including 'slopping out' and very limited time out of a single cell shared with another inmate. In our case, therefore, although the lack of association with other prisoners would not be regarded as serious enough to constitute a violation of **article 3**, unless it had a particularly harsh effect on a particular prisoner, the cumulative effect of those conditions, particularly the imposition of slopping out as a punishment, as opposed to an economic or security necessity, would in all likelihood result in the finding of a violation of **article 3**; the short-term detriment to the prisoners being offset by the fact that the conditions were imposed as a punishment and possibly with the intention to humiliate the prisoners.

Turning to forcing the prisoners to undertake work on football grounds, it is most unlikely that the court would feel that the necessary threshold had been met by this fact alone. Such work would appear to be a normal part of community service expected of a prisoner on release from detention, and although it might cause a good deal of embarrassment to the prisoners it is not likely to involve sufficient humiliation so as to constitute degrading treatment. However, the fact that the prisoners are chained together whilst travelling to and from the work could amount to such a violation. Although the handcuffing of prisoners is not inevitably in violation of **article 3** (*Raninen v Finland* **(1998) 26 EHRR 563**; *R (Faizovas) v Secretary of State for Justice, The Times,* **25** May **2009**), there could be a violation if such treatment is unnecessary with respect to the particular prisoner, or where the handcuffing would have a deleterious effect on the prisoner's mental or physical health. This would be the case particularly if the chaining of the prisoners was done with the deliberate intention of humiliating the prisoners.

Article 4 of the ECHR

Although **article 4** states that no one shall be required to perform forced or compulsory labour, **article 4(2)** excludes from the definition of forced or compulsory labour, work that is required to be done in the ordinary course of detention and work done during conditional release from such detention. Thus, although the prisoners in our case may feel that their subjection to army-type work is forced labour, it would be argued that such work is required in the ordinary course of prison detention. This would certainly be the case with the task of clearing the snow off football grounds, as this appears to be work done during conditional release, and such tasks would be regarded as the type of community services normally imposed on prisoners in such circumstances. This finding would not preclude the prisoners from claiming that the work is degrading within **article 3** (above).

Although the prisoners might not succeed in their claim under **article 4**, it might be argued that the imposition of army-type work and schedules is *ultra vires* the purpose and aim of the **Prison Act 1952**, and that the new rules are illegal on that ground. Thus, as the Home Secretary's powers are to pass regulations concerning the management of prisons and prisoners therein, it could be argued that the new rules are more appropriate to the armed forces and thus outside the powers granted by the Act.

Article 8 of the ECHR

The right to private and family life and correspondence is clearly engaged by the change to the rules and the prisoners can claim that the new rules impose an unnecessary and disproportionate interference with the prisoners' right to private correspondence and to contacts, especially with their family and legal advisers. Any interference with the prisoner's right needs to be in accordance with law and necessary in a democratic society for achieving a legitimate aim as required by **article 8(2)**.

As the new rules apply irrespective of the prisoner's need and content of the correspondence, they could be regarded as arbitrary (see, for example *Silver v United Kingdom* (1983) 5 EHRR 347). In addition, they may well be *ultra vires* the **Prison Act 1952** (see later). The new rules appear to have been passed with the legitimate aim of protecting the rights of others and of upholding prison security and discipline, although it is doubtful whether there was a pressing social need for their introduction and there does not appear to be a proportionate balance between the achievement of prison order and the grave interference with the prisoner's rights to correspondence, particularly if the prisoner's legal and family correspondence was subject to the new regulations. Such interference with the prisoner's legal correspondence would undoubtedly be in violation of **articles 6 and 8** of the Convention (see *Golder v United Kingdom* (1975) 1 EHRR 524 and *Campbell v United Kingdom* (1992) 15 EHRR 137), unless the courts could interpret the new rules so as to exclude any interference with legal correspondence and contacts. It is also likely that the courts would strike down the blanket penalty on visits as being an arbitrary and disproportionate interference with family and private rights.

The rules could also be challenged under more traditional grounds. It is questionable whether the prison authorities should use the withdrawal of fundamental rights as a form of punishment unless there are exceptional circumstances. This would reflect on the legality of the measures under the Prison Act as well as to their necessity, as surely other less intrusive methods of punishment could be employed. The courts could presume that any unnecessary interference with fundamental rights was not to be sanctioned by Parliament (see, for example *Raymond v Honey* [1983] AC 1 and *R (Daly) v Secretary of State for the Home Department* [2001] 2 AC 532), particularly as the **Prison Rules** themselves (in **Rules 34–35**) state that any interference with correspondence and contact rights must be proportionate and necessary.

Article 10 of the ICCPR

The **International Covenant on Civil and Political Rights 1966** is a UN treaty ratified by the United Kingdom government, but its rights are not scheduled under the **Human Rights Act 1998** and thus have no direct applicability under that Act. The terms of **article 10** are wider and possibly more generous than **article 3** of the European Convention and a court might regard certain conditions as a violation of a prisoner's inherent dignity even though it might not be of the opinion that the conditions are inhuman or degrading under **article 3**. Given the fact that the purpose of the Human Rights Act is to give effect to European Convention rights, it is likely that the domestic courts would rely on the established case law of **article 3** of the European Convention to resolve any dispute. In *A v Secretary of State for the Home Department (No 2)* [2006] 2 AC 221, the House of Lords accepted that in appropriate cases Convention rights could be interpreted as being in compliance with other, non-incorporated, rules of international law, in that case on the exclusion of torture evidence in legal proceedings. In our scenario it is unlikely that **article 10** of the International Covenant can add anything to the existing European case law and thus to the prisoners' claims. Further, although the UK is a party to the Covenant, it has not ratified the optional protocol allowing the Human Rights Committee to consider individual applications.

Conclusions

In conclusion, the prisoners could use **articles 3, 4, and 8** of the European Convention to mount challenges to the new rules in domestic proceedings. Although some of their claims under **article 3** are likely to fail, as is the claim under **article 4**, there is a strong possibility that the courts would declare the practice of slopping out and the chaining of the prisoners as contrary to **article 3**, in which case the court is likely to award damages for non-pecuniary loss as just satisfaction. The claim under **article 8** is also likely to succeed, as the new rules appear to impose an unnecessary and disproportionate interference with the prisoners' rights to correspondence and family life. Ironically, the prisoners' best chance of success may lie with the employment of traditional grounds of judicial review, as there is a strong case for claiming that the new rules, especially the introduction of army-type work, is *ultra vires* the main purpose of the **Prison Act 1952** and thus beyond the powers of the Home Secretary, whose main function is to make rules regarding the management of prisons and prisoners. Similarly, the new rules on correspondence may be thought to be irrational or illegal as they seek to use the infringement of prisoners' fundamental rights as a form of punishment.

Further reading

Cooper, J, *Cruelty: An Analysis of Article 3* (Sweet and Maxwell 2002), chs 1, 2, and 4.

Foster, S, *Human Rights and Civil Liberties*, 2nd edn (Longman 2008), ch 8.

Lazarus, L, *Contrasting Prisoners' Rights* (OUP 2004), chs 5–8.

Livingstone, S, Owen, T and Macdonald, A, *Prison Law*, 4th edn (OUP 2008).

9

The right to private life

Introduction

The areas of privacy and the protection of private life are taught on most civil liberties courses and are an increasingly topical area of human rights, particularly since the passing of the **Human Rights Act 1998.** Because of the traditional nature of domestic law, and the absence of a clear law of privacy, much academic discussion has centred on the lack of protection of individual privacy. As a result of this, and the recent development of privacy interests within this area, the topic has become a popular one with examiners. Thus, students need to possess a sound knowledge of this area and, in particular, need to be aware of continual changes in the law and to appreciate the relevant moral and legal arguments surrounding the law and its development.

Questions can be in essay or problem form and can cover a variety of areas, such as the nature and scope of privacy, the absence of a right to privacy in domestic law before the Human Rights Act, the development of privacy in the post-Human Rights Act era, and the protection of privacy and private life under the **European Convention on Human Rights.** In addition, as privacy and private life cover a number of key aspects of individual liberty, one may get tested in specific areas such as the law of confidence, press intrusion into private life, police and other surveillance, and private life and physical integrity. The questions in this chapter cover a number of those issues, including the right to private sexual life. Areas of privacy and private life may also appear in questions in other areas of human rights, such as police powers (arrest, search, and seizure) and freedom of expression (defamation and confidentiality).

Question 1

To what extent does the European Convention seek to protect the right to privacy, or the right to private life, and how effectively has the European Court of Human Rights guaranteed this right?

Commentary

This is a fairly broad question and the student needs to include a good deal of information in the answer. First, the question requires some appreciation of the theoretical basis of privacy protection and the importance of this right in the protection of human rights and individual liberty. The answer should then focus on the case law of the European Court (and, where appropriate) Commission for Human Rights under **article 8** of the European Convention in analysing the effectiveness of privacy protection under the Convention. Students should look at a variety of privacy aspects in this respect, but can choose which areas to concentrate on provided they look at cases that have raised essential privacy matters. Students can mention the full range of rights protected within **article 8**, including the right to family and home life where they complement the right to private life and privacy, but should concentrate on cases where privacy and private life are at issue.

The question calls for an analysis of the effectiveness of the Convention in protecting this right and as a consequence students should be aware of the principles underlying the protection of private life and focus their commentary on a critical appraisal of the Court's role and achievements in this area.

Answer plan

- Definition and scope of privacy and private life
- Examination of the scope and extent of privacy protection under the European Convention
- Examination of relevant European Convention case law illustrating the extent of protection
- Critical analysis of **article 8** and relevant case law in order to examine the extent and effectiveness of protection

Suggested answer

The right to privacy, or the right to private life, is at the heart of individual freedom and the right to be free from arbitrary state interference. Privacy includes the right to be let alone and the right to enjoy one's individual space, which the state or other individuals should not penetrate, including the right to enjoy one's property as well as being free from physical interference. However, in *Niemietz v Germany* (1992) **16 EHRR 97** the European Court held that the notion was not restricted to the person's inner circle, but includes the right to develop and establish relationships with other human beings.

Privacy or private life may also refer to the right of personal autonomy and human dignity, demanding the individual has the right to make choices about their life, such as whom they marry, or whether they have the right to die (*Pretty v United Kingdom* (2002) **35 EHRR 1**). Equally, the right to private life can complement the right to be free from inhuman or degrading treatment and thus protect a person from attacks on their person or personal dignity (*Costello-Roberts v United Kingdom* (1993) 19 EHRR 112). More specifically, the right to private life includes the right to choose and practice one's sexual orientation, and the right to be free from press intrusion or the right to withhold, or access, personal information.

Each state must ensure that an individual's right to privacy or private life is protected within its jurisdiction and **article 8** of the European Convention duly provides that everyone has the right to respect for his private and family life, his home, and his correspondence. **Article 8(2)** then stipulates that there may be no interference with the exercise of those rights *by a public authority* unless the restrictions are 'in accordance with law' and 'necessary in a democratic society' for the purpose of achieving legitimate aims such as the prevention of disorder or crime. Although the right to private life is enjoyed primarily as against the state, the state has a duty to protect these rights from violations by private individuals (*X v Netherlands* (1985) 8 EHRR 235). Further, the state has an obligation to provide the resources necessary for the enjoyment of these rights (*Marckx v Belgium* (1979) 2 EHRR 330).

The expression 'private life' clearly covers privacy issues relating to access to personal information (*Gaskin v United Kingdom* (1990) 12 EHRR 36), as well as interference with privacy by surveillance techniques (*Malone v United Kingdom* (1984) 7 EHRR 14) and press intrusion (*Von Hannover v Germany* (2005) 40 EHRR 1). The article also covers a variety of private and family interests, including the right to communicate private information with others (*Silver v United Kingdom* (1983) 5 EHRR 347), and the right to private sexual life (*Dudgeon v United Kingdom* (1982) 4 EHRR 149).

Further, although the right to private life is a conditional right and interferences are permitted under **article 8(2)**, the Court has insisted on strict procedural safeguards (*Klass v Germany* ((1978) 2 EHRR 214) and has made it clear that the state will be allowed a narrow margin of appreciation when its law and practice have interfered with private rights (*Dudgeon v United Kingdom* (above)).

With respect to sexual privacy, in *Dudgeon v United Kingdom* (above) the Court stated that the right to private life under **article 8** included the right to enjoy one's private sexual life, and that an individual's sexual life is one of the most intimate aspects of private life, and stressed that strong justification would be required to allow interference. A similar approach was taken in *Smith and Grady v United Kingdom* (2000) **29 EHRR 493** where it was held that the dismissal of armed forces personnel due to their sexuality constituted a disproportionate interference with their right to respect for their private lives. However, in *Laskey, Jaggard and Brown v United Kingdom* (1997) **24 EHRR 39** it upheld the applicants' convictions for assault for taking part in consensual acts of a sadomasochistic nature, noting that not every sexual activity carried out behind closed doors falls within the scope of **article 8**. Despite this ruling, the state's margin of appreciation will be limited where the criminal law has been used exclusively against one particular group based on its sexual orientation (*ADT v United Kingdom* (2001) 31 EHRR 33). Further, in *Sutherland v United Kingdom, The Times,* **13 April 2001** the European Commission refused to accept that society's preference for a heterosexual lifestyle constituted an objective justification for inequality of treatment under the criminal law.

The Convention has also extended its protection to transsexuals, although earlier cases had refused to interfere with domestic law that refused to recognize the private rights of transsexuals to marry and to choose their new sexual identity: see *Rees v United Kingdom* (1986) 9 EHRR 56, *Cossey v United Kingdom* (1990) 13 EHRR 62. However, in *Goodwin v United Kingdom* (2002) 35 EHRR 18 the Grand Chamber held that there had been a violation of **articles 8 and 12** of the Convention where the applicants had complained that they could not exercise their right to marry under **article 12** and were refused the right to change their sexual identity on various civil documents. The Court noted that the government had done nothing to respond to the Court's continual request to keep the need for legal reform under review, and could no longer benefit from the margin of appreciation in this area.

The Court has also been instrumental in protecting the right of correspondence, recognizing not only the right to communicate with friends or relatives, but also the right to carry on business communications (*Halford v United Kingdom* (1997) 24 EHRR 523 and *Amann v Switzerland* (2000) 30 EHRR 843). This protection has been notable in the context of prisoners' correspondence and in *Golder v United Kingdom* (1975) 1 EHRR 524 the Court upheld a prisoner's right to communicate with his lawyer and to access the courts for the purpose of bringing civil proceedings. It was also applied to more general correspondence in *Silver v United Kingdom* (1983) 5 EHRR 347, where a number of prison regulations interfering with the prisoners' right of correspondence were declared in violation of **article 8**, because they were not sufficiently accessible to be 'in accordance with law', and were excessive and disproportionate in relation to their legitimate aims of maintaining prison order.

The problem of state interference with the right of communication is perhaps most acute with respect to its use of surveillance devices, and in *Klass v Germany* (above) it was accepted that surveillance and other techniques struck at the heart of freedom of communication. The Court stressed that any such interference had to be justified in accordance with law and that the executive authorities should be subject to effective control, normally via the judiciary. The decision in *Klass* was applied in *Malone v United Kingdom* (above), where the Court found that the domestic law on telephone tapping did not satisfy **article 8(2)** because it was not publicly accessible and did not indicate with sufficient certainty the scope and manner of the relevant authorities' discretion. Further, in *Liberty v United Kingdom* (2009) 48 EHRR 1, it was held that there had been a violation of **article 8** when Liberty had had their telephone calls and other communications intercepted by the MOD. The power to intercept and read communications, under **s.3(2) of the Interception of Communications Act 1985**, was not in accordance with law because it gave an unlimited discretion and any safeguards against abuse were not made public or accessible.

However, the Court's primary concern in this area is with procedural safeguards as opposed to the substantive justification for such intrusions. Thus, in *PG and JH v United*

Kingdom, The Times, **19 October 2001** the European Court suggested that a member state would be afforded a good deal of discretion in this area provided the technique had a proper legal basis. Thus, although the Court has succeeded in putting into place proper safeguards for the use of such techniques, it has been reluctant to interfere with the substantive balance between individual privacy and the prevention and prosecution of crime. This reluctance is also apparent in the Court's willingness to allow illegally obtained evidence to be used in subsequent criminal trials (*Khan v United Kingdom* (2000) 31 EHRR 45).

With respect to surveillance and individual privacy the Court has also responded to the dangers of modern monitoring techniques, including closed-circuit television. Thus in *Peck v United Kingdom* (2003) 36 EHRR 41 the Court held that there had been a violation of the applicant's **article 8** rights when CCTV footage of him in a distressed condition had been released for use in various newspapers and television programmes without sufficient safeguards to ensure his anonymity. The disclosure of the footage had resulted in the applicant's actions being observed to an extent far exceeding any exposure to a passer-by or to security observation and to an extent surpassing that which the applicant could have foreseen. More recently, it has been held that the monitoring of an employee's use of emails and the internet was in violation of **article 8**, the practice not being in accordance with any law (*Copland v United Kingdom* (2007) 45 EHRR 37).

Cases such as *Peck* and *Copland* recognize the individual's right to control information relating to their personal life or image. In this respect the European Court has stressed the necessity of not only regulating other people's access to the individual's private information, but also of allowing the individual to access such personal information. Thus, in *Gaskin v United Kingdom* (above) it was held that a system that denied a person's access to information relating to his upbringing was an unnecessary restriction on the right to private life.

The Court has also been active in protecting individual privacy from press intrusion. In *Von Hannover v Germany* (above), the applicant, Princess Caroline Von Hannover, had unsuccessfully attempted to prohibit the publication of photographs taken by the German paparazzi. The Court held that the publication of the various photographs of her in her daily life clearly fell within the scope of her private life. Noting that the photographs had been taken without her consent and secretly, and that they made no contribution to a debate of public interest, it found a violation of **article 8**. Although the general public might have a right to information, including, in special circumstances, on the private lives of public figures, the protection of private life was essential to the development of every human being's personality and that everyone, including people known to the public, had a legitimate expectation that his or her private life would be protected. The decision illustrates the Court's desire to protect individual privacy from press harassment and disclosure of confidential and private information; although it was distinguished more recently in *Hachette Filipacchi Associes v France,* (2009) 49 EHRR 23, where the Court held that the newspaper's revelation of a pop singer's financial and personal problems was justified because it was not offensive and merely commented on information that was already in the public domain.

In conclusion, the European Convention protects a vast array of privacy interests within **article** 8 and the European Court has taken a dynamic approach to the protection of such interests. Although the right to private life is clearly a conditional right, the Court has made it clear that interferences with individual privacy must be justified on strong grounds. This reflects the Court's recognition of the importance of individual privacy and the need to protect it from unwarranted and uncontrolled intrusion.

Question 2

To what extent has the implementation of the **Human Rights Act 1998** led to the development of a domestic law of privacy? Do you agree that the current law provides adequate protection against intrusions into an individual's private life?

 Commentary

This continues to be a popular topic for essay-type questions, requiring the student to display knowledge of the domestic law in the pre-Human Rights Act era, as well as the legal developments—statutory and case law—since the passing of the Act. Although the question appears to concentrate on the current law, an appreciation of the former law is fundamental, as the question asks (implicitly) how the deficiencies of the old domestic law were remedied by the 1998 Act. The student also has to be aware of the jurisprudence of the **European Convention on Human Rights,** in particular the relevant case law under **article 8** of the Convention.

The answer should begin by briefly defining the term privacy and examining the scope of that right. Thus, the student should be aware of the theoretical justification and basis for privacy and the types of claims it can encompass, such as the right to personal and physical integrity, sexual privacy, the right to private correspondence and confidentiality, and freedom from interference with property rights. The student can then examine the extent to which English domestic law protected those interests via the traditional laws of trespass, assault, nuisance, defamation, and confidentiality. At this point the student should illustrate the inadequacies of the traditional law by using case examples where the courts refused to recognize a distinct breach of privacy and where the victim of privacy invasion was left unprotected.

The remainder of the answer should be dedicated to looking at the post-1998 Act era, examining the extent to which the Act's implementation has led to the development of a law of privacy, either under the Act's provisions or via the development of the existing or new common law actions. The answer should then conclude by considering the extent to which recent developments have provided adequate privacy protection, in particular whether it is the equivalent to that offered under **article 8** of the European Convention.

Answer plan

- Definition of privacy and the scope of the right to privacy
- Explanation of traditional common law position and the inadequacy of that protection
- Effect of the implementation of the **Human Rights Act 1998** and various developments in the common law and under statute
- Analysis of the extent and efficacy of the present legal position and its compatibility with the European Convention

Suggested answer

The right to privacy—the right to be let alone and the right to enjoy one's individual space as well as being free from physical interference—lies at the heart of individual freedom. The right is guaranteed under **article 8** of the European Convention and allows the individual to enjoy a private existence within the state and ensures the protection of personal autonomy, including the right to be free from attacks on one's person or personal dignity (*Pretty v United Kingdom* (2002) 35 EHRR 1). It can also include the right to choose and practice one's sexual orientation (*Dudgeon v United Kingdom*) (1982) 4 EHRR 149), and can be used in connection with the right to be free from press intrusion (*Von Hannover v Germany* (2005) 40 EHRR 1), or the right to withhold, or access, personal information (*Gaskin v United Kingdom* (1990) 12 EHRR 36).

Although various aspects of English law protected certain privacy interests, such as personal and real property (the law of trespass), and a person's reputation and confidential information (the laws of defamation and confidentiality), it failed to recognize the right to privacy as such. Consequently, in *Malone v Metropolitan Police Commissioner (No 2)* [1979] Ch 344, it was held that the plaintiff had no remedy when the police had tapped his telephone because **article 8** of the European Convention had not then been incorporated into English law, and the domestic laws of trespass and confidentiality had not been breached on the facts. As a consequence of this ruling the individual had to take proceedings under the European Convention (*Malone v United Kingdom* (1984) 7 EHRR 14). Similarly, in *R v Ministry of Defence, ex parte Smith* [1996] 1 All ER 257, the Court of Appeal held that individuals dismissed from the armed forces on grounds of their sexual orientation could not rely on the right to private life under **article 8** of the Convention, and again those affected needed to seek a remedy from the European Court (*Smith and Grady v United Kingdom* (2000) 29 EHRR 493).

The absence of a general right to privacy was most notable in the area of press intrusion. For example, in *Kaye v Robertson* [1991] FSR 62, it was confirmed that English law did not recognize the right of privacy and that the plaintiff could not sue under that heading, despite there being a 'monstrous invasion' of his privacy when he was interviewed by a reporter who had sneaked into his hospital room. Consequently, the individual had to rely on specific domestic laws to protect their privacy interests. In this respect some statute law was specifically designed to protect such interests and to comply with international law, (**Data Protection Acts 1988 and 1998**), while some common law remedies, such as the law of confidentiality, were already being developed so as to be consistent with the right to privacy (*HRH Princess of Wales v MGN Newspapers* (**Unreported, 8 November 1993**)). Nevertheless, cases such as *Malone, Smith* and *Kaye* (above) illustrated the need for a more general right to privacy.

The domestic courts have confirmed that there is still no specific common law action in privacy (*Secretary of State for the Home Department v Wainwright and others* [2004] 2 AC 406), and that the **Human Rights Act 1998** cannot be relied on so as to introduce a retrospective right to privacy. Nevertheless, the passing of the Act has allowed the courts to enhance the protection of private life. First, because **article 8** of the Convention has now been 'incorporated' into domestic law, a victim of a violation of **article 8** carried out by a *public authority* can bring an action under the Act. Thus in a case such as *Malone*, the claimant can rely directly on **article 8** and bring an action against the police authority. Secondly, although in *Wainwright* (above) the House of Lords confirmed that the Act does not create a new common law action of privacy, the 1998 Act will have some horizontal effect. As a consequence the courts (as 'public authorities' under the Act) will have a duty to develop and interpret the law to ensure that **article 8** rights are not unduly interfered with. More specifically, under **s.12(4)** of the 1998 Act the courts have a duty to take into account the contents of any privacy code in deciding whether to grant relief regarding the affected freedom of expression.

After the Act came into force the courts began to use their newly acquired powers to develop a law of privacy. For example, in *Douglas and others v Hello! and others* [2001] 2 WLR 992 Sedley LJ stated that the right to privacy could now be recognized and that the domestic law was now in a position to respond to an increasingly invasive social environment by affirming that everybody has the right to some private space. Further, in *Venables and Thompson v MGN* [2001] 2 WLR 1038 Dame Butler-Sloss held that although it might not be possible to rely on a freestanding application of privacy where the defendants were not public authorities, nevertheless the duty of the courts was to act compatibly with Convention rights in adjudicating upon existing common law causes of action.

Those cases seemed to suggest that the Act could have full horizontal effect and the courts were entitled to develop an independent law of privacy. However, in *Wainwright* (above) the House of Lords confirmed that those decisions did not establish a common law of privacy, but instead were confined to the development of the common law of confidentiality. Further, although the gap in the common law had been filled by the passing of the **Human Rights Act 1998**, which allowed individuals to bring actions against public authorities, it was not necessary to develop a law of privacy to apply to actions which occurred before the passing of the Act, or to create a common law right of privacy. However, the subsequent proceedings in *Wainwright v United Kingdom* (2007) 44 EHRR 40, where the European Court found a breach of **article 8** when the applicant's physical integrity had been violated by prison searches, suggest that common law remedies were not in conformity with the Convention. Notably, the Court found that there had been a breach of **article 13**—the right to an effective remedy at domestic law for breach of Convention rights—suggesting that common law remedies may be inadequate where the applicant is not eligible to claim directly under **article 8**.

Thus, whether domestic law has in effect developed a law of privacy depends largely on the extent to which the law of confidentiality, and other legal areas, have developed so as to fill the gaps evident in the pre-Act era. The laws of confidentiality, and the statutory protection of private information under the **Data Protection Act 1998**, were employed in *R v Wakefield LBC, ex parte Robertson* [2002] 2 WLR 889 to prohibit electoral authorities from passing on an individual's personal details for marketing purposes. In that case it was held that such a power was in clear contravention of **article 8**, and offended principles of proportionality. So too, surveillance powers, contained in various legislation passed as a result of cases such as *Malone* (above), could now be considered as part of a privacy law, as they contain restrictions on the use of such powers in line with **article 8** of the Convention.

Further, it is necessary to examine whether such laws comply with the principles and the case law of the European Convention, which have been 'incorporated' via the 1998 Act. With respect to the law of confidentiality, the courts are prepared to develop the law consistently with the basic notions contained in **article 8** (*X (Mary Bell) and another v News Group Newspapers and another* [2003] EMLR 37). Also, the courts are not required to give freedom of expression an enhanced status over and above the right to private life (*Douglas v Hello!* (above)). With respect to press intrusions into privacy, although the courts were initially unwilling to interfere with press freedom when individual privacy has been invaded (*A v B plc and another* [2002] 3 WLR 542 and *Theakston v MGN* [2002] EMLR 22), the situation was redressed to some extent by the House of Lords in *Campbell v MGN Newspapers* [2004] 2 AC 457, where it was held that the revelation of detailed information relating to the claimant's drug addiction constituted an undue interference with her right of enjoyment of private life. Further, in *Von Hannover v Germany* (2005) 40 EHRR 1, the European Court held that there was insufficient public interest to justify the persistent photographing of the former Princess Caroline of Monaco by the German paparazzi. As a result, more recent case law shows evidence of a shift from the public right to know to individual privacy (*McKennitt v Ash* [2007] 3 WLR 194 and *HRH Prince of Wales v MGN Ltd* [2007] 3 WLR 222).

There is little doubt that the current legal situation has enhanced the pre-Act position. For example, in cases such as *Kaye v Robertson* (above) the claimant would no longer have to rely on inappropriate laws aimed at protecting property or commercial interests. The courts also now have the power to subject public authority interference with privacy to greater scrutiny. For example, in *Peck v United Kingdom* (2003) 36 EHRR 41, it was held that the photographing of a distressed individual and the publication of such footage by newspapers and television companies was in violation of **article 8**. Importantly, the Court found that the applicant had been denied an effective remedy under **article 13** because the judicial review proceedings were incapable of adequately addressing the relevant privacy issues (*R v Brentwood Council, ex parte Peck* [1998] **CMLR 697**). The courts must now strike a correct balance between individual privacy and the public interest, and in *Wood v Commissioner of the Police of the Metropolis The Times,* **1 June 2009,** the Court of Appeal found that the taking and retention by the police of an individual's photograph as he left an area of protest was disproportionate because the police could provide no cogent reason for retention.

Since the coming into force of the 1998 Act the courts have interpreted various laws in the context of privacy claims, including cases involving physical and personal integrity (*Munjaz v Mersey Care NHS Trust; S v Airedale NHS Trust* [2006] **2 AC 148**); and the retention of DNA samples (*R v Chief Constable of South Yorkshire, ex parte LS and Marper* [2004] **1 WLR 2196,** successfully challenged in *S and Marper v United Kingdom* (2009) **48 EHRR 50**). Further, both the courts and Parliament have ensured that laws relating to sexual privacy are consistent with **article 8** of the European Convention. For example, following the decision in *Goodwin v United Kingdom* (2002) **35 EHRR 18** the House of Lords declared that the refusal of the law to recognize a transsexual's post-operative gender was contrary to **articles 8 and 14** of the Convention (*Bellinger v Bellinger* [2003] **2 AC 467**), and the **Gender Recognition Act 2004** now regulates such rights. Similar protection has been afforded by the courts in respect of those discriminated against on grounds of sexual orientation (*Mendoza v Ghaidan* [2004] **2 AC 557** and the **Civil Partnership Act 2004**).

At the very least, in the post-Human Rights Act era both the courts and Parliament must ensure that provisions empowering public authorities to encroach upon individual privacy are sufficiently clear, accessible, and certain. Thus, following defeats in Strasbourg in cases involving telephone tapping (*Malone* (above)) and other bugging devices (*Khan v United Kingdom* (2001) **31 EHRR 45**), such powers are now contained in relatively clear statutory form (**Regulation of Investigatory Powers Act 2000**). Also, these laws must strike a reasonable balance between the protection of privacy and competing legitimate aims. Despite the absence of a distinct law of privacy in domestic law, there is in place a flexible framework for the protection of privacy interests. These laws may not always achieve consistency with the European Convention (*Wainwright v United Kingdom* (above) and *S and Marper v United Kingdom* (above)), although such conflict may occur even where the state possesses a distinct law of privacy.

Question 3

Critically examine how the **European Convention on Human Rights** has protected individuals from covert surveillance by police and other authorities.

Commentary

This question concerns the protection of individual privacy from state and other surveillance. This is a popular area for examination and although this question centres on the European Convention, students should also expect questions relating to the domestic regulation of surveillance. It requires a fairly detailed knowledge of the area, and should not be attempted unless the student has a sound knowledge of the relevant Convention case law and a reasonable awareness of the domestic legal regulation of such practices.

To answer the question, the student must not only be aware of the essential case law of the European Court and Commission in this area, but also needs to appreciate the dangers of such surveillance techniques and the necessity for regulating their use. This will allow the student to discuss and comment on the scope, and limitations, of the Convention's protection in this area. The student can then allude to the current position in domestic law, describing how the law was introduced to address various decisions of the European Court in this regard. For this question, however, the student should concentrate on the principles and values of the Convention and its case law and should not give a detailed account of relevant domestic law.

Answer plan

- Explanation of various surveillance techniques, their utility, and the potential danger to individual liberty
- Examination of relevant Convention articles and case law of the European Court and Commission in the area
- Identification of the central principles and values evident from the cases and a critical evaluation of the scope and effectiveness of the Convention's protection
- Reference to relevant domestic statute and case law in illustration of the above principles

Suggested answer

The employment of covert surveillance techniques (such as telephone tapping, 'bugging' and the modern use of closed-circuit television surveillance), carried out, inevitably, without the individual's knowledge, involve a specifically sinister and grave interference with individual privacy and the enjoyment of such rights. In these cases, it is essential that such practices are only carried out with proper legal safeguards which restrict their use to the most essential cases and which provide the individual with a remedy in cases of their illegal use.

Article 8 of the European Convention provides protection against interference with the individual's right to private life, home, and correspondence and in *Klass v Germany* (1978) **2 EHRR 214** the European Court confirmed that the mere existence of legislation allowing telephone tapping by state authorities struck at freedom of communication and accordingly the power to carry out the activity must be 'in accordance with law' so that executive authorities are subjected to effective control. However, although the Court suggested that there should, ideally, be a system of judicial control, it was prepared to take a flexible approach, provided the domestic legislation had inbuilt safeguards against abuse.

The Court has stressed that the law should be couched in terms which give both the individual and the authority sufficient guidance as to the scope of the powers. Consequently, in *Amann v Switzerland* (2000) 30 EHRR 843, it was held that the tapping amounted to a violation of **article 8**, because the national law was not sufficiently clear to clarify the scope and conditions of the authorities' discretionary powers in this area. The principles in *Klass* and *Amann* were applied in *Malone v United Kingdom* (1984) 7 EHRR 14, where the applicant had brought an unsuccessful action against the police for tapping his telephone (*Malone v Metropolitan Police Commissioner (No 2)* [1979] Ch 344). The European Court held that the law regulating the practice, contained in government circulars that were not publicly accessible, did not satisfy **article 8(2)**. The Court stressed that telephone tapping required clear and accessible legal rules. In the present case it could not be determined what powers were incorporated in legal rules and what elements remained within the discretion of the executive and the police force. As a consequence Parliament passed the **Interception of Communications Act 1985**, which at least put telephone tapping on a statutory basis. These provisions are now contained in the **Regulation of Investigatory Powers Act 2000**, and such methods are supervised by an independent, and legally qualified, Interception of Communications Officer.

The Court has extended protection to practices other than the tapping of telephones in the private home, and in *Amann* (above), it held that **article 8** applied to interferences executed on business premises. Further, in *Halford v United Kingdom* (1997) 24 EHRR 523, it held that telephone calls made from business premises were covered by the notion of private life and correspondence under **article 8**. Thus, as such practices were not covered by legislation passed to conform to the decision in *Malone* (above); the interference was in breach of **article 8**. Further, in *Copland v United Kingdom* (2007) 45 EHRR 37 it was held that **article 8** applied to the monitoring of the employees' use of email and internet facilities at work.

With respect to covert surveillance in the United Kingdom, in addition to the decisions in *Malone* and *Halford* (above), the Court has also made rulings with respect to surveillance carried out by intelligence agencies such as MI5 (*Harman and Hewitt v United Kingdom* (1992) 14 EHRR 657)—leading to the passing of the **Security Services Act 1989**—and the placing of bugging devices on individuals and their property (*Khan v United Kingdom* (2001) 31 EHRR 45)—now contained in the **Police Act 1997** and the **Regulation of Investigatory Powers Act 2000**. Further, in *Perry v United Kingdom* (2004) 39 EHRR 3 the Court held that the secret filming of the applicant in a prison cell engaged the applicant's right to respect for his private life. In these cases, the Court not only found violations of **article 8**, but also held that the lack of regular domestic law in this area meant that the victim had been denied an effective legal remedy as required by **article 13** of the Convention. For example, in *Govell v United Kingdom* (1997) EHRLR 438 and *PG and JH v United Kingdom, The Times,* 19 October 2001 it was held that the domestic courts were not in a position to provide an effective remedy within **article 13** with respect to any complaint about abuse.

Despite the Court's insistence that such activities have a clear legal basis, it would appear that it will afford a member state a good deal of discretion when adjudicating upon the necessity and proportionality of such measures. Thus, in *Klass v Germany* (above) the Court accepted that such techniques were vital in protecting societies from sophisticated forms of espionage and terrorism, and that consequently states are in general justified in resorting to such methods. This deferential approach follows the Court's decision in *Leander v Sweden* (1987) 9 EHRR 433, where it was held that the state has a wide margin of appreciation when deciding the best means of securing a balance between individual privacy and national security. Thus, the Court's fundamental concern is with procedural safeguards rather than challenging the necessity of individual measures and their application. For example, in *PG and JH v United Kingdom* (above) the police had placed a covert listening device in the applicant's flat, using such information in subsequent criminal proceedings. The Court noted that the police lacked the statutory power to carry this out and found a violation of **article 8**. However, with regard to the use of the applicant's telephone, at this stage regulated by domestic law, it held that as the information had been obtained and used in the context of an investigation and trial concerning a suspected conspiracy to commit robbery, the measures were justified under **article 8(2)**.

Further, the Court is not prepared to find a violation of the applicant's right to a fair trial under **article 6** simply because such information has been used against the applicant in subsequent criminal proceedings (*Schenk v Switzerland* (1988) 13 EHRR 242). Thus, in *Khan v United Kingdom* (2001) 31 EHRR 45, although it held that the absence of domestic law regulating the use of bugging devices meant that there had been an unjustified interference with the applicant's private life and correspondence, it held that there had been no violation of **article 6** when such information had been used to convict the applicant. Although his conviction was based solely on the use of that unlawfully obtained evidence, there were sufficient safeguards in place to ensure that such information would not be admissible if it seriously prejudiced the applicant's right to a fair trial. Consequently, the European Court concerns itself with the overall fairness of the proceedings, rather than adopting a dogmatic exclusionary rule. This approach is also adopted by the domestic courts, and in *Martin v McGuiness, The Times*, 23 April 2003 it was held that evidence gathered by a private investigator in violation of **article 8** was admissible in personal injury litigation, provided the inquiries and surveillance were reasonable and proportionate in the circumstances.

The Court has also had the opportunity to rule on the compatibility of the modern phenomenon of closed-circuit television surveillance. In *Perry v United Kingdom* (above) the Court held that the secret filming of a prisoner in his cell, and the subsequent use of such images for identification purposes, amounted to an interference with his right to private life. The filming was not in accordance with law as the police had failed to follow the procedures set out in the relevant code and had not obtained the applicant's consent or informed him of his rights. Further, the filming had gone beyond the normal use of that type of camera and was thus disproportionate.

Although the Court appears to accept that such television surveillance is a necessary and increasingly normal practice, it is prepared to subject it to close scrutiny to ensure that it is not carried out unlawfully or unnecessarily. The legality of such techniques was challenged in *Peck v United Kingdom* (2003) **36 EHRR 41**, concerning the use by local authorities of closed-circuit television for the purposes of protecting public safety in the community. The applicant had been filmed by closed-circuit television, operated by a local council, walking down the street with a kitchen knife and attempting to commit suicide. The Council then issued a press feature in its CCTV News, containing photographs from the footage, which were later published in a local newspaper and used in a number of local and national television programmes, without the applicant's face being specifically masked. The European Court held that the disclosure of that footage constituted a serious interference with the applicant's right to respect for private life. Although it accepted that the interference was prescribed by law—it was allowed by **s.163 of the Criminal Justice and Public Order Act 1994**—and that it had a legitimate aim—public safety, the prevention of disorder and crime, and the protection of the rights of others, it held that the interference was not necessary in a democratic society. The Court stressed that the disclosure of private and intimate information could only be justified by an overriding requirement in the public interest and that such disclosure without the consent of the individual called for the most careful scrutiny. In the present case the disclosure of the material was not accompanied by sufficient safeguards to ensure anonymity and thus constituted a disproportionate and unjustified interference with the applicant's private life.

The decision in *Peck* confirms the Court's desire to protect individual privacy from unwarranted public exposure, as highlighted by the decision in *Von Hannover v Germany* (2005) **40 EHRR 1** with respect to press intrusion into private life. Further, the decision in *Peck* suggests that the Court is willing to rule on the necessity and proportionality of these particular surveillance techniques, albeit in exceptional cases. This approach is reflected in domestic case law, where the courts have insisted that the distribution of private images to the public should be monitored to ensure they do not impose a disproportionate interference on family and private life (*R (Ellis) v Chief Constable of Essex Police The Times,* **17** June 2003). At the same time, however, the courts have accepted the general legitimacy and necessity of such a practice (*R (Stanley and others) v Metropolitan Police Commissioner and another, The Times,* **22** October 2004).

The European Court and Commission have provided essential safeguards against unlawful and arbitrary use of surveillance. Cases such as *Klass* and *Malone* have insisted that such measures are controlled by the law, and this has led to domestic legislation, which places the techniques on a statutory footing and provides some element of judicial (or quasi-judicial) supervision. However, both the Convention organs and the domestic courts have displayed a good deal of deference to the state authorities in this area. Consequently, although the Convention and its case law have insisted on procedural protection from abuse, such practices appear to be regarded as essential to the protection of the public and their extent is, generally, best determined by the authorities themselves.

Question 4

(A)

How have the domestic courts attempted to balance the right of press freedom with the enjoyment of private life?

(B)

Norman is a former boy band member with the group Howzat! He left the group three years ago and is now 28. Last year he had an affair with a 17-year-old schoolgirl who now wishes to tell her story to the Daily Scum. He was telephoned by the newspaper, stating that next week it was to publish this story and another (true) story about his past affairs with several young women, along with photographs of him naked in a hotel room. For the next two days Norman was persistently followed by the newspaper's photographers, who took photographs of him and his current girlfriend.

Advise Norman as to the chances of him suppressing the stories, or suing for damages with respect to the stories or other tactics adopted by the newspaper.

 Commentary

This question concerns the balance between press freedom and the enjoyment of private life, most notably the privacy rights of those in the public eye. The question is in two parts, requiring an explanation and analysis of the law in the first part and its application to a specific scenario in the second. It is possible that each question might form a question in its own right, although the problem part below is quite limited and thus both parts are capable of being answered in examination conditions. The first part of the question requires a sound knowledge of the domestic law of (essentially) confidentiality, and how it has been adapted to protect privacy interests and in balancing such interests against press freedom and the public right to know. Students may also refer, briefly, to other areas, such as harassment, to support the answer. There have been a number of high-profile cases in this area, and the student should be aware of their existence, as well as the principles emerging from them. Some knowledge of the relevant case law of the European Court of Human Rights is also necessary. Given the two parts to the question, students should deal with the law as succinctly as possible, although some attempt should be made to take a critical approach.

The second part of the question requires an application of the law and principles identified in part one of the answer, as well as a discussion and application of any other relevant legal principles, such as harassment. Where the student is advising on areas already identified in part one, they should dedicate their time to interpreting the facts and giving specific advice, rather than repeating the basic legal principles. Accordingly, because of the way the question is split it might be permissible for the student to spend more time on part one.

The diagram below illustrates the procedure whereby the courts consider granting an interim injunction in such cases.

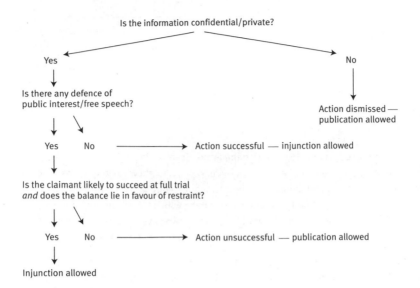

Is the information confidential/private?

Yes → Is there any defence of public interest/free speech?

No → Action dismissed — publication allowed

Yes No → Action successful — injunction allowed

Yes → Is the claimant likely to succeed at full trial *and* does the balance lie in favour of restraint?

Yes No → Action unsuccessful — publication allowed

Yes → Injunction allowed

Answer plan

- Explanation of press freedom and its importance in a democratic society
- Consideration of domestic law of confidentiality, both pre- and post-Human Rights Act, affecting the balance between press freedom and private life
- Identification of the relevant legal actions in confidentiality and other laws available to Norman, along with the impact of the **Human Rights Act 1998**
- Consideration of any defences available to the press to either action, with specific regard to the Human Rights Act
- Consideration of the likelihood of Norman succeeding in his action, together with advice on any likely remedy

Suggested answer

(A)

The 'incorporation' of **article 8** of the European Convention has allowed the courts to develop traditional legal principles, most notably the law of confidentiality, in line with **article 8**. This law, and other laws such as defamation, trespass, nuisance, and harassment (*Thomas v News Group Newspapers* [2002] EMLR 4), often involve a conflict between the protection of privacy interests and freedom of expression and must be applied in a manner which strikes an appropriate balance between such rights.

This dilemma is most acute when press freedom comes up against the private lives of 'public' figures, and in the post-Human Rights Act era the courts have confirmed that this area should be dealt with primarily within the law of confidentiality, rather than the development of a separate law of privacy (*Campbell v MGN* [2004] 2 AC 457). The use of confidentiality as a means of protecting privacy interests was recognized before the passing of the 1998 Act (*Stephens v Avery* [1988] 2 WLR 1280) and the wide defence of public interest has long been employed to justify intrusions into privacy on the basis of the public right to know (*Woodward v Hutchins* [1977] 1 WLR 760). Nevertheless, in *Robertson v Kaye and another* [1991] FLR 62 the Court of Appeal recognized that it was helpless to provide a remedy even in the face of 'a monstrous invasion' of the claimant's privacy.

The passing of the 1998 Act led the courts to accept an indirect law of privacy. Thus, in *Douglas and others v Hello! and others* [2001] 2 WLR 992 Sedley LJ stated that English law now recognized and protected a right of personal privacy and that the courts had a duty to protect the individual's right to some private space. This required the courts to take into account any countervailing Convention right, such as freedom of expression. **Section 12** of the **Human Rights Act** requires the Court to have special regard to **article 10** when granting relief that affects freedom of expression, and s.12(4) orders the court to consider both the public interest and the contents of any relevant privacy code. Accordingly, in *Douglas* (above) Sedley LJ held that both rights were to be balanced by the principles of legality and proportionality, and in *Re S (Publicity)* [2005] 1 AC 593, it was held that in deciding whether to grant an interim injunction a court should consider the magnitude of the interference proposed and whether there was a clear and proper interest in revealing the information.

This balance has tended to favour the protection of privacy when the claim of privacy is accompanied by a threat of physical harm to the claimant. Thus in *Venables and Thompson v MGN Ltd* [2001] 2 WLR 1038 it was held that on the facts there were compelling reasons to grant the injunctions, and that it was necessary to place the right to confidence above the right of the media to publish freely. (See also *Carr v News Group Newspapers Ltd* [2005] EWHC 971, and *X (Mary Bell) and another v News Group Newspapers and another* [2003] EMLR 37.) On the other hand, in less crucial cases, the courts have shown a reluctance to grant interim injunctions where violation of the claimant's privacy could be remedied at full trial (*Douglas v Hello!* (above)).

In particular, the courts have had to decide whether, and to what extent, a public figure enjoys the right to private life, and whether the public's right to know should override any such interest. Early case law suggested that press freedom and the public right to know would generally prevail. Thus, in *A v B plc and another* [2002] 3 WLR 542—a case involving the revelation of details of a professional footballer's extra-marital affairs—it was held that although a celebrity was entitled to a private life, he must expect that his actions would be more closely scrutinized by the media, and that even trivial facts could be of great interest to readers and other observers of the media. Further, the public had an understandable and legitimate interest in being told such information. This approach was adopted in *Theakston v MGN Ltd* [2002] EMLR 22, where the courts allowed the publication of a story of a television presenter visiting a brothel.

However, recent case law suggests that the courts will, in appropriate cases, favour individual privacy. First, in *Campbell v MGN* [2004] 2 AC 457 the House of Lords held that the revelation of detailed information relating to the claimant's drug addiction, including the publication of photographs of her visiting a rehabilitation clinic and details of her treatment, constituted an interference with her right of enjoyment of private life, which was not justified on grounds of public interest. Although the House of Lords accepted that there was a genuine public interest in receiving the information—the claimant had lied to the press about her drug addiction—the revelation of these specific details was held to be unwarranted. Further, in *Von Hannover v Germany* (2005) 40 EHRR 1 the European Court held that the persistent photographing of the former Princess Caroline of Monaco by the paparazzi was in violation of **article 8** of the Convention, the Court refusing to accept that there was any overriding public interest in the photographs.

Subsequently, in *McKennitt v Ash* [2007] 3 WLR 194 it was noted that there was a significant shift taking place between freedom of the press and individual privacy and that, even where there was a genuine interest in the media publishing articles and photographs, sometimes such interests would have to yield to the individual's right to private life. Equally, in *CC v AB* [2007] EMLR 11 the High Court appeared to override the principles established in *A v B plc* (above) and granted an injunction to stop the publication of a story about the claimant's adulterous relationship. In that case the court stressed that there was a clear difference between publication in the public interest and publication of matters that the public were interested in or curious about.

The courts will continue to take into account all the circumstances, including the extent of any intrusion and the importance of the public interest. For example, in *Jagger v Darling* [2005] EWHC 683 the court granted an injunction to stop the publication of CCTV footage showing the claimant engaged in sexual activities, finding that repeated publication of the images would only serve to humiliate the claimant. However, in *Browne v Associated Newspapers* [2007] 3 WLR 289 the court allowed the publication of some details of the claimant's homosexual affair, the court recognizing that there was a genuine public interest because of the claimant's position as a director of a global company and of allegations of abuse of the company's funds and facilities. This can be contrasted with the decision in *HRH Prince of Wales v Associated Newspapers Ltd* [2007] 3 WLR 222, where the Court of Appeal allowed a claim in confidentiality and copyright when the Prince's private diaries were taken and published, despite their apparently strong public interest content.

Present case law appears flexible and to some extent inconsistent, and although the existence of a *genuine* public interest in disclosure is vital, the decision in *HRH Prince of Wales* shows the courts' desire to protect individual privacy from press intrusion and public exposure.

(B)

The publication of the story and the photographs

The facts suggest that any information to be published by the newspaper is true; consequently, Norman must pursue an action in confidentiality, and not defamation; although the law of harassment will be considered with respect to the subsequent press tactics. Norman will bring a private action under the law of confidentiality, which has been used by the domestic courts to protect privacy interests (*Campbell v MGN* [2004] 2 AC 457). In particular, Norman will seek an interim injunction in order to prohibit the publication of the stories and the photographs.

First, the court will need to be satisfied that the information he is seeking to protect has a sufficient quality of confidence. Details of sexual encounters, even outside marriage, may attract protection (*Stephens v Avery* (above)). Further, although in *A v B plc and another* [2001] 1 WLR 2341 Lord Woolf CJ stated that there was a significant difference between confidentiality attaching to sexual relations in transient relationships as opposed to those within marriage or other stable relationships, it is clear that such relationships are still worthy of protection (*CC v AB* [2007] EMLR 11). In the latter case, therefore, an injunction was granted preventing the newspaper from publishing the details of the claimant's adulterous affair. Norman's case would appear to engage the law of confidentiality, albeit to a limited extent.

Secondly, the court would need to decide whether it would grant an interim injunction, and in doing so would need to consider both the strength of Norman's claim and any defence of public interest raised at full trial. **Section 12** of the **Human Rights Act 1998** requires the courts to have particular regard to freedom of expression in considering whether to grant relief affecting the exercise of this right, and **s.12(3)** provides that no relief shall be granted so as to restrain publication before trial unless the court is satisfied that the applicant is likely to establish that publication should not be allowed. This involves determining the strength of the parties' respective arguments (*Re S (Publicity)* [2005] 1 AC 593), and whether the claimant can be adequately compensated by compensation at full trial (*Douglas v Hello!* (above)).

Applying those principles to the present case, it is questionable that Norman will prevent publication of the stories. The stories relate to extra-marital and transient affairs, and it could be argued that as he is a well-known figure there may be some public interest in publication, at least pending the full trial; although the defendant would have to show more than mere public curiosity. More significantly, the strength of the claimant's interests are diminished by the fact that one girl now wishes to exercise her right to freedom of expression (*A v B plc* (above)). This contrasts with *CC* (above), where there was a vindictive desire by the defendant (the husband of the woman in the adulterous affair) to expose the claimant and to profit from the story. This factor would be particularly relevant in deciding the issue, and might suggest that the newspaper's defence of public interest was more likely to succeed.

However, Norman may have more success in stopping the publication of the photographs. **Clauses 3 and 4 of the Press Complaints Commission's Code of Practice** regulate the taking of photographs in a private place (a place where there is a reasonable expectation of privacy), and the courts are bound to consider such provisions under **s.12(4)**. Thus, in *Theakston* (above), the Court granted an injunction in respect of photographs taken of the claimant in a brothel, finding that there was a reasonable expectation that such photographs taken without consent would remain private. Such a finding would reflect the domestic courts' concern over the public dissemination of intimate and private detail (*Campbell v MGN* (above)).

The photographing of Norman and his girlfriend

Taking a person's photograph without their consent may amount to a *prima facie* breach of confidence (***HRH Princess of Wales v MGN* (Unreported, 8 November 1993)**) and may also violate the Press Complaints Commission's Code of Practice (above). We are not told where the photographs were taken, and the court must decide whether Norman and his girlfriend were in a private place and had a reasonable expectation of privacy (***R v Press Complaints Commission, ex parte Ford* [2002] EMLR 5**). More generally, the court would need to consider whether a fair-minded person would consider it offensive to disseminate such information (*Campbell v MGN Ltd* (above)). It would appear that the press behaviour in this case does not impact on individual privacy to the same extent as the photographs taken in *Campbell* and *Theakston* (above). Nevertheless, taking into account the decision in *Von Hannover* (above), it is possible that the courts would regard this tactic as an unnecessary method of exposing a public interest story and thus award damages.

Norman may also bring proceedings under the **Protection from Harassment Act 1997. Section 2** makes it an offence to pursue a course of conduct that amounts to harassment of another, and **s.3** provides a civil remedy for breaches of the Act, including damages for any anxiety and other loss caused by the harassment, and for the award of an injunction to restrain such conduct. In our case, the newspaper has pursued a course of conduct against Norman and his girlfriend, but whether that conduct is unreasonable or not depends on the circumstances of the case, and would be dependent on the court's findings in the confidentiality claim on whether the invasion was reasonable and in the public interest. Certainly, the taking of a person's photograph without their permission may amount to a breach of confidence or harassment (***Murray v Express Newspapers* [2008] 3 WLR 1360**), and the court's assessment on the press's tactics and the effect of such on the privacy of the individuals would be fundamental to the outcome of the case.

Question 5

To what extent has the **European Convention on Human Rights** been effective in promoting the enjoyment of the rights to private and family life of homosexuals and transsexuals?

 Commentary

This question covers the specific area of the right to private and family life of homosexuals and transsexuals and requires a very sound knowledge of the case law of the European Court of Human Rights, as well as recent judicial and statutory developments in domestic law. The student needs to be aware of the potential application of **articles 8, 12, and 14** of the

Convention, the case law of the European Court, and the impact that such cases have had on the protection of such rights.

The answer should begin by identifying the potential abuse of human rights in this area, as well as the relevant Convention articles that could be used in challenging such violations. The student should then chronicle the case law of the European Court, dealing, in turn, with both groups and explaining any shift of approach of the Court in these areas. The student can then examine any legislative or judicial changes at the domestic level, before drawing any conclusions as to the impact of the Convention on the enjoyment of such rights.

The question should concentrate on the principles and case law of the European Convention, rather than examining the current state of domestic law in this area, referring to any legislative or other changes in the context of Convention case law. Brief mention may also be made of the impact of EC Law in this area.

 ## Answer plan

- Identification of relevant Convention rights which protect the human rights of homosexuals and transsexuals

- Consideration and critical analysis of relevant case law of the European Court and Commission of Human Rights in both areas

- Explanation of changes in domestic law to comply with judgments of the Court and Commission

- Conclusions as to the effectiveness of the Convention case law and subsequent developments in protecting such rights

Suggested answer

In *Dudgeon v United Kingdom* (1982) 4 EHRR 149 the European Court recognized that the right to 'private life' under **article** 8 included the right to private sexual life, and described sexual life as one of the most intimate aspects of private life. Thus, the Court has stressed that any interference has to be justified on the most pressing of grounds, and not simply because a person's sexual choices are in conflict with the majority of that society.

Article 8 of the Convention, guaranteeing the right to private and family life, is supplemented by the right to marry under **article 12**, and by **article 14**, which guarantees the enjoyment of Convention rights free from discrimination on grounds of sex, or other status. Although **article 8** provides a general right to sexual life, much of the Convention case law in this area is concerned with the rights of homosexuals and transsexuals, who have suffered from the law's attempt to regulate their conduct or to exclude them from the general protection of the law.

With respect to homosexuals, although the European Court accepted that an individual had a *prima facie* right to choose and practice their own sexual orientation; it did not preclude regulation of non-heterosexual conduct. In *Dudgeon* (above) the

Court held that laws criminalizing homosexual acts, irrespective of the age of the participants, constituted an unjustified interference with the right to private life. Although the majority of the population may have disapproved of homosexuality, there was no evidence to suggest that the practice of homosexuality had been injurious to moral standards. Nevertheless, the Court accepted that the laws served a legitimate aim under article 8(2)—the protection of the rights and freedoms of others and the protection of morals—and that some degree of regulation via the criminal law can be necessary.

The Court was therefore more concerned with the proportionality of a particular measure, rather than questioning the legality of discriminatory treatment *per se* (*Modinos v Cyprus* (1993) 16 EHRR 485), and left a margin of appreciation in the hands of each state. However, the Court was prepared to subject such laws to intense scrutiny, and in *ADT v United Kingdom* (2001) 31 EHRR 33 it held that the application of criminal law (gross indecency) on the sole basis that the participants of the activities were male was in violation of article 8. This decision questioned the legitimacy of specific homosexuality offences and the offence of gross indecency was abolished by the **Sexual Offences Act 2003**.

The Convention began to offer a much narrower margin of appreciation to each state with respect to different age levels of hetero- and homosexual sex, and in *Sutherland v United Kingdom, The Times,* **13 April 2001** the European Commission held that the disparate age of consent in the law was in violation of **article 8,** leading to equalization in this area via the **Sexual Offences (Amendment) Act 2000.** In the Commission's view a disapproval of homosexual conduct and a preference for a heterosexual lifestyle did not constitute an objective and reasonable justification for inequality under the criminal law, and subsequent decisions indicate that the presumption is in favour of equality (*SL v Austria* (2003) 37 EHRR 39).

The European Court has also been instrumental in challenging discriminatory practices which have impacted on the civil rights of homosexuals. Thus, in *Smith and Grady v United Kingdom* (2000) 29 EHRR 493 and *Lustig-Prean and Beckett v United Kingdom* (2000) 29 EHRR 548 it held that the investigations into the applicants' sexual orientation, and their subsequent dismissals from the armed forces on the grounds of their sexual orientation, constituted grave interferences with the applicants' right to private life. The decision in *Smith and Grady* was particularly important as neither EC law (*Grant v South West Trains* [1998] IRLR 508) nor domestic sex discrimination law (*Macdonald v Ministry of Defence* [2004] 1 All ER 339) applied to discrimination on the grounds of sexual orientation. Article 8 has thus been instrumental in passing protective laws in this area (**Employment Equality (Sexual Orientation) Regulations 2003**). Any interference with the Convention rights of homosexuals could not thus be justified on the basis of society's negative attitude toward homosexuals, and in *Karner v Austria* (2004) 38 EHRR 24 the Court held that there was a violation of **articles 8 and 14** when a homosexual partner was refused his right to succeed a tenancy shared by him and his partner before his partner's death. Further, in *Mendoza v Ghaidan* [2004] 2 AC 557 the House of Lords was prepared to interpret the words 'living together as husband and wife' to mean 'living together as *if they were* man and wife' so as to avoid the discriminatory effect of an Act on same-sex partners. As a result the **Civil**

Partnership Act 2004, which gives legal recognition to same-sex (and other) relationships, provides general equality in the enjoyment of private and family life.

The European Court has, at times, sanctioned discriminatory state laws and practices, offering a limited margin of appreciation to member states. For example, in *Frette v France* (2004) 38 EHRR 1 it was held that it was permissible for the domestic authorities to refuse adoption rights to a homosexual applicant because of his choice of lifestyle. This decision appeared to be called into question in *EB v France* (2008) 47 EHRR 1, where the Court held that there had been a violation of **articles 8 and 14** when the applicant's request for adoption had been turned down on the grounds of the lack of paternal reference—the applicant was a homosexual living with another woman. The European Court found that the grounds for the refusal were based implicitly and unreasonably on her homosexuality and were *prima facie* in breach of **article 14.** Further, such grounds alone were not objectively justified as state law allowed applications from homosexuals. *Frette* was distinguished, although not expressly overruled, although the decision indicated that the Court will offer a limited margin of appreciation to states seeking to justify discriminatory practices.

Transsexuals have also benefited from the case law of the European Court. The traditional stance was reflected in *Corbett v Corbett* [1970] 2 All ER 33, where it was held that a person's sex was determined at birth and could not be changed subsequently, even by gender reassignment. This view was upheld by the European Court in *Rees v United Kingdom* (1986) 9 EHRR 56, where a female to male transsexual's request for the right to register his new sex on his birth certificate had been refused. The Court held that the right to respect for private life did not include a positive obligation on a state to give a person an unconditional right to label their chosen sexual identity, and that a balance had to be drawn between the interest of the individual and that of the public.

That decision was followed in *Cossey v United Kingdom* (1990) 13 EHRR 622 with respect to the right to marry, where the Court held that the biological approach adopted in domestic law was valid. The Court noted that state practice allowing such marriages was not uniform, and as a consequence there was no necessity for such a general right. This stance was modified in *B v France* (1992) 16 EHRR 1, where French law denying the right to change the sex of one's name on the birth certificate was held to be incompatible with the duty to respect private life, thus protecting transsexuals from wholly arbitrary interferences.

The Court continued its deferential approach in *Sheffield and Horsham v United Kingdom* (1999) 27 EHRR 163, where it noted the lack of any common European approach to legal recognition of post-operative gender status. In any case, the Court was not satisfied that by having to disclose their previous sexual identity they had suffered a substantial detriment so as to make any interference disproportionate to the aim of keeping correct records and of avoiding any possible deception. Further, in *X, Y and Z v United Kingdom* (1997) 24 EHRR 143, a female to male transsexual who had formed a relationship with a woman, and who had then had a child by artificial insemination, requested to register his name as the child's father on the birth certificate, but was refused. Despite finding that family life was no longer restricted to marriage-based relationships, and that there was now a clear trend towards the recognition of gender reassignment, it stressed that the community had an interest in maintaining a coherent system of family law that placed the best interests of the child at the forefront.

However, in those cases the Court warned the government that it should continue to monitor the situation and to consider changes in domestic law if and when necessary and in *Goodwin v United Kingdom* (2002) 35 EHRR 18 the Grand Chamber held that there had been a violation of **articles 8 and 12** of the Convention when the domestic law had refused to recognize the legal and civil status of the applicant. The Court held that the applicants had been subjected to a serious interference with their legal and Convention rights, causing feelings of vulnerability, anxiety, and humiliation. Further, the Court found no concrete or substantial detriment to the public interest, stressing that society should be expected to tolerate a certain inconvenience to enable individuals to live in dignity and worth in accordance with their chosen sexual identity. The Court also found a violation of **article 12**, holding that while it was for the state to determine the conditions under which a person could claim legal recognition as a transsexual, there was no justification for barring transsexuals from enjoying the right to marry under any circumstances.

The decision in *Goodwin* placed the onus on the state to show substantial justification for any interference and was followed in the domestic courts in *Bellinger v Bellinger* [2003] 2 AC 467, where the House of Lords held that domestic law which did not recognize the validity of a marriage undergone by a transsexual was incompatible with **articles 8 and 14**. This has led to changes in domestic law, giving civil and legal status to transsexuals (**Gender Recognition Act 2004**), although in *Grant v United Kingdom* (2007) 44 EHRR 1 the European Court held that, although the UK had acted swiftly to pass the **Gender Recognition Act 2004**, the applicant still remained a victim of the previous law and was entitled to the Convention's protection. Nevertheless, the European Court has rejected the claim that a transsexual should have the right to change her birth certificate until she had divorced in compliance with the registration system provided by the 2004 Act (*R v United Kingdom*, **Application No 35749/05**).

In conclusion, the European Convention has been instrumental in protecting both homosexuals and transsexuals from discrimination in the enjoyment of their Convention rights. In both cases, however, the European Court has had to overcome its own deferential approach, meaning that such groups had to endure decades of discrimination before benefiting from any changes in the law. Thus, the Convention and its principles of equality and human dignity have led to substantial changes in the status and rights of such groups; although the decision in *R* (above) denies complete equality.

Further reading

Clayton, R and Tomlinson, H, *Law of Human Rights*, 2nd edn (OUP 2009), ch 12.

Fenwick, H and Phillipson, G, *Media Freedom under the Human Rights Act* (OUP 2006), Part IV.

Rozenberg, J, *Privacy and the Press* (OUP 2004).

Sanderson, MA, 'Is von Hannover a step backward for the substantive analysis of speech and privacy interests?' [2004] EHRLR 631.

10

Freedom of expression

Introduction

Freedom of expression, or free speech, forms an essential part of the vast majority of human rights courses and students can normally expect at least one exam question in this area. Questions can be either in essay or problem form and can cover general matters such as the nature and importance of free speech, its protection under the European Convention and in domestic law, as well as notions such as press freedom and the public right to know. In addition, questions may concentrate on specific laws affecting free speech, such as defamation, confidentiality, official secrets, freedom of information, contempt of court, obscenity and indecency, and blasphemy laws. Even when answering questions in a substantive law area the student needs to be conversant with the principles of free speech if he or she is to offer a constructive and reflective answer.

As freedom of expression is a conditional right, the student needs to appreciate the ways in which it may be compromised, including the principles of legality and necessity governing any such interference. Also, because it often conflicts with other rights, students will not only need to appreciate how such rights are balanced, but also must be prepared for questions which require a knowledge of other human rights, such as privacy (confidentiality and defamation), the right to a fair trial (contempt of court), and freedom of religion (race or religious hatred laws and blasphemy). It is common, therefore, to mix free speech questions with other areas on the course and the student should be prepared for this. In particular, questions on free speech might require sound knowledge of freedom of assembly and public order law (dealt with, in this book, in Chapter 11).

Question 1

'Freedom of expression constitutes one of the essential foundations of a democratic society. . . This means that every formality, condition, restriction or penalty imposed in this sphere must be proportionate to the legitimate aim pursued.' (European Court of Human Rights in *Handyside v United Kingdom* (1976) 1 EHRR 737).

By the use of the case law of the European Court of Human Rights explain how freedom of expression has been upheld, and how the Court has used the 'margin of appreciation' to limit that freedom.

Commentary

The question requires a good knowledge of the jurisprudence of the European Convention with respect to the protection of freedom of expression. The student must first know why the European Court regards that freedom as an essential foundation of a democratic society, and this in turn requires an appreciation of the general values and theories of free speech. In addition, the student should be conversant with the principles of legality, necessity, and proportionality contained in **article 10(2)** of the Convention in order to justify any interference with this fundamental right, along with relevant case law to use in illustration. Finally, the student needs to be aware of the nature and significance of the doctrine of the 'margin of appreciation' and to use case examples to explain how the European Court has used the doctrine to adjudicate on cases involving the balancing of freedom of expression with other rights and interests.

Answer plan

- Explanation of the values of freedom of expression and its importance in democratic societies
- Explanation of how **article 10** of the European Convention seeks to protect freedom of expression
- Examination of the requirements of legitimacy and necessity employed by the Convention with respect to the restriction of that freedom
- Examination of relevant case law of the European Court to explain how and to what extent free speech has been upheld
- Explanation of the doctrine of margin of appreciation and its application in cases of free speech adjudication

Suggested answer

In *Handyside v United Kingdom* (1976) 1 EHRR 737 the European Court stated that freedom of expression constituted one of the essential foundations of a democratic society, forming one of the basic conditions for its progress and for the development of every man. This dictum recognizes the value of free speech in achieving individual autonomy and self-fulfilment. Consequently, the Court stressed that the protection afforded by **article 10** is applicable not only to information or ideas that are favourably received or regarded as inoffensive or as a matter of indifference, but also to those that offend, shock, or disturb the state or any sector of the population. In the Court's view, this accords with the demands of pluralism, tolerance, and broadmindedness without which there is no democratic society. However, the reference to 'a democratic society' recognizes that freedom of expression fulfils a wider public function in promoting democracy, allowing the free flow of views on matters of public interest and in discovering the truth.

Article 10 includes the right to 'hold opinions and to receive and impart information and ideas', and the European Court has extended its protection to commercial speech (*Autronic AG v Switzerland* (1990) 12 EHRR 485), and obscene and blasphemous expression (*Müller v Switzerland* (1991) 13 EHRR 212 and *Otto-Preminger Institut v Austria* (1994) 19 EHRR 34). However, **article 10** does not protect racist speech, particularly if it is aimed at the destruction of the rights of others as prohibited by **article 17** (*Glimerveen and Hagenbeek v Netherlands* (1980) 18 DR 187).

Article 10, paragraph 2 allows interference with the right provided the restriction is 'prescribed by law', pursues one of the legitimate aims listed within paragraph 2, and is 'necessary in a democratic society' for the furtherance of that legitimate aim. Freedom of expression, therefore, carries with it duties and responsibilities and has to be balanced against other rights such as an individual's privacy (*Von Hannover v Germany* (2005) 40 EHRR 1) as well as a number of social interests, such as public morality (*Handyside v United Kingdom* (above)). Nevertheless, any interference must possess the qualities of legality and necessity laid down in **article 10(2)**. Further, the Court is not faced with a choice between two conflicting principles, but with a principle of freedom of expression subject to a number of exceptions, which must be restrictively and narrowly construed (*Sunday Times v United Kingdom* (1979) 2 EHRR 245).

The Court must be satisfied that any interference is 'prescribed by law'. This protects free speech from arbitrary interference, insisting that the law must be identified and established (either in statute or the common law (*Sunday Times v United Kingdom* (above)), accessible, and formulated with sufficient certainty to enable people to regulate their conduct by it (*Silver v United Kingdom* (1983) 5 EHRR 347). Thus, although the Court has accepted that laws are inevitably couched in vague terms, and that their meaning and scope become apparent after it has been construed and applied by the courts (*Sunday Times v United Kingdom* (above)), it has refused to accept rules which are so vague that their meaning cannot be reasonably predicted. For example, in *Hashman and Harrap v United Kingdom* (1999) 30 EHRR 241 it held that the power to order a person to desist in conduct which is seen as wrong in the eyes of the majority of contemporary citizens failed to give sufficient guidance as to what conduct individuals were not allowed to partake in. Further, the Court must ensure that the restriction was imposed for a legitimate aim recognized by **article 10(2)**, although it will recognize a measure despite it being unequal in its application (*Gay News v United Kingdom* (1983) 5 EHRR 123).

Further, any violation of **article 10** must be 'necessary in a democratic society' for achieving the legitimate aim. Thus, there must exist a pressing social need for the restriction, the restriction in question must correspond to that need, and it must constitute a proportionate response to such a need (***Barthold v Germany*** (1985) 7 **EHRR 383**). Further, in *Handyside v United Kingdom* (above) it was held that the word 'necessary' did not mean 'useful' or 'convenient', thus protecting free speech from violations based on spurious and unsubstantiated grounds. Thus, the Court has held that a restriction should be strictly proportionate to its aim and that it should not go beyond what is strictly required to achieve that purpose (*Barthold v Germany* (above)).

However, this review goes hand in hand with the doctrine of the 'margin of appreciation', which leaves a certain margin of discretion to domestic authorities when passing, interpreting, and applying domestic laws that interfere with free speech (*Handyside v United Kingdom* (above)). This doctrine assumes that each state might take a variety of measures in attempting to balance free speech with other rights and interests, and that the Court should respect those measures provided they comply generally with principles enshrined in **article 10**.

The doctrine has been used cautiously and the margin of appreciation can be narrowed or widened depending on the circumstances of the case.

The state's margin of appreciation has been quite broad with respect to expression that conflicts with public morality, and the Court has been prepared to defer to the member state on whether such measures should exist and, largely, their extent. Thus, in *Handyside* (above) it stated that it was not possible to find a uniform conception of morals within the Council of Europe, and that the states, by reason of their direct and continuous contact with the vital forces of their countries, were in a better position than the international judge to give an opinion on the exact content of the requirements of morals, as well as to the necessity of any restriction or penalty intended to meet those requirements. The Court has taken a similar stance with respect to blasphemous speech (*Otto-Preminger Institut v Austria* (above) and **Wingrove v United Kingdom** (1996) 24 **EHRR 1**) and has held that it is within each state's discretion to have such laws (*Gay News v United Kingdom* (above)). These cases reflect the fact that it may be difficult to apply a common European standard in this area, and that the Court regards shocking and offensive speech as less important than other speech, such as political expression. Thus, in *Müller v Switzerland* (above), it was prepared to accept that causing gross offence to a society or its citizens was a legitimate aim, despite the traditional argument that such harm is not sufficient to justify restricting liberty.

In contrast, the Court has offered a much narrower margin of appreciation to speech that promotes a wider and more tangible public interest. Thus, in *Sunday Times v United Kingdom* (above) it held that in assessing whether any interference was based on sufficient reason, account must be taken of any public interest aspect of the case. Consequently, as free speech and press freedom are fundamental to the operation of democracy, it is prepared to apply the doctrine of proportionality to its fullest extent. For example, in *Sunday Times* it held that the granting of injunctions to stop a newspaper discussing impending litigation on the thalidomide disaster should not have been permitted unless it was *absolutely* certain that it would interfere with those proceedings. That decision can be explained on one of two bases. First, as the Court pointed out, the laws of contempt, as opposed to the laws of obscenity and indecency, displayed a much more common approach, allowing the Court to more easily judge the necessity of any particular interference. In such a case a more extensive European supervision corresponds to a less discretionary power of appreciation. Secondly, the duty of the press to inform the public on matters of great public interest was essential to democracy, and the Court will thus subject the measure to more intense scrutiny.

The Court is thus prepared to afford special protection to freedom of speech in the context of press freedom. For example, in *Thorgeirson v Iceland* (1992) 14 EHRR 843 the European Court held that when journalists publish articles directed at a matter of serious public interest in an attempt to draw popular attention to matters of legitimate public concern, any penalty imposed on such a person had to be strictly proportionate. This suggests that excessive penalties, including excessive damages in defamation actions (*Tolstoy v United Kingdom* (1995) 20 EHRR 442) might have a chilling effect on press freedom, and should be subjected to very close scrutiny by the Court. Similarly, in *Jersild v Denmark* (1994) 19 EHRR 1 the conviction and fining of an employee of a broadcasting company for assisting the expression of unlawful racist speech on a television show was held in violation of **article 10**. Although the views of the group were not protected by **article 10**, the punishment of a journalist for assisting in the dissemination of such statements would seriously hamper the contribution of the press in discussion of matters of public interest. Consequently, such speech is guarded most zealously, and the state's margin of appreciation is narrower.

As with the United States Supreme Court (*New York Times v Sullivan* (1964) 376 US 254), the European Court has given enhanced protection under **article 10** to those who question and criticize government and public officials. For example, in *Castells v Spain* (1992) 14 EHRR 445 it stressed that in the democratic system, the actions or omissions of the government must be subject to close scrutiny not only by the legislative and judicial authorities but also via the press and public opinion. Thus, with respect to defamation actions, in *Lingens v Austria* (1986) 8 EHRR 407 the Court noted that freedom of the press afforded the public the best means of discovering and forming an opinion of the ideas and attitudes of political leaders and that as a consequence the limits of acceptable criticism of an individual are wider with respect to a politician than as regards a private individual. However, the Court has not gone so far as to prohibit public figures from taking actions in defamation and in *Steel and Morris v United Kingdom* (2005) 41 EHRR 22 it accepted that large public corporations should not be excluded from defending their reputation. The Court will also allow a narrow margin of appreciation if the restriction takes the form of prior restraint (*Observer and Guardian v United Kingdom* (1991) 14 EHRR 153).

The European Court has extended the protection of **article 10** to almost all forms of expression, and has, despite the doctrine of the margin of appreciation, required strong justification for any restriction with that right. However, the Court is more likely to offer states limited deference where the speech genuinely serves the public interest. This is evident in the recent judgment in *Von Hannover v Germany* (above), where the Court held that a celebrity's privacy had been violated when the paparazzi persistently photographed her whilst shopping and socializing. In the Court's view the public did not have a genuine public interest in receiving such information, distinguishing this case from those such as *Lingens* (above). It appears, therefore, that some speech may be more important than others, and that such a factor will dictate the margin of appreciation afforded to the domestic authorities.

Question 2

To what extent does English common law protect freedom of expression? How has the passing of the **Human Rights Act 1998** enhanced free speech and do you feel that domestic law is now consistent with the case law of the **European Convention on Human Rights**?

Commentary

This question requires a knowledge of relevant domestic law both pre- and post-Human Rights Act. As it requires consideration of whether the law is compatible with **article 10** of the Convention, it also demands a sound knowledge of the case law and jurisprudence of the European Court of Human Rights in this area. The question covers a good deal of ground and the student should select case and other examples that illustrate the fundamental characteristics of the domestic system, as well as the essential case law of the Convention.

The answer should begin by exploring the pre-Human Rights Act position and considering whether in the absence of a domestic bill of rights domestic law recognized such a right, and if so, the extent and effectiveness of such protection. Reference can be made to decisions of the European Court to illustrate the effectiveness or otherwise of domestic protection. The student can then move on to the post-Act era, explaining the 'incorporation' of **article 10** into domestic law and, in particular, the protection afforded to freedom of expression by **s.12** of the 1998 Act. The answer should include the essential case law under **s.12** and the principles emanating from such cases, as well as cases on various aspects of free speech in the post-Act era, examining whether those cases are in general conformity with the European Convention and the Court's case law.

Answer plan

- Explanation of the theory of free speech protection and its constitutional importance
- Examination of the status of free speech at common law and examples of its recognition, enforcement, and the limitations of that protection

- Explanation of the 'incorporation' of **article 10** of the Convention into domestic law by the 1998 Act, in particular via **s.12** of the Act
- Examination of the post-Human Rights Act case law
- Analysis of present domestic law to assess its compatibility with the European Convention with respect to the values and principles of free speech upheld by **article 10** of the Convention, along with relevant case law

Suggested answer

Before the **Human Rights Act 1998**, freedom of expression existed as a residual freedom. In other words, one was allowed to exercise freedom of speech provided that it did not infringe any of the restrictions in statute or the common law, such as the criminal laws of obscenity and indecency, and civil laws such as defamation and confidentiality. Although freedom of expression was not protected in a bill of rights, there was evidence of its acceptance by the courts as a fundamental constitutional right. As a consequence, the courts would seek to protect it from arbitrary and unnecessary interference by interpreting legislative and common law restrictions in a manner that would ensure the greatest possible enjoyment of free speech.

For example, the courts would strike down administrative actions that unlawfully interfered with freedom of expression. Thus, in *Wheeler v Leicester County Council* [1985] AC 1054 a local council had acted unlawfully by penalizing a rugby club when it had refused to persuade their players not to tour South Africa, the court assuming that the Council had no statutory power to penalize the club for its opinions. The courts would thus insist on substantial justification for any interference and in *R v Secretary of State for the Home Department, ex parte O'Brien and Simms* [2000] 2 AC 115 a policy restricting journalists visiting prisoners and using the content of such interviews for the purposes of publication was declared *ultra vires* the **Prison Act 1952**. In that case, Lord Steyn noted that the starting point was freedom of expression, which in a democracy is a primary right and without which an effective rule of law is not possible.

The courts insisted that freedom of expression was as well protected at common law as under **article 10** of the European Convention on Human Rights, and in *R v Secretary of State for the Home Department, ex parte Brind* [1991] AC 696 the House of Lords stressed that the courts would start with the presumption that any interference with freedom of expression was unlawful. Thus, the fact that in that case it was held that **article 10** of the Convention, and the doctrine of proportionality, could not be directly employed in the domestic courts was not seen as a disadvantage. Similarly, in *Attorney-General v Guardian Newspapers (No 2)* [1998] 3 All ER 852 the House of Lords held that an injunction could not be granted restraining the publication of information on matters of government unless there was evidence of an overriding public interest outweighing the public interest in the free dissemination of information.

Despite this approach, the position of freedom of expression before the Human Rights Act was regarded as unsatisfactory. In *Brind* (above) the courts had rejected the possibility of relying on **article 10** of the Convention directly and subjecting restrictions to the doctrine of proportionality. This led to defeats before the European Court of Human Rights in areas such as contempt of court, where the European Court of Human Rights held that the domestic courts had failed to give sufficient weight to freedom of expression when granting injunctions prohibiting a newspaper from commenting on impending legal proceedings (*Sunday Times v United Kingdom* (1979) 2 EHRR 245). The government suffered other defeats with respect to the disclosure of press sources (*Goodwin v United Kingdom* (1996) **22 EHRR 123**) and prior restraints (*Observer and Guardian v United Kingdom* (1991) 14 EHRR 153), thus showing the inconsistency of domestic judges in protecting free speech.

The coming into operation of the **Human Rights Act 1998** provided the opportunity to enhance free speech protection. The domestic courts are now allowed to refer to relevant Convention case law when resolving free speech disputes and are able to apply the doctrine of proportionality in deciding whether any interference with free speech is 'necessary in a democratic society.' This should at least ensure that the domestic courts are applying the same weight to freedom of expression as does the European Court of Human Rights. In addition, **s.12** of the Human Rights Act requires the courts to have particular regard to freedom of expression where it grants relief that might affect the exercise of the Convention right to freedom of expression. More specifically, **s.12(2)** provides that if a respondent in free speech proceedings is neither present nor represented, then the court should not grant relief unless it is satisfied that the applicant has taken all practicable steps to notify the respondent, or that there are compelling reasons why the respondent should not be notified.

The Act also seeks to control interferences with free speech via prior restraint, which is viewed by the European Court as the most dangerous form of restriction (*Observer and Guardian v United Kingdom* (above)). **Section 12(3)** thus provides that a court should not restrain publication before trial unless it is satisfied that the applicant is likely to establish that publication should not be allowed. This is intended to favour publication by modifying the rule in *American Cyanamid v Ethicon Ltd* [1975] AC 396—the balance of probabilities test—which was adopted to decide where the balance of convenience lay before granting the order. In *Cream Holdings v Banerjee and another* [2005] 1 AC 253 it was held that the purpose of **s.12(3)** was to emphasize the importance of freedom of expression at the interim stage and set a higher threshold for granting interim orders against the press than the *American Cyanamid* criteria. Hence, as a general rule the courts should be very slow to make such orders where the applicant had not demonstrated that he would probably succeed at trial. Further protection of free speech was recognized in *Green v Associated Newspapers* [2005] 3 WLR 281, where the Court of Appeal confirmed that an interim injunction would be refused in defamation cases unless the defence of fair comment or justification is bound to fail.

However, the courts have recognized that freedom of expression is not an absolute right. Thus, although **s.12** provides that the courts must have *particular regard* to the importance of this Convention right, this does not give free speech an absolute or even superior status over and above other Convention rights. For example, in *Douglas* *v Hello!* [2001] 2 WLR 992 the Court of Appeal held that **s.12(4)** requires the court to consider **article 10** of the Convention in its entirety, and not to give freedom of speech additional weight over and above any competing right, such as the right to private life. Equally, the court's task under **s.12(3)** was to apply its mind to how one right was to be balanced against another right, without building in additional weight on the one side (*Re S (Publicity)* [2005] 1 AC 593).This reflects the wording of **s.12(4)**, which requires the court not only to consider whether publication would be in the public interest, but also whether it would violate any relevant privacy code. Nevertheless, the courts have confirmed that one can start with the premise that any interference with free speech is unlawful and that the grounds for interference have to be established convincingly (*Venables and Thompson v MGN* [2001] 2 WLR 1038). This accords with the case law of the European Court of Human Rights (*Sunday Times v United Kingdom* (above)).

Whether freedom of expression has been enhanced in the post-Human Rights era, can only be answered by examining the relevant case law. In many areas, such as national security, the courts appear to remain deferential. For example, in *R v Shayler* [2002] 2 WLR 754 the House of Lords refused to imply a public interest defence into the **Official Secrets Act 1989**, believing that the special position of those employed in the security and intelligence services made it inappropriate to offer such a defence, even where the information in question was of great public interest. Although this decision might be regarded as conservative, it is probably consistent with the European Court's stance in this area (*Leander v Sweden* (1987) 9 EHRR 433).

A more controversial deference was shown in *R (Prolife) v BBC* [2004] 1 AC 185, where the courts upheld a ban on a proposed election broadcast on the grounds that it violated taste and decency. In that case the House of Lords held that the courts should be reluctant to interfere with the broadcasting authority's decision and that it was not appropriate for the court to conduct its own balancing exercise between the requirements of political speech and the protection of the public from undue distress. This decision does not appear to conform to the case law of the European Court with respect to political speech (*Lingens v Austria* (1986) 8 EHRR 407). Further, in *R (Animal Defenders International) v Minister of Culture, Media and Sport* [2008] 2 WLR 781 it was held that the **Communications Act 2003**, which prohibits political advertising, was compatible with **article 10**, despite the Minister making a declaration of incompatibility when introducing the Bill, believing it to be inconsistent with the European Court's case law (*VgT Verein gegen Tierfabriken v Switzerland* (2002) 34 EHRR 4).

The courts have been more liberal in areas such as the law of confidentiality and defamation where they are satisfied that there is a true public interest in publication. This has allowed them to refuse interim injunctions in cases where free speech conflicts with the commercial confidences of the claimant (*Cream Holdings* (above)). However, they have been less generous where freedom of expression has conflicted with individual privacy, even that of public figures, and have stated that the public have a very limited interest in publication of details of such individuals' private lives (*McKennitt v Ash* [2007] 3 WLR 194 and *HRH Prince of Wales v Associated Newspapers Ltd* [2007] 3 WLR 222). So too, in the law of defamation the courts have been prepared to extend the defence of qualified privilege to the press to conform to the Convention case law (*Lingens v Austria* (above)). Although they have insisted on the press employing strict standards of professional journalism (*Galloway v Telegraph Group Ltd* [2005] EMLR 7), subsequent case law confirms that the defence should not be denied on these grounds where there is a true and strong public interest in publication (*Jameel v Wall Street Journal Europe* [2007] 1 AC 359).

In conclusion, domestic law is now equipped to apply the principles of legality and necessity that are employed by the European Court to ensure that interference with free speech is not incompatible with **article 10**. In addition, in areas such as the law of confidentiality there is some evidence to suggest that freedom of expression is given greater weight than in the past, particularly with respect to the granting of temporary injunctions. However, in other areas such as national security and public morality, there appears to be little evidence of fundamental, or indeed any, change. This probably justifies the conclusion that, on the whole, freedom of expression has not been greatly enhanced in the post-Human Rights Act era.

Question 3

(A)

To what extent are the laws of defamation a justifiable interference with free speech and freedom of the press?

(B)

Arnold, a freelance journalist, began investigating the private and professional affairs of Sir Graham Forrester, an MP and former government minister. On the basis of information given to him by Sir Graham's ex-personal secretary, Arnold submitted an article to the Sunday Scum, which alleged that, whilst chairman of the 'Family Values' Committee, Sir Graham had been involved in an affair with the 18-year-old daughter of a neighbour. Acting on the same source, he also submitted an article to the same newspaper, which alleged that his wife allowed him to entertain prostitutes in the family home. Sir Graham was telephoned by the newspaper's editor, and asked for his comments on the allegations, but he simply told them that he had no comment other than he would sue if they published 'these lies'. Sir Graham now wishes to sue the newspaper in defamation in connection with these articles. Advise Sir Geoffrey as to what remedies are available to him and the likelihood of him succeeding in an action for defamation.

 Commentary

This question requires a sound appreciation of the law of defamation and how it impacts on freedom of expression, press freedom, and the public right to know. The first part of the question is not an opportunity to write all you know about the law of defamation, but rather to identify the purpose of the law and its potential impact on freedom of expression. Therefore, the student should be careful to identify the law's most central rules, supported by relevant case law, in order to assess whether the law strikes an appropriate balance between the achievement of its aims and the protection of free speech. Reference should be made to **articles 8 and 10** of the European Convention, along with the case law of the European Court in this area.

The second part of the question requires the student to apply the issues identified in part one to the particular facts of the scenario, advising on the potential success of a defamation action, including any likely defences. Again, the student should centre on issues affecting the law of defamation and freedom of the press and the public interest in freedom of expression. As part one of the question requires the discussion of a number of issues, it might be wise to spend more time on that part, and to allude to those principles and cases when giving advice.

Answer plan

- Explanation of the aims of defamation laws and their impact on freedom of expression

- Explanation and analysis of the extent of those laws, the penalties for infringement, and any available defences

- Conclusions as to the necessity and proportionality of those laws and defences and their compatibility with the **Human Rights Act 1998** and the **European Convention on Human Rights**

- Consideration of the necessary ingredients of an action in defamation and whether they exist in this case

- Explanation of the likely remedies open to Sir Graham and whether they would be granted

- Explanation of any defences available to the newspaper and their possible success

Suggested answer

(A)

The law of defamation protects an individual's reputation from untrue statements that either subjects them to ridicule, hatred, or contempt, or which lower that person's reputation in the eyes of right-thinking members of society (*Sim v Stretch* (1936) 52 TLR 669). Article 10(2) of the European Convention provides that freedom of expression can be restricted to protect the rights or reputations of others; a person's right to reputation being part of his or her private life (*Tammer v Estonia* (2003) 37 EHRR 43). However, such laws must strike a proper balance between these competing fundamental rights and domestic law should not unreasonably halt the flow of political and other public interest discussion (*Lingens v Austria* (1986) 8 EHRR 407), or award damages so excessive as to impose a chilling effect on free speech (*Tolstoy v United Kingdom* (1975) 20 EHRR 442). Further, in *Steel and Morris v United Kingdom* (2005) 41 EHRR 22 the Court stressed the importance of equality of arms between those who publish and powerful claimants.

Domestic law contains attempts to ensure that defamation actions do not unduly interfere with press freedom. First, in certain contexts the law might regard freedom of expression as so vital that it will bar an individual from taking action. For example, **article 9 of the Bill of Rights 1689** protects parliamentary debates by providing that freedom of speech and debates or proceedings in Parliament cannot be impeached or questioned, and this immunity has been upheld by the European Court (*A v United Kingdom* (2003) 36 EHRR 51). Further, in *Derbyshire County Council v Times Newspapers* [1993] AC 534, it was held that democratically elected bodies were not able to sue in defamation, noting that such an action would stifle public criticism of its activities.

Secondly, the common law has protected freedom of expression in this area from prior restraint. Thus, in *Bonnard v Perryman* [1891] 2 Ch 269 it was held that no temporary orders pending full trial will be given where the defendant intends to raise the defences of justification and/or fair comment unless it was clear that such a defence would fail at the trial. This extends to the defence of qualified privilege, and has been accepted as a necessary safeguard to free speech and thus compatible with **articles 8 and 10** of the Convention (*Green v Associated Newspapers* [2005] 3 WLR 281). The presumption against prior restraint is, however, offset by potentially large damages awards, which may have a chilling effect on freedom of expression. This danger was recognized by the European Court in *Tolstoy Miloslavsky v United Kingdom* (above) where it was held that an award of £1.5m constituted a disproportionate interference with freedom of expression and the domestic courts are now empowered to give juries strict guidance on the acceptability of damage awards (*Grobbelaar v News Group Newspapers* [2002] 1 WLR 3024). Nevertheless, in *Independent News and Media plc and another v Ireland* (2006) 42 EHRR 46, the European Court held that high awards are acceptable provided domestic law provides sufficient safeguards against disproportionate damages.

Because the law of defamation has such a potentially damaging impact on free speech and press freedom, it is essential that suitable defences are available in such actions. In addition to providing absolute immunity, the law may also provide a defence of qualified privilege, which will be lost if the defendant has acted maliciously or in bad faith. This defence applies, *inter alia*, to fair and accurate reports of both parliamentary proceedings and *bona fide* public meetings held for a lawful purpose and to discuss matters of public concern. Further, in *Turkington v Times Newspapers Ltd* [2001] 2 AC 277 a press conference attracted qualified privilege, their Lordships recognizing that such forums had become an important vehicle for promoting discussion on matters of public concern.

The defence is also available where the defendant has a legal or moral duty to impart information and conveys it to a person who has a similar duty to receive it (*Beech v Freeson* [1972] 1 QB 14). Initially the courts refused to extend the defence to the press (*Blackshaw v Lord* [1984] QB 1), but in *Reynolds v Times Newspapers* [1999] 4 All ER 609 it was held that the defence might be used by the press in appropriate circumstances to justify the publication of public interest information; although the House of Lords stressed that there was no defence of public interest *per se*, and refused to give political information immunity, irrespective of the circumstances. Whether the defence was available depended on factors such as the seriousness of the allegation, the nature of the information (including the urgency of the matter), and the extent to which the subject matter was of public concern. In addition, they stressed the need for the press to display responsible journalism, requiring it in most cases to check its sources and to seek the comments of the potential claimant before publication. This case follows the case law of the European Court, which insists that domestic law makes allowance for the fact that the plaintiff was a public figure (*Lingens* (above)).

The courts have applied the defence with caution and in *Loutchansky v Times Newspapers Ltd and others (No 2)* [2002] 1 All ER 652 it was held that, although the public had an interest in the promotion of a free and vigorous press, the press had a corresponding duty to act responsibly. Consequently, to set the standard of journalistic responsibility too low would encourage too great a readiness to publish defamatory material. In that case it was also held that the defence could not be used in relation to facts of which the defendant was unaware at the time of publication; and the Court of Appeal's approach was affirmed by the European Court: *Times Newspapers v United Kingdom,* [2009] EMLR 14. This caution has been shown in subsequent cases, and in *Galloway v Telegraph Group Ltd* [2005] EMLR 7 it was held that a newspaper was not under a moral or social duty to make the allegations about an MP's unlawful associations without any attempt at verification and without putting to him what they were proposing to publish. However, in *Jameel v Wall Street Journal* [2005] 2 WLR 1577 the House of Lords held that, although the public interest test established in *Reynolds* was more stringent than proving that the public would be interested in the matter, the defence should not be denied simply because the press had departed from one of its obligations to ensure professional journalism—the main factor being whether the public interest test had been satisfied.

Outside the defence of qualified privilege, the press will have to rely on the defences of fair comment and justification. This will often involve the press proving the substantial truth of the statement, a factor which the House of Lords recognized as being capable of stifling public criticism (*Derbyshire County Council* (above)). Although the European Court has accepted that this burden of proof is not necessarily inconsistent with **article 10** (*McVicar v United Kingdom* (2000) 35 EHRR 22), it has stressed that the law of defamation should provide greater protection to speech which attacks politicians (*Lingens* (above)), and large corporations (*Steel and Morris v United Kingdom* (above)), particularly where the statements are part of general public discussion.

(B)

If Sir Graham intends to bring an action in defamation, it must be established that the allegations contained in the stories would lower Sir Graham's reputation in the eyes of right-thinking members of society (*Sim v Stretch* (above)). There would appear to be little doubt that such allegations would so harm Sir Graham's reputation, ruining his career as an MP and causing him to be castigated in the eyes of the public. Further, this could cause him financial harm, as he may find it difficult to hold a position of authority and responsibility in the future.

Sir Graham is advised to seek an interim injunction, prohibiting the publication of the allegations pending the full trial of the action. However, the courts will be reluctant to grant such an order where the defendant will rely on the defences of justification, fair comment, and qualified privilege at the trial (*Bonnard v Perryman* (above)). This rule has been upheld by the Court of Appeal as a necessary restriction on the claimant's right to vindicate their reputation (*Green v Associated Newspapers* (above)), and will mean that the injunction will be refused unless the court is satisfied that the defences are bound to fail at the full trial, which given the fact that the information was received from an ex-employee, appears unlikely.

Accordingly, Sir Graham is advised to maintain an action in defamation for damages, compensating him for the harm caused to his reputation. Such damages could also reflect any interference with his right to private life, as guaranteed by **article 8**, and can be substantial in a case such as the present where great financial and other harm is likely to be caused (***The Gleaner Company and another v Abrahams*** [2004] 1 AC 628). However, any award must not be so great as to have a chilling effect on freedom of expression (***Tolstoy Miloslavsky v United Kingdom*** (1995) 22 EHRR 442).

The newspaper would seek to rely on a number of defences at full trial. First, it will seek to rely on the defence of justification. The newspaper will have to prove the truth of the sting of the allegation, rather than the truth of every allegation made in the stories. Thus, if the neighbour's daughter was 20 rather than 18, that would not defeat a defence of justification, whereas if the affair was with a mature woman who was not a neighbour's daughter, a defence of justification would fail. Similarly, **s.5 of the Defamation Act 1952** states that where more than one defamatory comment is made about a person and not all of them are justified, the defence is still available if the words not proved to be true do not materially injure the plaintiff's reputation having regard to the truth of the remaining charges. Thus, if the allegations about the prostitutes are proved to be true, then the newspaper could rely on **s.5** even if the story about the neighbour's daughter was untrue, the reputation of Sir Graham already being irreparably damaged.

As the newspaper's allegations could not be described as opinion, it could not rely on the defence of fair comment (***Silkin v Beaverbrook Newspapers Ltd*** [1958] 1 WLR 743), and it would have to rely on the defence of qualified privilege. The defence can be used where the defendant has a duty to impart information and does so to a person who has a duty to receive it (*Beech v Freeson* (above)), but is not available if it can be proved that the defendant has acted maliciously or in bad faith, which is unlikely in the present circumstances because the newspaper at least relies on information given by a third party.

Since *Reynolds v Times Newspapers* (above) the press has been allowed to rely on the defence provided the court is satisfied that the 'duty-interest test' had been satisfied. The court would first need to be satisfied that there was a sufficient public interest in the publication, which seems to be clear, as the claimant is a current MP, a former cabinet minister, and a former chairman of a Family Values Committee, making the allegations particularly appropriate for public debate. The court would also consider factors such as the seriousness of the allegation—in this case it is particularly serious, which might act against the newspaper—but also the nature of the information and the extent to which the subject matter was of public concern, which in the present case would favour publication.

To rely on this defence, newspapers must exercise the attributes of professional journalism (*Loutchansky v Times Newspapers Ltd and others (No 2)* (above)), although the essential question is whether there is a public interest in publication (*Jameel v Wall Street Journal Europe* (above)). Further, in *Reynolds* (above) the House of Lords held that the courts should pay regard to particular factors such as the source and status of the information, the steps taken to verify it, the urgency of the matter, and the tone of the article. All these factors appear to favour the press in our case as the source appears reliable, and the public interest would be best served by the instant publication of the matter.

More specifically, regard should be had as to whether the defendant had sought comment from the claimant, and whether the article contained the gist of the claimant's side of the story. Sir Graham was approached and told the editor that he had nothing to say, apart from his threat to sue. Thus, given the public interest in the information, and the facts that the newspaper appears to be relying on a reliable source and to have given the claimant an opportunity to comment, I would advise Sir Graham that his action in defamation would be met with a successful defence of qualified privilege.

Question 4

To what extent does domestic law relating to government confidentiality and official secrets provide for a defence of 'press freedom' and the public right to know? How has the **Freedom of Information Act 2000** impacted on this area?

 Commentary

This question covers the area of official secrecy and freedom of expression and requires a sound knowledge of the **Official Secrets Acts**, the common law of confidentiality and the **Freedom of Information Act 2000**. These three areas often generate questions in their own right, but this question combines them and requires the student to assess the law's impact on press freedom and the public right to know. Consequently, the answer does not require an in-depth knowledge of the law, but rather expects the student to identify its central characteristics and the general concerns with respect to free speech and freedom of information.

The answer should begin with a brief explanation of the aims of and need for secrecy laws and the difficulty in maintaining a balance between national security and public safety on the one hand, and press freedom and the public right to know on the other. The answer should then concentrate on those aspects which impact on press freedom and the public right to know, rather than giving a general account of the law. Students should provide case examples in illustration and should draw on the case law of the European Court of Human Rights in order to assess the compatibility of the respective laws with free speech norms. Finally, the student can assess the impact of the **Freedom of Information Act** in this area, before concluding as to whether domestic law achieves a proportionate balance between state security and press freedom.

Answer plan

- Explanation of the rules and aims of the common law of confidentiality and the **Official Secrets Acts**

- Consideration of the need to balance national security with press freedom and the public right to know

- Consideration of the extent to which the above laws accommodate any press freedom defence

- Consideration of the impact of the **Freedom of Information Act 2000** on the above

- Conclusions as to whether the present law adequately protects press freedom and the public right to know

Suggested answer

Although the workings and activities of government and other public agencies are undoubtedly in the public interest of free speech and democratic accountability, government will argue that the disclosure of such information is detrimental to effective government and national safety. The law and the courts will, therefore, have to balance these two fundamental issues. Under **article 10(2)** of the European Convention freedom of speech can be compromised on grounds of national security, territorial integrity, public safety, the prevention of disorder and crime, and the prevention of the disclosure of information received in confidence, all of which potentially promote the machinery of government. Such restrictions have to be prescribed by law and are necessary in a democratic society, although in *Leander v Sweden* (1987) 9 **EHRR** 433 it was accepted that the state would be given discretion not only with respect to the necessity and proportionality of such laws, but also as to their clarity and certainty.

The government's power to defend national security is contained in specific official secrets legislation and the private law of confidentiality, which, along with the law of contempt of court, can be employed by public authorities in an attempt to safeguard national security, either by criminalizing the disclosure of sensitive information or by employing the civil law against individuals and the press to use prior restraint to stop its dissemination. In addition it is important to provide the public with access to public information, a right which is not specifically protected under **article 10** of the Convention (*Leander* *v Sweden* (above)), but which is now covered under the **Freedom of Information Act 2000**, which came into force in 2005.

The **Official Secrets Act 1989** was passed in order to liberalize the **1911 Act**, which made it an offence for specified persons to disclose any official information without lawful authority, irrespective of the nature or content of the information or of any potential damage caused on disclosure. The law was discredited when a jury acquitted a senior civil servant charged with passing on unauthorized information relating to the sinking of the *General Belgrano* during the Falklands war (*R v Ponting* [1985] **Crim LR 318**). The 1989 Act creates particular categories of information that might attract liability—security and intelligence, defence, international relations, and crime and special investigation powers—and imposes liability only where the disclosure of the information would be damaging to those interests. It was hoped that this would create a defence of public interest, allowing the defendant to argue that any breach, for example, exposed government incompetence. Such a claim had been clearly rejected by the House of Lords in *Chandler v DPP* [1964] **AC 763**, where it was held that whether an activity was 'prejudicial to the interests of the state' was to be determined by reference to the views of the present government and not by the courts applying an objective standard to that question.

However, although the law of confidentiality has allowed defences of public interest and prior publication (*Attorney-General v Guardian Newspapers (No 2)* [1990] **1 AC 109**, below), the 1989 Act does not recognize a public interest defence. This rule was established in *R v Shayler* [2002] **2 WLR 754**, where a former member of the security service had been charged with unlawful disclosure of documents and information, contrary to **ss.1 and 4** of the Act. The defendant had argued that his disclosure was justified in the public interest because he alleged that the security services had been involved in a plot to kill a head of state and that they had been guilty of gross incompetence. The House of Lords held that there was no right for the defendant to show that the disclosure was, or, in his opinion, might be, in the public interest and that such a finding was not incompatible with **article 10** of the European Convention or its case law (*Leander v Sweden* (above) and *Klass v Germany* (1978) **2 EHRR 214**).

The House of Lords recognized the special duties owed by persons employed in the services as justifying the lack of any public interest defence, but added that despite such deference the courts would insist on adequate safeguards to ensure that any restriction on free speech did not exceed what was necessary to achieve national security. The ban on disclosure was not absolute and was tempered by the right under **s.7(3)(a)** of the Act to make disclosure to appropriate staff if one had concerns about illegality, misbehaviour, irregularity, maladministration, or incompetence. Further, a person had the right under **s.7(3)(b)** to seek official authorization to make disclosure, any refusal being subject to judicial review; although in *A v B*, [2009] **3 All ER 416** it was held that any appeal against refusal must be made to the Investigatory Powers Tribunal. Given that the European Court's principal concern is to ensure procedural safeguards against abuse (*Klass* (above)), the decision is probably consistent with the case law of the Convention. More promisingly, it has been held that the reverse burden of proof contained in the 1989 Act was incompatible with the right to a fair trial: *R v Keogh* [2007] 1 WLR 1500.

The courts have been more receptive to the notion of press freedom when interpreting the common law of confidentiality. The government may rely on the duty of confidentiality to ensure that its servants do not breach their duties of loyalty (*Attorney-General v Blake* [2001] 1 AC 268; *Blake v United Kingdom* (2007) 44 EHRR 29). This duty can then be imposed on the press if it intends to disclose such information, making it guilty of contempt if it publishes that information. Further, such publications are subject to prior restraint in the form of interim injunctions; although in *Attorney-General v Guardian Newspapers (No 2)* (above), the House of Lords held that a public body could only maintain an injunction to prevent a breach of confidence if it could prove that there was an overriding public interest justifying an interference with freedom of expression. Further, if information had entered the public domain it could no longer be the basis of an injunction to preserve confidentiality. Thus, as the information in question—the publication of Peter Wright's book *Spycatcher*—had already entered the public domain, there was no public interest overriding free speech. (See also *Lord Advocate v Scotsman Publications Ltd* [1990] 1 AC 812.) The position was clarified by the European Court of Human Rights in *Observer and Guardian v United Kingdom* (1991) 14 EHRR 153, where it was held that the granting of injunctions before the book entered the public domain was necessary in a democratic society to preserve national security, as the domestic courts had weighed the conflicting public interests before granting the orders. However, the Court held that injunctions granted after the information had entered the public domain were unnecessary and disproportionate to the need to protect the efficiency and reputation of the security service. Those injunctions prevented the newspapers from carrying out their right and duty to inform the public about matters of great and legitimate public concern.

The decision suggests that judges, both domestic and European, will be loath to interfere when there is a true conflict between the public interest in defending national security and the public interest in receiving information on governmental matters. Thus, the European Court did not appear to conduct a full inquiry into whether prohibiting any breach of confidence would be offset by the public interest in receiving information about possible illegal conduct on behalf of the government. In this respect, therefore, the decision is more favourable to press freedom than the ruling in *Shayler*, which upholds the restriction on dissemination because of the position of the informant, and irrespective of any public interest in publication.

The law of contempt can be employed in conjunction with confidentiality to prevent the disclosure of information covered by an existing injunction safeguarding confidentiality. In *Attorney-General v Times Newspapers* [1992] 1 AC 191 it was held that the publication of such matter could constitute an interference with the administration of justice and, thus, the publication of extracts of *Spycatcher*, after two newspapers had been injuncted for breach of confidence, constituted contempt of court. These actions can deny the press a public interest defence under the law of confidentiality, and the public interest defence under s.5 of the **Contempt of**

Court Act 1981. This threat was mitigated by the decision in *Attorney-General v Newspaper Publishing Ltd* [1997] 3 All ER 159, where it was held that a trivial breach of a court order was insufficient to attract liability for contempt. However, in *Attorney-General v Punch and Steed* [2003] 1 All ER 301 the House of Lords held that a breach of an order did not have to cause a risk of damage to national security. The purpose of any order was the prevention of publication pending the confidentiality proceedings, so that a deliberate breach would prejudge the issues and thus constitute contempt.

Thus, the courts have fallen short of establishing any clear defence of press freedom where the threat to national security can be balanced proportionally with freedom of expression and the public right to know. This has been exacerbated by the absence of a right to freedom of information, both in domestic law and under the European Convention. Thus in *Leander v Sweden* (above), the European Court held that **article 10** does not require the facilitation of free speech and does not impose an obligation on government to provide an open forum to achieve the wider dissemination of views. This interpretation has been accepted by the domestic courts (*R Persey and others v Secretary of State for Environment, Food and Rural Affairs* [2003] QB 794).

With the passing of the **Freedom of Information Act 2000** it was hoped that the public would acquire a substantive right of access to information, which would not only protect their own privacy interests, but would allow the public access to the workings of government. Thus, **s.1** of the Act provides a general right of access to information held by public authorities and entitles any person making such a request to be informed in writing whether it holds the information, and, if so, to have it communicated to him. The Act is enforced by an Information Commissioner, who, under **s.50**, has the power to receive complaints with respect to the way that complaints have been dealt with, and to make, normally, binding decisions on such matters. Notably the Act has been used to gain access to information relating to the expenses claims made by Members of Parliament (*Corporate Officer of the House of Commons v Information Commissioner,* [2009] 3 All ER 403). The Act contains a number of exceptions, some of which are absolute, while others allow publication where the authority in question considers that the public interest in disclosure outweighs the public interest in maintaining the exemption. In particular, **s.23** of the Act completely exempts information supplied by, or which relates to, the intelligence and security services, and **ss.35–36** provide, respectively, an absolute exemption for information relating to the formation of government policy, and a limited immunity with respect to information whose release might cause damage to the workings of government.

The passing of the **Freedom of Information Act** is, therefore, unlikely to enhance access to the workings of government covered in the current laws of official secrecy and confidentiality. Press freedom, therefore, will continue to be protected on a limited basis, allowing publication where no identifiable harm has been caused by the dissemination of government information. This does not permit a true balance between press freedom and national security, although does not appear to be in violation of **article 10**.

Question 5

(A)

What deficiencies of the domestic law of contempt were exposed by the decision of the European Court of Human Rights in *Sunday Times v United Kingdom*? To what extent are those laws now consistent with **article 10 of the European Convention on Human Rights**?

(B)

In June 2009, Sir Joseph Cranberry, a former Cabinet Minister, was facing charges of fraud connected with his financial and political dealings. His trial was due to take place on 22 June, and on 2 June the *Daily Tribune* published an article about corruption in public life. The article focused on a number of incidents over the previous 10 years, involving politicians and other public officers who had been charged with offences involving fraud. The article concluded that 'fraud and deceit in public life is of epidemic proportions' and that 'many politicians had been proved to be constitutionally incapable of telling the truth'. The article also referred to a case last year when a well-known politician had been acquitted of a variety of theft and deception charges and concluded, 'Let us hope that juries have learnt from that lesson, and do not let abusers of public office off the hook.' On reading the article, the trial judge decided to abandon the trial and referred the matter to the Attorney-General. The *Daily Tribune* has now heard that they will face contempt charges in connection with the article. Advise the newspaper as to any defences it might have and the likely outcome of the proceedings.

 Commentary

This question covers the specific area of contempt of court, a popular area for examination in both essay and problem-type questions. The student requires a sound knowledge of the domestic law and of the relevant case law of the European Court of Human Rights in this area. The first part of the question should begin with a very brief explanation of the aims of contempt laws and their impact on free speech, moving speedily on to a critical analysis of the domestic law via the 'thalidomide' case, including a summary of both the domestic proceedings and the decision of the European Court. The answer should then assess the compatibility of the current law with that case and **article 10** of the Convention, highlighting matters of concern with respect to free speech and using cases in illustration.

The second part of the question requires the specific application of the law to the factual situation, rather than any critical analysis, and students should identify the central issues raised by the scenario and give precise and constructive advice based on their knowledge of the law. Most of the legal issues raised by the case will have been identified in part one of the answer; thus the student should avoid giving any detailed explanation of the law in the second part, unless absolutely necessary.

Answer plan

- Brief examination of the aims of contempt law and its impact on freedom of expression and the public right to know
- Explanation of the pre-1981 Act situation, the 'thalidomide' litigation and the changes made to the law by the 1981 Act
- Critical analysis of the Act's provisions and their application in post-1981 Act case law to consider their compatibility with the Convention and the decision in *Sunday Times*
- Conclusions as to the compatibility of present law with **article 10** of the Convention and relevant case law
- Consideration of whether the relevant newspaper articles would constitute contempt under present law
- Consideration of any defences available to the press and their likely success in this case
- Conclusions as to the likely success of any contempt proceedings

Suggested answer

(A)

The law of contempt of court safeguards the individual's fundamental right to a fair trial by preventing the publication of information which might influence the outcome of legal proceedings (*R v Taylor* (1998) 93 Cr App Rep 361) and protects the public's confidence in the impartiality and independence of the judicial process. These aims are contained in **article 10(2)** of the European Convention—the rights of others and the impartiality and independence of the judiciary—and must be balanced with the fundamental right of freedom of expression and, in particular, public debate on impending judicial proceedings.

The domestic law of strict liability contempt came under attack as a result of the decision of the European Court in *Sunday Times v United Kingdom* (1979) 2 EHRR 245), and those laws underwent statutory change. The case involved the publication of two articles, which commented on the thalidomide affair before impending litigation between parents and a company had been resolved. The House of Lords granted injunctions, finding that one of the articles had prejudged the case (*Attorney-General v Times Newspapers* [1974] AC 273). The European Court held that the injunctions were not 'necessary in a democratic society' and was particularly critical of the fact that English law had formulated an absolute rule that made it unlawful to prejudge issues in pending cases. The issue was a matter of undisputed public concern and the public and the families could only be deprived of this information if it appeared absolutely certain (as opposed to there being a 'real risk') that its diffusion would have presented a threat to the authority of the judiciary.

The judgment led to the passing of the **Contempt of Court Act 1981**, which addressed the strict liability rule, and in particular the questions of the necessary risk of prejudice and the lack of a defence where prejudice is caused by public interest discussion. **Section 2** now provides that the strict liability rule only applies in relation to publications that create a *substantial* risk that the course of proceedings in question will be *seriously* impeded or prejudiced. This is intended to reflect the European Court's concern that strict liability could be established if there was merely a real risk, and that in cases which raise public interest issues liability should only be imposed where it was 'absolutely certain' that proceedings would be prejudiced.

The Court of Appeal examined the scope of the new test in *Attorney-General v News Group Newspapers* [1987] 1 QB 1, where it was noted that both elements, although overlapping, must be met in each case. In particular, it was held that a substantial risk was one that was 'not minimal' or 'not insubstantial', rather than one that was 'weighty'. In addition, the effect of the publication on the particular proceedings had to be potentially serious; thus there must be some risk that the proceedings in question will be affected and, if so, that likely effect must be serious. Allowing liability where the risk of prejudice is 'not insubstantial' appears to give too little weight to freedom of expression, but in practice the courts have tended to apply the test liberally in favour of free speech. Thus, in the above case it held that the *News of the World* was not in contempt when it published an article about an individual's behaviour that was the subject of a libel trial due to take place in 10 months' time; it was not possible to say that there was a serious risk that the course of justice would be seriously prejudiced by such publication.

Equally, the courts have taken a liberal approach in deciding whether there is evidence of serious prejudice. Thus, in *Attorney-General v ITN and others* [1995] 2 All ER 370 it was held that the defendants were not guilty of contempt when they published the fact that a person arrested for murder and attempted murder had recently escaped from jail in Belfast where he was serving a life sentence for murder. Given that the trial would not take place for nine months, and the ephemeral nature of a single news item on TV news, no contempt had been committed. (See also *Chief Constable of Greater Manchester Police v Channel 5 Broadcast Ltd* [2005] EWCA Civ 739.)

Nevertheless, in *Attorney-General v Hislop and Pressdram* [1991] 1 QB 514 there was contempt when *Private Eye* published an article making allegations against an individual three months before a defamation action between the parties was to begin; there was a substantial risk that the jurors would remember the allegations and might be seriously prejudiced against her. The courts have thus taken a flexible approach, considering all the circumstances. Thus, in *Attorney-General v Times Newspapers, The Times*, 12 February 1983, although the *Sun* newspaper was not in contempt of court when they referred to someone facing charges of theft from Buckingham Palace as 'a glib liar with a long-standing drug problem', the *Daily Star* was in contempt when they had written an article asserting that he had admitted to stealing wine from the Queen.

The law is only likely to be tested where the publication serves a strong and genuine public interest, as in the *Sunday Times* case. In this respect, s.5 of the Act provides a public interest defence by giving protection to publications constituting a discussion in good faith of public affairs or other matters of general public interest where the risk of impediment or prejudice is merely incidental to the discussion. Again, the provision has been interpreted quite liberally in favour of free speech and in *Attorney-General v English* [1983] 1 AC 116 the Court of Appeal held that it was not proper to ask whether an article could have been written without the offending words. Further, it accepted that a discussion of public affairs could take place beyond abstract debate, and could include examples drawn from real life. Further, in *Attorney-General v Times Newspapers* (above) an article about someone who broke into the Queen's bedroom fell within s.5 even though the person was named, as it formed part of a discussion of public concern, namely the Queen's personal safety. However, where the article relates clearly and closely to the legal proceedings it will be easier for the Attorney-General to show that the risk of prejudice is more than merely incidental (*Attorney-General v TVS Television Ltd and Southey and Sons, The Times,* 7 July 1989).

It is, therefore, questionable whether the law complies with **article 10** where the public interest in publication is overwhelming despite the potential prejudice. However, the decision in *Sunday Times* does not give absolute protection to press freedom and in **Worm v Austria (1998) 25 EHRR 454** the Court stressed that that the domestic courts are the appropriate forum for determining a person's guilt and that it was essential that the public had confidence in the courts' capacity to carry out that function. Accordingly, the press must not overstep the bounds imposed in the proper administration of justice and prejudice the chances of a fair trial. On the other hand, in *News Verlags v Austria* **(2001) 31 EHRR 8** it was held that an injunction restraining the publication of a photograph of a right-wing extremist facing trial was disproportionate because the defendant had courted publicity in the past and the offences with which he was charged were directed against democracy.

Thus, the domestic courts must construe s.5 very liberally in order to comply with Convention case law. So too the common law offence of causing intentional interference with the administration of justice (*Attorney-General v News Group Newspapers* [1989] 2 All ER 906), which remains untouched by the *Sunday Times* judgment and which contains no public interest defence, and will need to be developed in accordance with principles of press freedom.

(B)

The newspaper will either face contempt charges under the **Contempt of Court Act 1981**, where liability for contempt is strict, or under the common law for intentional contempt. Liability is based on interfering with the impartiality and independence of the judicial system, and the fact that in our case the criminal trial has been abandoned as a result of the judge's assessment of the pre-trial publicity on Sir Joseph's right to a fair trial will be a relevant, though not decisive, factor (*Attorney-General v MGN* [1997] 1 All ER 456).

Under the 1981 Act, the court will need to be satisfied under s.2 that the article created a substantial risk that the criminal proceedings would be seriously impeded or prejudiced. There is no question that the criminal proceedings were not active, as such proceedings start with the issue of a warrant and end with the discontinuance of the trial. It is not sufficient if one of those factors exists, but not the other (*Attorney-General v News Group Newspapers* (above)), and in the context of criminal proceedings the court would have to be satisfied that not only would the article have a likely influence on the jury, but also that such an influence would materially and substantially prejudice the defendant's, or prosecution's, case.

In *Attorney-General v News Group Newspapers* (above) the Court of Appeal stated that for a risk to be substantial it had to be 'not minimal or insubstantial'. Further, it held that in assessing whether that substantial risk would cause serious prejudice, it was permissible to take into account factors that were considered at the first stage. Thus, some factors, such as the proximity of the article to the trial, are relevant at each stage. The court in our case would ask whether there was a substantial risk that one or more of the jury would encounter the article, remember it, and be affected by it, so that they could not put it out of their mind during the trial. The court could then refer to a number of factors such as the likely readership of the article, the proximity of publication of the article to the trial, whether the case had attracted the public interest, and the language used in the article. Because the article is written in a national newspaper, discusses a matter of public interest, is written in a strident manner, and appears only three weeks before the trial, there would appear to be a substantial risk that the jurors would encounter the article and remember it at the time of the trial.

The court would then address the question of whether the article would cause the jury to be *prejudiced* against Sir Joseph and whether that prejudice would be *serious*. The court would consider similar factors to those considered at the first stage and the public profile of the defendant and the issue under discussion, as well as the tone and language used in the publication. In *Attorney-General v Hislop and Pressdram* (above) the defendants were held to be in contempt when they published allegations of fraud and deception against an individual three months before a defamation trial between the parties was due to begin. In particular, the court noted that the articles went further than fair and temperate criticism and amounted to plain abuse. In this case, although the defendant is not specifically mentioned, the tone of the article is quite strong as is the potential for serious prejudice, particularly as it appears to call upon juries to convict politicians facing criminal charges. Further, the timing of the article is critical, as opposed to *Attorney-General v ITN and others* (above), where the publication appeared nine months before the murder trial.

If the court finds the newspaper in contempt, it may rely on s.5 of the 1981 Act, if the publication was made as part of a discussion in good faith of public affairs, or other matters of general public interest, and where the prejudice to the proceedings is merely incidental to that discussion. In *Attorney-General v English* (above) it was held that a discussion of public affairs could take place beyond abstract debate and could include examples drawn from real life. In our case, therefore, the use of specific examples, including the allusion to Sir Joseph's case, might be acceptable. However, in *Attorney-General v TVS Television Ltd and Southey and Sons* (above) it was stressed that the main thrust of the article must not consist of a discussion of the proceedings. In our case, the article does discuss wider issues over and above the impending trial, but the warning given to the jury not to acquit might be seen as unacceptable and make the likelihood of prejudice central to, rather than incidental to the discussion. Accordingly, a court might reject a public interest defence in such circumstances.

Such is the tone of the article that it may be regarded as an intentional interference with the administration of justice under common law. In such a case the newspaper would not be able to avail itself of any public interest defence, although the court would have to be satisfied that the defendants intended to prejudice proceedings, or saw such interference as an inevitable consequence of the publication (*Attorney-General v News Group Newspapers* (above)). It is uncertain that the newspaper saw with virtual certainty that Sir Joesph's trial would be prejudiced (***Attorney-General v Sport Newspapers* [1991] 1 WLR 1194**), unless there is evidence of a personal vendetta (*Hislop* (above)).

Question 6

To what extent is English law on the disclosure of press sources consistent with notions of press freedom and **article 10 of the European Convention on Human Rights?**

 Commentary

This question concerns an essential aspect of press freedom—the right of journalists and newspapers to refuse to name their sources—and is a reasonably popular area for examination. It should not be attempted unless the student has a very good knowledge of this specific area, particularly of the case law of both the European Court of Human Rights and the domestic courts. However, it does require a broad knowledge of notions of free speech and press freedom and an appreciation of the importance of those principles in this context.

The answer should begin by identifying the importance of press freedom and the dangers posed to that concept (and to the public's right to know) by the compulsory disclosure of its sources. The student can then examine the domestic law in this area, contained in **s.10 of the Contempt of Court Act 1981,** and in particular the domestic case law to see whether it complies with free speech and **article 10**. At this point the student should analyse the case law of the European Court, before making a comparison with domestic decisions and identifying any difference in approach between the two courts. The answer should conclude by examining the legal position in the post-Human Rights Act era to consider whether domestic law is compatible or not.

 Answer plan

- Explanation of the dangers of the disclosure of press sources and the cases where it might be necessary to do so
- Examination of the domestic legal position under **s.10 of the Contempt of Court Act 1981**
- Critical examination of the domestic case law under **s.10,** both pre- and post-Human Rights Act
- Examination of the principles underlying **article 10** of the Convention and the case law of the European Court of Human Rights in this area
- Conclusions as to the compatibility of the domestic law with the principles and case law of the European Convention

Suggested answer

The European Court of Human Rights has offered special protection to press freedom and the right of the press to impart information, thereby serving the public interest in the free flow of information (*Sunday Times v United Kingdom* (1979) **2 EHRR 245**). This recognizes the importance of press freedom to the maintenance of a democratic society, the press having a duty to inform the public (*Jersild v Denmark* (1994) **19 EHRR 1**).

An essential aspect of press freedom is that journalists are not forced to divulge their sources, lest the confidence between the press and those who supply information to it is compromised and the disclosure then has a chilling effect on the free flow of information and ideas. The European Court has noted that the protection of journalistic sources is one of the basic conditions for press freedom (*Goodwin v United Kingdom* (1996) **22 EHRR 123**). On the other hand, there will be cases where such disclosure will serve both the public interest, such as the detection of crime (*BBC v United Kingdom* (1996) **84-A DR 129**), and the rights of individuals, who may, for example, wish to identify a source with a view to taking civil action against that source or other persons. Consequently, both **article 10** of the Convention and domestic law will allow the principle of non-disclosure to be compromised in necessary cases. Nevertheless, press disclosure should be ordered only in exceptional cases, and the state is given a very narrow margin of appreciation (*Goodwin v United Kingdom* (above)).

Under **s.10 of the Contempt of Court Act 1981** no court may require a person to disclose (nor is any person guilty of contempt of court for refusing to disclose) the source of information contained in a publication for which he is responsible unless the court is satisfied that disclosure is *necessary* in the interests of justice or national security or for the prevention of disorder or crime. This ensures that requests for orders are subjected to the tests of necessity and proportionality and in *Re an Inquiry under the Company Securities (Insider Dealing) Act 1985* [1988] 1 All ER 203 it was held that **s.10** required that the disclosure was 'really needed' to achieve any of those listed reasons. Despite this, in *Secretary of State for Defence v Guardian Newspapers* [1985] AC 339 the House of Lords ordered a newspaper to disclose the source of a leaked document containing allegations that Parliament had been misled on the issue of the storing of nuclear weapons, despite there being no evidence of any harm caused to national security and where the ministry had failed to carry out internal investigations into the leak. This deference was particularly evident where disclosure was required in the context of terrorism (*DPP v Channel Four Television Company Ltd* [1993] 2 All ER 517).

Such cases suggested that the domestic courts were not prepared to give sufficient weight to press freedom and that their approach was not consistent with the principles of free speech expounded by the European Court in cases such as *Sunday Times* (above). This can be illustrated by the decision in *X v Morgan Grampian (Publishers) Ltd* [1991] AC 1, which was then challenged before the European Court in *Goodwin v United Kingdom* (above). An individual had disclosed a company's financial affairs to a journalist and the company had obtained an injunction in the law of confidence prohibiting its publication. The company then sought an order forcing the journalist to disclose the source of his information so that it could take legal action against the informant and when he refused he was committed for contempt. The House of Lords held that the phrase 'the interests of justice' included contemplated legal proceedings and that the plaintiffs had established the need to identify the informant; the public having no legitimate interest in the business of the plaintiffs.

That decision was successfully challenged in *Goodwin v United Kingdom* (above). The Court stressed that without legal protection of the right of the press to protect its sources, its ability to provide reliable and accurate information would be adversely affected. Accordingly, any interference with that right would require an overriding requirement in the public interest. Although the interference with the applicant's freedom of expression was prescribed by law and related to the legitimate aim of preserving the company's legal claim, the restriction was not necessary in a democratic society because the main element of damage to the company had already been redressed by the original injunction. The additional benefit of unmasking the culprit and allowing the legal action against him was not sufficient to outweigh the vital public interest in maintaining the confidentiality of the press source.

The decision suggested that the domestic courts were attaching too little significance to the notions of press freedom and to violations of the principles of non-disclosure. This was borne out in *Centaur Communications v Camelot* [1998] 2 WLR 379, where the courts ordered the disclosure of documents that led to the identification of a press source. An employee of Camelot supplied a journalist with detailed information on the company's accounts and the company sought the return of the document in order to identify and take necessary legal action against the employee. Although the Court of Appeal accepted that the decision of the European Court in *Goodwin* could be considered, it held that the interests of the company in ensuring the loyalty of its employees and ex-employees outweighed the public interest attached to the protection of press sources. The Court of Appeal distinguished *Goodwin* on the grounds that in *Camelot* there was a *continuing* threat of damage caused by the presence of a disloyal employee, which needed to be addressed in order to restore confidence within the company and its employees.

The decision in *Camelot* was criticized for attaching too much weight to the company's commercial interests, while neglecting to promote a wider public interest in allowing the free flow of information. Specifically, the courts were often prepared to order such disclosure before the claimant had conducted a full inquiry into the breach of confidence (*Secretary of State for Defence v Guardian Newspapers* (above) and *Camelot* (above). In contrast, in **Saunders v Punch [1998] 1 WLR 986**, where a firm had already received an injunction prohibiting an article that disclosed confidential legal correspondence, the Court refused a further order requiring the defendant to reveal its sources. It held that although there was a great public interest in preserving the confidentiality of legal correspondence, in this case the Court's original injunction had gone a long way in protecting the claimant's interests.

In the post-Human Rights Act era the courts must develop the law in compliance with Convention rights, and **s.12** of the 1998 Act requires the courts to have special regard to freedom of expression when granting any relief that would interfere with such a right. This duty is heightened when the information is of a journalistic nature (**s.12(4)**). In **John v Express Newspapers [2000] 3 All ER 257** the Court of Appeal seemed to adjust the balance in favour of press freedom and non-disclosure. In this case a journalist had destroyed a confidential legal document that had come into his possession, but an order requiring the newspaper to disclose the identity of the source was still sought. The court ordered disclosure even though the firm had failed to conduct an internal inquiry, but on appeal it was accepted that the judge had attached insufficient significance to the failure to conduct an internal inquiry and too much significance to the threat posed to legal confidentiality. The Court stressed that when the press was being required to depart from its normal professional practice, the public interest in such an order had to be clearly demonstrated.

This approach was adopted in **Ashworth Security Hospital v MGN Ltd [2002] 1 WLR 2033**, where the House of Lords stated any court should be satisfied that the case for disclosure was so important that it overrode the public interest in protecting journalistic sources. In *Ashworth* (above), disclosure was ordered when a hospital employee had supplied medical information on a mental patient to a third party and the defendants had published an article detailing confidential information. The House of Lords held that the present case was exceptional and was the only means of discovering the source of the information, an internal inquiry having failed to identify the employee. This decision was qualified by subsequent proceedings in **Mersey Care NHS Trust v Ackroyd, The Times, 26 February 2007**, where the Court of Appeal took into account a change in circumstances since the original order, and the public interest in investigating the hospital's procedures, in refusing a request to disclose the third party's source.

The question of whether disclosure will be ordered will be determined on a case-by-case basis, which has led to some inconsistency in this field. For example, in *Interbrew SA v Financial Times and others* [2002] **EMLR 24** an order was granted ordering a newspaper to produce documents identifying a person who had provided the newspaper with deliberately misleading financial material relating to the claimants. It was held that although the court must start with a presumption that it is contrary to the public interest to require disclosure, the right of the claimant to identify a disloyal employee overrode the general interest in non-disclosure. Although the court is still prepared to order disclosure, more recent cases (most notably *Ackroyd*, above) indicate such that disclosure will be exceptional, and that the courts are no longer willing to grant such orders simply because they would assist the claimant in furthering their commercial or other interests. This stance may, of course, waiver in cases involving terrorism, where one would expect the courts to show more deference to national security and other public interest claims: although in *An Application by D* [2009] **NICty 4**, the Northern Ireland High Court refused to order the disclosure of a journalist's sources when that would have put her life at risk. In general, however, the current situation compares favourably with the traditional stance taken by the courts in this area (*Guardian Newspapers* (above)), and provided the courts use the orders in only exceptional cases, it would appear that the law is generally compatible with **article 10**.

Question 7

Do the UK's obscenity and indecency laws serve any legitimate purpose? In your view, do you feel they strike a proportionate balance between freedom of expression and the achievement of any legitimate aims?

 ## Commentary

This question concerns the compatibility of domestic law restricting obscene and indecent material with the principles of freedom of expression. It remains a popular area for examination and students need to be conversant with the statutory and common law rules on obscenity and indecency as well as the relevant case law of the European Court and Commission of Human Rights in this area. This question requires the student to take a reflective approach and the answer should avoid simply detailing the relevant law and should attempt to assess the law's aims and their compatibility with free speech norms. Students are especially prone to making such a mistake in this area, going into unnecessary detail on the legal components of the offences without highlighting the potential for unnecessary interference with free speech.

The answer should begin by clearly identifying the purpose, or purposes, of the respective laws, and tying those purposes with the legitimate aims identified in provisions such as **article 10(2)** of the European Convention. This will require an examination of different legal provisions, including the distinction between obscenity and indecency offences in this respect. The student should then identify the potential for interference with free speech, and by considering basic notions of free speech, and in particular the case law under **article 10** of the European Convention, the student can then address the question of whether the law achieves a proper and proportionate balance in this area.

 ## Answer plan

- Explanation of the aims and objectives of domestic laws relating to the control of obscene and indecent speech and expression

- Examination of specific statutory and common law offences with a view to assessing the above

- Identification of the restrictions on free speech imposed by such measures

- Examination of the case law of the European Court and Commission of Human Rights in this area

- Analysis of whether current law strikes a proper and proportionate balance between the control of obscene and indecent material and free speech

Suggested answer

Domestic law attempts to regulate and penalize the dissemination of obscene and indecent speech. Some laws (for example, the **Obscene Publications Acts 1959/64**) regulate *obscene* expression—material likely to deprave or corrupt the likely readership. However, other offences (such as the **Indecent Displays (Control) Act 1981**) apply to *indecent* material—which cause, or are likely to cause, shock and offence and which are considered lewd and disgusting. The European Court of Human Rights has accepted that 'speech' within **article 10** of the Convention applies to views which shock and offend (*Handyside v United Kingdom* (1976) 1 EHRR 737): accordingly any interference with such speech must comply with the requirements of legitimacy and necessity laid down by the European Court.

Such laws might prevent physical harm caused by the publication and dissemination of such speech. Although a general link between obscene speech and incitement to criminal behaviour was not established by the Williams Committee (*Report of the Committee on Obscenity and Film Censorship*, Cmnd 7722, 1979), some publications might incite acts harmful to others, even though such a result is not a prerequisite of liability under that legislation (*Whyte v DPP* [1972] AC 849). This type of material was at the heart of the government's *Consultation on the Possession of Extreme Violent Pornography* (2005), and **s.63 of the Criminal Justice and Immigration Act 2008** makes it an offence being in possession of such material.

More generally, such laws are seen as necessary to prevent harm to society's morals. This objective is apparent in the offence of corrupting public morals (*Shaw v DPP* [1964] AC 220), and outraging public decency (*Knuller v DPP* [1973] AC 435), where the courts have assumed the role of the protectors of public morality. Also, the **Obscene Publications Acts**, which make it an offence to publish (or have in one's possession for publication) an article that is likely to deprave and corrupt its likely readership, assumes that some actions, or thoughts, are contrary to general public morals. Such objectives are difficult to reconcile with notions of broadmindedness, pluralism, and tolerance, which the European Court insists underpin the notions of democracy and free speech (*Handyside v United Kingdom* (above)). However, the Court accepted that it was legitimate to restrict such speech where it was likely to deprave and corrupt vulnerable sectors of society, such as the young.

The restriction of such material also protects society or individuals from shock or offence. For example, offences under the **Indecent Display (Control) Act 1981**—of displaying any indecent material in public—assumes that such material will upset individual or group morality or sensibilities. This also informs the powers of broadcasting authorities under the **Communications Act 2003** to preserve taste and decency. This would appear to be a weak basis for interfering with free speech, as expression is restricted because it has a nuisance value, rather than causing any tangible harm.

Such laws may also protect individual dignity and integrity. The traditional feminist argument against pornography is that such material constitutes violence against women in itself, without the need to prove any link between the distribution of such material and the commission of sexual offences. Based as it is in the protection of human dignity, it would appear to be a substantial argument in favour of restriction, although the argument is not directly reflected in any domestic laws.

If such laws are to comply with **article 10** of the European Convention the law has to be sufficiently certain and predictable, it must pursue a legitimate aim within **article 10(2)**, and its application must meet a pressing social need and be proportionate (*Handyside v United Kingdom* (above)). The European Court has given a wide margin of appreciation in this area, accepting that the national authorities are often better placed than the international judge to assess the necessity of such laws and their proportionality (*Handyside* (above) and *Müller v Switzerland* (1991) 13 EHRR 212).

There are a number of free speech concerns with respect to the **Obscene Publications Acts**. First, liability is based on the *likely* effect of the publication and ignores the specific intention of the author. Thus, it is not possible to adduce evidence as to the publisher's real intention in determining whether an article is obscene (*R v Penguin Books* [1961] Crim LR 176), although s.4(2) allows expert evidence when relying on the public good defence, below, and this appears to be compatible with **article 10** (*Hoare v United Kingdom* [1997] EHRLR 678). Secondly, the wording of the Act appears vague and subjective, although the courts have clarified that 'deprave and corrupt' does not cover publications which are lewd, crude, and disgusting (*R v Anderson* [1972] QB 304) and that rather it refers to a real social evil (*Knuller v DPP* (above)). More significantly, in *Handyside* (above) the European Court regarded the test as sufficiently certain to be 'prescribed by law'. Thirdly, the offence is committed irrespective of whether publication is likely to incite criminal or other harmful conduct. Thus in *Whyte v DPP* (above), it was held that the Act was *principally* concerned with the effect of the material on the mind of the reader. This would appear to violate free speech norms, although in *Handyside* (above) the Court recognized the importance of protecting vulnerable sectors of society from this type of harm, and this view has been re-stated by the Court of Appeal (*R v Perrin* [2002] EWCA 747). Fourthly, it is uncertain who, and how many, should be in danger of corruption. The Act requires a significant proportion of the likely readership, which means neither just a few, nor on the other hand, all, of its readers (*R v Calder and Boyars* [1969] 1 QB 151) and in *R v Perrin* (above) it was held that it was sufficient that there was a likelihood of vulnerable persons seeing the material.

Such concerns are offset to some extent by the availability under s.4 of a public good defence. This provides that a person shall not be convicted if it is proved that the article in question is justified as being for the public good on the grounds that it is in the interests of science, literature, art, or learning, or of other objects of general concern. The defence is only considered once the court has established that the article is obscene (*R v Calder and Boyars* (above)) and, in *DPP v Jordan* [1977] AC 699 the House of Lords insisted that 'other objects of general concern' must relate to the specific objects of science, literature, etc, listed in s.4. Further, in *Attorney-General's Reference (No 3 of 1977)* [1978] 3 All ER 1166, it was held that the defence of 'learning' could not allow expert evidence to the effect that the publication provided information to the readers about sexual matters, without making a contribution to scholarship. Nevertheless, it has been held that 'other objects of general concern' cover discussions on social problems (*R v Calder and Boyars* (above)) and the presence of such a defence appears fundamental to the European Court's assessment of the Act's compatibility with **article 10** (*Handyside* (above)). In *R v Perrin* (above), the Court of Appeal held that the offence was prescribed by law, and pursued a legitimate aim for the purpose of **article 10(2)**, adding that there was no public interest to be served by allowing profit through the supply of material that most people would regard as pornographic or obscene. This reflects the jurisprudence of the European Court and Commission, especially where there is no public interest quality to the expression (*Hoare v United Kingdom* (above)).

There would also appear to be little doubt that offences aimed at protecting children from the harm caused by obscene and indecent expression is compatible with **article 10**. The **Protection of Children Act 1978** makes it an offence to take, distribute, publish, or be in possession of an indecent photograph or image of a child (under 18 years of age). Although this offence can be committed by the mere possession of such material, and the intention in making the photograph is not relevant in determining whether it is indecent, the domestic courts have concluded that the offence is clearly compatible with article 10 (*R v Smethurst, The Times*, 13 April 2001).

However, there is concern as to the compatibility of other obscenity and indecency laws. For example, in *Shaw v DPP* (above), the House of Lords recognized the common law offence of conspiring to corrupt public morals. As the offence lacks a public good defence, prosecutors can bypass the safeguards of the 1959 Act by bringing these proceedings. Further, in *Knuller v DPP* (above) the House of Lords confirmed the existence of the common law offence of outraging public decency, which again has no public good defence. This latter offence created liability on the basis of indecency rather than obscenity, although in *Knuller* the House of Lords stressed that causing outrage went beyond merely shocking the public. This appears to be consistent with the case law of the European Court (*Müller v Switzerland* (above)), which has held that offensive and indecent material could be regulated by domestic law, provided it grossly offended the sexual propriety of persons of ordinary sensibility. Further, the offence may be compatible with article 10 despite the speech possessing clear artistic merit. Thus, in *S and G v United Kingdom*, **Application No 17634** the Court held that there had been no violation of article 10 when the applicants had been prosecuted for displaying an exhibit at an art gallery, despite the facts that the offence did not require a specific intent and that the applicants had no public good defence. The defendants could have argued that the exhibit did not outrage public decency and thus the prosecution fell within the state's margin of appreciation.

Public authorities also have the power to regulate broadcasts that offend taste and decency. Although such powers do not create criminal or other liability, they can in some cases take the form of prior restraint and thus deny access to information and ideas. These dangers were evident in the House of Lords' decision in *R (Prolife Alliance) v BBC* [2004] 1 AC 185, concerning the BBC's decision in refusing to broadcast the claimant's party political video that graphically illustrated the abortion process. The Court of Appeal [2002] 1 All ER 756 held that the broadcasters had failed to give sufficient weight to political expression and that a truthful and unsensational election broadcast could only be rejected on the grounds of taste and decency in the rarest of circumstances. However, the House of Lords held that it was not appropriate for the courts to carry out its own balancing exercise between the requirements of political speech and the protection of the public from being unduly distressed. This decision shows remarkable deference to the authorities in the control of such speech, and may be in conflict with the European Court's case law, which insists that the media has a duty to broadcast on matters of public interest (*Jersild v Demark* (1994) 19 EHRR 1).

Despite the above criticisms, the current law appears to be generally compatible with the European Convention, provided the laws are used against pornography, or other expression lacking any real public interest content. However, where they are used to suppress 'worthy', artistic, or political speech, they should be used reasonably and cautiously.

Further reading

Clayton, R and Tomlinson, H, *The Law of Human Rights*, 2nd edn (OUP 2009), ch 15.

Fenwick, H, *Civil Liberties and Human Rights*, 4th edn (Routledge 2007), chs 5–8.

Fenwick, H and Phillipson, G, Media Freedom and the Human Rights Act (OUP 2006).

11

Freedom of religion, association, and peaceful assembly

Introduction

This chapter covers **articles 9 and 11 of the European Convention on Human Rights**, which guarantee the right to religion, association, and peaceful assembly. They are included in the 'democratic' rights of the Convention and complement freedom of speech and expression, which has been covered in the preceding chapter.

These areas are frequently covered in human rights courses and topical matters such as the right to wear religious dress, proscription of terrorist groups, and the control of political protest will mean that they remain a popular area for examination. Questions can be essays or problems, although it is more usual for questions on religion and association to be in essay form. Questions on the domestic law of freedom of assembly lend themselves to problem questions, although examiners often ask questions on the compatibility of domestic law with the right to demonstrate.

Students need to be aware of the case law of the European Convention in these areas, in addition to any relevant domestic regulations on matters such as religious freedom, proscription, and the variety of public order laws that restrict freedom of peaceful assembly. They also need to appreciate the conditional status of these rights and the relationship between each of the rights themselves, and other rights, such as freedom of speech, as well as the values that each right upholds.

Question 1

How effective has **article 9 of the European Convention on Human Rights** been in upholding the objectives and values of freedom of religion?

Commentary

This question is quite broad, requiring the student to possess a general knowledge of **article 9**, its objectives, and the case law of the European Court and any relevant domestic decisions post **Human Rights Act 1998**. The question is relatively straightforward, although the student needs to spend some time explaining the scope and underlying values of the article before launching into any relevant case law. The answer should examine such case law in the light of the identified objectives and values and should not just contain a list of cases with facts and decisions—the purpose is to examine the effectiveness of that case law in facilitating the enjoyment of this right. The student may choose from a variety of decisions, but should include the central case law of the European Court and Commission in any high-profile domestic cases such as ones on religious dress and corporal punishment in schools.

 Answer plan

- Explanation of the wording of **article 9** of the European Convention and the objectives and values of the right to freedom of thought, conscience, and religion
- Consideration of the case law of the European Court and assessment of the effectiveness of its protection in this area
- Critical examination of the post-Act case law on **article 9** in the domestic courts
- Conclusions as to the effectiveness of **article 9** in achieving religious freedom

Suggested answer

Article 9 of the European Convention provides that everyone has the right to freedom of thought, conscience, and religion, including the freedom to change one's religion or belief and freedom, either alone or in community with others. This aspect of **article 9** is absolute and the qualifying provision in **article 9(2)** does not apply to the enjoyment of the basic freedom of religion, etc. The article then provides the right of an individual (in public or private) to *manifest* his religion or belief, in worship, teaching, practice, and observance. This aspect is subject to **article 9(2)**, which allows for interferences provided they are prescribed by law and necessary in a democratic society in the interests of public safety, the protection of public order, health or morals, or the protection of the rights and freedoms of others. Thus, **article 9(2)** recognizes that in a democratic society, where several religions coexist, it may be necessary to place restrictions on the right to manifest one's religion in order to ensure that everyone's beliefs are respected. This is complemented by **article 17** of the Convention, which safeguards against the destruction of other persons' Convention rights.

The right to freedom of thought, conscience, and religion complements the right to private life, freedom of expression, and freedom of association and public assembly. Thus, in ***Kokkinakis v Greece* (1993) 17 EHRR 397** the European Court stated that **article 9** enshrined one of the foundations of a democratic society and was one of the most vital elements that go to make up the identity of believers and their conception of life. This would give special protection to religious views, although in *Kokkinakis* the Court stressed that the values underlying **article 9** were also essential for atheists, agnostics, and sceptics. **Article 9** is thus essential to the maintenance of a pluralist society.

The basic right under **article 9** would appear to apply irrespective of any manifestation of those views, as required in rights such as freedom of expression. Therefore, **article 9** is concerned with the prohibition of religious or other persecution based solely on one's beliefs. Further, the European Court and Commission have made it clear that not all views and opinions fall within the scope of **article 9**. Thus, although the article is not limited to religious beliefs or convictions, the Court has stressed that it does not cover every opinion and conviction of the individual. In *Arrowsmith v United Kingdom* (1978) 3 EHRR 218, although the European Commission accepted that pacifism was a philosophy protected by **article 9**, it held that the distribution of leaflets seeking to persuade military personnel not to serve in Northern Ireland did not constitute the 'practice' of her beliefs within **article 9**. In that case, the leaflets reflected the applicant's views on British involvement in Northern Ireland rather than the views of pacifism. Further, in *Pretty v United Kingdom* (2002) 35 EHRR 1 the European Court rejected the applicant's claim that her belief in the right to die fell within **article 9**, stressing that the term 'practice' did not cover each act that was motivated or influenced by a religion or belief. The applicant's views merely reflected her commitment to the principle of personal autonomy under **article 8**.

The European Court has insisted that any interference with the right to manifest one's religion or beliefs will be in violation of **article 9** unless that interference is prescribed by law and necessary in a democratic society for the achievement of one of the legitimate aims laid down in **article 9(2)** (*Kokkinakis v Greece* (above)). In that case the Court held that **article 9** included the right to convince others of one's religion, and that proselytism could only be restricted if it took the form of exerting improper pressure on people in distress or in need, or the use of violence or brainwashing. The Court has also held that interference will not be justified simply on the grounds that the applicant's beliefs are contrary to the established religion in that country (*Manossakis v Greece* (1996) 23 EHRR 387).

The Court has offered a wider margin of appreciation in cases where the manifestation of religious or other views are inconsistent with fundamental democratic features of that society. Thus, in *Kalac v Turkey* (1997) 27 EHRR 552 the dismissal of the applicant from the armed forces for voicing religious views conflicting with national principles of secularism was justified under **article 9**. The applicant had a particular allegiance to the state because of his position, and the dismissal was not the result of any manifestation of the normal forms of religious practice, such as prayer. More controversially, in *Sahin v Turkey* (2005) 41 EHRR 8 the Court upheld the interests of national unity in favour of religious views. In that case it held that there had been no violation of **article 9** when the applicant had been suspended from university for wearing a Muslim headdress at university, contrary to that university's rules. In the Court's view the ban on religious wear was proportionate to the protection of the rights of others and of public order, and necessary to preserve secularism in the country's educational institutions; even though the Court accepted that the rule was not enforced in all universities. (The decision in *Sahin* was followed more recently in *Atkas and others v France,* **Application No 43563/08.**) This conservative approach has also been taken with respect to **article 11** and the proscription of political organizations. Thus, in *Refah Partisi Erbakan Kazan and Tekdal v Turkey* (2003) 37 EHRR 1 the Court held that the dissolution of the applicant's party on the grounds that it had become a centre of activities against the principles of secularism was within the state's margin of appreciation and thus justified.

The balance between religious practice and other interests was considered in *R (Begum) v Denbigh High School* [2007] 1 AC 100. It was claimed that a school uniform policy that precluded the wearing of the Muslim jilbab was in violation of the girl's rights under **article 9** (and **article 2 of the First Protocol,** guaranteeing the right to education in conformity with a parent's religious convictions). In the House of Lords it was held that the girl had not been excluded on grounds of religious belief but rather for her failure to abide by a clearly articulated and reasonable school uniform policy. The essential question was whether that policy struck a fair balance between the girl's interests and the interests of others, including the school and its other pupils. In the present case the policy pursued a legitimate aim and accommodated the views and practices of all religions. The approach was followed in *R (Playfoot) v Millais School Governing Body, The Times,* **23 July 2007** with respect to a decision by a school to refuse permission to a schoolgirl to wear a purity ring demonstrating her religious commitment to celibacy before marriage. However, in *R (Watkins Singh) v Aberdare Girls' High School Governors* [2008] EWHC 1865, it was held that the refusal of a school to allow a girl to wear a 'Kara'—a slim bracelet expected to be worn by Sikhs at all times—was contrary to the **Race Relations Act 1976**; as opposed to cases involving religious dress (*Begum*) the Kara was less visible and ostentatious and did not interfere with the general uniform policy.

Thus, in general the domestic courts have been prepared to compromise freedom of religion when it is in conflict with the public interest or the rights of others. For example, in *R (Williamson) v Secretary of State for Employment* [2005] 2 AC 246 the House of Lords held that a ban on corporal punishment in all schools did not violate the rights of teachers and parents under **article 9** and **article 2 of the First Protocol,** which guarantee the rights of parents to have their children educated in conformity with their religious and philosophical convictions (*Campbell and Cosans v United Kingdom* (1982) 4 EHRR 243). Parliament was entitled to make an exception to those rights on the basis that they interfered with the child's right not to be subject to inhuman and degrading treatment contrary to **article 3**. Accordingly, a broad blanket rule on prohibition (**Education Act 1996**) was within the state's margin of appreciation. A similar approach has been taken in other cases where there has been a conflict between religious practice and public health or safety (*R (Swami Suryanada) v Welsh Ministers* [2007] EWCA Civ 893 and *Ghai v Newcastle City Council, The Times,* 18 May 2009).

Article 9 imposes a positive obligation on the state to allow individuals the right to manifest and enjoy their beliefs peacefully and without undue interference (*Dubowska and Skup v Poland* (1997) 24 EHRR CD 75). This might impose a duty on some private individuals, such as employers, to ensure that an individual enjoys his right to thought, conscience, and religion. Thus, in *Ahmed v United Kingdom* (1981) 4 EHRR 126 the European Commission accepted that an employer should not place unreasonable obstacles in the way of their employee's right to manifest his religion, although an employee would in general have to take into account their contractual obligations in carrying out those rights. A similarly wide area of discretion was given in *Stedman v United Kingdom* (1997) 23 EHRR CD 168, where the European Commission held that there was no violation of **article 9** when the applicant had been dismissed for refusing to work on Sundays.

Both the European Court and Commission have accepted that a state may impose criminal liability for blasphemy and that such law would serve the legitimate aim identified in **article 10(2)** of the Convention of protecting 'the rights of others'—that is the right to enjoy one's religion (*Gay News v United Kingdom* (1983) 5 EHRR 123 and *Otto-Preminger Institut v Austria* (1994) 19 EHRR 34). The Court has indicated that member states would be given a wide margin of appreciation in this area, reflecting the fact that the need to protect religious followers from gross offence would vary from state to state (*Wingrove v United Kingdom* (1996) 24 EHRR 1). However, **article 9** does not impose a positive obligation upon states to protect religious sensibilities and followers had no right to demand that the state operated a law of blasphemy so as to protect their religious beliefs and activities (*Choudhury v United Kingdom* (1991) 12 HRLJ 172). On the other hand, the Court has imposed strict obligations on the state to ensure that religious observers are protected against violent attacks from counter-religions (*Members of the Gldani Congregation of Jehovah's Witnesses v Georgia* (2008) 46 EHRR 30).

Although **article 9** is accepted as central both to the enjoyment of individual liberty and to the principles of a modern democracy, the European Court and Commission have allowed individual member states a generous margin of appreciation when balancing religious rights with other rights or social interests. This approach is mirrored in the post-Human Rights Act era and, as can be seen from cases such as *Sahin*, *Begum* and *Choudhury*, this may leave the religious and other views of minority groups inadequately protected.

Question 2

To what extent does both the **European Convention on Human Rights** and English law provide sufficient protection to religious groups and followers against blasphemous and other offensive or harmful speech?

Commentary

This area of law concerns the balance between the right to protect one's religion and religious sensibilities from blasphemous and other offensive speech and the right to freedom of expression. However, the question itself is asking the student to comment on the adequacy of protection afforded to religion and religious followers and this must be the focus of the answer. Thus, although the student should appreciate the free speech arguments, the answer must concentrate on analysing the law and the case law for the purpose of seeing whether it gives sufficient weight to the religious rights argument.

The answer should begin by identifying the potential conflict between free speech and the enjoyment of religious freedom and the aims of offences such as blasphemy (now abolished in domestic law by virtue of **s.79 of the Criminal Justice and Immigration Act 2008**) and incitement to racial and religious hatred. The student should then examine each offence in turn, identifying relevant domestic law, and the case law of the European Court and Commission, in assessing its compatibility with the values of the Convention and general human rights norms. The answer can then draw some conclusions with respect to the domestic law and the Convention case law as to whether sufficient protection is given to religious freedom.

Answer plan

- Appreciation and consideration of the potential conflict between **articles 9 and 10** of the Convention

- Consideration of the (now abolished) domestic law of blasphemy and other offences seeking to regulate religiously offensive speech in the context of a critical examination of relevant case law of the European Court and Commission where **articles 9 and 10** are in conflict

- Critical commentary on the scope of domestic law and Convention case law and whether they provide sufficient protection against such speech

Suggested answer

In a democratic, tolerant, and pluralist society freedom of expression will include the right to impart information and ideas that shock and offend (*Handyside v United Kingdom* (1976) 1 EHRR 737). However, freedom of expression may be compromised provided any such restriction serves a legitimate aim and is necessary and proportionate. One such aim is the protection of religious freedom, which is guaranteed under **article 9** of the European Convention, and identified as a legitimate aim in **article 10(2)**—the 'protection of the rights of others'. This appears to legitimize domestic state laws that regulate speech or conduct which attacks either the religion or the right of individuals to practise their religion. The absence of such laws might seriously affect the right to religious observance, arguably imposing a duty on the state to provide protection in this area (*Members of the Gldani Congregation of Jehovah's Witnesses v Georgia* (2008) **46 EHRR 30**).

Some legal systems will attempt to protect either the tenets of the country's religion, or the sensibilities of its members via a specific law of blasphemy, which not only protects public safety and prevents disorder or crime, but also, more specifically, guarantees freedom of religion and religious enjoyment.

The domestic law of blasphemy does, therefore, offer some protection to religious followers against grossly offensive or outrageous expression. However, the case law in this area insists on a proportionate balance between free speech and freedom of religion. For example, in *Otto-Preminger Institut v Austria* (1994) **19 EHRR 34** the European Court held that religious followers could not expect to be exempt from all criticism and that they must tolerate and accept the denial by others of their religious beliefs and even the propagation by others of doctrines hostile to their faith. However, the Court also noted that the state may have a responsibility to ensure the peaceful enjoyment of **article 9** rights by the holders of those beliefs, recognizing that the effect of certain criticism might inhibit such believers from exercising their rights. In that case, therefore, it held that a film that depicted God as senile, Jesus as feeble-minded, and Mary as a wanton woman constituted a provocative portrayal of objects of religious veneration and that the seizing of the film was a proportionate response to ensure religious peace in that region and to protect some people from an unwarranted and offensive attack on their religious beliefs.

Furthermore, the Convention machinery has offered each state a wide margin of appreciation with respect to whether, and how, it wishes to regulate blasphemous speech. Thus, in *Otto-Preminger* (above) the Court held that the state is better placed than the international judge to assess the need for blasphemy laws and of their application in particular circumstances because it was not possible to discern a common European conception of the significance of religion in society. Further, in *Otto-Preminger* it noted that the concept of blasphemy could not be isolated from the society against which it is being judged, as well as the population where publication was to take place, which in that case were strongly Catholic (see, more recently, *IA v Turkey* (2007) **45 EHRR 30**).

This approach does not force the state to pass and maintain blasphemy laws, but, in cases where one's religious beliefs are recognized under such laws, one can expect a generous level of protection from the Convention when that right comes into conflict with freedom of expression. For example, in *Gay News v United Kingdom* (1983) **EHRR 123**, the European Commission accepted that it may be necessary in a democratic society to attach criminal sanctions to material that offends against religious feelings, provided the attack is serious enough. Furthermore, it upheld the applicant's convictions (in *R v Lemon* [1979] **AC 617**) even though the offence was based on strict liability, thus ignoring the intention of the author and publisher in publishing the work. This approach was maintained in *Wingrove v United Kingdom* (1996) **24 EHRR 1**, where the Court upheld the domestic authorities' refusal to give a video licence to a short film that described the ecstatic and erotic visions of Jesus Christ of a sixteenth century nun and which the authority felt would risk violating domestic blasphemy laws. The Court held that the interference corresponded to a legitimate aim—the protection of Christians against serious offence in their beliefs—and was proportionate despite the fact that the law did not treat all religions alike. Although there was little scope for restrictions on political speech (see the recent case of *Kunstler v Austria* (2008) 47 EHRR 5), a wider margin of appreciation was available in relation to matters liable to offend intimate personal convictions in the sphere of morals and religion. However, the Court will not sanction restrictions which are simply hostile to a religion without being abusive (*Tatlav v Turkey*, Application No 50692/99, judgment of the European Court, 2 May 2006).

This would suggest that the European Court would back any reasonable restriction on blasphemous speech imposed by regulatory agencies such as broadcasting authorities, who have a power to regulate material on grounds of taste and decency. Indeed, the domestic courts have indicated that they would provide these agencies with a wide area of discretion in this area (*R (Prolife) v BBC* [2004] 1 AC 185).

In addition, the Court has not insisted that domestic blasphemy laws apply equally to all religions. In *R v Chief Metropolitan Stipendiary Magistrate, ex parte Choudhury* [1991] 1 QB 1006, the Court of Appeal held that English blasphemy law only applied to protect the Anglican faith, and in *Choudhury v United Kingdom* (1991) 12 HRLJ 172 the Commission held that **article 9** did not contain a positive obligation upon states to protect religious sensibilities and that the right to freedom of religion does not require adherents of all religions to bring legal proceedings in respect of scurrilous abuse. As a consequence, the applicants had no right to demand that the state operated a law of blasphemy so as to protect their religious beliefs. Further, the Commission reasoned that the unequal application of blasphemy laws did not discriminate against the applicants because as there was no positive obligation of a state to protect the right to be free from offence under **article 9**, it could not be a breach of **article 14** to deny someone protection. Consequently, the state appears to possess discretion whether to enact blasphemy laws, and to choose which religions to protect under such laws; in 2008 the English law of blasphemy was abolished by **s.78 of the Criminal Justice and Immigration Act**. This situation would be remedied by the introduction of a freestanding right to equality under the law (as contained in optional **Protocol 12** of the Convention), but at present the protection of religious beliefs from such attacks remains within the discretion of the individual state.

This position is mitigated to some extent by the existence in domestic law of certain race or religious hatred crimes, which might indirectly protect individuals from racial and religious discrimination and protect their right to freedom of thought, conscience, and religion under **article 9**. For example, **ss.18–23 of the Public Order Act 1986** create a number of offences relating to the incitement of racial hatred—defined under **s.17** as hatred against a group of persons defined by reference to colour, race, nationality (including citizenship), or ethnic or national origins. These provisions did not apply specifically to religious groups, although some such groups (such as Sikhs and Jews) have been held to come within the terms 'race' and 'ethnic or national origins' (*Mandla v Dowell Lee* [1983] 2 AC 548). However, **s.1 of the Racial and Religious Hatred Act 2006** amends the 1986 Act and it is now an offence to use threatening, abusive, and insulting words or behaviour where that person intends to stir up religious hatred, or where such hatred is likely to be stirred up (**s.18** of the 1986 Act). This does not provide protection against offensive or insulting attacks *per se* and will require religious hatred to ensue. Moreover, it is a defence that the defendant did not intend his words or behaviour, or the written material, to be, and was not aware that it might be, threatening, abusive, or insulting (**s.18(5)**). These qualifications protect true freedom of speech and under **s.7** of the Act no proceedings may be brought without the consent of the Attorney-General.

Further, racially, and religiously, aggravated public order offences were introduced via the **Crime and Disorder Act 1998**, which provided for increased penalties for certain public order offences where at the time of committing the offence, or immediately before or after doing so, the offender demonstrates towards the victim of the offence hostility based on the victim's membership (or presumed membership) of a racial group, or where the offence is motivated (wholly or partly) by hostility towards members of a racial group based on their membership of that group. This principle was extended by **s.28 of the Anti-terrorism, Crime and Security Act 2001**, where the commission of the offence was activated on the grounds of religious hatred, including the victim's membership of a religious group (a group of persons defined by religious belief or lack of religious belief, **s.28(4)**). This gives greater protection than the old law of blasphemy which only protected the religious observer from outrageous attack (*R v Lemon* (above)), and which allowed the court to find that the object under attack was not religion, but other social matters, such as media morality (*R (Green) v Westminster Magistrates' Court* [2008] HRLR 12).

Domestic courts will be mindful of the need to uphold freedom of expression, although case law thus far suggests that the courts will show a limited tolerance to such speech. Thus, in *Norwood v DPP, The Times,* 30 July 2003, it was held that the display of a poster containing, in very large print, the words 'Islam out of Britain' and 'Protect the British People' constituted an aggravated offence under **s.5 of the Public Order Act 1986** of displaying an insulting sign likely to cause harassment, alarm, or distress. The appeal court held that the sign was plainly unreasonable, indicating a public expression of attack on all Muslims in this country as opposed to an intemperate criticism against the tenets of the Muslim religion. This decision was upheld by the European Court of Human Rights (*Norwood v United Kingdom* (2005) 40 EHRR 11), who held that the speech was not protected by the Convention as it was a general and vehement attack against a religious group, linking the group as a whole with grave acts of terrorism, and thus incompatible with the values of the Convention, notably tolerance, social peace, and non-discrimination. That reflects the Court's intolerance of hate speech (*Glimerveen and Hagenbeek v Netherlands* (1980) 18 DR 187) and thus provides some protection to the right of religious observance.

In conclusion, **article 9** of the Convention offers a limited and inconsistent protection against blasphemous and other religiously offensive speech. The absence in **article 9** of a positive right to defend one's religion and beliefs from verbal attack militates against full and effective protection in this field; a situation compounded by the unequal application of domestic blasphemy laws. This is to an extent mitigated by the growth of racially and religiously aggravated offences, which at least outlaw unreasonable and insulting attacks against religion and religious followers.

Question 3

Critically examine the extent to which the European Court of Human Rights has safeguarded the fundamental right of political association. In your opinion are domestic restrictions in this area compatible with the European Convention and its case law?

 Commentary

This question requires a sound knowledge of the nature and scope of the right of political association and an appreciation of the values and principles underlying that right. As the question refers to political association there is no need to consider trade unions, although they can be mentioned when referring to the general right of association. Although the question asks how successfully the European Court has upheld that right, the student needs to appreciate the theoretical and democratic arguments with respect to the right of association so as to critically analyse the Court's role and success in this area. The second part of the question requires a sound knowledge of domestic law, in particular relevant anti-terrorism laws. Students should concentrate on the general compatibility of those laws with the principles identified in the first part of the question. Both questions could form a question in their own right and thus the student must be careful to cover all aspects clearly but analytically. Consequently, the question does not require an in-depth explanation of the legal area and the case law, but rather an appreciation of the relevant values and a critical assessment of the law.

The answer should begin with a brief, but incisive explanation of the right to political association, its democratic and other values, and its conditional status within the Convention. The student should then examine the case law of the European Court in this area so as to assess the Court's attitude and the extent to which it is prepared to uphold the right of association in the light of the dangers some associations pose to the state. In particular, the student should appreciate the nature of proscription and the danger it poses to democratic values. The second part of the question can then examine domestic provisions in this area, in particular those relating to the proscription of terrorist organizations. The answer should assess the compatibility of such provisions with **article 11** of the Convention and the values of political association, referring back to the principles identified in part one of the question.

Answer plan

- Explanation of the theory and value of the fundamental rights of association, including its relationship with democracy and other Convention rights

- Consideration as to the extent and efficacy of the European Court's case law in the light of the democratic and other values that the freedom purports to uphold

- Explanation of the conditional status of that right within the Convention and the need to limit that right in order to protect individual and collective interests

- Explanation of various domestic laws restricting the right of association, and their rationale

- Consideration of the compatibility of relevant domestic law with the **Human Rights Act 1998**, supported by any relevant post-Act case law

Suggested answer

Article 11 of the European Convention states that everyone has the right of association, expressly including the right to form and join trade unions. 'Association' includes political parties (*United Communist Party of Turkey v Turkey* (1998) 26 EHRR 121), where the Court recognized that such parties are essential to the proper functioning of a democracy, and that **article 11** must be considered in the light of **article 10**, particularly in relation to political parties, because of their essential role in ensuring pluralism.

The Court has attached special significance to the political views of the speaker (*Vogt v Germany* (1995) 21 EHRR 205), and will safeguard associations more vehemently where the group in question has a democratic mandate, as opposed to those forming for social purposes (*Anderson v United Kingdom* (1998) 25 EHRR CD 172). The Court will subject any restriction on the right of political association, particularly any form of proscription, to the closest scrutiny.

Consequently, proscription cannot be sanctioned simply because the group's views conflict with established political orthodoxy and any interference by the national authorities has to be based on compelling evidence. For example, in *United Communist Party of Turkey v Turkey* (above), the dissolution of a political party on the basis that it used the word 'communist' in its name was in violation of **article 11**. Although it had advocated a separate Kurdish nation, the group's dissolution because of the use of the word 'communist', and because its constitution and programme contained statements likely to undermine territorial integrity and national unity, was not necessary in a democratic society. Although the party advocated different views from the government on the Kurdish problem, there was insufficient evidence that it advocated division of the Turkish nation.

This decision was upheld in *Socialist Party v Turkey* (1998) 27 EHRR 51, where the Court held that the same principles applied even if proscription was based on the group's activities after formation.

The Court has also taken a robust approach with respect to measures that interfere with the individual's enjoyment of association. Thus, in *Vogt v Germany* (above), it held that the dismissal of a teacher simply because she was a member, and had taken part in the activities, of the German Communist Party, violated **article 10**. There was insufficient evidence to support the necessity of the dismissal: her work as a teacher had been satisfactory and she had never acted in a way that was inconsistent with the compulsory declaration of allegiance to the German constitutional order. However, in *Ahmed v United Kingdom* [1999] **IRLR 188** it held that the prohibition of certain local authority officers from holding political office was proportionate to the aim of securing public confidence in public officers and the performance of their duties.

There will be exceptional cases where the Court is satisfied that an organization poses a sufficient threat to the values of that society to warrant proscription and it must distinguish such threats from those cases where the views of the group are simply unpopular or inconsistent with other, democratic, majority views. One method may be to employ **article 17**, which provides that nothing in the Convention gives any person or group any right to engage in any activity or perform any act aimed at the destruction of any of the rights and freedoms in the Convention. This could be used to justify the proscription of groups whose purposes and activities are either violent, or incite violence, or are otherwise inconsistent with the enjoyment of others' Convention rights. Thus in *Refah Partisi Erbakan Kazan and Tekdal v Turkey* (2002) **35 EHRR 2** the Grand Chamber of the European Court confirmed that political parties whose leaders incite others to use violence could not rely on the Convention to protect them from resultant sanctions.

However, the Court has made it clear that violence is not a prerequisite of proscription and that an association may be restricted for wider purposes. Thus in *Refah Partisi* (above) it held that although political parties who campaign for changes to the legal or constitutional structure are allowed the protection of **article 11**, any such change had to be compatible with the fundamental principles of democracy. In this case the Court held that the dissolution of the applicant's party on the grounds that it had become a centre of activities against the principles of secularism, was within the state's margin of appreciation. Noting that the party sought to institute a system of Sharia law, the Court held that such a system was incompatible with the state's role as the guarantor of individual rights, and would infringe the principle of non-discrimination between individuals.

In domestic law, proscription has been reserved for the most extreme groups who pose major threats to public order or the security of the state. Instead, domestic law attaches criminal liability to words or behaviour that cause, or are likely to cause, particular harm. For example, with respect to right-wing groups with racist agendas, the law instead makes provision for specific offences that seek to protect individuals or groups. Thus, **s.18 of the Public Order Act 1986** makes it an offence to incite racial hatred, and **s.1 of the Racial and Religious Hatred Act 2006** contains a similar offence of inciting religious hatred. In addition, some public order offences, such as using threatening, abusive, or insulting words or behaviour likely to cause alarm and distress, can now be committed in a racially (**Public Order Act 1986**), or religiously (**Anti-terrorism, Crime and Security Act 2001**) aggravated form. These provisions are enforced stringently by the courts (*Norwood v DPP, The Times*, 30 July 2003). However, they do not make a person liable by association only, even though their views might not attract the protection of **articles 10 and 11** of the European Convention (*Norwood v United Kingdom* (2005) 40 EHRR 11).

Nevertheless, there are certain provisions that criminalize association with a particular group. For example, **s.1 of the Public Order Act 1936** makes it an offence to wear a uniform in any public place or at any public meeting that signifies association with any political organization or the promotion of any political object. In *O'Moran v DPP* [1975] QB 864, it was held that although the wearing of a uniform required some article of clothing, as opposed to, for example, a lapel badge, it covered the wearing of a beret. Further, the wearing of a uniform could be associated with a political association either through evidence of previous association, or, as in the present case, from the circumstances surrounding the wearing of the uniform. This provision overlaps with **s.13 of the Terrorism Act 2000** (see below), and its potential use against peaceful and lawful groups, such as animal activists, would be a disproportionate interference with **article 11**, although the consent of the Attorney-General is required for any prosecution.

Further, **s.2 of the Public Order Act 1936** prohibits the formation of military or quasi-military organizations—those organized or trained to be employed for the use or display of physical force in promoting any political object. The provision also covers organizations concerned with usurping the functions of the police or the armed forces, and makes it an offence for any person to take part in the control or management of that association, or, as a member of that association, to take part in the organization or training of members. The provision—which was employed in *R v Jordan and Tyndall* [1963] **Crim LR 124** against an extremist right-wing paramilitary group—appears compatible with **articles 11 and 17** of the Convention, and, again, any prosecution requires the consent of the Attorney-General.

The proscription of terrorist groups is now covered by the **Terrorism Act 2000**, and **s.3** identifies proscribed groups as those listed in **Schedule 2** of the Act, the Secretary of State having the power to add to that list if he believes that it is concerned in terrorism—that it commits or participates in acts of terrorism, prepares for terrorism, promotes or encourages terrorism, or is otherwise concerned in acts of terrorism. 'Terrorism' is defined under **s.1** as the use or threat (for the purpose of advancing a political, religious, or ideological cause) of action designed to influence the government or to intimidate the public or a section of the public, which involves serious violence against any person or serious damage to property, endangers the life of any person, or creates a serious risk to the health or safety of the public or a section of the public. This could cover environmental groups or animal activists, who represent a genuine and strongly supported cause. Such groups are subject to a range of public order offences, and the use of proscription powers might be an unnecessary restriction on the lawful activities of that group.

This wide power of proscription, although subject to parliamentary approval (under **s.123**), is not subject to judicial review. Instead, **s.5** establishes the Proscribed Organisations Appeal Commission, which hears appeals against the Secretary of State's refusal to remove an organization from that list and in *R v Secretary of State for the Home Department, ex parte Kurdistan Workers Party and others* [2002] EWHC 644 (Admin) it was held that this procedure must be used to challenge any decision.

Once a group is proscribed, **s.11** of the Act makes it an offence to belong, or profess to belong, to a proscribed organization and under **s.12** it is an offence to solicit support for, to arrange, manage, or assist in managing a meeting which he knows is to support or further the activities of a proscribed organization, or to address any such meeting in order to encourage support for such. **Section 13** of the Act then makes it an offence to wear an item of clothing, or wear, carry, or display an article in such a way or in such circumstances as to arouse reasonable suspicion that the person in question is a member or supporter of a proscribed organization. The provision might apply to a person who, for example, holds up a placard expressing views in agreement with that group and **s.1 of the Terrorism Act 2005** creates the offence of directly or indirectly encouraging or inducing an act of terrorism. Such encouragement could consist of an act which the public could understand as glorifying such an act, thus blurring the distinction between incitement to violence and lawful support.

Although the state's margin of appreciation is narrow with respect to the dissolution of political parties and the enjoyment of the right of association, the European Court is willing to sanction proscription in cases where the association threatens democratic values. The distinction between those cases, and ones where the ideology of the group is simply inconsistent with established orthodoxy, might be difficult to apply in practice. With respect to domestic law, proscription has been reserved for the most extreme groups who have practised violence as their main agenda. Current laws appear to be consistent with the European Convention, although, the *potential* application of those laws to groups with a legitimate agenda, but whose members have employed violent means, might threaten **article 11**. Further, the new offence of 'glorifying' terrorism needs to be employed cautiously.

Question 4

'The Courts have consistently stated that under English law there is no right to demonstrate.'

To what extent, if at all, would you qualify that statement in the light of post-Human Rights Act case law?

 Commentary

This is a fairly traditional question regarding the legal status of the right to demonstrate in domestic law. Although the student must begin by looking at the historical status of that right, and the general unwillingness of the law to provide it with formal protection, the question must now be answered in the light of recent developments, particularly the passing of the **Human Rights Act 1998**. The student may draw on a number of statutory and common law restrictions on the right to demonstrate, but should include examples which best illustrate the issue of inadequate, or increased protection. Although the case law of the European Court of Human Rights will have a bearing on the domestic protection of this right, students should not provide a full and analytical account of the case law of the European Court and Commission.

Students should explain the traditional residual position with respect to freedom to demonstrate and should take a critical approach to that position, using examples to illustrate the law's lack of support for the fundamental right to take part in peaceful assembly. The student should then move on to more recent developments and in particular consider the impact of the **European Convention on Human Rights** and the **Human Rights Act 1998** on the central proposition contained in the quote. Examples should be given where the courts have upheld the right to demonstrate, but the student should also include examples where the traditional position has been maintained.

The student can also comment, where appropriate, on recent proposals for reform and conclude by examining the truth of the quote and by comparing the traditional position with the post-Human Rights Act era, examining the necessary evidence to see whether it is possible to conclude that the statement can now be qualified.

 ## Answer plan

- Explanation of the importance of the right to demonstrate and of the residual and insecure nature of that right at common law
- Examples where courts and Parliament interfered or failed to secure the right to demonstrate
- Examples where Parliament or the courts gave support and recognition to the right to demonstrate
- Explanation of the impact of the European Convention and **Human Rights Act 1998** on the right to demonstrate
- Conclusions with respect to the efficacy of domestic law protection and the truth of the quote

Suggested answer

In *Hubbard v Pitt* [1976] **QB 142** Lord Denning stated that the right to assemble for the purpose of deliberating upon public grievances was not prohibited as long as it was done peaceably and in good order and without threats or incitement to violence or obstruction. This only bestows a right provided the law is not broken, and given the variety of offences that can be transgressed while demonstrating, provided little protection against arbitrary interference. The absence of a constitutional guarantee of freedom of peaceful assembly made the right to demonstrate a notional one, given the proliferation of public order laws that existed, and still exist, to ensure public safety and the enjoyment of private interests.

The right to demonstrate relied heavily on the courts and their willingness to apply these laws in a manner that was consistent with fundamental rights. Traditionally, the courts displayed reluctance to accommodate the right to demonstrate. In *Arrowsmith v Jenkins* [1963] 2 QB 561 it was held that the offence of obstruction of the highway might be committed without any specific intention to obstruct on behalf of the demonstrator; here the obstruction had occurred because of her presence and the motive of the speaker was irrelevant. This view was tempered in *Hirst and Agu v Chief Constable of Yorkshire* (1987) 85 Cr App R 143, where it was held that the courts needed to consider the reasonableness of the protester's actions and thus balance the right to protest with the need for good order. Nevertheless, the courts did not have to consider the European Convention, or the proportionality of any interference.

Further, the courts allowed the police wide discretion in how they balanced public order and individual liberty. Thus, in *Nicol and Selvanayagam v DPP* [1996] Crim LR 318 the police were allowed to arrest demonstrators for disrupting an angling competition by blowing horns, as their conduct, although not unlawful, was likely to cause a breach of the peace because on the facts the anglers were on the verge of using force against the protestors. Further, in *R v Morpeth Ward Justices, ex parte Ward* (1992) 95 Cr App R 215, it was held that provocative disorderly behaviour (in this case protesting against a pheasant shoot) which is likely to have the natural consequence of causing violence to the demonstrators, can constitute a breach of the peace. This illustrated the law's overriding concern with preserving the peace rather than the reasonableness of each party's actions.

Police discretion was particularly prevalent in cases where the demonstrator was charged with obstruction of a police officer in the execution of his duty (now contained in s.89 of the Police Act 1997). Thus, in *Duncan v Jones* [1936] 1 KB 218, although a demonstrator might not have caused any obstruction, or provoked a breach of the peace, she might nonetheless be arrested for obstruction if she was prepared to take the risk that a disturbance would result from her conduct. This conflicted with the principle in *Beatty v Gillbanks* (1882) 15 Cox CC 138—that a person cannot be punished for acting lawfully if he knows that in so doing he will induce another person to act unlawfully. Further, the courts were reluctant to subject police discretion to any real substantive review. For example, in *Piddington v Bates* [1961] 1 WLR 162, it was held that the police were entitled to restrict the number of pickets at a factory entrance, and in *Moss v McLachlan* [1985] IRLR 76 police were entitled to arrest striking miners for refusing to turn back when travelling to a colliery, the police being entitled to apprehend a breach of the peace because of previous disorder that had occurred at the collieries.

A number of statutory provisions allow the police to regulate marches and assemblies; then making it an offence to disobey any resultant orders. For example, ss.11–14 of the Public Order Act 1986 require organizers to give notice of public processions and allow the police to impose conditions on both processions and assemblies. These powers extend to banning processions in advance (s.13) and the courts have been unwilling to challenge the use of these powers where the police have apprehended serious public disorder (*Kent v Metropolitan Police Commissioner, The Times,* 15 May 1981). Further, ss.14A–14C of the 1986 Act allow a chief police officer to apply to the local council for an order prohibiting the holding of all trespassory public assemblies in a specific area where that assembly might result in serious disruption to the life of the community, or significant damage to land or buildings of historical or scientific significance. Such provisions appear to impose liability irrespective of any unlawful conduct, although they have been construed to accommodate freedom of peaceful assembly (*DPP v Jones and Lloyd* [1999] 2 All ER 257).

After the **Human Rights Act 1998**, courts are obliged to take into account the case law of the European Court (**s.2**) and have the power to declare legislative provisions incompatible with a Convention right (**s.4**). In particular, restrictions have to be prescribed by law and necessary in a democratic society for the purpose of achieving any legitimate aim, such as public safety.

A number of decisions in the post-Act era appear to provide greater protection for freedom of assembly. For example, in *Redmond-Bate v DPP, The Times*, 23 July 1999, the High Court restricted the effect of *Duncan v Jones* (above) by insisting that a police officer would have to concentrate on the *source* of the potential trouble when arresting someone for obstruction. Also, speech was not actionable simply because it offended the audience. Lord Justice Sedley held that speech included the irritating, contentious, and provocative, provided it did not tend to provoke violence, and that freedom only to speak inoffensively was not worth having. Again, in *Percy v DPP, The Times*, 21 January 2002, it was held that behaviour which was an affront to other people (desecrating a national flag) was not outlawed and that peaceful protest will only constitute an offence where the conduct goes beyond legitimate protest.

Further, in *DPP v Jones and Lloyd* (above) it was held that the public could have a right to use the highway for the purpose of conducting a peaceful assembly, provided that was a reasonable and usual activity and consistent with the primary right to use the highway for passage and repassage and that in the present case the defendants' activities (a silent roadside protest) were peaceful and non-obstructive and therefore not unlawful. A similar approach was taken in *Westminster CC v Haw* [2002] EWHC 2073, where the High Court refused to grant the local authority an order to remove a protester from the area outside Parliament because in its view the protester was exercising his fundamental rights, and that in all the circumstances his presence was reasonable.

Domestic law continues to impose substantial restrictions on the right to demonstrate. First, Parliament may pass legislation which gives the judges no choice but to sanction the actions of the authorities. Thus, following the decision in *Haw*, Parliament enacted **s.132 of the Serious Organized Crime and Police Act 2005**, which makes it an offence for any person to organize or take part in a demonstration in a designated area (extending 1,000 yards from Parliament), unless police authorization has been given. The Police Commissioner can then impose such conditions as, in his reasonable opinion, are necessary for the purpose of preventing, *inter alia*, hindrance to persons wishing to enter or leave the Palace of Westminster. These powers are subject to judicial review, and in *DPP v Haw, The Times*, 11 September 2007 (**Admin**) the High Court struck down vague and unworkable conditions imposed on Mr Haw's protest.

(Clause 32 of the Constitutional Reform and Government Bill 2009 abolishes this offence, proposing that the provisions of the **Public Order Act 1986** apply to the area.) In contrast, in *R (Brehony) v Chief Constable of Greater Manchester Police, The Times,* **15 April 2005,** the police had acted lawfully under **s.14 of the Public Order Act 1986** when they moved the protest to another location during the busy Christmas shopping period. Further, in *Austin v Commissioner of Police of the Metropolis* [2006] 2 WLR 372 it was held that the power to impose conditions under **s.14** could include a power to bring the procession to an end and that it was not necessary that the police had **s.14** in mind when issuing any directions.

Secondly, the courts have offered the authorities a wide margin of appreciation when achieving public order. For example, in *R (Gillan) v Commissioner of Police of the Metropolis and another* [2006] 2 AC 307 there had been no violation of **article 10 or 11** when the police used their powers of stop and search under **s.44(4)(b)** of the Terrorism **Act 2000** to search people who were on their way to attend an arms fair to take part in a peaceful protest. The threat posed by terrorism provided the necessary justification for any violation of the claimants' rights and there was enough evidence that the arms fair was an occasion that warranted the use of their powers; the Joint Committee on Human Rights questioned the validity of these powers and asked for their clarification.

Outside the context of terrorism, a more generous approach is evident and in *R (Laporte) v Chief Constable of Gloucestershire and others* [2007] 2 WLR 46 it was held that the police had violated **articles 10 and 11** when they prevented the passengers of a coach from reaching the site of a demonstration. The House of Lords held that no such power existed unless they anticipated a clear breach of the peace; and that, on the facts, no such belief was present as they were unable to identify which (if any) of the passengers were a threat. In any case, the police could have dealt with any threat at the place of demonstration. That decision casts doubt on *Piddington v Bates*, above, although the police do still have a general power when they do, reasonably, anticipate a breach of the peace (*Austin* (above)); the power was used in that case to detain demonstrators for seven hours.

The Joint Committee on Human Rights (above) has concluded that, in general, domestic law facilitates peaceful protest and is compatible with the Convention. However, it points to specific provisions, such as the powers of stop and search in terrorism laws, and the control of demonstrations outside Parliament (above), which it considers are in need of clarification or abolition. In any case, it is difficult to gauge whether domestic law is compatible with the European Convention as the European Court has granted a wide margin of appreciation to the state with respect to the enforcement of public safety (*Chorherr v Austria* (1993) 17 EHRR 358). However, laws must be clearly prescribed by law (*Hashman and Harrap v United Kingdom* (1999) 30 EHRR 241) and must not impose disproportionate interferences on entirely peaceful protest (*Steel v United Kingdom* (1999) 28 EHRR 603).The courts now have the tools to ensure that any restrictions on this right comply with the case law of the European Court, although cases such as *Gillan* suggest that any assertion of a right to peaceful demonstration should be taken with caution.

Question 5

Jack Morrisey is the head of a protest group called 'Rebels against Cruelty', concerned with the killing of animals for human consumption. Three weeks ago he and four members of the group were campaigning on a pavement in Leavington when they were confronted by local butchers, who started swearing at them. Several members of the group started chanting, referring to the butchers as 'murdering bastards'. A police officer arrived on the scene and asked the group to move along because they were causing an obstruction, and when they refused to move Jack was arrested for obstruction of the highway, and the other members for obstruction of a police officer.

The next day Jack distributed leaflets in Leavington with pictures of pigs with their heads cut off. The leaflet stated that the group intended to hold a silent protest outside a farmer's house in the Boventry countryside and the Chief Constable, on reading the leaflet, immediately applied for an order to prohibit the assembly of any persons on the land of the farmer, or on any adjoining highway. The group nevertheless proceeded to the lane outside the farm and lined up along the grass verge of the lane. When the police arrived they were asked to move and when they refused to do so Jack, together with four other members of the group, was arrested for taking part in a trespassory assembly. In addition, other members of the group, armed with banners, were stopped en route to the farm and told to turn back. When they refused they were arrested.

Jack now wishes to organize a procession through the streets of Boventry to launch the group's 'Meat is Murder' campaign and applied to the police giving two weeks' notice. The police gave permission for the procession but imposed the following conditions: that the number of marchers be restricted to **200**, that due to the busy shopping period the procession must circle and not enter Boventry shopping precinct, and that during the procession the protesters must not distribute leaflets likely to distress the public.

Advise Jack and the others as to the legality of the police action and whether they are likely to be found guilty of any offence.

 Commentary

This problem question covers a number of legal provisions and requires a sound knowledge of public order law and the impact of the **European Convention on Human Rights** and the **Human Rights Act 1998** in this area. In particular, it requires the student to be conversant with the scope and wording of certain statutory provisions under the **Public Order Act 1986**, as well as a number of other offences and the powers of the police to deal with a breach of the peace.

Students are advised to deal with each issue in turn, as indicated by the request for advice at the end of the question and to create sub-headings to ensure that this is done clearly and visibly. As the question covers a number of issues, there will be some pressure on the student to cover everything in the allotted time. Consequently, the relevant law should be dealt with clearly but precisely, leaving sufficient time to advise the parties on the facts in each scenario. Case law can be used to illustrate the answer, but students are advised to keep the facts of such cases to a minimum, extracting the principles and applying them clearly to the facts.

Answer plan

- Consideration of the laws relating to obstruction of the highway and breach of the peace and their application in the present case

- Consideration of the powers under **s.14A of the Public Order Act 1986** and the legality of the order in this case

- Consideration of the scope of **ss.14A–C** of the 1986 Act and the legality of the protester's arrest at the pig farm and of the arrest of those proceeding to the site

- Consideration of the powers under **ss.11–12** of the 1986 Act to control public processions and the legality of the above conditions

Suggested answer

The arrests in Leavington

Section 137 of the Highways Act 1980 makes it unlawful to wilfully obstruct a highway without lawful authority and for the officer to arrest Jack the court must be satisfied that Jack had caused an obstruction, that it was wilful, and that obstruction was unreasonable (*Nagy v Weston* **[1965] 1 WLR 280**).

This obstruction must not be *de minimis* and the court must be satisfied that Jack's presence had interfered with the public's right to use the highway, which would include the pavement. Consequently, there would have to be some evidence that as a result of the protest and the altercation the public could not use the pavement effectively. The court would then consider whether that obstruction was unreasonable—for example, whether pedestrians were forced to use the busy road to walk on as opposed to using another viable route, and could take into account the fact that Jack and the other members were taking part in a political protest (*Hirst and Agu v Chief Constable of West Yorkshire* **(1987) 85 Cr App 143**). Thus, under **s.12 of the Human Rights Act** the court would take into account Jack's (and the butcher's) freedom of expression in determining whether the obstruction was unreasonable (*Westminster CC v Haw* **[2002] EWHC 2073**).

Jack may be guilty of the offence even if he did not intend to cause an obstruction (*Arrowsmith v Jenkins* **[1963] 2 QB 561**) provided the obstruction occurs because of his presence. In our case, therefore, he may be arrested even though his real intention is to protest. In the post-Act era the police must discover the source of the trouble (*Redmond-Bate v DPP, The Times,* **23 July 1999** and thus consider whether the butchers were at least partly to blame for the incident. The police must not assume that Jack is to blame and there must be sufficient evidence to conclude that there was an obstruction and that Jack had caused it.

Under **s.89 of the Police Act 1997** it is an offence to obstruct a police officer in the execution of his duty and it would be argued in this case that he reasonably apprehended an obstruction of the highway and that by refusing to move along they have obstructed him in his efforts to deal with it. Alternatively, the officer may have reasonably apprehended a breach of the peace and that by refusing to move, the members have obstructed his efforts to deal with it (*Duncan v Jones* [1936] 1 KB 218). A breach of the peace is an act or threatened act which either actually harms a person, or in his presence his property, or is likely to cause such harm, or which puts someone in fear of such harm being done (*R v Howell* [1982] QB 416). That covers the situation where a person is either inciting a breach of the peace by his conduct or words, or where such words or behaviour are likely to result in another person committing a breach of the peace. The officer must, therefore, reasonably believe that the members were about to use violence towards the butchers, or that the butchers were about to use violence.

Further, the words or conduct of the demonstrators must interfere with the rights of others and be unreasonable (*Nicol and Selvanayagam v DPP* [1996] Crim LR 318). Consequently, the officer must be satisfied that he reasonably apprehended a breach of the peace, and also direct his attention to the source of the trouble (*DPP v Redmond-Bate* (above)). In *Redmond-Bate* the source of the trouble was the actions of onlookers and not the protesters, although in our case both factions appear to be using inflammatory language. Although the words and conduct must be more than annoying (*Percy v DPP, The Times*, 21 January 2002), calling people 'murdering bastards' would incite others to violence and might then justify the arrests. However, the officer may have to have been present at the incident to draw such conclusions and for the arrests to be lawful.

The banning of the trespassory assembly

Section 14A(1) of the 1986 Public Order Act allows a chief police officer to apply to the local council for an order prohibiting the holding of all trespassory public assemblies in that area. Section 14A(9) defines an assembly as one of two or more persons and assuming that there will be at least two demonstrators, the legality of this order is dependent on the chief police officer's reasonable belief that such an assembly is intended to be held on land to which the public has no, or a limited, right of access and that the assembly is either likely to be held without the permission of the landowner or to conduct itself in a way which would exceed that permission or the limit of such access. If the land outside is a public highway, their attendance would have to go beyond their right of access (*DPP v Jones and Lloyd* [1999] 2 All ER 257).

The group was to hold a silent protest 'outside the farmer's house', so the chief police officer must have contemplated that this was either on the farmer's land, or on the highway but constituting an unreasonable use. Further, there must be a reasonable belief that the assembly might at least result in serious disruption to the life of the community. This could include blocking a public highway if such an obstruction would seriously disrupt rural or community life, but the meeting would have to seriously affect community life, rather than the rights of the landowner. At the very least the police must have evidence of potential trespass and disruption; for example a *reasonable and objective* belief that the demonstrators will not keep to their silent protest and might go onto the farmer's land, or into his house, and take part in other unlawful and disruptive activities.

The arrests for taking part in a trespassory assembly

Section 14B(1) makes it an offence for a person to organize such an assembly knowing that it is prohibited by an order, and, under **s.14A(2)**, for a person to take part in such an assembly knowing that it is prohibited. Further, under **s.14B(4)** a constable in uniform may arrest without warrant anyone whom he reasonably suspects to be committing such an offence. Following *DPP v Jones and Lloyd* (above) it is insufficient that they are simply in breach of the order, whether that was made on reasonable suspicion or not. Thus, the question is whether lining up on a grass verge is in excess of their right of access.

In *Lloyd and Jones* the police had arrested a group who had assembled on a grass verge on the roadside and the House of Lords held that the defendant's actions constituted a peaceful, non-obstructive assembly consistent with their limited right of access to the highway. Thus, in the absence of any evidence to suggest that this was causing an unreasonable obstruction of the highway, they would not be taking part in a trespassory assembly. Further, if the police had no reasonable evidence to suggest that they were taking part in a trespassory assembly, the arrests and subsequent detentions would constitute a violation of **article 5** of the European Convention.

The arrests for obstruction for not turning back

Under **s.14C** a police constable has the power to stop persons from proceeding to a trespassory assembly where he reasonably believes that a person is on his way to a prohibited assembly. The constable may stop that person and direct him or her not to proceed in the direction of the assembly, and any person who refuses to comply with a direction which he knows has been given to him is guilty of an offence and a constable in uniform may arrest without warrant anyone he reasonably suspects to be committing an offence (**s.14C(4)**). This is in addition to the police's power to preserve the peace, which can be used to stop protesters from reaching particular destinations (*Moss v McLachlan* [1985] IRLR 76) provided any detention is not unreasonable in length and there exists a reasonable apprehension that those arrested are likely to threaten the peace (*R (Laporte) v Chief Constable of Gloucestershire and others* [2007] 2 WLR 46). The police would have reasonable grounds to suspect that the protesters were on their way to the relevant area because they were holding banners and moving in the direction of the farm. However, despite *Jones and Lloyd* (above), **s.14C** talks about *suspicion* that someone is on his way to an assembly prohibited under that section, without expressly requiring that the order is lawful. In all likelihood the officer is required to have a reasonable suspicion that the protesters were about to act in breach of that order by exceeding their right of access on the land. In addition, given the now limited discretion afforded to the police with respect to anticipating and preventing a breach of the peace (*Laporte* (above)), the courts would require evidence that the protesters were to exceed their right to be on the land or to act in breach of the peace.

The legality of the conditions imposed on the procession

Jack appears to have complied with **s.11 of the Public Order Act 1986**, which imposes a duty on the organizer of a procession to give advance notice to the police six days before the date when it is intended to hold the march. Despite that, the police have a further power under **s.12** to impose conditions on a procession. The conditions must be imposed by the chief police officer in the area, who must reasonably believe that serious public disorder, serious damage to property, or serious disruption to the life of the community may be caused by the procession, or that the purpose of the assembly is the intimidation of others. The officer can have regard to the time, place, and circumstances in which the procession is to be held and may give to the organizer and those taking part such conditions which appear to him necessary in order to prevent such (**s. 12(1)**). This can prescribe the route of the procession and prohibit it from entering any public place specified in those directions.

Such powers are subject to judicial review and they must comply with the **Human Rights Act 1998** by being necessary and proportionate. The courts have allowed a wide margin of discretion to the police under this section, and under **s.14** with respect to conditions imposed on public assemblies in *Broadwith v DPP* [2000] **Crim LR 924**, and in *R (Brehony) v Chief Constable of Greater Manchester Police, The Times,* **15 April 2005**, where it was held that the police must give basic reasons for their use. In our case the police do not appear to have given any reasons for imposing the conditions, and have not identified which of the statutory reasons is applicable in this case. Consequently, there appears to be no reason why the number of protesters should be limited and why the procession should not enter the shopping precinct. Further, the condition that they should not distribute leaflets which are likely to cause distress to the public could be regarded as both insufficiently clear to be prescribed by law (*Hashman and Harrap v United Kingdom* (1999) 30 EHRR 241 and a disproportionate interference with reasonable and peaceful protest (*Steel v United Kingdom* (1999) 28 EHRR 603).

Further reading

Clayton, R and Tomlinson, H, *The Law of Human Rights*, 2nd edn (OUP 2009), ch 16.

Fenwick, H, *Civil Liberties and Human Rights*, 4th edn (Cavendish Routledge 2007), ch 8.

Fenwick, H and Phillipson, G, 'The Right to Protest, the Human Rights Act and Judicial Responses' [2000] PL 627.

Joint Committee on Human Rights, *Demonstrating Respect for Rights? A Human Rights Approach to Policing Protest* 2008–09 HL 47/HC 320.

Mead, D, 'The Right to Peaceful Protest under the European Convention on Human Rights' [2007] EHRLR 345.

Index

A

Absolute rights 26, 57
  death penalty and 68–71
  derogation and 64
  life, right to *see* Life, right to
  margin of appreciation and 30
  torture *see* Torture, freedom from
Access to justice, right to
  fair trial *see* Fair trial, right to
  prisoners 49
African Charter on Human and People's
  Rights 13
'Age of Enlightenment' 8
American Convention on Human Rights 13
Anti-terrorism provisions 9
  detention of terrorists 23
Arbitrary interference
  court's power to safeguard against 56
  free speech and 161, 165
  peaceful assembly and 207
  protection from 10, 136
  transsexuals and 157
Aristotle 8
Armed forces
  court martials and 109, 111
  sexual privacy 29, 41, 137, 141
Arrest, arbitrary 97, 101
Association, freedom of 8, 61
  animal activists 205
  Article 11, 58, 61, 193, 202–6
  conditional right 58
  individual's enjoyment, interference
    with 203–4
  military organizations, formation of 205
  paramilitary groups 205
  police, organizations usurping function
    of 205
  political parties, proscription of 203, 206
  political protest, control of 193, 196
  proscription and 204–6

  public order offences 204–5
  quasi-military organizations 205
  racial hatred, offence to incite 200–1, 204
  religion *see* **Religion, freedom of**
  terrorist groups, proscription of 193, 205–6
  trade unions, right to form 203
  uniforms, wearing of 205
  war and 36
  see also **Peaceful assembly, right to**
Asylum seekers
  torture and 80
Artificial insemination
  prisoner's right 123

B

Bankrupts
  refusal of permission to consult solicitor 111
Bentham, Jeremy
  utilitarian view 8
Bills of Rights
  aims of 17–19
  anti-democratic 17–19
  content of 16
  domestic 8, 9–10, 15
  human rights and 15–19
  'notwithstanding' clause 18
  'rogues' charter 18
Blasphemy 42, 117
  protection from 197–201
  see also **Religion, right to freedom of**
British Constitution 45, 52
Broadcasting authorities
  taste and decency, preservation of 189, 191
Bugging devices *see* **Surveillance techniques**

C

Canadian Charter of Fundamental Rights
  'notwithstanding' clause 18

Children
  adult-like trials 106, 111–12
  corporal punishment 81, 196
  detention of minors 98
  human rights abuses of 25
  life sentences for murder 30
  obscenity offences to protect 190–1
  unborn child's right to life 30, 65
Civil and political rights 9–10
  life, right to *see* **Life, right to**
  social and economic rights
    distinguished 10
  see also **International Covenant on Civil and Political Rights**
Civil liberties 5–8, 15–19
Closed-circuit television *see* **Surveillance techniques**
Clothing
  fundamental right to 7, 9
Committee of Ministers 23
Conditional rights 57
  Articles 8-12, 26, 28
  association, freedom of *see* **Association, freedom of**
  expression, freedom of *see* **Expression, freedom of**
  margin of appreciation and 30
Confidentiality, law of
  data, statutory protection of 142, 143
  European Convention
    compliance with 143
    development in line with 150
  expression, freedom of 165
  national security 173–7
  official secrets *see* **Official secrets**
  press freedom and 176
  prior publication defence 175
  privacy, right to 135, 140, 141, 142–3
  private lives of 'public' figures 151, 167
  public interest defence 175, 176
Confiscation orders 116
Conscience, freedom of *see* **Religion, right to freedom of**
Contempt of court, law of
  disclosure of information, prevention of 179–83
  fair trial and 179–183
  journalistic sources, protection of 166, 183–7
  national security 174

ongoing litigation, comments by newspapers 50, 162–3, 165–6, 179
  public interest defence 176, 181, 183
  'serious prejudice' 180
  strict liability rule 179–80
  'thalidomide' litigation 162–3, 165–6, 179–80
Contra bones mores conduct 33
Control orders 111
Corporal punishment
  birching 83, 84
  children and 81, 196
  'inhuman and degrading' treatment 196
  judicial 83, 84
Correspondence
  legal 126–7, 133
  medical 127
  prisoners' rights 120, 126, 128, 132–4, 138
  private, right to 138, 140
Council of Europe 22, 39
  death penalty and 70, 71
  public morality, uniform conception of 162
Court martials 108, 111
Cultural relativism
  doctrine of 11

D

Data protection 49, 142, 143
Damages 24, 34, 125
  acceptable, guidance to juries 170
  disproportionate 170
  excessive 163, 169, 170, 172
Death penalty 25, 63, 67, 68–71
  abolition of 70, 76, 79
  contravention of Convention on Human Rights 76–80
  extradition and 76–80, 92
  International Covenant on Civil and Political Rights 69
  persons under 18, 69
  pregnant women 69
  Protocol 6 Convention on Human Rights 70, 76, 79
  Protocol 13 Convention on Human Rights 70, 76
  torture, freedom from and 70
Defamation 140, 141
  absolute immunity 170
  corporations, speech attacking 171

damages and 172
definition 169
democratically elected bodies and 170
excessive damages, effect on press
    freedom 163, 169, 170
expression, freedom of 165
fair comment, defence of 171, 172
interim injunctions, refusal of 166, 172
justification, defence of 171, 172
law of 169–73
politicians, speech attacking 171
press freedom *see* **Press, freedom of**
prior restraint 166, 170
public figures and 163
qualified privilege defence 168, 170–2
reputation and 171–2
Deportation
    AIDS sufferers and 94
    diplomatic assurances of receiving state 93
    fundamental rights, risk of infringement by
        receiving state 91–2
    human rights abuse 50
    'real risk' factor 92–4
    Sri Lankan Tamils 93
    terrorism 92
    torture and 81, 92
Derogation, power of
    absolute rights and 64
    Article 15, 36–9, 64, 103, 105
    emergencies threatening life of nation 36–9,
        55, 82, 105
    fair trial, right to 103, 105
    judicial control and 36–7
    limitations 36–7
    public emergency 36, 105
    terrorism and 101–5
    war and 36–9, 55, 82
Detention
    Article 5, 97, 101–5
    'closed evidence' 104
    derogation and 37–8, 103–5
    fixed term, detention after expiry 97–8
    foreign terrorist suspects 53–4, 55, 103–5
    lawful detention by competent court 97
    legal assistance during, right to 107
    life-sentence prisoners
        judicial supervision of release on expiry of
            tariff 100
    protection on deprivation of liberty
        compensation for unlawful 97
            continued lawfulness, right to
                question 97
            judicial authority, right to be brought
                before 97
        removal of person from state 91
        terrorist offences 101–3
        without trial 27–8
Die, right to 30, 44, 65, 136, 195
Discretionary Lifer Panel 127
Discrimination, freedom from 8
    Article 14, 40–4, 155
    tax relief and 43–4
    Widowed Mother's Allowance 43
DNA samples
    retention of 144
'Due process' rights 9
    fair trial *see* **Fair trial, right to**
    liberty *see* **Liberty and security, right to**
    retrospective criminal law *see* **Retrospective
        criminal law, freedom from**
Dworkin, Ronald 7, 9, 40

E

Economic and social rights 10
    civil and political rights distinguished 10
    see also **International Covenant on
        Economic, Social and Cultural Rights**
Education, right to
    corporal punishment 81, 196
    fundamental right, as 7, 9
    school uniform policy
        'Kara' bracelets 196
        Muslim headdress 195, 196
        purity rings, wearing of 196
Employment, right to 7
Enforcement
    European Convention on Human Rights
        and 13
    judicial method 13–14, 15
    non-judicial methods 14–15
    see also **European Court of Human Rights**
Environmental hazards
    protection against 65
Equality
    rule of law and 8, 9
    see also **Discrimination, freedom from**
European Commission of Human Rights
    11, 14, 21, 23
European Committee on Torture 128

European Convention on Human Rights 7, 9,
12, 13, 14, 19, 21, 26, 27, 2s7
aims of 22–3
Article 1 13, 23, 25, 26
Article 2 *see* **Life, right to**
Article 3, *see* **Torture, freedom from**
Article 4 *see* **Slavery, freedom from**
Article 5 *see* **Liberty and security, right to**
Article 6 *see* **Fair trial, right to**
Article 7 *see* **Retrospective criminal law,
freedom from**
Article 8 *see* **Private and family life, right
to** 13, 32
Article 9 *see* **Religion, right to**
Article 10 *see* **Expression, freedom of**
Article 11 *see* **Association, freedom of**
Article 13 25, 77, 79–80
Article 14 *see* **Discrimination, freedom from**
Article 15 26, 27, 36–9 *see also* **Derogation,
power of**
Article 17 60
Article 19 23
Article 28 23
Article 31 23
Article 33 24
Article 34 13, 24
Article 35 13, 24
Article 38 24
Article 41 13, 24
Article 43 23
Article 46 23
Article 47 23
conditional rights 26
death penalty 70
enforcement bodies under 23
Preamble 22
Protocol 6 70, 76
Protocol 1, Article 1 43
Protocol 11 25
Protocol 12 43, 44
Protocol 12, Article 1 43
Protocol 13 70, 76
Protocol 14 25
restrictions on rights
'in accordance with law' 32–3
'necessary in a democratic society' 33–4
'prescribed by law' 32–3
proportionality of restriction 34–5

European Convention on the Prevention of
Torture 14, 119
European Court of Human Rights 13, 21, 23
Chambers of the Court 23
Committees of the court 23
decisions binding in international law 24
friendly settlement between States, giving
effect to 24
Grand Chamber 23
international human rights, establishing
norms 25
just satisfaction award 24
legality, establishing norms 25
'margin of appreciation' and 26
proportionality
establishing norms 25
restriction on rights 34–5
success of 25–6
European Prison Rules 119
European Social Charter 10
Euthanasia 30, 44
Expression, freedom of 7, 9, 23, 31, 34, 36, 49,
58, 61
Article 10 58, 159–64
blasphemous speech 162, 197–201
commercial speech 161
conditional right 58, 159, 166
defamation *see* **Defamation**
free speech, value of 160–1
Human Rights Act 1998
enhancement of protection 166–8
individual privacy and 161, 167
intelligence services 167
interference with right
common law presumption 165
'necessary in a democratic society'
requirement 161–2, 166
'prescribed by law' requirement 161
prior restraint 166
substantial justification for 165, 167
introduction to 159
government criticism, enhanced protection
of 163
'margin of appreciation' and 162–4
national security and 167, 173–7
obscenity and *see* **Obscenity**
parliamentary proceedings 170
political speech 167

press freedom *see* **Press, freedom of**
prior restraint 166, 170
prisoner's right to 123, 124, 126
privacy interests, conflict with 150–1
private life right and 143
proportionality doctrine and 162–3
public corporations 163
public interest defence 167, 172
public morality 161, 162
public official criticism, enhanced protection
   of 163
racist speech 161, 163
religion *see* **Religion, freedom of**
reputation, right to 169
tobacco advertising ban 53
Extradition
   death penalty and 76–80
   human rights abuse 50
   torture and 81, 84–5

F

Fair trial, right to 54
   access to the courts, right of 107
   accusations
      language accused understands 107
      prompt detailed information, right to 107
   Article 6 7, 9, 23, 105–9
   'civil rights and obligations', interpretation
      of 107–8
   'criminal charge', interpretation of 108
   control orders 111
   court martials 109, 111
   defence, right to time and facilities for
      preparation of 107
   detention, right to legal assistance during 107
   equality of arms 107
   evidence, right to access and present 106–7,
      112
   free legal assistance 107, 113
   'impartial court or tribunal'
      hearing before, right of 106, 110
      interpretation of 108–9
      strict approach of courts 109
   interpreter, free legal assistance of 107
   interrogation, right to legal assistance
      during 107

judicial decisions, impartiality of 109
legal representation, right to 106, 107, 113
participation, effectively in
   proceedings 106–7, 111–12
presumption of innocence 106, 112
presumption of liberty 106
prison disciplinary proceedings 108, 109,
   111, 113, 127
public hearing 106, 110
reasonable time, right to hearing within 106
representation in person 107
retrospective criminal law *see* **Retrospective**
   criminal law, freedom from
self-incrimination, right against 106, 112
silence, right 106, 112–13
violations of right
   bias of government 111
   convictions based on biased juror 113
   defence witnesses, refusal to allow 113
   delay of proceedings 113
   executive sentences 113
   legal aid denied 113
   legal representation denied 113
   party's inability to present case 112
   public authorities, proceedings against 111
   refusal of permission to consult
      solicitor 111
   silence, erosion of right to 112–13
'Five techniques'
   torture and 83
Food
   deprivation of 83
   force feeding 125
   prisoners rights to decent 122
   right to 7, 9
Force feeding 125
Free speech *see* **Expression, freedom of**

G

Gender reassignment 54
   see also **Transsexuals**
Grand Chamber
   advisory opinions, requests for 23
   appeal court 23
Gross indecency
   abolition of offence 156

H

Habeas corpus 38
Handcuffing 132
'High Contracting Parties' 22
Home Secretary
  'public authority' 131
  'public body' 131
Homosexuals
  adoption rights 157
  age limits 44, 156
  armed forces 29, 156
  civil partnerships and 156
  civil rights, discriminatory practices and 156
  Convention rights 155–7
  criminal law, regulation via 156
  gross indecency, abolition of 156
  legal recognition of relationships 156
  Northern Ireland legislation 33
  tenancy, right to inherit 54, 156
Human rights
  bills of rights and 15–19
  civil liberties distinguished 7
  economic 10
  enforcement of 5–19
  meaning of 7
  nature of 7
  protection of
    anti-democratic notion 16–19
    constitutional problems of 16–19, 51–6
    post-Human Rights Act 1998 47, 50–1
    pre-Human Rights Act 1998 47, 48–50
  social 10
  violation of *see* **Violation of rights**
  war and 36–9
Human Rights Act 1998 21, 25
  constitutional issues and 52–5
  declarations of incompatibility and 51, 54, 55, 58, 61, 167
  expression, freedom of 166–8
  extension of courts' powers to protect rights 56
  introduction to 45–6
  prisoners' rights, challenges under 119, 120, 123
  privacy, right to and 142–4
  protection of rights
    extension of courts power 56
    post-Act 47
    pre-Act 47 52–3
  reasons for passing 50–1

statutory interpretation, courts' increased
  powers of 51
rights based system 51
violations, proceedings for 87–90
Human Rights Committee 12, 14, 25, 134
Human Rights Council 11

I

Immigration policies
  torture and 92, 94
Indecency
  expression, freedom of and 165
  gross, abolition of offence of 156
Information, freedom of
  legislation 177
  see also **Date protection**
Inhumane treatment
  absolute right 30
Injunctions 153
Intelligence services
  expression, freedom of 167
  surveillance and 146
International Covenant on Civil and Political Rights 9, 12, 14, 131
  Article 4 15
  Article 6 69
  Article 10 130, 133–4
  Article 26 40–1, 43
  Article 28 12
  Article 41 12
  death penalty
    generally 69
    pregnant women 69
  inherent dignity 130, 133
  Optional Protocol, Article 1, 12
  prisoners' rights 119
  state reporting mechanism 120
International Covenant on Economic, Social and Cultural Rights 10, 12
  Article 1 12
  Article 3 12
  Article 6 12
  Article 7 12
  Article 8 12
  Article 9 12
  Article 11 13
  Article 12 13
  Article 13 13

Article 14 13
Article 16 13
International treaties 9
Investigatory Powers Tribunal 175

J

Joint Committee on Human Rights 210
Jones, Timothy 27
Judicial review 49
    act of proscription by Home Secretary 59–61
    case law examples 122–3
    minimum prison term, reasons for 123
    prison authorities and 122–3
    prisoners' rights
        executive sentencing 123
        legal claims 120
        recall 123
        release 123
    privacy issues and 144
    public processions, police powers subject
        to 215
    upholding prisoner's Convention rights 123,
        130
    violation of rights, challenging 58–61
Just satisfaction 90
    compensation remedy under Convention 13,
        24, 123
    Human Rights Act 1998 and 88, 90, 123
    judgment as 24
    non-pecuniary loss, damages for 134
    prisoners' rights and 123
    see also **Damages**

L

Legality, principle of
    Convention rights, interference with 7, 31,
        41
    death penalty under Convention 67, 76
    expression, freedom of 168
    judicial review and 123
    press intrusion 151
    prisoners' rights, restrictions on 124
    private life, right to 154
    public processions, conditions imposed 215
Legitimacy, principle of 14, 19, 51, 57
Liberty and security, right to
    arbitrary arrest 97

Article 5 7, 8, 23, 24, 54, 97–100, 101–5
    detention *see* **Detention**
    detention without trial 27–8
    fixed term of imprisonment, detention after
        expiry 97–8
    lawful arrest to bring person before
        competent authority 98
    lawful detention by competent court 97
    life-sentence prisoners 100
    minors, detention of 98
    poll tax defaulters 98
    protection on deprivation of liberty
        compensation for unlawful 97, 100
        continued lawfulness, right to question 97,
            99–100
        judicial authority, right to be brought
            before 97, 99
    suspected terrorists, detention of 98, 102–3
    terrorism *see* **Terrorism**
    unlawful entrants 98
    unsound mind, persons of 98
    vagrants, detention of 98
Life, right to 7, 8, 9, 22, 44
    absolute right 30, 64, 70–1
    Article 2 7, 8, 9, 22, 63–71, 72–6, 77–80,
        87–90
        negative duty on state 65
        positive duty on state 65, 73
    case law 64–7
    death penalty 63, 67, 68–71
    deaths caused by acts of state 65
    definition 64
    derogation and 37, 68, 70–1
    die, right to 30, 65
    extradition and 76–80
    introduction to 63
    peacetime compromise of right 68–9
    prisoners' rights 126
    scope subject to judicial application 64–5
    state's duty to investigate deaths
        67, 72, 75
    state's duty to safeguard lives of those in
        detention 73–4
    state's obligation to protect 65, 71–6, 76–80,
        90
    suicides in prison 66
    unborn child and 30, 65
Locke, John
    'social contract' notion 7, 8

M

Magna Carta 48, 110
'Margin of appreciation', doctrine of 26, 28,
    30, 34, 138
    absolute rights and 26, 30
    Article 15 and 26
    conditional rights and 30
    expression, freedom of 162–4
    'Margin of error' 28
    'necessary in democratic society' 29
    obscenity laws and 189
    press freedom *see* **Press, freedom of**
    private life and 29
    proportionality and 34
    public morality and 29
    religion and 197
    universal enforcement of rights, threat to 29
'Margin of error' *see above* 'Margin of
    appreciation', doctrine of
Marital rape 117
Marry, right to
    Article 12 13, 128, 138, 155, 158
    homosexuals, civil partnerships and 156
    transsexuals and 44, 155, 158
Mental health
    legislation incompatible with Convention on
        Human Rights 55
    prisoners 90, 129
MI5 surveillance 146
Minors
    detention of 98
    see also **Children** *and* **Young offenders**
Miscarriage of justice
    prisoner's right to freedom of expression 123
Movement, freedom of 7
    war and 36
Murder
    children, life sentences for 30
    prisoners, life sentence
        judicial supervision of release 100

N

National origin
    discrimination against 8
National security
    expression, freedom of 167, 173–7

press sources, non-disclosure of 184–5
    terrorism *see* **Terrorism**
Natural justice principles
    'due process' rights upholding 9
    English law principle and 95, 106
    fair trials 110, 111
    life, arbitrary taking of 69
    prison authorities and 122
'Necessary in a democratic society'
    Convention rights, interference with 21, 29,
        33, 34
    expression, freedom of 159, 161–3, 168–9,
        174, 185, 188, 189
    fair trial, right to a 104
    necessity, doctrine of 53, 56
    prisoners' rights 133
    private life, right to 147–8
    surveillance techniques 145, 148
Newspapers
    ongoing litigation, comments
        by 50, 162–3
    see also **Press Intrusion**
Noise
    torture and 83
Nuisance 140, 150

O

Obscenity laws
    broadcasting authorities
        taste and decency, preservation of 189,
            191
    children 190–1
    'deprave or corrupt', words likely to 34, 189,
        190
    expression, freedom of 165
    indecent material
        display of 189
        regulation of 188–91
    'margin of appreciation' 189
    pornography 189, 191
    public decency, outraging 189, 191
    public good defence 49, 190
    public morals, conspiracy to corrupt 189,
        191
    obscene expression, regulation
        of 188–91
    Williams Committee 188

Official secrets
  categories covered by legislation
    crime, information on 175
    defence information 175
    intelligence 175
    international relations information 175
    security 175
  confidentiality *see* **Confidentiality, law of**
  information, freedom of 177
  legislation 174, 175
  legislation compatible with Convention on
    Human Rights 55, 175–6
  official authorisation to disclose 175
  public interest no defence 175

P

Parliamentary sovereignty 45, 49, 50, 53, 54,
  56
Parole Board 127
Peaceful assembly, right to 9, 23
  arbitrary interference 207
  breach of the peace and 208, 210, 213
  conduct of demonstrators 213
  demonstrate, restrictions on right to 209–10,
    213
  highway, offence of obstruction of 208, 212
  highway, right to use 209
  leaflets, distribution of 57, 58, 61, 195, 211,
    215
  legislation based restrictions 49
  pickets, restricting numbers 208
  police officer, obstructing 208, 209, 212–13
  public processions
    banning, police powers 208
    conditions, imposition of 208, 215
    judicial review of police powers 215
    requirement of advance notice 208, 215
  restrictions on
    'prescribed by law' 209, 210
    'necessary in a democratic society' 209
  silent roadside protest 209
  'stop and search' powers 210
  striking miners 208
  trespassory public assemblies 209, 213–14
  words of demonstrators 213
  see also **Association, freedom of**

Penal policy 30
Photographs
  publication of 139, 152–4
  see also **Press, freedom of**
Plato 8
Police authorities
  civil actions against
    blanket ban prohibiting 111
    duty of care owed by police 111
  prisoners
    liability for attacks on 88–90
    medical care, provision of 89
    self-harm, duty to safeguard from 89
Poll tax defaulters 98
Pornography
  Consultation on the Possession of Extreme
    Violent Pornography 189
  obscenity laws 189, 191
**Press Complaints Commission's Code of
  Practice**
  photographs, regulating the taking of 153,
    154
Press, freedom of
  absolute immunity 170
  bona fide public meetings, reporting
    of 170
  confidentiality *see* **Confidentiality, law of**
  damages
    excessive, effect of 163
    libel actions and 34
  defamation law 170–3
  duty to inform public 163, 172–3
  election broadcast, ban on 167
  fair comment, defence of 171
  freedom of speech and 163–4
  injunctions 151–4
  journalism, need for professionalism 168,
    171, 173
  journalistic sources, protection of 166, 183–7
  justification, defence of 171
  margin of appreciation and 29–30, 162–4
  parliamentary proceedings, reporting of 170
  photographs, publication of 139, 152–4
  politicians and 163
  press conferences 170
  prisoners, restrictions on reporting interviews
    with 165

private individuals *see* **Private life, right to**
'public' figures, private lives of 151–4, 164
public interest defence 152–4, 163–4, 167–8, 175
qualified privilege defence 170–1
restrictions and 34
Press intrusion 139, 141, 143, 148
  case law and 149–54
  photographs, publication of 139, 152–4
  tactics of press 149, 152
Prison complaints system 121
Prison conditions
  intolerable 93–4
  'Soering principle' and 93
  unlawful 93–4
Prisoners' rights
  access to courts 123, 126–7, 129, 138
  accommodation, right to decent 122
  assault by police 88, 123
  chaining of prisoners 132,l 134
  clothing, right to 122
  conjugal visits 128, 129
  correspondence 120, 126, 129, 134, 138
  court protection of 122
  detention *see* **Detention**
  disciplinary proceedings 108, 111, 113, 127
  discipline in prisons 120, 124, 125, 127, 129
  domestic law claims
    assault 120
    Human Rights Act 1998 120, 124
    judicial review 120
    negligence 120, 123–4
  drug withdrawal symptoms, medical care for 88, 89
  fair trial *see* **Fair trial, right to**
  fair trial, violation of right to
    refusal of permission to consult solicitor 111
  food, right to decent 122
  free speech 128
  handcuffing 132, 134
  human rights abuses of 25, 50
  ill-treatment, states' obligation to prevent 89
  inmates, protection from fellow 128
  international law claims under
    European Convention on Human Rights 120
    International Covenant on Civil and Political Rights 120
  journalists, visits from 49
  judicial protection of 119
  life-sentence prisoners, release of 100
  marriage 128
  mental health problems 90, 129
  mentally disabled prisoners 129
  physically disabled prisoners 129
  prison complaints system 121
  prison conditions 88–90, 124–5, 128, 131
  prison searches 143
  Prisons Ombudsman 121
  prisoner, definition of 119
  recall 120, 123
  release 120, 123, 127, 129
  restrictions on
    legality of 124
    proportionality 124
  'slopping out' 89, 125, 131, 134
  suicides in prison 90, 128
  torture and 81, 126, 128, 129, 131
  vindication of 119, 125
  vote, right to 125, 126, 128
Prisons Ombudsman 121
Privacy, right to
  absence of specific right in English law 141, 142
  Human Rights Act 1998
    development of law under 142–3
    effect of 142
  individual privacy
    case law and 149–54
    press intrusion *see* **Press intrusion**
    private information, right to control 139
    strong justification for interference with 139–40
    public interest, balance between 141, 143, 144
  laws protecting certain rights
    assault 140
    confidentiality 135, 140, 141, 142
    defamation 141, 150
    nuisance 140, 150
    trespass 141, 150
  personal integrity cases 144
  physical integrity cases 144
  press intrusion *see* **Press intrusion**
  privacy interests, protected
    confidential information 141
    personal property 141

person's reputation 141
real property 141
private space, right to 142
'public' figures and 151–2
see also **Private and family life, right to**
Private and family life, right to 7, 13, 31,
32, 50
Article 8 13, 32, 42, 91, 132–4, 137, 141,
145
conditional right 140
confidentiality, right to 135, 140, 141, 142,
150
correspondence see **Correspondence**
defamation and private life 135, 141
female prisoners separation from their
babies 124
homosexuals see **Homosexuals**
individual privacy
press intrusion see **Press intrusion**
private information, right to control 139
strong justification for interference
with 139–40
public interest, balance between 141, 143,
144, 167
margin of appreciation and 29, 138
personal autonomy, right to 136, 141
personal information, right to withhold 141
photographs 139, 152–4
press intrusion see **Press intrusion**
prisoners' rights 126,132–4
privacy, definition of 141
'public' figures and 149–54, 167
religion see **Religion, freedom of**
removal of persons from a state 91
reputation, right to 169
sexual orientation see **Sexual orientation**
sexual privacy see **Sexual privacy**
surveillance techniques see **Surveillance
techniques**
telephone tapping see **Telephone tapping**
transsexuals see **Transsexuals**
**Property rights, freedom from interference
with** 7, 8, 9, 140
Proportionality, doctrine of
Convention rights, interference with 21, 25,
27, 28, 34–5, 49–51, 53
derogation and 37
expression, freedom of 162–3, 166
judicial review proceedings 123

press intrusion 151
prisoners' rights, restrictions on 124
surveillance techniques 147
**Proscribed Organisations Appeal
Commission** 205
Protection of rights
courts, constitutional difficulties 51–6
post-Human Rights Act 1998, 47, 50–1
pre-Human Rights Act 1998 47, 48–50,
52–3
traditional common law system 46–50, 52–3
see also **Natural justice principles**
Public decency
offence of outraging 189, 191
public good defence 191
Public emergency
Article 15 European Convention on Human
Rights 27, 103–5
derogation, power of 36, 55
'Public' figures
private lives and 149–54
Public morals
conspiracy to corrupt 189, 191
proportionality and 34
protection of public morality 29
public good defence 191
Punishment
inhuman or degrading see **Torture, freedom
from**

Q

Qualified privilege defence
bona fide public meetings, reporting of 170
parliamentary reporting 170
press conferences 170
public interest information, justification for
publishing 168, 170–1

R

Race
discrimination 8
racial hatred, offences relating to 200–1
racist agendas, groups with 204
racist speech 161, 163
Rawls
'social contract' notion 8

Religion, right to freedom of 23
absolute right to basic freedom 194
Article 9 42, 193–7, 198–202
blasphemous speech *see* **Blasphemy**
conditional right 31
corporal punishment 196
counter-religions, protection against attacks
from 197
discrimination and 8
interferences with right to manifest
employers and 197
'necessary in a democratic society'
194, 195
'prescribed by law' 194, 195
safeguarding other persons' rights 194
manifest, individual's right to 194
'margin of appreciation' and 195–7
pacifism philosophy, protection of 195
pluralist society, maintenance of 194–5
proselytism 195
religious dress 193, 195, 196
religiously aggravated offences 200–2
school uniform policies
'Kara' bracelets 196
Muslim headdress 195, 196
purity rings 196
see also **Association, freedom of** *and*
Expression, freedom of *and*
Private and family life, right to
Retrospective criminal law, freedom from
Article 7 48, 114–18
blasphemy and 117
confiscation order and 116
'criminal offences', interpretation of 115
derogation and 37, 115
foreseeing consequences of action, principle
of 116–17
licences in addition to fixed sentences 116
marital rape, criminalisation of 117
penalties and 115–16
'Rogues' charter 18
Rule of law, doctrine of
bills of rights and 17, 19
equality and 9
fundamental ideals of 32
prisoners' rights 122

S

Security, right to 7, 8, 23
Self-determination 65
see also **Die, right to**
Separation of powers
bill of rights and 18
breach of 55
constitutional principle 2
Human Rights Act 1998, effect of 52
life-sentence prisoners 100, 127
Servitude *see* **Slavery, freedom from**
Sex discrimination 8
Sexual minorities
human rights abuses of 25
Sexual orientation
discrimination and 144
homosexuals *see* **Homosexuals**
right to choose 135, 141, 144, 154–8
transsexuals *see* **Transsexuals**
Sexual privacy 137–8, 140, 144, 152, 153,
155–8
see also **Sexual orientation**
Shelter
fundamental right, as 7, 9
Slavery, freedom from 7, 8, 23, 132
derogation and 37
prisoners' rights 129, 132
Sleep
deprivation of 83
'Slopping out' 89, 125, 131, 134
'Soering' principle 67, 69, 76, 78, 79, 84–5,
91–4
Speech, right to free *see* **Expression, freedom of**
'Spycatcher' 176
State reporting 26, 120
State sovereignty, doctrine of 11
universal protection of human rights
and 27–30
Strip searches 125
Suicide
legislation compatible with Human Rights
Convention 55
prisoner's life, duty to safeguard 89–90
Surveillance techniques 137, 138–9
arbitrary use of 148

bugging devices 144, 145, 146, 147
closed-circuit television 139, 145, 147, 148
e-mails, monitoring employees' 139
espionage 147
illegally obtained evidence, use in criminal
  trials 139
internet, monitoring employees' use of 139
legal safeguards against abuse of 145–7
listening devices 147
MI5 surveillance 146
proportionality 147, 148
secret filming 146, 147
statutory powers and 144
telephone tapping see **Telephone tapping**
terrorism 147

T

Telephone tapping 32, 48, 50, 138–9, 141, 144
  business premises 146
  private home 146
  statutory basis for 146
Terrorism
  Article 15 and 35
  definition of 205
  derogation of rights 36, 37–9, 103–5
  deportation and 92
  detention of terrorists 23, 100–5
  foreign nationals detention 53–4, 55, 103–5
  'glorifying' terrorism, offence of 206
  liberty and security, right to 101–3
  'Soering principle', relaxation of 94
  'stop and search' powers 210
  surveillance techniques 147
  terrorist groups see **Association, freedom of**
  torture and 83
  treatment of suspected terrorists 24
'Thalidomide' litigation 162–3, 165–6, 179–80
Thought, freedom of see **Religion, right to**
  freedom of
Tobacco
  advertisements, ban on 53
Torture, freedom from 7, 8, 22, 24, 30, 63
  absolute nature of right 82, 83, 86, 94

Article 3 69, 77–80, 81–93, 87–90, 92–4,
  131–2
case law 82–6
corporal punishment see **Corporal**
  punishment
death penalty and 69 70
definition of 82, 83, 131
'degrading' treatment
  definition of 83
  examples of 84, 88–90
deportation see **Deportation**
derogation and 37
examples of 83
extradition and 77–80
'five techniques' 83
food, deprivation of 83
force feeding 125
humiliation of victim 131
ill-treatment, states obligation to prevent
  89–90
'inhuman' treatment
  definition of 83, 131
  examples of 83–4, 88–90
mental suffering 83, 131
noise and 83
physical suffering 83
prisoners' rights 126, 131–2
psychiatric disturbances 83
reasonable chastisement defence 85
sleep, deprivation of 83
strip searches 125
wall-standing 83
Trade unions 203
  see also **Association, freedom of**
Transsexuals 29
  arbitrary interference, protection from 157
  civil status for 44
  equality of 157–8
  marry, right to 44, 55, 138, 157, 158
  post-operative gender, legal recognition
    of 144, 157
  sexual identity, right to change 138
Trespass
  privacy, right to 141, 150
'Trump rights' 10

U

Ultra vires actions 49
  expression, freedom of 165
  judicial review 131
  prison authorities actions 122–3
United Nations Minimum Standards on the
  Treatment of Prisoners 14
United Nations
  Economic and Social Council 11
United Nations Charter 11, 13
  Article 1 11
  Article 68 11
  Preamble 11 40
United Nations Commission on Human
  Rights 12
United States Constitution 17
Universal Declaration of Human Rights 11, 12
USA Bill of Rights 45

V

Violation of rights
  Article 13 77, 79–80
  challenging 58–61

deportation *see* **Deportation**
fair trial, right to 111–13
incarceration and 124
incompatibility, declaration of 58–60
prosecution mechanism 58, 61
remedy before national authority 77, 79–80
'victims' of 72, 87–90
Voting
  prisoners' rights 125, 126, 128

W

Wall-standing
  torture and 83
War
  Article 15 27, 36, 55
  death penalty in times of 70
  derogation, power of 36–9, 55, 82
Williams Committee
  film censorship 188

Y

Young offenders 112, 127